The Disk Compression Book

Matthew Harris

que

The Disk Compression Book

Copyright ©1993 by Que® Corporation.

All rights reserved. Printed in the United States of America. No part of this book may be used or reproduced in any form or by any means, or stored in a database or retrieval system, without prior written permission of the publisher except in the case of brief quotations embodied in critical articles and reviews. Making copies of any part of this book for any purpose other than your own personal use is a violation of United States copyright laws. For information, address Que Corporation, 201 W. 103rd St., Indianapolis, IN 46290.

Library of Congress Catalog No.: 93-84805

ISBN: 1-56529-288-X

This book is sold *as is*, without warranty of any kind, either expressed or implied, respecting the contents of this book, including but not limited to implied warranties for the book's quality, performance, merchantability, or fitness for any particular purpose. Neither Que Corporation nor its dealers or distributors shall be liable to the purchaser or any other person or entity with respect to any liability, loss, or damage caused or alleged to be caused directly or indirectly by this book.

96 95 94 93   4 3 2 1

Interpretation of the printing code: the rightmost double-digit number is the year of the book's printing; the rightmost single-digit number, the number of the book's printing. A printing code of 93-1, for example, shows that the first printing of the book occurred in 1993.

Trademarks

All terms mentioned in this book that are known to be trademarks or service marks have been appropriately capitalized. Que cannot attest to the accuracy of this information. Use of a term in this book should not be regarded as affecting the validity of any trademark or service mark.

Publisher: David P. Ewing

Associate Publisher: Rick Ranucci

Managing Editor: Corinne Walls

Marketing Manager: Ray Robinson

Credits

Publishing Manager
Joe Wikert

Acquisitions Editor
Thomas F. Godfrey III

Product Director
Timothy S. Stanley

Production Editor
William A. Barton

Editors
Sara Allaei
Jo Anna Arnott
Elsa M. Bell
Sara Black
Jane Cramer
Kelly Currie
Don Eamon
Lorna Gentry
Louise Lambert
Mary Morgan
Greg Robertson
Brad Sullivan
Vickie West

Technical Editors
Christopher Denny
Mitch Milam
Eric D. Rudder

Book Designer
Amy Peppler-Adams

Graphic Image Specialists
Teresa Forrester
Dennis Sheehan
Sue VandeWalle

Production Team
Danielle Bird
Angela Bannan
Claudia Bell
Laurie Casey
Charlotte Clapp
Brook Farling
Michelle Greenwalt
Heather Kaufman
Bob LaRoche
Sandra Shay
Amy Steed
Tina Trettin
Lillian Yates
Michelle Worthington

Indexer
Joy Dean Lee

Dedication

To my parents, Mark and Lorraine, who gave me each: a love of science and a love of books.

Acknowledgements

This book is the result of long hours of hard work by many individuals. The efforts of each of these people have earned them the author's deepest gratitude:

Rick Ranucci, Associate Publisher, for the opportunity to write this book.

Bill Barton, production editor on this book, for his hard work and kindly editorial assistance.

To all the Que staff who worked on this book, my heartfelt thanks for your efforts and assistance in making this the best book possible.

Finally, thanks to **Greg Conti** of Jennings and Co. for his assistance in organizing meetings and contacts; to Product Managers **Anne Galdos**, **Ramu Sheshadri**, and **Anita Habeich** of Stac Electronics for sharing their valuable time and knowledge; to **Stac Electronics** for providing copies of the Stacker software; and to **Anatoly Tikhman**, President, and **Chuck Runquist**, VP Product Support, of **Vertisoft Systems, Inc.**, for providing copies of the SPACEMANager software. Special thanks to these persons and organizations for their invaluable help in putting this book together.

About the Author

Matthew Harris, a consultant living in Oakland, California, has been involved with the microcomputer industry since 1980. He has provided technical support, training, and consulting services to the 1990 International AIDS Conference, the University of California at San Francisco, and many private companies. A certified hardware technician, Mr. Harris began programming applications for IBM PCs and compatibles in 1983 and has written both commercially distributed applications and in-house applications for many clients. He also has taught classes on DOS and programming. Mr. Harris is co-author of Que's *Using FileMaker Pro 2.0 for Windows* and is a contributor to Que's *Using Paradox 4.0*, *The Paradox Developer's Guide*, and *Using MS-DOS 6*. He can be reached via CompuServe 74017,766.

Contents at a Glance

Introduction 1

Part I: Understanding Disk Compression

1 Understanding and Using Disk Compression 9
2 Comparing DoubleSpace and Stacker 33

Part II: Using DoubleSpace

3 Installing DoubleSpace 51
4 Configuring and Optimizing DoubleSpace 71
5 Using DoubleSpace 93
6 Using the DoubleSpace Utilities 115
7 Troubleshooting DoubleSpace 135
8 Beyond DoubleSpace: Using SPACEMANager 149

Part III: Using Stacker

9 Installing Stacker 171
10 Configuring and Optimizing Stacker 203
11 Using Stacker 241
12 Using the Stacker Utilities 267
13 Troubleshooting Stacker 287

Part IV: Appendixes

A Glossary 301
B Using the Microsoft Stacker to DoubleSpace Conversion Disk 307
C The "Grandfather" Backup Technique 319

Index 321

Contents

Introduction 1
    What Is Disk Compression? 1
    Who Should Read This Book? 1
    What Computers Can Use Disk Compression? 2
    What Does This Book Cover? 2
        Part I: Understanding Disk Compression 2
        Part II: Using DoubleSpace 3
        Part III: Using Stacker 3
        Part IV: Appendixes 4
    Conventions Used in This Book 4
        Special Typefaces and Representations 4
    Keys and Key Combinations 5

I Understanding Disk Compression

1 Understanding and Using Disk Compression 9
    Understanding the Disk Storage System 10
        Disk Drives 10
        The Disk Operating System: DOS 10
        The DOS File System 11
    What Disk Compression Can and Cannot Do 14
        Disk Compression on a Network 14
        What Compresses? 14
    How Disk Compression Works: An Overview 18
        The Disk Compression Algorithm 18
        Software Disk Compression 20
        Hardware Disk Compression 21
    Adding Compressed Disks: An Overview 22
        Preparing To Add Disk Compression 22
        Creating the Compressed Disk 23
        Making the Compressed Disk Available 26
    Using a Compressed Disk 26
        Using a Compressed Hard Disk 27
        Using Compressed Removable Media Disks 28
        Using Disk Cache Programs 28
    Potential Difficulties in Using Disk Compression 29
        Lost Device Drivers 29

      Deleted Compressed Volume 30
      Memory Usage and Memory Conflicts 30
      Compressed Removable Media 31
      Loss of DOS Uninstall 32
   Summary 32

2 Comparing DoubleSpace and Stacker 33
   Comparing Features 33
      Device Driver Preloading and System File Synchronization 36
      Installation 37
      Compressed Disk Sizes 38
      Disk Compatibility 38
      Removable Media 39
      Memory Consumption 40
      Compression Levels and Recompression 41
      Reporting, Diagnostic, and Maintenance Tools 42
      Disk Repair Utilities 44
      Integration with Windows 44
      Security 46
      System Requirements 46
   Deciding Which Compression Program To Use 47
   Summary 47

II Using DoubleSpace

3 Installing DoubleSpace 51
   Changes Made by DoubleSpace Setup 51
      Files Added to Boot Disk Root Directory 51
      Changes to CONFIG.SYS and AUTOEXEC.BAT 52
      Compressed Volume Files 52
   How DoubleSpace Exchanges Drive Letters and Volume Labels 53
      Drive Letters 53
      Volume Labels 54
   Preparing To Install DoubleSpace 54
   Running Express Setup 56
   Running Custom Setup 59
      Compressing an Existing Drive 60
      Creating a New Empty Compressed Drive 63
   Converting to DoubleSpace from Another Disk Compression
      Program 66

Converting from Stacker to DoubleSpace 66
Converting from Other Disk Compression Programs 66
Summary 70

4 Configuring and Optimizing DoubleSpace **71**

Relocating DoubleSpace in Memory 71
    Using DBLSPACE.SYS and DBLSPACE.BIN 72
    Using DBLSPACE.SYS To Relocate the DoubleSpace
        Device Driver 72
Improving DoubleSpace Performance by Using SMARTDRV.EXE 76
Changing the Estimated Compression Ratio 79
    Changing the Estimated Compression Ratio
        at the Command Line 79
    Changing the Estimated Compression Ratio by Using the
        DoubleSpace Menus 80
Changing DoubleSpace Drive Letter Assignments 81
    Understanding the DBLSPACE.INI File 82
    Editing DBLSPACE.INI 85
Adjusting the Last Drive Letter 86
Adjusting the Number of Removable Media Drives 87
Creating a DoubleSpace RAM Disk 88
    Compressing the RAM Disk by Using AUTOEXEC.BAT 89
    Compressing the RAM Disk by Copying the Compressed Volume 90
Summary 91

5 Using DoubleSpace **93**

Performing File Management on Compressed Drives 93
    Using the DIR Command on DoubleSpace Drives 95
    Using the CHKDSK Command on DoubleSpace Drives 96
Getting Information about Your Compressed Drives 97
    Obtaining Information at the DOS Prompt 97
    Obtaining Information by Using the DoubleSpace Menus 99
    Obtaining Information from the Windows File Manager 100
Mounting and Unmounting Compressed Drives 101
    Mounting and Unmounting from the DOS Prompt 102
    Mounting and Unmounting by Using the DoubleSpace Menus 104
Using DoubleSpace with Removable Media 105
    Compressing Removable Media 106
    Using Removable Media 108
Backing Up Your Compressed Drives 110

Using Disk Utilities with DoubleSpace 110
Using the DoubleSpace Help System 111
    Context-Sensitive Help 111
    The DoubleSpace Help Menu 112
    Navigating the Help System 112
Summary 113

6 Using the DoubleSpace Utilities 115

Creating Additional Compressed Drives 115
    Compressing an Existing Drive 116
    Creating a New Compressed Drive from Free Space 120
Changing the Size of a Compressed Drive 125
    Changing Drive Size from the DOS Prompt 126
    Changing Drive Size by Using the DoubleSpace Menus 126
Deleting a Compressed Drive 127
    Deleting a Compressed Drive from the DOS Prompt 127
    Deleting a Compressed Drive by Using the DoubleSpace Menus 128
Defragmenting a Compressed Drive 129
    Defragmenting a Drive from the DOS Prompt 129
    Defragmenting a Drive by Using the DoubleSpace Menus 130
Checking the Integrity of a Compressed Drive 131
    Using DoubleSpace CHKDSK from the DOS Prompt 131
    Running DoubleSpace CHKDSK by Using
        the DoubleSpace Menus 132
Formatting a Compressed Drive 133
    Formatting a Compressed Drive from the DOS Prompt 133
    Formatting a Compressed Drive by Using
        the DoubleSpace Menus 133
Summary 134

7 Troubleshooting DoubleSpace 135

Preventing Problems 135
    Memory Manager and Upper Memory Conflicts 135
    STACKS Statement in CONFIG.SYS 136
    Write-Delay Disk Cache 137
    Other Precautions 138
Solving Drive Letter Problems 139
    Local Drive Letter Problems 139
    Network Drive Letter Problems 139
Solving Windows Swap File Problems 139

Contents **xi**

Examining Lost Clusters 141
    What Causes Lost Clusters? 141
    Repairing Lost Clusters 142
Examining Cross-Linked Files 142
    What Causes Cross-Linked Files? 142
    Repairing Cross-Linked Files 143
Solving Problems in Changing a Compressed Volume's Size 144
Recovering a Deleted Compressed Volume File 146
Correcting Corrupt CVF or Damaged CVF Error Messages 147
Correcting Chronic Disk Read Errors 148
Summary 148

8 Beyond DoubleSpace: Using SPACEMANager 149

What is SPACEMANager? 149
    Multiple Compression Levels 150
    Automatic Mounting of Removable Media 151
    Improved Windows Integration 152
    Improved Free Space Reporting 152
How SPACEMANager Works 152
Installing SPACEMANager 153
    Changes Made by SPACEMANager Installation 153
    Preparing To Install SPACEMANager 155
    Performing the Installation 156
Using SPACEMANager 159
    Starting SPACEMANager 159
    Enabling SelectCompress 162
    Setting Compression Levels 162
    Making Removable Media Usable on Computers
        without DoubleSpace 163
    Compressing a Floppy Disk from Windows 165
    Using SUPERX Exchangeable Removable Disks 165
    Enabling and Disabling Automatic Mounting
        of Removable Disks 166
Summary 168

III Using Stacker

9 Installing Stacker 171

Changes Made by Stacker Setup 171
    Files Added to Boot Disk Root Directory 172

    Changes to CONFIG.SYS and AUTOEXEC.BAT 172
    Stacker Volumes 173
  How Stacker Assigns Drive Letters and Volume Labels 174
    Assigning Drive Letters 174
    Assigning Volume Labels 175
  Preparing To Install Stacker 175
  Running Express Setup 177
    Starting Express Setup at the DOS Prompt 178
    Starting Express Setup from Windows 179
    Completing Stacker Express Setup 182
  Running Custom Setup 184
    Starting Custom Setup at the DOS Prompt 185
    Starting Custom Setup from Windows 187
    Completing Stacker Custom Setup 189
  Making a DOS 6 Start-up Disk Containing Stacker 194
  Converting to Stacker from Another Disk Compression Program 195
    Converting from DoubleSpace to Stacker 195
    Converting from Other Disk Compression Programs 199
  Summary 202

10 Configuring and Optimizing Stacker 203

  Understanding the Stacker Initialization File: STACKER.INI 203
    Examining the STACKER.INI Commands 206
    Editing STACKER.INI 214
  Freeing Conventional Memory 218
    Using STACHIGH.SYS and DBLSPACE.BIN 218
    Using Stacker with EMS Memory 222
    Disabling Automatic Removable Disk Mounting 222
  Redirecting DOS Disk Commands to Stacker 222
  Improving Stacker Performance by Using SMARTDRV.EXE 223
  Tuning Stacker Compression Levels 226
    Setting Compression Levels by Using the Stacker Tuner
      Utility 226
    Setting Compression Levels by Using STACKER.INI 228
  Changing the Expected Compression Ratio 228
    Changing the Expected Compression Ratio by Using
      the Stacker Toolbox 229
    Changing the Expected Compression Ratio by Using
      the Windows Stackometer 230

Changing Stacker Drive Letter Assignments	231
Adjusting the Number of Removable Media Drives	233
Creating a Stacker RAM Disk	234
Compressing the RAM Disk by Using CONFIG.SYS	235
Compressing the RAM Disk by Using AUTOEXEC.BAT	236
Compressing the RAM Disk by Copying the Compressed Volume	237
Creating the Stacker Program Group in Windows	238
Summary	239

11 Using Stacker 241

Performing File Management on Compressed Drives	241
Using the DIR and SDIR Commands on Stacker Drives	242
Using the CHKDSK and CHECK Commands on Stacker Drives	244
Getting Information about Your Compressed Drives	245
Obtaining Information at the DOS Prompt	246
Obtaining Information by Using the Stacker Toolbox	247
Obtaining Information from Windows	248
Mounting and Unmounting Compressed Drives	252
Mounting a Compressed Drive	253
Unmounting a Compressed Drive	255
Using Stacker with Removable Media	256
Mounting Removable Disks Automatically	256
Compressing Removable Media	257
Using Removable Media	259
Using Passwords	260
Backing Up Your Compressed Drives	262
Using Disk Utilities with Stacker	263
Using the Stacker Help System	264
Summary	265

12 Using the Stacker Utilities 267

Creating Additional Compressed Drives	267
Compressing Drives by Using the Stacker Toolbox	267
Compressing Drives by Using the CREATE Utility	273
Changing the Size of a Compressed Drive	275
Removing a Compressed Drive	276
Defragmenting a Compressed Drive	279
Defragment a Drive by Using the Stacker Toolbox	280
Defragment a Drive by Using the Stackometer	281

Checking the Integrity of a Compressed Drive 281
Using Stacker CHECK from the DOS Prompt 282
   Using Stacker CHECK from the Stacker Toolbox 284
Summary 285

13 Troubleshooting Stacker 287
Preventing Problems 287
   Memory Manager and Upper Memory Conflicts 287
   STACKS Statement in CONFIG.SYS 288
   Write-Delay Disk Cache 289
   Other Precautions 290
Solving Drive Letter Problems 290
   Local Drive Letter Problems 291
   Network Drive Letter Problems 291
Solving Windows Swap File Problems 291
Examining Lost Clusters 293
   What Causes Lost Clusters? 293
   Repairing Lost Clusters 294
Examining Cross-Linked Files 294
   What Causes Cross-Linked Files? 294
   Repairing Cross-Linked Files 295
Recovering a Deleted Compressed Volume File 296
Correcting Write-Protected Drive Error Messages 297
Correcting Chronic Disk Read Errors 298
Summary 298

IV Appendixes

A Glossary 301

B Using the Microsoft Stacker to DoubleSpace Conversion Disk 307
Preparing To Convert 307
Making the Stacker to DoubleSpace Conversion 309
   Performing the Conversion 309
   After the Conversion 313
Converting Stacker Compressed Removable Media to DoubleSpace 314
   Converting from the DOS Prompt 314
   Converting by Using the DoubleSpace Menus 315
   Converting If Insufficient Working Room Is Available 315

C The "Grandfather" Backup Technique 319

Index 321

Introduction

Welcome to *The Disk Compression Book*. This book is intended to help you understand and use the disk compression products that take advantage of new features in DOS 6. Its several chapters and appendixes explain how disk compression increases the amount of data you can store on your disks and shows you how to install and configure disk compression software for the greatest safety and ease of use.

What Is Disk Compression?

Disk compression is the term given to any technique used to reduce the amount of space that data occupies on a disk. Using disk compression enables you to store more data on the same disk.

Disk compression software does not actually increase the size of your disk. Instead, disk compression reduces the size of your data. As you store data on a disk, disk compression software makes that data smaller, with no loss of information. When you access your data, the compression software restores the data to its original state. After you install disk compression software, it attaches itself to DOS and operates automatically, without much further thought or effort on your part. You use your computer just as you did before.

Who Should Read This Book?

Both experienced disk compression users and those relatively new to disk compression should find this book helpful in understanding how DoubleSpace and Stacker 3.1 integrate with DOS 6 to accomplish their tasks. This book makes no assumptions about your background or experience with disk compression software, although it does assume at least a basic knowledge of your computer's hardware and DOS operations (as well as Windows operations if you use Windows).

If you are new to disk compression, pay special attention to the first chapter of the book. This chapter summarizes how disk compression works. Chapter 2 compares the DoubleSpace and Stacker compression programs; you may want to examine this chapter closely if you have not yet decided which disk compression product is right for you. More experienced users, or those who want to deal with practical matters immediately, can go directly to Part II or Part III, depending on the product you intend to use.

Because DOS 6 is the current DOS version at this writing, and because DoubleSpace and Stacker 3.1 both require DOS 6, this book assumes that you use DOS 6.

What Computers Can Use Disk Compression?

To use DoubleSpace or Stacker 3.1 disk compression, your computer must run DOS 6 and have at least 640K of RAM, a hard disk, and a floppy disk drive. Some memory-usage options of Stacker and DoubleSpace require an 80386 or higher CPU, at least 1M of RAM, and software for XMS and EMS memory management. Both Stacker and DoubleSpace support a fully Microsoft-compatible mouse.

DoubleSpace and Stacker 3.1 both can be used on networks. Every network computer using disk compression, however, must have its own copy of the software; you cannot share disk compression software over a network.

What Does This Book Cover?

This book covers DoubleSpace version 1 (supplied with DOS 6), SPACEMANager version 1.5, and Stacker version 3.1. The book is divided into three major parts: Part I is about "Understanding Disk Compression." Part II concerns "Using DoubleSpace." Part III involves "Using Stacker." Three appendixes constitute a fourth and final part of the book.

Part I: Understanding Disk Compression

The first part of this book explains how disk compression works in relation to your disk storage system and concludes with a comparison of the Stacker and DoubleSpace products.

Chapter 1, "Understanding and Using Disk Compression," begins with a brief review of disk storage and the DOS file system. The chapter then examines what disk compression actually can and cannot do; explains the theory behind disk compression; offers an overview of creating and using compressed disks; and concludes by describing difficulties you may encounter if you add disk compression to your system.

Chapter 2, "Comparing DoubleSpace and Stacker," compares the various features found in these two disk compression programs. This chapter also describes in detail the system requirements for DoubleSpace and Stacker.

Part II: Using DoubleSpace

Part II of the book provides practical information and instructions on installing and using DoubleSpace.

Chapter 3, "Installing DoubleSpace," describes the changes DoubleSpace makes to your system and outlines the rules DoubleSpace uses for exchanging drive letters. Suggestions and recommendations help you prepare to install DoubleSpace. The chapter then guides you through the actual installation, explaining each option in the process. The chapter also covers how to convert data from another disk compression program to DoubleSpace.

Chapter 4, "Configuring and Optimizing DoubleSpace," describes how to relocate DoubleSpace in memory and how to safely improve your disk system's performance by using a disk cache. The chapter discusses adjusting how DoubleSpace assigns drive letters; examines the DBLSPACE.INI file and its configuration commands; and explains how to create and compress a RAM disk.

Chapter 5, "Using DoubleSpace," explores file management for compressed drives; describes how to obtain information about your DoubleSpace compressed disks; and describes how to use compressed removable disks (such as floppy disks). The chapter then explains how to back up your compressed drives. The chapter concludes by providing information on DoubleSpace's Help system.

Chapter 6, "Using the DoubleSpace Utilities," provides step-by-step instructions on how to create additional compressed drives after you install DoubleSpace and how to change the size of a compressed drive. The chapter also describes when and how to use the DoubleSpace defragmenting utility.

Chapter 7, "Troubleshooting DoubleSpace," explores common problems and ways to prevent them. The chapter describes how to resolve conflicts in drive letter assignments and how to deal with Windows swap files. How to repair lost clusters and cross-linked files also is covered.

Chapter 8, "Beyond DoubleSpace: Using SPACEMANager," introduces and examines the SPACEMANager add-in product for DoubleSpace. The chapter describes SPACEMANager, walks you through the SPACEMANager installation process, and explains how to use the most important SPACEMANager features.

Part III: Using Stacker

Part III of *The Disk Compression Book* provides practical information on installing and using Stacker.

Chapter 9, "Installing Stacker," describes the changes Stacker makes to your system and discusses Stacker's rules for exchanging drive letters. The chapter offers several pre-installation recommendations and guides you through an actual installation, explaining all the options available. A special section shows you how to create a DOS start-up disk containing the Stacker device driver files.

Chapter 10, "Configuring and Optimizing Stacker," examines the STACKER.INI file and the Stacker configuration commands. The chapter explains how to make Stacker use less conventional memory and how to adjust Stacker's compression levels. The chapter also describes how to adjust Stacker drive letter assignments, how to compress a RAM disk, and how to increase the accuracy of free space reports by changing the expected compression ratio.

Chapter 11, "Using Stacker," describes file management for Stacker compressed drives; how to obtain information about your compressed disks; how to use removable disks; how to set and enter passwords for your Stacker drives; and how to back up your compressed drives. The chapter ends with information about the Stacker Help system.

Chapter 12, "Using the Stacker Utilities," offers step-by-step instructions for creating additional compressed drives or changing the size of a compressed drive after you install Stacker. The chapter then covers when and how to use the Stacker defragmenting utility.

Chapter 13, "Troubleshooting Stacker," explores several common problems and how to avoid them. Problems and solutions dealt with in this chapter include those involving drive letter assignment conflicts, Windows swap files, lost clusters and cross-linked files, and chronic disk read errors.

Part IV: Appendixes

Appendix A is a glossary of many of the terms used in this book.

Appendix B, "Using the Microsoft Stacker to DoubleSpace Conversion Disk," explains how to use the optional conversion disk available from Microsoft, beginning with several preparatory guidelines and proceeding through the conversion process itself.

Appendix C, "The 'Grandfather' Backup Technique," describes a backup routine that enables you to restore any file to its condition on any given day for a period of up to three months past.

Conventions Used in This Book

This book uses certain conventions to help you better understand the techniques and information presented. The following sections describe these conventions.

Special Typefaces and Representations

Words appearing in all uppercase characters represent DOS, DoubleSpace, and Stacker 3.1 commands and file names, such as CHKDSK, DBLSPACE, STACKER, or CONFIG.SYS.

Special typefaces also are used in this book, as described in the following table.

Typeface	Meaning
italics	New terms or phrases being defined; also variables in syntax lines.
boldface	Information you type at the prompt or in a text box.
`special typeface`	Words or messages that appear on-screen.

Several different paragraph formats provide special information related to but separate from the main text. These paragraphs appear in shaded boxes set off from the main text or as marginal notes with distinctive icons to alert you to their presence.

Cautions warn the reader of hazardous procedures (for example, activities that alter files beyond recovery).

Warnings indicate that the procedures described are extremely dangerous (for example, activities that delete or reformat disks).

Tips suggest easier or alternative ways to execute a procedure or describe shortcuts to simplify or speed up the processes described in the text.

Notes indicate additional information you may want to consider while using the described features.

Sidebars

Sidebars also are used throughout the book to provide additional information. Sidebars are set off in shaded boxes from regular text and include their own heads.

Figures appear throughout the book as visual aids to help illustrate certain procedures. Figures are offset from the text, and figure captions appear in the margins, below the figures.

Keys and Key Combinations

Most keys are represented in the book just as they appear on your computer's keyboard. The arrow keys, however, are represented by name (for example, *the up-arrow key*). The Print Screen key is abbreviated PrtSc, Page Up as PgUp, Insert as Ins, and so on. (These key names may be spelled out or abbreviated differently on your keyboard.)

A plus sign (+) connecting two keys indicates that you press and then hold the first key while pressing the second key. Ctrl+Break, for example, indicates that you press and hold the Ctrl key and then press the Break key while still holding Ctrl. If key combinations are not connected by the plus sign, do not hold any of the keys; press and release each key in the order listed (for example, End Home).

PART I

Understanding Disk Compression

1. Understanding and Using Disk Compression
2. Comparing DoubleSpace and Stacker

CHAPTER 1

Understanding and Using Disk Compression

Disk compression is the name given to data compression as applied to computer disk drives. *Data compression* is simply the process of squeezing information to take up less storage space. Compressing data is like squashing a foam rubber mattress into a tight roll. The rolled-up mattress takes up less room in your closet, so you can fit more items in the closet. The mattress has not been permanently changed—it regains its original properties as you unroll it. Squashing the foam rubber makes the mattress smaller, because foam rubber contains many air spaces. As you press out the air, the mattress becomes smaller and takes up less room.

Of course, you do not compress data by physically squeezing it. And, unlike foam rubber, your data does not spring back into its original shape without help. A sort of "air" *is* present in your disk files, however—in the form of repeated sequences of bytes—and your disk files can be compressed by removing this "air." *Decompressing* the data returns it to its original form. Disk compression software can both compress and decompress data.

Data compression is a widely accepted technology used in many applications. In fact, if you own a tape backup or a backup utility such as Norton Backup or Central Point's PC Backup, you already use data compression; these products all use the same patented technology under license from Stac Electronics, the publishers of the Stacker disk compression program.

This chapter begins with a review of how your computer's disk storage system works so that you can better understand how the DoubleSpace and Stacker disk compression programs enhance that storage system. The chapter then discusses what disk compression can and cannot do for you and describes in basic form the process used to compress data on a disk. This chapter also outlines what happens as you install a disk compression program and create compressed disk drives, whether you use Stacker or DoubleSpace. The chapter concludes with a discussion of potential difficulties you may encounter on installing disk compression.

Understanding the Disk Storage System

The *disk storage system* is the combination of hardware and software in your computer that is responsible for storing and retrieving information on disks. This section briefly reviews the components of your computer's disk storage system. (For a more complete description of your computer's hardware components and operating system software, you may want to read *Introduction to Personal Computers*, by Kathy Murray, and *Using MS-DOS 6*; both books are published by Que.)

Disk Drives

A *disk drive* is the physical unit that holds the computer disk. The disk drive spins the computer disk and writes and reads information to and from the disk. The *read/write head* is the part of the disk drive that actually reads or writes information on the disk. The disk drive moves the read/write head across the surface of the disk in small, precise steps.

Although disks and disk drives come in many different types and sizes, all drives can be categorized as either removable media or nonremovable media.

A *removable media* disk drive is one from which you can remove the disk (media). Removable media disk drives are used to transport information or software from one computer to another or to store infrequently used information. The most common type of removable media disk drive is the floppy disk drive that is standard on almost every computer. Removable media disk drives also include CD-ROM drives, Floptical drives, and Bernoulli drives; these removable drive types are briefly described in the Glossary in Appendix A, at the end of this book.

A *nonremovable media* disk drive—frequently called a *fixed disk drive*—is one from which the disks cannot be removed; its disks are "fixed" in place. The disks and the disk drive are constructed together as a single unit and usually take significantly less time to store or retrieve information than do removable media drives. Fixed disk drives are generally used to store data you access frequently.

To make it easier to find a specific piece of information on a disk, the disk's surface is divided into specific regions, and the information stored on the disk is kept track of region by region. First, the disk's surface is divided into concentric circular regions, called *tracks*. Then the disk's surface is sliced like a pie so that each track is divided into individual regions called *sectors*. Sectors are the smallest whole part of the disk that the drive can read or write; a single sector is usually 512 bytes long. The capability to access specific sectors on a disk is built into your disk drive's hardware.

The Disk Operating System: DOS

The software that provides the instructions necessary to operate your computer's disk drive hardware is called the *disk operating system*. The *DOS* in the name *MS-DOS* stands for *Disk Operating System*. You are probably familiar with some of the disk services DOS provides to you through the DOS command line (such as the DIR, MKDIR, or CHDIR commands). DOS provides similar services to your software programs—as well as several services not available from the command line. To access information on your computer's

NOTE:
The terms *nonremovable media disk drive*, *fixed disk drive*, and *hard disk drive* (or *hard disk*) all mean essentially the same thing. For simplicity and to reflect common usage, the term *hard disk* is used in the rest of this book.

disk, an application asks DOS to retrieve, add to, or change information on the disk. DOS keeps track of where each file is located on the disk, whether the disk is full, and all other aspects involved in controlling the disk drive. To make DOS useful on many different computers, its designers did not try to give DOS absolute control over a computer's disk and other hardware. Instead, just as an application relies on DOS to provide services for controlling the computer's hardware, DOS in turn relies on yet another group of software instructions to handle the most hardware-specific details of its services.

BIOS

BIOS is an acronym for *Basic Input/Output System*. Your computer's BIOS software handles the most hardware-specific level of operations within your computer. BIOS provides services to DOS in much the same way that DOS provides services to applications. Although DOS handles most of the work involved in keeping track of where specific information is recorded on a disk, DOS uses the BIOS disk services to select the actual head, track, and sector while reading or writing information on a disk.

Figure 1.1 shows how your computer's hardware, BIOS, DOS, and applications relate to one another. BIOS directly controls the hardware; DOS fits between BIOS and the application and uses the simple BIOS services to provide complex services for the application.

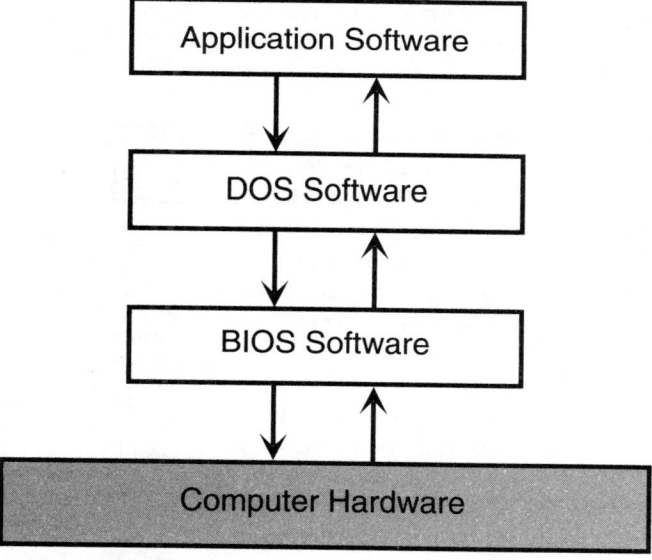

Fig. 1.1

How your computer's hardware, BIOS, DOS, and applications fit together.

Device Drivers

A *device driver* is a special type of software that contains instructions for controlling—or *driving*—a particular hardware device. DOS loads the device driver into memory and then uses the instructions in the device driver to provide services for a particular piece of hardware. Device drivers also are used to replace or enhance existing DOS services.

Figure 1.2 shows how device drivers fit into the relationship with DOS, BIOS, and your hardware and software. An application asks for a specific service from DOS. If the service involves a device controlled by a device driver or a DOS service replaced by a device driver, DOS passes the service request to the device driver. The device driver controls the hardware directly or uses BIOS services to complete the requested service.

The DOS File System

The methods DOS uses to keep track of and organize the files on a disk are collectively known as the *file system*. You are undoubtedly familiar with how the DOS file system helps you organize files on your disk by using disk directories and subdirectories. The DOS disk directory and subdirectory services may be the most obvious aspect of the DOS file system. These visible parts of the system, however, rest on a hidden foundation.

Disk Clusters and File Chains

A disk *cluster* is a group of disk sectors treated as a single unit. Depending on the specific disk drive, disk clusters typically contain two, four, or eight disk sectors. All clusters on a disk are numbered sequentially, beginning with the clusters on the outermost tracks of a disk. DOS groups disk sectors together into clusters for several reasons. The most important of these reasons is that DOS can manage all the information on a disk by referring to specific cluster numbers without being concerned with specific track and sector numbers. DOS uses BIOS services to determine the actual head, track, and sector numbers for a particular disk cluster, as necessary.

Most disk files need more than one disk cluster to store an entire file. DOS keeps track of which clusters belong to which files by joining the disk clusters together in a *file chain*—much like stringing paper clips together to form a chain. DOS connects the clusters in a file chain by writing the number of the next cluster in the chain at the end of each cluster. DOS uses a special code to indicate the last cluster in a file chain.

A certain file, for example, may occupy two clusters on a disk. If cluster #5 is the first cluster in the chain and cluster #27 is the second cluster, DOS writes the number "27" at the end of cluster #5 and the end-of-chain code at the end of cluster #27.

The clusters belonging to a file chain need not be sequential. DOS can fit a file's information on a disk wherever an empty cluster exists. If no single area of the disk is large enough to hold a file, DOS can store individual pieces of the file wherever the disk has room.

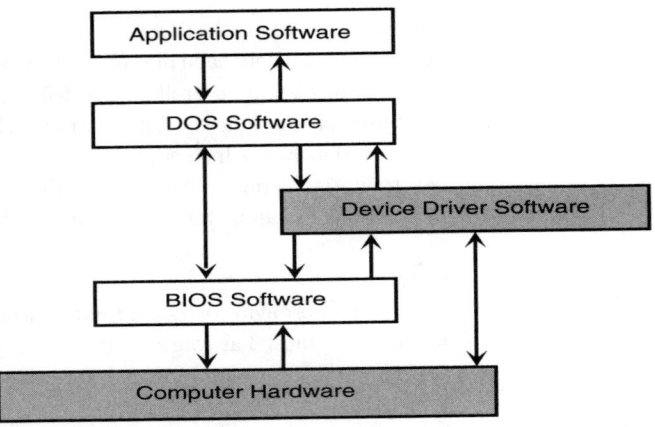

Fig. 1.2

How a device driver adds hardware control to DOS.

In DOS versions 5 and 6, the DOS documentation—and the messages displayed by DOS utility programs such as CHKDSK—refer to disk clusters as *allocation units*. A disk cluster and an allocation unit are the same thing.

The File Allocation Table

DOS uses a *File Allocation Table (FAT)* to keep track of which disk clusters are in use and which disk clusters are available. The FAT is a list of all the clusters on a disk. The FAT itself is stored on the disk in a special area DOS sets aside as it formats the disk. Whenever DOS writes new information onto the disk, it first looks in the FAT to locate an unused disk cluster. DOS writes the new information onto that unused cluster and then marks the cluster's entry in the FAT to indicate that the cluster is now in use.

If you erase a file, DOS changes the FAT entries for each cluster in the file chain to indicate that the cluster is no longer in use.

File Attributes

DOS can assign a file several properties, or *attributes*. The file's attributes are stored with the file's directory entry. DOS's ATTRIB command enables you to view or change a file's attributes. DOS also uses a *directory entry* to record a file's name, size, the date and time the file was last changed, and the number of the first cluster in the file chain.

Usually, you need not be concerned about a file's attributes, although knowing something about these attributes can be useful. The various file attributes are described in the following list:

- **Archive.** The archive attribute indicates whether the file has been backed up since it was last changed.
- **System.** The System attribute indicates that a file is part of the computer's operating system.
- **Hidden.** The Hidden attribute instructs DOS not to include the file in the directory displays produced by using the DIR command.
- **Read-Only.** The Read-Only attribute indicates that a file is not to be changed or erased. DOS refuses to delete or alter any file assigned a Read-Only attribute.

Drive Letters

DOS uses a letter of the alphabet, followed by a colon, to indicate the particular disk drive in use. This symbol is called the *drive letter*. On almost every computer, the first disk drive is a floppy disk, indicated by the drive letter A. Many computers also have a second floppy disk drive, indicated by the letter B.

On computers with a hard disk, DOS uses the letter C to indicate the first (or only) hard disk in the computer. The first hard disk is always C, even if the computer has no drive B. DOS assigns the next available drive letter—D, E, F, and so on—to every additional physical or logical disk drive it recognizes.

Physical and Logical Disk Drives

By using the drive letter system, DOS can control a disk drive even if the drive is not physically present in the computer. A *physical* disk drive is a disk drive that is actually present in your computer, such as your floppy drive or hard disk. A *logical* disk drive, however, is a drive that is not physically present in the computer.

A logical disk drive may be a drive on a computer connected to yours by a network, or it may be a device with which DOS can communicate *as if* that device were a disk drive. DOS often communicates with this second type of logical disk drive through a device driver.

Disk Partitions

Early versions of DOS had an internal limit of 32M as the largest amount of hard disk space DOS could control for a single disk drive. To use all the space on disk drives with capacities greater than 32M, a single physical drive was divided into two or more logical drives. Dividing a physical disk into logical drives is called *partitioning* the drive.

Disk partitioning works by grouping consecutive tracks together on the disk's surface and assigning each group a DOS drive letter. DOS then accesses each disk partition as if the partition were a separate disk drive by using the drive letter for that specific partition. Disk partitions can be any size, up to the limit for your version of DOS. Usually, a disk is partitioned so that the first partitions are as large as possible, with the last partition made up of whatever tracks are left.

What Disk Compression Can and Cannot Do

Disk compression software enables you to use available disk space more efficiently so that you can store more programs and files on your hard disk. Both Stacker and DoubleSpace essentially double the data you can store in a given amount of disk space. You also gain some incidental benefits from adding disk compression to your system. Disk compression cannot, however, solve all your disk storage problems. Knowing just what to expect from disk compression software may save you from frustration and disappointment later.

Disk Compression on a Network

Both Stacker and DoubleSpace work quite well on a network, with only one restriction. You cannot compress the hard disk designated as the network's file server on a client/server network such as Novell. You can, however, compress any workstation's local disks.

If your computer is connected to a DOS-based or peer-to-peer network—such as Lantastic or Windows for Workgroups—you can -use Stacker or DoubleSpace on any computer in the network. Disk compression does not affect how computers on a DOS-based network use the disk, whether the disk is local to the user or is accessed by using the network.

What Compresses?

Ideally, both DoubleSpace and Stacker can compress all your files to half their original size and, thereby, double the amount of information you can store on a disk. The *compression ratio* measures how much a file is compressed—that is, how much smaller the compressed file is than the uncompressed file.

If a compressed file is half the size of the uncompressed file, the compression ratio is 2 to 1 (written as *2:1*). This means that two units of data in the compressed file now take up only as much space as one unit of data in the uncompressed file. If the compression ratio is higher—3:1, for example—the file is compressed to an even smaller size. A lower compression ratio—such as 1.5:1—indicates that the file is not compressed as much.

Both Stacker and DoubleSpace are assumed to compress every file at a 2:1 compression ratio—the overall average result of the compression technique used—which is why the publishers of DoubleSpace and Stacker both claim the programs "double your disk space." In practice, however, some files compress more than others. The actual compression ratios may be greater or smaller than the anticipated 2:1.

The data on a disk is compressed by removing redundant sequences of bytes (a method described more fully in the following section). Some files contain more redundancy than

NOTE:

In DOS version 4 and later, the limit for a single disk drive was raised from 32M to 4G. Partitioning a hard disk, therefore, usually is no longer necessary. Understanding disk partitioning and logical disk drives, however, is still important if using Stacker or DoubleSpace. Both DoubleSpace and Stacker work by creating additional logical disk drives for every compressed drive you create.

others, however, and a few files have no redundancy at all. Files with many repetitive byte sequences—for example, the bitmap graphic files produced by such programs as Windows PaintBrush—compress a great deal more than do files lacking such redundancy—for example, the files containing your software programs. Even if a file compresses exceptionally well, both Stacker and DoubleSpace have a maximum compression ratio of 16:1.

This maximum compression ratio of 16:1 actually is an arbitrary limit Stacker and DoubleSpace impose on themselves. Both programs compress and decompress files *on-the-fly*, which means the compression/decompression operation takes place at the same time the file is read from or written to the disk. No separate action is required from either the user or an application. For on-the-fly disk compression to work without excessive delays, however, the compression/decompression process must occur very quickly. The designers of Stacker and DoubleSpace have therefore made a trade-off between compressing your data to the maximum extent possible and reducing the time required to compress the data.

Even if you do not get exactly twice as much storage space by compressing your data, the difference between this theoretical doubling and the actual increase is probably very small. If many of your files compress at greater than 2:1, you may even end up with more than twice your available storage space.

Many types of data files do compress at or greater than 2:1. The following list describes several that often yield a compression ratio of 2:1 or better. (Generally, Stacker provides slightly higher compression ratios than does DoubleSpace. Differences between DoubleSpace and Stacker are discussed in Chapter 2, "Comparing DoubleSpace and Stacker.")

- **Text and Document Files.** Text and document files created by using a word processing program or a text editor usually compress quite well. Ratios often are as high as 3:1 or 4:1.
- **Database files.** Database files created in programs such as Microsoft's Access, Borland's Paradox, Claris' FileMaker for Windows, dBASE, and others usually have a fairly high compression ratio, depending on the type of information stored in the file (numbers, text, sound, or pictures) and how the file itself is structured. Expect database files to have typical compression ratios ranging from about 2:1 (for Access and FileMaker files) to 3.5:1 or higher (Paradox, dBASE, or other databases). Access and FileMaker files usually contain less blank space than Paradox or dBASE files and do not compress as much.
- **Spreadsheet files.** Spreadsheet files generated by programs such as Microsoft's Excel, Lotus 1-2-3, or Borland's Quattro generally have compression ratios of about 2.5:1.
- **Graphics Files.** A graphics file may contain either pictures you draw by using a program such as MS PaintBrush or CorelDRAW or pictures scanned in from a photograph or other source. Graphics files that compress well include bitmap graphics files (BMP or PCX), Encapsulated PostScript (EPS) files, most Tagged Image Format File (TIFF) files, Windows Meta File (WMF), and several other

The compression ratios for the different file types discussed in this section are averages only. Because the exact contents of any file are likely to vary, each file of a given type can have a different compression ratio. Some files may compress more—or less—than those averages listed.

formats. A few types of graphics file do not compress well. These include the Graphics Interchange Format (GIF) files and a special variation of TIFF file. As explained later in this section, data in these files is already compressed and usually cannot be compressed much further.

- **CADD Files.** Computer Aided Drafting and Design (CADD) files also compress very well. CADD files use a variety of formats and are produced by programs such as AutoCAD, Generic CADD, AutoSKETCH, and others. Almost all CADD file formats compress at 2:1 or better.

Files with high compression ratios often compress so much because they contain information that is inherently redundant. Bitmap graphics files, for example, compress very well, because bitmap files store pictures by storing information about every dot that makes up a picture. Most pictures have many white dots, black dots, or dots of the same color all located together in the picture, so there is much redundant information to remove.

Just as some file types have a certain amount of built-in redundancy, others have very little redundancy. The following list describes several file types that do not yield very high compression ratios; frequently, these types of files have compression ratios of less than 2:1, although a few may come close to 2:1.

- **Font Files.** Font files contain information needed to display different character typefaces on both your computer screen and printer. The TrueType fonts for Windows 3.1, for example, are font files. Many font files have compression ratios just less than 1.5:1. Bitmap fonts, however, compress more like bitmap graphics files and achieve compression ratios closer to 2.5:1.
- **Program Files.** Computer programmers usually design software applications to contain as little redundancy as possible. Software applications are designed explicitly to reuse as many programmed steps as possible and to share internal data as often as possible. Compression ratios for program files (which end in EXE or COM extensions), therefore, are relatively low—usually less than 2:1—although some do have higher ratios.
- **Windows and Windows DLL Files.** Windows program files have low compression ratios for the same reasons as other program files. Dynamic Link Library (DLL) files contain program instructions stored in a special form usable by any Windows application. DLL files are essentially a type of program file and exhibit compression ratios similar to those of other program files.
- **Encrypted Files.** Many programs enable you to protect the confidentiality of files created in that program by enabling you to enter a password to encrypt the file. Most encryption schemes eliminate or severely reduce the amount of redundancy in a file. Encrypted files tend toward extremely low compression ratios. Encrypted Paradox and Access database files, for example, have compression ratios barely greater than 1:1. Some encrypted files do not compress at all.
- **Sound Files.** Sound files contain digitized sound. The Windows 3.1 Sound Recorder, for example, records and plays back digitized sound by using WAV files.

If you write computer programs, you may be interested to know that not only do program source files have an average compression ratio of greater than 2:1, but object files also tend toward compression ratios somewhat greater than 2:1.

The compression ratio for most WAV files is around 1.5:1. Many sound-sampling boards or software applications compress the sound data as it is sampled. These sound files are already partially compressed and cannot be compressed much more.

- **Video Files.** Video files, such as the Microsoft AVI files, contain digitized video information and have low compression ratios for reasons similar to those for digitized sound.
- **Files Already Compressed.** Many types of files contain information that is already compressed. These files always display low compression ratios if used with either Stacker or DoubleSpace—often close to 1:1—because neither DoubleSpace nor Stacker can compress data that is already compressed. Some files are already compressed because the established standard for the file specifies that its data be compressed according to a particular compression technique. The popular GIF graphics file format, for example, already compresses its data by removing redundant patterns of dots in the picture stored in the file. Other files may already be compressed because a special utility program is used on them. You may be familiar with such programs as the popular PKZIP shareware program, used to compress files before transmitting them over a modem or putting them into a historical archive. Unlike files compressed by DoubleSpace or Stacker, files compressed by utilities such as PKZIP are not compressed or decompressed automatically and thus are not available for immediate use. To compress or decompress such a file, you must manually apply the utility. These types of programs are known as *file-by-file* compression programs. Files already compressed by file-by-file compression programs usually have extremely low compression ratios on a DoubleSpace or Stacker compressed disk.

Even though a particular file does not compress well or is already compressed, putting such a file on a Stacker or DoubleSpace compressed disk causes no harm, though you may not benefit much either. Some files, however, should not be placed on a DoubleSpace or Stacker compressed disk. These files either do not work right on a compressed disk or unacceptably reduce your computer system's performance. Never place on a compressed disk the files described in the following list.

- **Windows Permanent Swap Files.** If running on a 386 or higher computer, Microsoft Windows can improve its performance by using some disk space as if the space were additional memory. This disk space that Windows uses in place of memory is called a *swap file*. Windows can set aside a fixed amount of disk space—usually fairly large—and reserve this space permanently for use as a swap file. This is the fastest and most efficient configuration for the Windows swap file. Windows uses BIOS to access this permanent swap file, however, and thus bypasses the DoubleSpace or Stacker device driver. If the permanent swap file is on a Stacker or DoubleSpace compressed disk, Windows misreads the file, which results in error messages from Windows. Permanent swap files cannot be placed on a compressed drive; they must always be placed on an uncompressed drive. For more information about Windows swap files, refer to your Windows

If you are considering using Stacker or DoubleSpace disk compression to increase the amount of information you can store on your hard disk, and you work in desktop publishing or multimedia, you may discover that many of the file types with low compression ratios—fonts, sound, and video—are exactly the files you want to compress. Adding DoubleSpace or Stacker to your system can give you more storage space on your disk, but you may not experience as dramatic an increase as a user who has mostly word processing documents and spreadsheets to compress. To learn more about multimedia, you may want to read *Windows 3.1 Multimedia*, by Roger Jennings, also published by Que.

- **Windows Temporary Swap Files.** Windows has an alternative to using a permanent swap file—the temporary swap file. Windows uses the temporary swap file in much the same way that it uses the permanent swap file. With a temporary swap file, Windows creates and accesses the swap file by using DOS. Because Windows uses DOS for the temporary swap file, Windows can successfully use a temporary swap file placed on a Stacker or DoubleSpace compressed drive. Windows accesses its swap file so frequently and moves such large blocks of data, however, that the additional time required to compress and decompress the data in the swap file may noticeably degrade Windows' performance on your system—unless you have an exceptionally fast computer. For this reason, your Windows temporary swap file should usually be placed on an uncompressed drive. Refer to the appropriate chapters in this book on installing DoubleSpace or Stacker for information on setting up these products with Windows.
- **Other Files Accessed through BIOS.** With the exception of the Windows permanent swap file, few applications now access disks through BIOS. Those few programs that do still use BIOS to access data files or other disk information may not work correctly if placed on a compressed disk—and may even damage the disk. Such programs should not be allowed to read or write information on your DoubleSpace or Stacker compressed drive. The chance of encountering such programs is very small, however, so you need not be overly concerned. If you are uncertain about any application, check with its publisher to learn if it uses BIOS to access the disk.

How Disk Compression Works: An Overview

This section explains the theory behind the technology used to compress your disks and then describes the two methods used to implement that technology.

The Disk Compression Algorithm

An *algorithm* is a technical name given to the specific steps for solving a problem or accomplishing a particular task. If you follow a recipe to bake a cake, you are using an algorithm—the recipe—to provide you with the necessary steps to bake the cake. The basic algorithm used by both Stacker and DoubleSpace is the *Lempel-Ziv compression algorithm*. The Lempel-Ziv algorithm for data compression—abbreviated LZ—is named after its two Israeli inventors and was first published in 1977.

The LZ algorithm uses a simple idea to compress data—that of finding repeating sequences of characters in a file and replacing the repeated sequence with a *token*, which is a one-character symbol that represents the repeated character sequence. The repeated sequence of characters is stored only once. As the data is decompressed, the tokens in the file are replaced by copies of the repeated sequence they represent. Because the compressed data is not permanently changed and is easily restored to its original condition, the LZ algorithm is referred to as a *lossless* compression algorithm.

The LZ algorithm uses the following basic steps to compress data:

1. Take a series of characters (called a *string*) from the file.
2. Starting at the beginning of the string, take a two- to four-character sequence and compare it to every other series of characters in the string, moving through the string one character at a time.
3. The first time a matching sequence of characters is found in the string, create a new token and replace the repeated sequence of characters with the new token. The second time a matching sequence of characters is found in the string, replace the repeated sequence of characters with the same token used before.
4. Repeat steps 2 and 3 until all the repeated character sequences in the string are replaced by tokens.
5. Repeat steps 1 through 4 until all the data file has been compressed.

Each new token created is stored in a *dictionary* of tokens, along with the sequence of characters the token replaces. Whenever you need to know what characters a particular token replaces, you can look up that token in the dictionary.

The following example applies the steps of the LZ compression algorithm to a text sample. The text compressed in this example is the following quote from *Through the Looking Glass*, by Lewis Carroll:

```
If you think we're wax-works, you ought to pay, you know. Wax-works
weren't made to be looked at for nothing. Nohow!
```

Using the entire sample as the string for testing, the first repeating sequence of characters identified is the four-character sequence "_you" (the underscore represents a space character).

The Greek letter α is chosen as the token to replace the repeated sequence, and the repeated sequence "_you" is entered in the dictionary. Table 1.1 shows the completed token dictionary.

After replacing the repeated sequence with the token, the sample text now looks as follows:

```
If α think we're wax-works,α ought to pay,α know. Wax-works weren't made
to be looked at for nothing. Nohow!
```

Now the string is examined again for repeating patterns. The next repeating pattern identified is the two-character sequence "_t" (again, the underscore indicates a space character in the repeated sequence). The Greek letter β is chosen as the token for this repeated sequence, and both the token and the characters it represents are entered in the dictionary (see table 1.1).

After replacing the repeated sequence with the β token, the sample text appears as follows:

```
IfαβhinkΒ we're wax-works,α oughtβo pay,α know. Wax-works weren't madeβo be
looked at for nothing. Nohow!
```

Again, the string is examined for repeating patterns. Another pattern is found and another token created. After replacing the repeated sequence with the χ token, the sample looks like the following line:

```
Ifαβ χk we're wax-works,α oughtβo pay,α know. Wax-works weren't made βo be
looked at for notχg. Nohow!
```

By continuing to apply the algorithm until no more repeating sequences are found, the final result (using Greek letters as tokens) looks as follows:

```
Ifα β χkδe'εδφγ,α ought βηpay, kιwϑWϕγδeεn'λmade βηbe looked aλfor
ιtχgϑNohow!
```

The completed token dictionary is shown in Table 1.1 To restore the compressed data to its original form, each token in the compressed string is replaced by the original sequence of characters it replaces.

Table 1.1 Sample Compression Dictionary

Token	Characters for Token*	Token	Characters for Token*
α	_you	γ	orks
β	_t	η	o_
χ	hin	ι	no
δ	_w	ϑ	._
ε	re	λ	t_
φ	ax-w		

An underscore in this column stands for a space character.

The original quote was 116 characters in length, and the compressed result is only 77 characters in length. The compressed version of the sample was reduced in size by 34 percent and has a compression ratio of about 1.5:1. Although this example is used because of its obvious repeated character sequences, the technique can be applied to any data.

A great deal of variation is possible in exactly how you carry out the steps of the LZ algorithm. You could, for example, allow a token to contain another token. Although both Stacker and DoubleSpace are based on the LZ compression algorithm, each varies in the specific details used to carry out the LZ compression. Stacker, for example, uses a patented variation of the LZ technology, called LZS. Specific differences in features between DoubleSpace and Stacker are described in Chapter 2, "Comparing DoubleSpace and Stacker."

With the theory behind the Stacker and DoubleSpace disk compression algorithm firmly in mind, you can better understand how that theory is put into action.

Software Disk Compression

In software disk compression, all on-the-fly compression and decompression of your data is accomplished by a software program stored in your computer's memory. The software

Understanding and Using Disk Compression 21

instructions for data compression and decompression are part of the device driver that makes the compressed disk drive accessible to DOS. (Refer to the first section of this chapter for a description of device drivers.)

With software disk compression, your computer's Central Processing Unit (CPU) must perform all the steps involved in compressing or decompressing your data. While the CPU carries out the instructions in the compression software, DOS and any application that may be running are slowed down by as much time as your CPU needs to perform the compression or decompression process.

The delay inherent in using software disk compression may or may not be noticeable. If your computer is an older, slower model—such as an 8088 or 80286—the time the CPU needs to perform the disk compression and decompression steps may be very noticeable as an overall slowdown in your computer's performance.

On faster computers—such as an 80386 or 80486—the delay involved usually is not noticeable, although it is often still measurable. Some computers experience enough improvement in disk performance to completely compensate for any delay involved in compressing the data. If you own a computer with an 80386 or higher CPU that runs at a speed of 33Mhz or faster, you are unlikely to notice any delay at all.

Most on-the-fly disk compression schemes you encounter are likely to involve software disk compression. DoubleSpace disk compression and decompression is available only in software form, and Stacker disk compression is predominantly installed so that compression and decompression are performed by software.

Hardware Disk Compression

You can add to your computer a special hardware accessory that increases the speed of data compression on older, slower computers. Most modern computers, however, do not benefit from hardware-based disk compression.

DoubleSpace does not use a compression co-processor board. Only Stacker makes available a co-processor option.

To add hardware-based compression to your computer, you install an expansion card that contains the compression hardware. Because the purpose of this expansion card is to assist your CPU, this type of card also is known as a *co-processor* card. This hardware compression co-processor is essentially another, albeit miniature, computer dedicated to the single task of compressing and decompressing data. The co-processor contains all the instructions necessary to apply the compression algorithm to any data. Because the co-processor is an expansion card, with its own memory and other resources, it operates independently of your computer's CPU. If this independent co-processor runs faster than the CPU, the amount of time your system needs to compress or decompress data is reduced.

A device driver is required, however, even if a compression co-processor is used. The device driver makes the compressed disks available to DOS as logical disk drives and controls the compression co-processor. The device driver for a compression co-processor usually requires much less memory than does a device driver for software-only compression, as the driver itself does not actually perform the compression or decompression.

Hardware compression technology was successful initially because the increase in speed usually justified the additional expense involved in using a compression co-processor. Contemporary computers, however, operate so fast that any delay caused by using software-only compression is barely noticeable—if at all. Some newer computers, in fact, operate far faster than a co-processor and derive no benefits from using a co-processor card—and may even be slowed down by one.

An 80386 computer with a speed of 25Mhz to 33Mhz can software-compress data about as fast as can the same computer with a Stacker co-processor installed. If your computer is an 80386 or 80486 with a speed greater than 40Mhz, your CPU can compress data faster by using software instead of a Stacker compression co-processor.

Adding Compressed Disks: An Overview

This section offers an overview of what happens as you add disk compression to your computer system. The section describes how a compressed disk is created and made accessible to you through DOS. The information in this section applies generally to both DoubleSpace and Stacker. See Chapter 3, "Installing DoubleSpace," for details on how DoubleSpace creates a compressed disk; see Chapter 9, "Installing Stacker," for details on how Stacker creates a compressed disk.

This book covers only Stacker software. Except as described in this section, the Stacker co-processor board is not covered, because the co-processor is substantially more expensive than Stacker alone and is of little benefit in contemporary computers. The remainder of the book assumes that you use Stacker (or DoubleSpace) software only.

Preparing To Add Disk Compression

Adding disk compression to your computer system does not require extensive preparation. Certain tasks, however, need to be performed before you actually add disk compression capabilities to your computer.

If your system has more than one hard disk or any hard disk with more than one partition, deciding beforehand which disks or partitions to compress may help the task go more smoothly. For each disk drive or partition you choose to compress, you also must decide whether to compress all the files and free space already on the drive—the usual choice—or to compress only the free space on the drive. How (and why) to compress free space on a drive is discussed in the following section, "Creating the Compressed Disk."

Before creating a compressed disk, make sure that your disk drives and partitions are in good shape. Use the DOS CHKDSK command to test the integrity of the cluster allocations on your disk. If CHKDSK reports lost clusters, lost allocation units, or cross-linked files, take the appropriate action to recover the lost clusters and repair or replace the cross-linked files before you compress the disk. See Chapter 7, "Troubleshooting DoubleSpace," and Chapter 13, "Troubleshooting Stacker," for more information on dealing with lost clusters and cross-linked files. Refer to your DOS manual for information about the CHKDSK utility program, or use HELP CHKDSK.

CHKDSK tests only the integrity of your disk's logical organization. Several disk diagnostic programs—such as Gibson Research's SpinRite II, Central Point's PC Tools, or Norton Disk Doctor—test your disk for actual defects in the disk's surface. If you own such a disk testing program, use the program to test your disk before you compress that disk.

After you test your disk drives and partitions for reliability, you are almost ready to create a compressed disk. First, however, you need to back up all the files on each disk or partition you intend to compress. Adding disk compression introduces a major change

Before you use any low-level disk diagnostic or repair utility, first make sure that your diagnostic software is compatible with the type of disk drive you have and with the particular version of DOS you use. Incompatible versions may result in damage to your disk drive if used. Check with the diagnostic utility manufacturer or with your computer dealer if you are uncertain whether a particular disk diagnostic program is compatible with your hardware and DOS version.

to your computer system. Disk compression software significantly extends the capabilities of DOS and alters how information is stored on your disk drives. The importance of backing up all your files before any such major change cannot be over stressed. You are unlikely to experience problems working with disk compression, but if you do, a current backup may make all the difference between an inconvenience and a tragedy.

After you protect your data by making a current backup, you are ready to create one or more compressed disks on your computer.

Creating the Compressed Disk

Before you create a compressed disk, you must copy the disk compression program files from the distribution disks to your hard disk. The DOS 6 Setup program copies the DoubleSpace files to your disk as you install DOS 6. To copy the Stacker program files, you must use the Stacker Setup program. (See Chapter 9, "Installing Stacker," for details.)

DoubleSpace and Stacker both begin creating a compressed drive by setting aside their own working space on the disk or partition. This working space is not compressed, and it takes up about 1M on a bootable disk and substantially less on a nonbootable disk. (The exact amount of working space required depends on whether you use DoubleSpace or Stacker.) Because the working space must remain uncompressed, both Stacker and DoubleSpace retain access to the original, uncompressed disk drive. The original disk drive is referred to as the *uncompressed drive*, or the *uncompressed volume*. (A *volume* is just another term for a disk partition or other logical disk drive.) After the working space has been set aside, the disk compression software uses all the remaining space on the uncompressed volume to create one large file. This large file stores all your compressed data and is called the *compressed drive*, or the *compressed volume*.

Figure 1.3 shows a schematic representation of a disk drive after the compressed volume file is created. The figure represents an 80M drive with 2M of working space and 78M of physical space used for the compressed volume file. The compressed volume can store up to 156M of information—twice the physical space used by the compressed volume file.

Because the compressed drive is actually a large file stored on the uncompressed volume, the uncompressed volume also is referred to as the *host drive*.

Both DoubleSpace and Stacker protect the compressed volume file from accidental alteration or erasure by applying the DOS file attributes Hidden, System, and Read-Only. As discussed earlier in this chapter, the Read-Only and System file attributes prevent you from erasing the file. The Hidden file attribute prevents the file name from appearing if you use the DOS DIR command to display a list of files in the disk directory, so you usually are not even aware of the compressed volume's presence.

After the compressed volume file is created, the disk compression program compresses every existing file on the disk and moves the compressed data to the compressed volume file. (If you use only free space to create a compressed volume, this step is

> **NOTE:** Stacker's documentation calls the compressed volume the *Stacker volume*, or *Stacker drive*, while the DoubleSpace documentation calls it the *Compressed Volume File (CVF)*. All these terms refer to the same thing—the large file that stores your compressed data files.

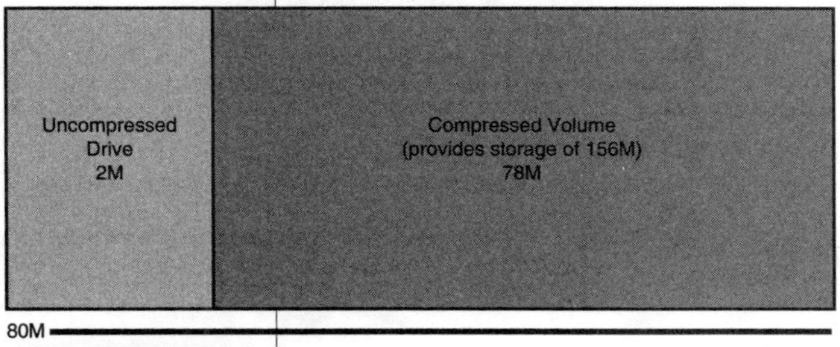

Fig. 1.3

An 80M hard disk showing both uncompressed and compressed volume.

skipped.) The compressed volume file is directly used only by DOS and your disk compression device driver—Stacker or DoubleSpace. You and your applications access data files stored in the compressed volume indirectly, through the logical disk drive created by the disk compression device driver.

Whenever DOS reads or writes data to the compressed disk drive, the disk compression device driver determines where to read or write the data in the compressed volume file. The disk compression device driver creates a logical disk drive from the compressed volume file. You and your applications access compressed data files on this logical drive through regular DOS services, just like you access data files on any other disk drive.

Whenever your computer starts up and loads DOS into memory, DOS assigns drive letters to all the physical and logical drives it detects. DOS assigns these drive letters on a first-come, first-served basis, so your newly created compressed volume is assigned the next available drive letter. If you have drives A, B, and C, for example, and you compress drive C, the new compressed volume receives the drive letter D. Usually, however, you want the compressed logical drive to replace the uncompressed physical drive or partition. The disk compression device driver, therefore, switches the drive letters of the uncompressed drive and the compressed volume so that you work with the compressed volume by using the same drive letter you used for the previously uncompressed drive.

If you compress drive C by using Stacker, for example, DOS assigns drive letter C to the original physical, uncompressed volume and then assigns drive letter D to the compressed logical volume. Immediately after DOS assigns drive letters, the Stacker device driver exchanges the compressed volume's drive letter for that of the uncompressed volume. After the exchange, drive letter C refers to the compressed volume, while drive letter D refers to the uncompressed volume. You continue working with all your files and programs on drive C, just as you did before you compressed the disk. By exchanging drive letters, DoubleSpace and Stacker eliminate the need for you to reinstall or reconfigure any software already on your disk.

Figure 1.4 shows a schematic representation of a physical disk drive containing a compressed volume. The figure indicates the drive letters assigned by DOS, before any drive letter exchanges take place. (The figure uses the same 80M disk drive as shown in figure 1.3.)

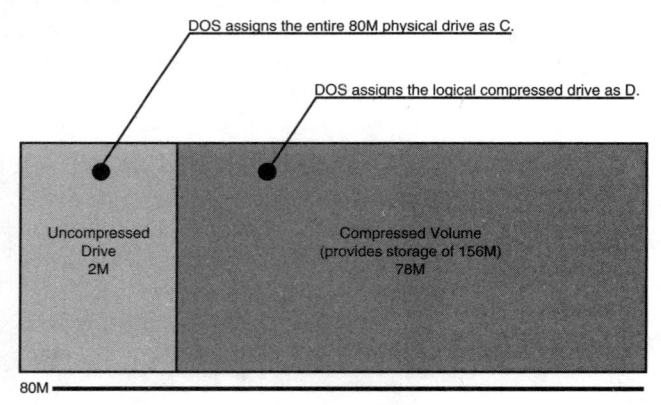

Figure 1.5 depicts the same physical and compressed drive, but with the drive letters swapped by Stacker. Figure 1.6 shows the same drive letters as swapped by DoubleSpace.

DoubleSpace and Stacker use different rules and schemes for exchanging drive letters, which is why the uncompressed drive in figure 1.5 is drive D, but the uncompressed drive in figure 1.6 is drive H. How DoubleSpace and Stacker reassign drive letters is detailed in Chapter 3, "Installing DoubleSpace," and Chapter 9, "Installing Stacker," respectively.

Both DoubleSpace and Stacker enable you to override how the program exchanges, or swaps, the drive letters. Chapter 4, "Configuring and Optimizing DoubleSpace," and

> Do not change the compressed volume's file attributes or attempt to edit or change the compressed volume file in any way. If you alter or delete this file, you may lose all the data stored in the compressed volume.

Fig. 1.4

A compressed 80M hard disk showing the drive letters DOS assigns, before any drive letter exchanges.

Chapter 10, "Configuring and Optimizing Stacker," provide specifics on how to alter the way drive letters are exchanged.

Stacker and DoubleSpace also affect the volume labels on your compressed and uncompressed disks. How DoubleSpace and Stacker alter volume labels is detailed in Chapter 3, "Installing DoubleSpace," and Chapter 9, "Installing Stacker," respectively. You also may use the LABEL command to change the volume label on the Stacker or DoubleSpace compressed drives.

Figure 1.7 shows how the compressed volume increases your available storage. All your compressed files are stored inside the single large compressed volume file.

The available storage space on the compressed volume is approximately twice the size of the compressed volume file. In the figure, an 80M hard disk is compressed, with 2M set aside for the uncompressed volume. (The 2M in the uncompressed volume is reserved for the working space required by the disk compression software, plus a bit more for any files you may want to store on the uncompressed volume.)

The remaining amount of space on the drive, 78M, is used for the compressed volume. At an anticipated compression ratio of 2:1, the 78M compressed volume yields 156M of storage. Assuming that the 80M drive is drive C before it is compressed, the 156M compressed volume becomes drive C after the disk compression device driver swaps the drive letters.

If your disk has multiple partitions, you must compress each partition separately. Stacker or DoubleSpace creates additional logical drives for every compressed volume you create. The disk compression's device driver then exchanges drive letters between compressed and uncompressed volumes for every physical partition you compress.

Both DoubleSpace and Stacker enable you to create more than one compressed volume on a single physical disk or partition. If you create multiple compressed volumes in a single disk or partition, each compressed volume is assigned its own drive letter. The respective chapters on installing Stacker and DoubleSpace provide more specific information about how drive letters are exchanged if a single disk or partition has multiple compressed volumes.

Whether using DoubleSpace or Stacker, you can choose to create your compressed disk from just the free space on a partition or disk. You normally use this free space option

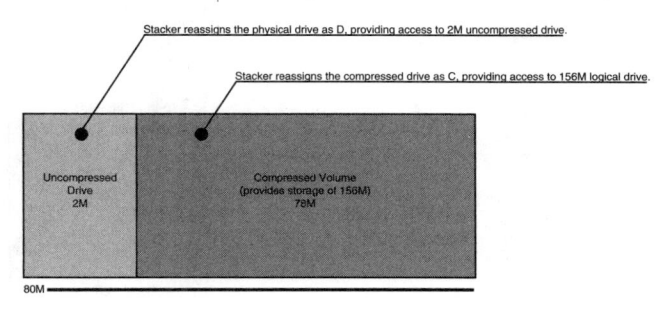

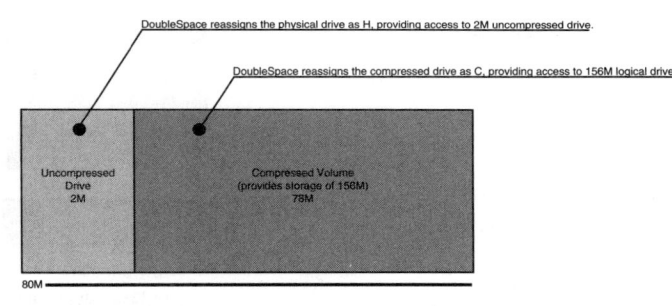

Fig. 1.5, top

A compressed 80M hard disk showing drive letters as exchanged by Stacker.

Fig. 1.6, bottom

A compressed 80M hard disk showing drive letters as exchanged by DoubleSpace.

only on a blank disk or partition—such as a new disk, a previously unused partition, or a floppy disk or other removable media. You also can create a compressed drive from free space on a disk if you want to leave your existing files uncompressed for any reason.

Making the Compressed Disk Available

The final step either DoubleSpace or Stacker performs after creating your first compressed drive is to add its disk compression device driver to your system. If you use DoubleSpace or Stacker 3.1, the disk compression device driver is placed in the root directory of your boot disk—in the uncompressed portion of the disk if your boot disk is compressed. The disk compression device driver must always go on a disk's uncompressed portion, because DOS cannot use the compressed volume until the device driver is loaded.

As DOS loads into memory on start-up, it searches the root directory of the boot drive. If DOS finds the DoubleSpace or Stacker 3.1 device driver, it loads the device driver into memory, making available to you any compressed volumes on any disk or partition.

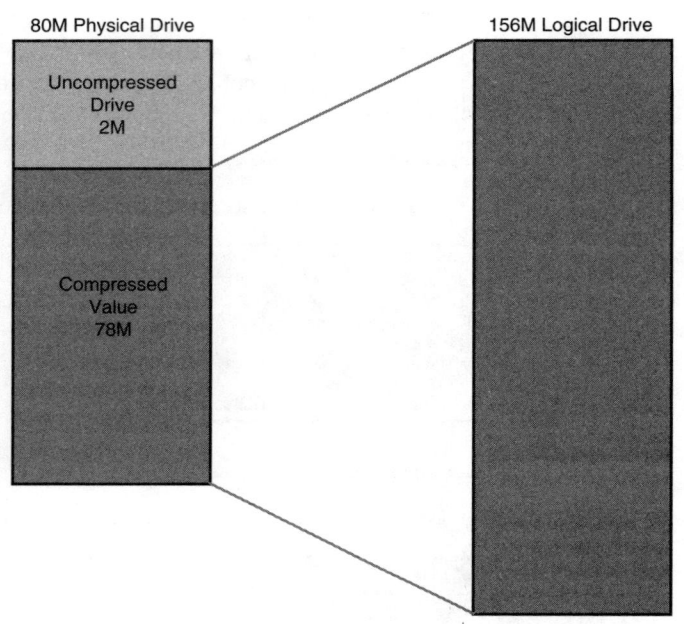

Fig. 1.7

How the compressed volume file increases available disk storage.

Using a Compressed Disk

For disk compression to be truly useful, it must not intrude in any way on your normal use of a disk. You should never be aware that anything special is happening with your disk. This kind of operation is called a *transparent* operation, because you cannot "see" the program operating. Although both Stacker and DoubleSpace are primarily transparent, a few situations, described in this section, may require you to use your compressed disks a little differently than you use an uncompressed disk. Usually, however, you do not notice DoubleSpace or Stacker in operation.

As you use disk compression, remember that the free space reported by DOS or the disk compression utilities as available on a compressed drive is merely an approximation. Because different files compress at different ratios, the disk compression software can only estimate how much space actually is available on the compressed volume.

Stacker and DoubleSpace determine the amount of available space on a disk drive by using the estimated compression ratio of 2:1. If the compressed volume has 512K of physical space free, for example, the free space reported for the compressed disk is 1M. Because neither DoubleSpace nor Stacker can determine exactly how much a file can be compressed until the file actually is compressed, the actual amount of data you can store

Understanding and Using Disk Compression 27

NOTE:
Although DoubleSpace and Stacker are compatible with almost every type of disk drive, neither DoubleSpace nor Stacker 3.1 can be used with boot disks that require a device driver to be loaded before the boot disk can be read. DOS 6 loads the Stacker 3.1 or DoubleSpace device driver before processing your CONFIG.SYS file—which contains the statements that load other device drivers. As soon as the compression device driver loads, DOS 6 tries to read the disk as if it were a compressed drive. Because the device driver needed to access the disk's hardware is not yet loaded, however, DOS cannot read the compressed drive. If your boot disk drive requires a device driver to read the disk, you can still use disk compression, but you must take one of the following steps:

• *Partition the disk so that the boot partition is not compressed.* (Refer to the documentation that came with your disk drive or consult with your dealer to determine the appropriate method for partitioning your drive.)

• *Create a compressed volume from free space only.* This has the same effect as partitioning the disk so that the boot partition is not compressed.

may differ from the amount of free space reported. If, for example, you add to the compressed volume several files that do not compress well, these files occupy more space than estimated, and the compressed volume may fill up faster than anticipated. If instead you add to the compressed volume several files with high compression ratios, the files occupy less space than estimated.

Both Stacker and DoubleSpace enable you to specify the compression ratio used to estimate free space. Use this option if you find that the file types you store consistently tend toward compression ratios higher or lower than 2:1. Chapter 4, "Configuring and Optimizing DoubleSpace," and Chapter 10, "Configuring and Optimizing Stacker," describe how to change the estimated compression ratio.

Using a Compressed Hard Disk

DoubleSpace and Stacker both work on almost any type of hard disk drive. They are compatible with IDE, SCSI, MFM, RLL, ESDI, and VLB (VESA Local Bus) disk drive controllers. (The initials IDE, SCSI, MFM, and so on represent the names of the different device control or data recording standards that disk controllers use.) You need not be concerned with how these devices work, however, as Stacker and DoubleSpace deal with them correctly through your computer's BIOS.

Using Disk Compression with DOS Versions Prior to DOS 6

If you use a version of DOS earlier than version 6, you cannot use DoubleSpace without upgrading to DOS 6. DoubleSpace works only with DOS 6 and is supplied with your purchase of DOS 6. DoubleSpace uses special new features in DOS 6 that automatically load the disk compression device driver. Stacker 3.1, however, works with any version of DOS from version 3.2. Stacker 3.1 also can use the new feature in DOS 6 to automatically load its disk compression device driver. If used with earlier versions of DOS than 6, Stacker installs device drivers that load through the CONFIG.SYS file.

If you use a version of DOS prior to version 4, you may need to divide your compressed volume into two or more drives, because these earlier DOS versions have a 32M partition limit. If, for example, you run DOS 3.3 and use a 32M hard disk (the maximum limit for that version of DOS), adding disk compression gives you about 60M of disk space. This is greater, however, than DOS 3.3's 32M limit. To use all this space, you must divide the compressed drive into two 30M compressed drives. Although the total compressed space still is 60M, dividing it into two logical drives keeps the individual volumes within the 32M limit. Stacker automatically divides the compressed volume and creates additional logical drives if necessary. Because DoubleSpace works only with DOS 6, which has no 32M limit, DoubleSpace does not need to deal with the problem.

Backing Up Compressed Hard Disks

When you back up your hard disk, make sure that you back up the files on your compressed drive just as you normally back up those on any other hard disk—whether you use a tape backup, the DOS BACKUP or MSBACKUP programs, or a third-party backup program. Make sure also that you back up any files on your uncompressed volumes, except any hidden files that contain your compressed volumes.

You may, for example, have a compressed drive C and an uncompressed drive D, the latter containing the compressed volume file. You back up all your files on drive C as you would any other drive. You also back up the files on your uncompressed drive D, except for the hidden file that contains the compressed volume's data. (Refer to the documentation of your backup program to determine how to exclude files from a backup. See also Chapter 3, "Installing DoubleSpace," and Chapter 9, "Installing Stacker," for details about Stacker and DoubleSpace hidden compressed volume files.)

Using Compressed Removable Media Disks

The least transparent aspect of disk compression involves the use of compressed removable media disks, such as floppy disks. To use a compressed floppy disk, for example, you must explicitly establish a connection between DOS, the device driver, and the compressed volume on the floppy disk. This process is called *mounting* the drive. (Your hard disk drives also must be mounted, but this occurs automatically.) Every time you remove a compressed floppy disk from the floppy drive, you must first *unmount* the disk; that is, you must sever the connection to DOS for the mounted disk in the drive.

Bernoulli drives, Floptical drives, and Syquest drives are other types of removable media that must be mounted or unmounted.

Using Disk Cache Programs

Cache comes from a French word meaning "pocket." A *disk cache* is an area of memory—a pocket—set aside to hold information from the disk. A disk cache is used to speed a computer's disk performance. Most disk cache programs install themselves as a device driver and use part of your computer's RAM to hold the disk data.

The disk cache works by assuming that the disk location containing the information you want next is near the last location from which you read data. As the disk is read, the disk cache device driver loads data from the disk into the cache, specifically including areas immediately before and after the current reading position. The next time the disk is read, the disk cache device driver searches the cache memory for the disk information before actually reading from the disk. If the desired disk data is found in the cache, the time required to actually reposition the drive's heads is saved, improving the disk system's performance.

Many different cache programs are available. DOS and Windows include a cache program called SMARTDRV; other popular cache programs are Norton's NCache and Golden Bow's VCache. Almost all disk cache programs are compatible with disk compression software. (If you use DoubleSpace, however, you must use SMARTDRV version 4.1, supplied with DOS 6.)

A special type of disk cache uses a technique called *write-behind*, or *write-delay*, caching. Whenever data is written to a disk by using this technique, only the data in the cache is changed initially. Data is actually written to the disk only after the cache is full or your computer is idle for a set period of time—usually 2 to 5 seconds.

> **NOTE:**
> If you own an 80386 or higher computer, upgrading to at least DOS 5 is highly recommended. The many improvements in memory usage and memory management in DOS 5—and, by inheritance, DOS 6—greatly enhance your computer's performance.

> **NOTE:**
> Stacker disk compression software includes a special feature that automatically mounts and unmounts removable media. DoubleSpace does not have a corresponding utility, but the DoubleSpace add-in program, SPACEMANager, provides the same function. (Specific differences between Stacker and DoubleSpace are described in Chapter 2, "Comparing DoubleSpace and Stacker.") Using removable media disks with Stacker is described in Chapter 11, "Using Stacker." The disk mounting utility in SPACEMANager is described in Chapter 8. "Beyond DoubleSpace: Using SPACEMANager."

The write-delay cache technique saves the time normally required to physically access a disk while writing to it, just as a regular cache saves time by accessing the disk fewer times while reading it. Write-delay caches have a certain inherent danger, however. If a power failure occurs or your computer is accidentally rebooted, and the cache contains information not yet written to the disk, data loss or corrupted files may result. Most disk caches that use write-delay caching—including SMARTDRV—enable you to selectively disable the write-delay caching on specific disk drives. Whether you use the additional performance write-delay caching delivers, however, always remain aware of its potential drawbacks.

If using disk caching on compressed drives, cache the host drive for the compressed volume file. If using Stacker, for example, and you have a compressed drive C and an uncompressed drive D (which contains the compressed volume file), you want to cache drive D and exclude drive C from caching.

Because Stacker and DoubleSpace each contain their own caches, caching the compressed drive itself has little effect. Caching the host drive for the compressed volume file, however, speeds up the compressed drive's operation. The use of disk caches with DoubleSpace or Stacker is detailed in the programs' configuration and optimization chapters (chapters 4 and 10, respectively).

Potential Difficulties in Using Disk Compression

As a rule, using disk compression is a straightforward and easy process. Adding disk compression to your computer system does increase its complexity, however, and you do need to consider a few special issues that may complicate your use of this technology.

Lost Device Drivers

If your disk compression device driver becomes corrupted or is accidentally deleted from your boot disk, your compressed volumes may be temporarily inaccessible. If DOS cannot load the device drivers, it can read only the uncompressed portion of any disk drive. If you use DoubleSpace or Stacker 3.1 on your boot disk, your CONFIG.SYS and AUTOEXEC.BAT files usually are stored on the compressed volume. Other device drivers your system needs also may be stored on your compressed drive. If the compressed drive becomes unavailable, therefore, these crucial files also are unavailable.

If you experience difficulty accessing your compressed volumes because of a problem with the disk compression device driver, keeping on hand a floppy disk from which you can reboot your system is helpful. This bootable floppy disk should contain the disk compression device drivers and any other device drivers your system needs to operate. You can create this bootable floppy disk by using the DOS SYS command. The SYS command puts the disk compression device drivers on the boot floppy for you. (Refer to your DOS documentation for more information on creating a bootable floppy disk.) Even though the DoubleSpace or Stacker 3.1 (with DOS 6) device drivers load automatically, your bootable floppy still needs a CONFIG.SYS file and an AUTOEXEC.BAT file to load any additional device drivers your system requires.

You also may want to consider storing copies of your disk diagnostic and repair programs—including the DOS CHKDSK program and your disk compression diagnostic and repair utilities—on an uncompressed disk or a floppy disk. That way, your disk troubleshooting software is always available, even if your compressed volumes are not.

Deleted Compressed Volume

As discussed earlier in this chapter, the file containing the compressed volume is assigned System, Hidden, and Read-Only attributes. These attributes prevent the file containing the compressed volume from appearing in normal directory listings and also saves the file from being deleted. You can, however, use the DOS ATTRIB command—or another disk tool, such as Norton Utilities or Central Point PC Tools—to alter file attributes on your disk. Some troubleshooting procedures may, in fact, require you to change the file attributes of the compressed volume file.

If you do change the attributes of the compressed volume file, you risk accidentally deleting the compressed volume, which causes the loss of all its data.

If you use DOS 5 or 6 or certain third-party disk utilities, you may be able to undelete a compressed volume—if your undelete utilities are stored on an uncompressed disk or on a floppy disk. Refer to your DOS documentation for information on the DOS UNDELETE command. If you cannot undelete an accidentally erased compressed volume file, your only recourse is to re-create the compressed volume and restore all your files from a backup.

> Never alter the file attributes of a compressed volume file unless specifically directed to do so as part of a troubleshooting procedure. If you do change the file's attributes, always remember to change them back to System, Hidden, and Read-Only. Casual experimentation with your compressed volume file or its attributes may result in the complete and irrevocable loss of your data.

Memory Usage and Memory Conflicts

Whether you use DoubleSpace or Stacker, your computer must load a device driver into memory before the compressed volume is read. Although the Stacker and DoubleSpace device drivers do not require much memory, what memory they do use may not leave enough for some of your applications. Running out of memory is likely to be a problem only if you must load a number of device drivers, if you set aside sizable amounts of memory for disk cache programs or RAM disks, or if you use many TSR (Terminate-Stay-Resident) programs—or some combination of these factors.

Its first 640K of RAM, referred to as *conventional memory*, is the part of your computer's memory most in demand. Most DOS programs use this memory area. Device drivers and TSR programs also normally load into this part of your computer's memory. If you load many device drivers and TSR programs, conventional memory space may be severely reduced because the device drivers and TSRs continuously occupy memory.

Beginning with DOS 5, however, DOS gained the capability to load device drivers into other areas of memory so that more of this first 640K is available for other uses. Various ways have been developed to use memory beyond 640K and are implemented by programs such as 386MAX, QEMM-386, and EMM386 (which is supplied with DOS). Programs that enable device drivers and other programs to use memory areas beyond conventional memory are called *memory managers*.

Most memory manager techniques—including those built into DOS—use the 384K memory area directly above conventional memory, but still within the first 1M of memory. This area is known as the *upper memory area*. The upper memory area is used mainly to store the memory addresses of your computer's various hardware devices, such as its video display board. Most memory managers can exclude or include specific ranges of memory addresses to avoid conflicts with the parts of upper memory actually used by hardware devices.

If you need more conventional memory space, both DoubleSpace and Stacker can be loaded into upper memory. Unfortunately, because most memory managers attempt to load the device drivers into the upper memory area, the upper memory area may become crowded. The upper memory area may also become crowded if many hardware devices are installed in your computer. If the upper memory area is too crowded, it may not have enough room for the disk compression device driver. Even if enough room is available to load the disk compression device driver into upper memory, the various device drivers may begin to conflict with each other if upper memory is crowded.

If device drivers in upper memory conflict, you may receive sporadic but chronic read errors as you read from your compressed volumes. If the conflict between the device drivers is severe, the data on your compressed volume may even become corrupted. The data on your compressed volume also may become corrupted if your memory manager includes or excludes incorrect areas of the upper memory.

Memory conflict problems are almost always resolvable; once resolved, they tend to stay resolved. The best insurance against this type of problem is to back up all your files before you install the disk compression software. If you load device drivers into upper memory and are concerned about possible conflicts, back up your files frequently during the first weeks after you install disk compression software. After you determine that the software is working correctly, you can return to your original backup schedule. See Chapter 4, "Configuring and Optimizing DoubleSpace," and Chapter 10, "Configuring and Optimizing Stacker," for more information about loading the disk compression device drivers into upper memory.

Compressed Removable Media

If you plan to compress removable media disks, such as floppy disks, you must remember that only computers using the same type of disk compression can read those disks. If you use DoubleSpace to compress a floppy disk, for example, only computers using DoubleSpace can read files on that floppy disk.

Stacker disk compression includes a utility program, called Stacker Anywhere, that alleviates this problem. Computers on which Stacker disk compression is not installed can use the Anywhere program to read Stacker compressed floppy disks. Chapter 11, "Using Stacker," describes the Stacker Anywhere utility program in detail.

DoubleSpace does not include a similar utility. The SPACEMANager accessory for DoubleSpace, however, does provide a utility called SuperExchange that offers the same capabilities as the Stacker Anywhere program. Chapter 2, "Comparing DoubleSpace and Stacker," describes the specific differences between Stacker and DoubleSpace, and

Chapter 8, "Beyond DoubleSpace: Using SPACEMANager," describes the SPACEMANager accessory.

Loss of DOS Uninstall

Another potential problem involves DOS upgrades and the DOS Uninstall program. The DOS 6 Setup program that installs your DOS upgrade creates a special "uninstall" disk. The Setup program stores critical information about your computer system and boot disk on this uninstall disk before placing the new version of DOS on your computer.

If you discover that the new version of DOS is somehow incompatible with your existing programs or computer hardware—unlikely but not impossible—you can use the DOS Uninstall program to revert back to your original version of DOS. The Uninstall program uses the information on the uninstall disk to restore the version of DOS you used before upgrading.

If you add disk compression to your system after upgrading to a new DOS version, however, you cannot use the uninstall disk to revert to your previous version of DOS. The disk compression software so alters your disk drive's contents that the data on the uninstall disk is no longer valid for restoring the previous DOS version. Even if you already use disk compression and upgrade to a later version of DOS, the uninstall disk created during DOS setup becomes invalid, and you cannot uninstall the upgrade.

Summary

This chapter first reviewed the physical components of a disk drive and how your computer's BIOS and DOS work together to control the disk drives. The chapter then described how the capabilities of DOS are enhanced by using device drivers and reviewed how DOS organizes the space on a disk to manage files and directories. This chapter also introduced you to disk compression software and explored what disk compression can and cannot do. The chapter explained the technology behind disk compression and discussed how a compressed disk is created and how disk compression affects your system. Finally, the chapter described some difficulties you may encounter in using disk compression.

The next chapter compares DoubleSpace and Stacker, feature by feature, and offers information to help you choose the disk compression system that is right for you.

CHAPTER 2

Comparing DoubleSpace and Stacker

This chapter examines and compares the DoubleSpace and Stacker features and operating characteristics. The features you can add to DoubleSpace by using the SPACEMANager enhancement product also are discussed. (Chapter 8, "Beyond DoubleSpace: Using SPACEMANager," describes SPACEMANager in more detail.) The chapter concludes with a discussion intended to help you choose the disk compression software that is right for you.

Comparing Features

This section describes the important features of Stacker and DoubleSpace, including the features that SPACEMANager adds to DoubleSpace.

Table 2.1 summarizes the features discussed in this section. The first column of the table lists the feature; the next two columns indicate whether the feature is present in Stacker or DoubleSpace. The last column in the table is for SPACEMANager's features. Because SPACEMANager is an enhancement to DoubleSpace, the blank spaces indicate either that SPACEMANager does not add this feature or that DoubleSpace already has the feature.

The discussions following table 2.1 cover the features in the same order they are presented in the table.

NOTE: You can install and use only one disk compression scheme on your computer at a time. Installing both Stacker and DoubleSpace on your system is impossible. SPACEMANager and DoubleSpace, however, can be installed together because SPACEMANager is designed to enhance DoubleSpace's capabilities. SPACEMANager does not work on disks compressed by Stacker or with the Stacker software.

Table 2.1 Summary of DoubleSpace and Stacker Features

Feature	Stacker 3.1	DoubleSpace	SPACEMANager
Automatic system file synchronization	Yes	NA	
Preload device driver with DOS 6	Yes	Yes	
Adjustable estimated compression ratio	Yes	Yes	
Setup from Windows	Yes	No	No
Automatic configuration of CONFIG.SYS and AUTOEXEC.BAT	Yes	Yes	Yes
Express Setup for all hard disks	Yes	No	
Custom Setup for individual disks	Yes	Yes	
Maximum compression when setting up	Yes	Only one compression level	No
Smallest disk (uncompressed capacity)	360K	720K	
Maximum disk size (uncompressed capacity)	1G	256M	
Maximum compressed disk size	2G	512M	
Required working space on boot disk	1M	1.2M	
Required working space on nonboot disk	100K	.65M (approx. 670K)	
Compatible with standard disk utilities	Yes	Yes	
Automatic handling of disk cache	Yes	Use SMARTDRV 4.1 (supplied with DOS 6)	

Comparing DoubleSpace and Stacker

Feature	Stacker 3.1	DoubleSpace	SPACEMANager
Makes compressed removable media readable on any computer	Yes	No	Yes
Compress removable media with existing files	Yes	Yes	
Load device drivers in upper memory	Yes	Yes	
Compression cache in EMS	Yes	No	
Recompression of existing compressed drive for maximum compression	Yes	No	No
Integrated utilities	Yes	No	Yes
Compression report based on file type	Yes	No	Partial
Internal integrity checks	Yes	Yes	
Tuning: Balance compression against speed	Yes	No	Yes
Tuning: Based on file type	No	No	Yes
Change compressed disk size (larger or smaller)	Yes	Yes	
Compatible with standard disk repair utilities	Yes	Yes	Yes
Windows graphical display of compressed disk information	Yes	Yes (via File Manager only)	Yes (provides new utility)
Automatic update of Windows information utilities	Yes	No	No

continues

Table 2.1 Continued

Feature	Stacker 3.1	DoubleSpace	SPACEMANager
Automatic installation of Windows program group	Yes	NA	Yes
Password protection	Yes	No	
On-line Help	Yes	Yes	Yes
Mouse interface for DOS utilities	Yes	Yes	Yes
Automated removal of compression	Yes	No	
Compatible with operating environments other than DOS	Yes	No	No

Device Driver Preloading and System File Synchronization

System files are the files that your computer needs to start up, load DOS, and configure itself. These files include special DOS files, your CONFIG.SYS and AUTOEXEC.BAT files, and any device drivers your system needs to operate. As your computer starts up, DOS loads from your hard disk, processes your CONFIG.SYS file, and then loads device drivers into memory. If your boot disk is compressed, however, a problem arises, because DOS cannot read from a compressed disk until the device driver for the compressed disk is loaded into memory. Before DOS 6, the only way to resolve this problem was to keep duplicate copies of all your system files and device drivers on the uncompressed portion of your boot disk. DOS 6 solves the problem by *preloading* (loading ahead of time) the device driver for the compressed disk.

With DOS 6 and DoubleSpace or Stacker 3.1, you need only the DOS system files and the disk compression device driver on the uncompressed portion of your boot disk. After the DOS system files load into memory, DOS loads the disk compression device driver. DOS can then read the remaining system files from the compressed volume. DoubleSpace relies on the DOS 6 preloading capability and cannot be used with any version of DOS prior to DOS 6. Stacker 3.1, however, can be used with DOS 3.2 or any later version. If you use Stacker 3.1 with versions earlier than DOS 6, however, you must keep copies of all your system files on the uncompressed portion of your boot disk, because earlier versions of DOS cannot preload the disk compression device driver.

Because your system files are likely to change from time to time, Stacker automatically updates the copies of these files on the uncompressed part of your boot disk whenever the copies on the compressed volume change. Stacker automatically maintains copies of CONFIG.SYS, AUTOEXEC.BAT, and any device drivers named in your CONFIG.SYS file.

NOTE: System file synchronization applies only to versions of DOS prior to DOS 6. If you use DOS 6 and either DoubleSpace or Stacker 3.1, you need not be concerned with this issue.

Installation

As you may expect, you install both DoubleSpace and Stacker from the DOS command line. You can start the installation process for Stacker from inside Windows, but Stacker exits Windows to complete the installation process. DoubleSpace cannot be installed from Windows. The program files for DoubleSpace are installed in the DOS directory on your hard disk at the time you install your DOS 6 upgrade. The Stacker program files are copied onto your hard disk during Stacker's setup process.

Stacker and DoubleSpace both offer you the choice of an express setup or a custom installation. DoubleSpace and Stacker carry out their express setups quite differently; the custom setups for Stacker and DoubleSpace, however, have much more in common with one another than do the express setups.

DoubleSpace offers you the choice of Express or Custom Setup the first time you run the DoubleSpace program only. If DoubleSpace finds at least one compressed hard disk on your system when it starts, the DoubleSpace utility program starts instead of the Setup program. DoubleSpace Express Setup compresses only drive C. If your system includes other hard disk drives or partitions, you must compress each additional drive manually. If you want to compress several disk drives or partitions at once, therefore, you may find Stacker's Express Setup easier to use than DoubleSpace's. Stacker's Express Setup automatically compresses all hard disks or disk partitions on your computer. If you started the Stacker installation from Windows, Stacker Express Setup also prepares Windows to set up a program group for the Stacker Windows utilities.

Use the Custom Setup option with either DoubleSpace or Stacker to compress selected hard disk drives, create a compressed drive by using only free space, or compress floppy disks or other removable media. If you perform a Custom Setup, Stacker and DoubleSpace enable you to set certain advanced options for the compressed drive you create. The options offered by DoubleSpace and Stacker differ slightly. In Stacker, you use the advanced options to select how much space to leave uncompressed on the disk, set the estimated compression ratio, and adjust the cluster size used by the compressed drive. The Custom Setup options in DoubleSpace enable you to select how much space to leave uncompressed on the disk and the drive letter for the new uncompressed drive. The compressed drive letter is always exchanged so that it has the same drive letter as the original uncompressed disk. These options are described more fully in Chapter 3, "Installing DoubleSpace," and Chapter 9, "Installing Stacker."

Whether you choose an Express or Custom setup, Stacker compresses all the files on the new compressed disk using its maximum compression. Stacker offers three different compression levels; DoubleSpace uses only one compression level. Notice that the SPACEMANager enhancement to DoubleSpace adds two additional compression levels to DoubleSpace's standard compression. Refer to Chapter 8, "Beyond DoubleSpace: Using SPACEMANager," for more information.

Compressed Disk Sizes

Both DoubleSpace and Stacker require that a certain amount of uncompressed working space be available on each disk or disk partition you compress. As Stacker or DoubleSpace compress a disk, the correct amount of working space is left uncompressed. Neither disk compression scheme can compress a disk that does not have at least the minimum amount of working space available. Because the working space requirements for Stacker and DoubleSpace are different, the smallest capacity disk you can compress with each product is different. The working space requirements are greatest for a compressed boot disk.

Notice in table 2.1 that Stacker requires approximately 1M of working space for a boot disk and only about 100K of working space for other disks. DoubleSpace, on the other hand, requires more room: 1.2M for a boot disk and .65M (approximately 670K) for other disks. Because of DoubleSpace's working space requirement, the smallest disk you can compress with DoubleSpace is a 720K floppy disk. You can use Stacker to compress 360K floppy disks, however, because Stacker's working space requirement is less. Because 360K floppy disks are not as common as they once were, however, this difference may not be important to you.

The maximum drive size that Stacker or DoubleSpace can compress is probably more important to you than the minimum drive size. The maximum drive size you can compress is related to the size of the disk cluster used for the compressed volume. Both DoubleSpace and Stacker have a limit to how many disk clusters they can track. To use the space on larger compressed volumes, Stacker uses larger cluster sizes. Because each cluster then represents more information, a larger disk can be used for the same number of clusters. Stacker can use disk clusters from 4K to 32K in size; DoubleSpace uses only 8K clusters. Stacker, therefore, can access much larger compressed volumes than can DoubleSpace.

The difference in the maximum compressed volume size may be significant if the drives you want to compress are very large. Remember, however, that you cannot compress disk drives on network servers—where most very large hard disks are used. DoubleSpace can handle compressed drives up to 512M, so the largest capacity uncompressed disk drive to which you can apply DoubleSpace compression is 256M. You can compress hard disks with uncompressed capacities greater than 256M (such as 300M or 400M) by using DoubleSpace, but you must create several compressed volumes on the hard disk—each with its own drive letter—because no single DoubleSpace compressed volume can exceed 512M. Because Stacker uses larger cluster sizes, it can handle compressed volumes up to 2G. Using Stacker, you can create a single compressed drive from an uncompressed drive up to 1G in size.

Disk Compatibility

Both Stacker and DoubleSpace are compatible with IDE, ESDI, SCSI, MFM, and RLL hard disk drives, and almost all types of removable media, including floppy disks, Floptical disks, Syquest drives, and Bernoulli drives. DoubleSpace and Stacker can even be used to compress RAM disks. Compressing RAM disks is described in Chapter 4, "Configuring and Optimizing DoubleSpace," and in Chapter 10, "Configuring and Optimizing Stacker."

> **NOTE:**
> DoubleSpace cannot use disks compressed by Stacker; similarly, Stacker cannot use disks compressed by DoubleSpace or the DoubleSpace/ SPACEMANager combination. The Stacker and DoubleSpace disk compression schemes are not compatible with each other. Exchanging files on compressed removable media between computers that use different compression schemes is possible, however, by using utilities such as Stacker Anywhere or SPACEMANager's SuperExchange. These utilities are discussed more fully in the following section of this chapter and in Chapter 8, "Beyond DoubleSpace: Using SPACEMANager," and Chapter 11, "Using Stacker."

One restriction does exist on the type of hard disk drive you can compress. If your hard disk requires that a device driver be loaded before DOS can read from it, and the hard disk also is your boot disk, you cannot compress the disk. Many SCSI disk drives, for example, require a device driver (loaded through CONFIG.SYS) to enable DOS to access the disk. Because DOS 6 preloads the disk compression device driver *before* processing the CONFIG.SYS file, DOS tries to read from the compressed volume before the device driver necessary for controlling the disk's hardware has been loaded. DOS is, therefore, unable to access the disk at all.

Of course, neither DoubleSpace nor Stacker can compress a disk that does not have enough working room. If your disk is very full, you may need to delete some files so that Stacker or DoubleSpace has enough working space to compress the disk.

Removable Media

If you use removable media, you have some special concerns. Using compressed removable media is one area in which the operation of your disk compression software becomes more visible. To access any compressed volume, the disk compression device driver must mount the compressed volume, associating the compressed volume with a DOS drive letter. Your hard disks and hard disk partitions are automatically mounted at the time you start your computer.

The entire purpose of removable media disk drives is to enable you to remove a disk and replace it with another—essentially providing unlimited storage as well as a way to transfer or distribute programs and data to a number of different computers. Because you can insert a removable media disk at any time, your disk compression software must be capable of mounting a compressed removable disk at any time—not only when your computer starts. Your disk compression software also must be capable of unmounting a compressed removable disk whenever the disk is removed from its drive so that another compressed removable disk can be mounted.

Both DoubleSpace and Stacker have commands to manually mount and unmount compressed removable disks. Manually mounting or unmounting a removable disk is potentially irksome, especially if you need to access files on a compressed removable disk while running another application. Often, you must quit the application, mount the removable disk, and then restart the application.

To reduce the inherent inconvenience of using compressed removable disks, Stacker includes a special feature known as *Stacker AutoMount*. This feature is built into the Stacker device driver. Stacker AutoMount automatically recognizes and mounts removable disks compressed by Stacker so that the removable disk is available whenever needed, just like a regular removable disk. If you change disks in the drive, Stacker AutoMount unmounts the old disk and mounts the new compressed removable disk as you use your DOS applications or Windows. Stacker permits manual mounting and unmounting of compressed disks from the DOS command line only.

DoubleSpace by itself does not have a feature equivalent to Stacker AutoMount. You must always mount or unmount DoubleSpace compressed removable disks manually, either from the DoubleSpace menus or by using the DoubleSpace command-line equivalent. SPACEMANager, however, adds the ability to automatically mount or unmount removable disk drives to DoubleSpace. SPACEMANager provides a TSR program called *SuperMount*. If loaded into memory, SuperMount automatically recognizes and mounts removable disks compressed by DoubleSpace. If you change disks in the drive, SuperMount unmounts the old disk and mounts the new compressed removable disk. You can use SPACEMANager's SuperMount to mount or unmount removable drives automatically while you use your DOS applications or Windows. SPACEMANager's Windows utility also enables you to manually mount or unmount a compressed removable drive while running Windows, even if SuperMount is not loaded into memory.

Removable media—floppy disks in particular—often are used to transfer or distribute programs or data from one computer to another. An inherent problem of using compressed removable disks is that a computer without disk compression cannot read the compressed disk. A compressed removable disk also is unreadable if the other computer uses a different disk compression scheme than that used to compress the removable disk.

To overcome this problem, Stacker includes a utility program called *Stacker Anywhere*. You load Stacker Anywhere from the DOS command line. Stacker Anywhere mounts the compressed removable disk on a computer that does not use Stacker disk compression. Stacker places the Stacker Anywhere utility on every removable disk you compress. Stacker Anywhere is discussed more fully in Chapter 11, "Using Stacker."

DoubleSpace alone does not provide a way for a computer that does not already use DoubleSpace to mount a removable disk compressed by DoubleSpace. You can, however, add this feature to DoubleSpace through SPACEMANager's *SuperExchange* utility. Similar to Stacker Anywhere, SPACEMANager's SuperExchange loads into memory from the DOS command line and enables a computer that does not use DoubleSpace compression to mount a DoubleSpace compressed removable disk. SuperExchange is discussed more fully in Chapter 8, "Beyond DoubleSpace: Using SPACEMANager."

Memory Consumption

Even though disk compression software consumes a certain amount of your computer's memory, you can load the disk compression device drivers so that they do not use as much conventional memory. Unless you alter the memory locations they use, both DoubleSpace and Stacker require approximately 44K of conventional memory. If you own an 80386 or higher computer and use a memory manager program—such as 386MAX, QEMM386, or EMM386 (which is provided with DOS)—you can load the DoubleSpace or Stacker device drivers into upper memory. The disk compression device drivers still take up as much memory as they did before; they just are not using conventional memory.

If your system has EMS memory or uses a memory manager to simulate EMS memory, the Stacker disk compression device driver can put its buffers into EMS memory. (A *buffer* is an area of memory used to store information temporarily.) Stacker uses its buffers to hold the data being compressed or decompressed. If Stacker loads its buffers into EMS memory, the remaining portion of the device driver occupies only about 26K of conventional memory. To free up more conventional memory, you can choose to leave the Stacker AutoMount feature out of the device driver if you do not often use compressed removable media. Instructing the device driver to load without the AutoMount feature reduces the amount of memory the Stacker device driver requires. You still can mount compressed removable disks, but you must do so manually. Loading the Stacker device driver without the AutoMount feature is described in Chapter 10, "Configuring and Optimizing Stacker."

If your computer has extended memory and an XMS memory manager—such as the HIMEM.SYS supplied with DOS—you may be able to load the disk compression device drivers into upper memory. DoubleSpace automatically adds the necessary commands to load its device driver into upper memory as you compress the first disk drive on your computer, and DoubleSpace sees that HIMEM.SYS is loaded in your CONFIG.SYS file.

Compression Levels and Recompression

All disk compression software products make a trade-off between compressing data as much as possible and keeping the time required for the data's compression within reasonable limits.

Stacker offers three different levels of compression, because some computer users may not mind if data compression takes longer in return for a higher compression ratio. For some users with high-performance computers, the additional time required to compress data further may not be particularly noticeable. When you install Stacker, you select whether you want the best speed and standard compression, less speed and better compression, or the best compression with the least speed. Stacker provides utilities that enable you to change the compression level later. Stacker also enables you to *restack*, or recompress, all the files on a disk. If you recompress all the files on a disk or create a new compressed drive, Stacker always applies the maximum compression level to the files on the drive.

In contrast to Stacker's multiple compression levels, DoubleSpace offers only one compression level, which is approximately equivalent to the Best Speed, Standard Compression level in Stacker. (The actual compression ratios tend to be somewhat lower than Stacker's.) If you already use DoubleSpace but believe you can benefit from multiple compression levels, consider enhancing DoubleSpace by adding SPACEMANager. SPACEMANager adds two compression levels: *Ultra I*, which provides higher compression at some sacrifice of speed, and *Ultra II*, which provides the highest compression and the lowest speed. SPACEMANager also enables you to select a compression level of *None* for files that do not compress much or at all.

The compression level you set for Stacker affects all files on your compressed volume. If you select Best Compression, all files added to the disk later are compressed at the highest Stacker compression level. As existing files on the hard disk are modified or copied, they, too, are compressed at the highest compression level. Instructions for setting Stacker's compression levels are described in Chapter 9, "Installing Stacker," and in Chapter 10, "Configuring and Optimizing Stacker."

NOTE: If you add SPACEMANager to your DoubleSpace disk compression, be aware that SPACEMANager requires an additional 62K of conventional memory for all its features: SuperMount, SuperExchange, and FortuneTeller. These SPACEMANager utilities are described more fully in Chapter 8, "Beyond DoubleSpace: Using SPACEMANager."

NOTE: Any computer using DoubleSpace can read disks compressed by the DoubleSpace/SPACEMANager combination, even if that computer does not have SPACEMANager installed.

If using the Ultra levels of compression in SPACEMANager, however, you apply the compression level based on the file's extension. SPACEMANager thus enables you to use the file extension to control which compression level is applied to which type of file. You can select EXE files to receive the Ultra II maximum compression, for example, because these files normally are written to your disk only once—usually as you install new software. You can use SPACEMANager to select a compression level of None for files that end with ZIP, because these files are already compressed and cannot be compressed much more. By using no compression for these files, your computer saves the time and effort of attempting to compress a file that cannot be further compressed. SPACEMANager's capability to select compression levels based on file extensions is potentially very useful, though setting up this feature can be time-consuming. How to select compression levels in SPACEMANager is described in Chapter 8, "Beyond DoubleSpace: Using SPACEMANager."

Reporting, Diagnostic, and Maintenance Tools

As you use your compressed disks, you may need information about the files on the compressed volume or about the compressed volume itself. You also may need to know the host drive for the compressed volume, the compression ratios for various files, how much room is left on a compressed volume, whether the actual overall compression ratio is higher or lower than the estimated compression ratio, and so on. You may need to test the internal integrity of your compressed volumes and ensure that the clusters on a compressed volume are correctly chained together, just as you would for an uncompressed disk drive. Occasionally, if you need more room on the uncompressed part of your disk, you may want to reduce the size of a compressed volume. Conversely, you may want to increase the size of a compressed volume if you end up needing less space on the uncompressed part of your disk. Both DoubleSpace and Stacker provide reporting, diagnostic, and maintenance tools to perform these tasks.

DoubleSpace provides a single program to carry out all its information, diagnostic, and maintenance procedures. This program is the same one you use to create new compressed drives or to alter the size of a compressed volume. You use the DoubleSpace program by starting it from the DOS command line and then making choices from its menus. You also can issue commands to DoubleSpace by using command-line switches to instruct DoubleSpace to perform a specific activity. SPACEMANager also enhances the reporting tools available to DoubleSpace.

Stacker provides several separate utilities for carrying out its information, diagnostic, and maintenance procedures. Although these utilities each can be run separately, Stacker also includes the Stacker Toolbox, which provides an overall menu system for invoking the specific utilities. As in DoubleSpace, you use the Stacker utilities by starting them from the DOS command line and then making choices from menus. Also as in DoubleSpace, you can use command-line switches to command the Stacker utilities to perform a specific activity.

The tools used to obtain information about DoubleSpace or Stacker drives while running Windows are described in the section "Integration with Windows," later in this chapter. Stacker's and DoubleSpace's reporting and informational tools cover the most essential information about your compressed volumes. The simplest tools provided with both Stacker and DoubleSpace are those used to list all the drives on your system, indicating which drives are compressed and reporting the following information about each compressed volume:

- Compressed volume's free and used space.
- Name of the compressed volume file.
- Host drive for the compressed volume.
- Actual compression ratio.
- Estimated compression ratio.
- Overall compression ratio.
- Compression ratio for specific files.
- Compression ratio for specific file types.

The actual compression ratio for specific files and the overall compression ratio information can be provided through the DOS DIR command. DOS 6 adds a switch to the DIR command to show the overall compression ratio and the compression ratio of each file listed in the directory display of a compressed volume. Chapter 5, "Using DoubleSpace," describes how to use the DOS DIR command with DoubleSpace compressed volumes. This new switch in the DIR command works with both DoubleSpace and Stacker 3.1. Stacker also provides the SDIR utility as an alternative to the DOS DIR command. Chapter 11, "Using Stacker," describes how to use the Stacker SDIR utility and the DOS DIR command with Stacker compressed volumes.

Stacker provides a reporting function that displays a report of the files on your disk, showing the overall compression ratio, file compression by file type, space used and space free on the compressed volume, and the estimated compression ratio. DoubleSpace does not provide this type of report. SPACEMANager, however, adds a similar capability to DoubleSpace.

Although obtaining information about how well files compress and how much space is left on your drive is important, the diagnostic and maintenance tools for your compressed disks are probably even more important. Both Stacker and DoubleSpace contain diagnostic tools similar to the DOS CHKDSK utility. Like DOS CHKDSK, these disk compression utilities examine the integrity of the logical structure of your compressed volume and report lost clusters, cross-linked files, and other problems.

In DoubleSpace, you check the integrity of your disk either through the DoubleSpace program itself or simply by issuing the DOS CHKDSK command. If you use DOS CHKDSK on a DoubleSpace compressed volume, it invokes the DoubleSpace disk-checking utility after performing the standard DOS disk checking. Checking the integrity of DoubleSpace compressed volumes is described in Chapter 7, "Troubleshooting DoubleSpace."

If you use Stacker 3.1, the DOS CHKDSK command recognizes the compressed volume and can invoke the appropriate checking routine for the Stacker compressed volume, just as it does for a DoubleSpace drive. Stacker also provides the CHECK utility to test the logical integrity of your Stacker compressed volumes. Checking the integrity of Stacker compressed volumes is described in Chapter 13, "Troubleshooting Stacker."

Occasionally, you need to change the size of a compressed volume. If your compressed volume becomes full and the uncompressed portion of the drive has enough room, you can increase a compressed volume's size. If you need more room on the uncompressed portion of your disk drive, you may want to reduce the size of your compressed volume. Both Stacker and DoubleSpace enable you to change the size of a compressed drive. To make a compressed volume smaller, you may need to defragment the drive. Defragmenting a compressed volume is different from defragmenting an uncompressed drive. Both DoubleSpace and Stacker provide their own utilities—special versions of Norton Speed Disk—to defragment their compressed volumes.

Both DoubleSpace and Stacker enable you to alter the estimated compression ratio for specific compressed volumes. Changing the estimated compression ratio changes the amount of free space reported. Remember that the free space reported on a compressed volume is an estimate, based on the estimated compression ratio. If the difference between the actual overall compression ratio and the estimated compression ratio is great, the free space reported for your compressed volume is correspondingly inaccurate. Changing the estimated compression ratio to match the actual average compression ratio may increase the accuracy of your free space reports. Chapter 4, "Configuring and Optimizing DoubleSpace," and Chapter 10, "Configuring and Optimizing Stacker," describe changing the estimated compression ratio in more detail.

Disk Repair Utilities

If your hard disk develops a problem, you may need to use one or more disk repair utilities, such as Symantec's Norton Utilities, Central Point's PC Tools, Gibson Research's SpinRite, or others. These disk repair tools are compatible with both DoubleSpace and Stacker compressed volumes, as long as they also are compatible with your DOS version and your computer's hardware.

You do not normally use disk repair utilities directly on your compressed volumes. Instead, you use the disk repair utilities on the uncompressed volume. You want to repair the physical disk drive—which contains the compressed volume—rather than attempt to repair the logical disk drive created by the disk compression device driver. Repairing your compressed volumes is described in Chapter 7, "Troubleshooting DoubleSpace," and Chapter 13, "Troubleshooting Stacker."

Integration with Windows

During the past few years, many computer users have switched to Windows and seldom, if ever, perform tasks at the DOS command line. If you are one of these users, the degree to which your disk compression installation, information, and maintenance tools are available from within Windows may be important to you. DoubleSpace, for example, cannot be installed from inside Windows; in fact, the DoubleSpace utility program cannot be used from inside Windows at all. SPACEMANager cannot be installed from Windows either, although SPACEMANager does provide a Windows version of its enhancement tools.

STOP

Before you use any disk repair utility, you must carefully check to make sure that the disk repair utility is compatible with the version of DOS you use and compatible with your computer's hardware. Using disk repair tools that are not compatible with your DOS version and disk hardware may result in the permanent loss of some or all data on your hard disk.

Stacker does enable you to start the installation process from inside Windows, although Stacker must exit Windows to complete the installation and compression of your disk drives. If you start the Stacker installation from inside Windows, Stacker sets up Windows so that you are asked if you want to create a Stacker program group the next time you run Windows. If you add the program group, Stacker creates a Windows program group containing all the Stacker Windows utilities and adds a new **S**tacker menu to the Windows File Manager. The Stacker Windows utilities consist primarily of the Stacker Tuner and the Stacker Stackometer.

The Stacker Tuner enables you to adjust the compression levels for a disk, as described in the section "Compression Levels and Recompression," earlier in this chapter. The Stackometer is similar to the Stacker Toolbox. You use the Stackometer to view your compressed drive's overall compression ratio, free space, and fragmentation. The Stackometer operates in real time, updating its displays for free space and overall compression as conditions on your compressed volumes change. The Stackometer also provides access to Stacker's defragmenting tool and enables you to change the estimated compression ratio and adjust the selected compression level. Using the Stackometer is described more fully in Chapter 11, "Using Stacker."

If you have Windows installed on your computer before you upgrade to DOS 6, and you install at least one of the Windows versions of the DOS Microsoft Anti-Virus utility or the Microsoft Backup utility at the time you upgrade to DOS 6, the DOS Setup also adds a new **T**ools menu to your Windows File Manager. This new **T**ools menu provides access to the only Windows tool built into DoubleSpace: an information report for DoubleSpace compressed drives that graphically shows the amount of used and free space on a compressed volume, indicates the overall compression ratio for the drive, and enables you to see compression ratios for specific files. The DoubleSpace information choice in the File Manager also shows which drive is the host drive for the compressed volume.

For more information and greater control of your DoubleSpace compressed drives while in Windows, you can add several capabilities to DoubleSpace by using SPACEMANager. SPACEMANager has a full Windows interface, giving you access to all of SPACEMANager's features through Windows. SPACEMANager provides the same information as does the File Manager **T**ools menu and displays compression ratios for specific types of files. SPACEMANager also provides a way to mount and unmount removable disks without leaving Windows and without installing SPACEMANager's SuperMount TSR.

DoubleSpace alone cannot mount or unmount removable disks from inside Windows. Instead, you must exit Windows, manually mount or unmount the removable disk, and then restart Windows. You cannot manually mount or unmount removable disks from inside Windows by using Stacker either. The Stacker AutoMount feature, however, automatically mounts and unmounts removable drives in Windows as well as in DOS. If you remove the AutoMount feature from the Stacker device driver, you cannot mount removable drives with Stacker from inside Windows.

Security

Stacker offers a security feature not found in DoubleSpace, even if SPACEMANager is added. Stacker enables you to protect specific compressed volumes on hard drives or removable disks by using a password. Whenever a password-protected compressed volume is mounted, Stacker asks for the password. You—or the person using your computer—are asked to enter a password for each password-protected compressed volume mounted.

You can select two different levels of password security for your compressed volumes. You can specify a read-only password or a read-write password. The read-only password enables data on the compressed volume to be read, but it does not permit any data on the compressed volume to be changed. The read-write password permits data to be read from and written to the compressed volume. Using Stacker password protection is described in Chapter 11, "Using Stacker."

System Requirements

Having briefly examined the similarities and differences between Stacker and DoubleSpace, you now need to look at the hardware and software required to use Stacker, DoubleSpace, or SPACEMANager.

DoubleSpace

If your computer runs DOS 6, you have everything you need to use DoubleSpace. Because DoubleSpace is supplied with DOS 6, its program files are installed automatically on your hard disk along with the other DOS 6 programs and utilities. The DoubleSpace device driver requires about 44K of memory, whether loaded into conventional or upper memory.

Stacker

Stacker 3.1 has the following system requirements:
- 640K conventional memory.
- 44K RAM occupied by the device driver, whether placed in conventional or upper memory; 26K occupied by the device driver if buffers are put in EMS.
- 2.9M disk space *before* compression for the Stacker programs. This is in addition to the required working space for the compressed volume.
- DOS 3.2 or a later version.
- DOS 6 to preload device driver.

SPACEMANager

SPACEMANager 1.5 has the following system requirements:
- 640K conventional memory.
- 80286 or higher processor.
- 250K or more XMS memory for multiple compression levels.

- 1.5M disk space *before* compression for the SPACEMANager program files.
- DOS 6 with DoubleSpace disk compression active. SPACEMANager is not compatible with the OS/2 compatibility box.
- DOS 3.31 or higher for SuperExchange.
- 505K free conventional memory for installation program.

Deciding Which Compression Program To Use

Choosing software that is appropriate for you is much like choosing an automobile or a bicycle. After the basic criteria of mechanical soundness and ability to provide transportation are satisfied, the remaining criteria relate to personal preferences and the specific uses to which you put the vehicle. Making a choice between Stacker and DoubleSpace depends mostly on your own preferences and the specific goals you want to meet by adding disk compression to your computer system. If, for example, you want to compress a 600M drive into only one compressed volume, you must use Stacker; DoubleSpace cannot handle a single compressed volume that large.

You may prefer DoubleSpace if your needs are simple. One of DoubleSpace's great advantages is that it is supplied with DOS 6 without any additional cost. If you do not need compressed volumes greater than 512M, do not make heavy use of compressed removable disks, or are not the kind of user who is interested in "tweaking" software performance, DoubleSpace could be a good choice for you. DoubleSpace also may be a good choice if you are upgrading a large number of computers to DOS 6 and you want to add disk compression to all of them.

SPACEMANager enhances DoubleSpace. You may want to add SPACEMANager to your DoubleSpace system for extra fine control of the disk compression software. SPACEMANager not only adds different compression levels to DoubleSpace, but also enables you to select the compression level based on a file's extension. You also may want to add SPACEMANager if you start out using DoubleSpace and then discover that you use Windows often or use removable media frequently.

If your needs are more complex—such as manipulating large compressed drives, relying heavily on removable media, and desiring fine control of the disk compression software—you may want to choose Stacker instead. Stacker also may be a good choice if you use Windows predominantly or are concerned about the security of your compressed volumes. Stacker compresses files somewhat better and faster than DoubleSpace, so Stacker is a good choice if you want the best in both speed and compression. On faster computers, however, Stacker's greater speed may not be noticeable.

Summary

This chapter summarized the various features of DoubleSpace and Stacker, beginning with the installation of the disk compression software. Stacker's and DoubleSpace's upper and lower limits for compressed disks were described, along with those features of Stacker and SPACEMANager that make removable media easier to use. Loading the DoubleSpace and Stacker device drivers into upper memory to free up more conventional memory also was discussed.

You learned, too, that Stacker and SPACEMANager offer different compression levels and further learned about the reporting and diagnostic tools provided with Stacker, DoubleSpace, and SPACEMANager. Compatibility with other disk repair utilities, the system requirements for each product, and how DoubleSpace, SPACEMANager, and Stacker integrate with Windows also were discussed. The chapter included a discussion of the password security feature unique to Stacker and concluded with a discussion on choosing the right disk compression program for you.

The next chapter begins Part II of the book and describes how to install the DoubleSpace disk compression program on your computer.

PART II

Using DoubleSpace

3. Installing DoubleSpace
4. Configuring and Optimizing DoubleSpace
5. Using DoubleSpace
6. Using the DoubleSpace Utilities
7. Troubleshooting DoubleSpace
8. Beyond DoubleSpace: Using SPACEMANager

CHAPTER 3

Installing DoubleSpace

To use DoubleSpace, you must have DOS 6. You do not need to copy additional files to your hard disk to set up DoubleSpace because DOS 6 Setup copies all DoubleSpace files into the DOS directory on your hard disk at the time you install DOS 6. This chapter describes how DoubleSpace alters your computer's setup, assigns drive letters, and alters disk volume labels. The chapter also discusses how to prepare to add DoubleSpace to your computer system and provides step-by-step instructions for both Express and Custom Setup. Finally, the chapter describes how to convert from other disk compression programs to DoubleSpace.

Each time you run the DoubleSpace program, it searches your computer system for compressed disks. If your computer has no DoubleSpace compressed drives, DoubleSpace enters its setup mode and enables you to choose between the Express and Custom installation routines described in this chapter. If your computer does have a DoubleSpace compressed disk drive, DoubleSpace instead loads the menu-driven utility described in Chapter 5, "Using DoubleSpace," and Chapter 6, "Using the DoubleSpace Utilities."

Changes Made by DoubleSpace Setup

DoubleSpace must make changes in your computer's configuration to operate. This section describes the changes DoubleSpace makes and how they affect your computer.

Files Added to Boot Disk Root Directory

In addition to any compressed volume files you create, DoubleSpace adds two files—DBLSPACE.BIN and DBLSPACE.INI—to the root directory of your boot disk. DoubleSpace puts these files in the uncompressed part of your boot disk because DOS and DoubleSpace must be able to read them at a time when your compressed volumes are not accessible.

The DBLSPACE.BIN file is the DoubleSpace device driver; it provides access to your compressed drives. Whenever DOS starts up, it looks for the DBLSPACE.BIN file in the root directory of your boot disk, and if it finds this file, DOS loads it into memory. The DBLSPACE.INI file contains information the DoubleSpace device driver needs when it loads into memory during your computer's start-up. DBLSPACE.INI tells the DoubleSpace device driver how many drive letters to use and how to assign drive letters to the compressed and uncompressed drives. Chapter 4, "Configuring and Optimizing DoubleSpace," describes the contents of the DBLSPACE.INI file.

As DoubleSpace puts the DBLSPACE.BIN and DBLSPACE.INI files on your boot disk, it gives them Hidden, System, and Read-Only file attributes. Normally, you are not aware of these files, because the Hidden attribute prevents them from appearing in most directory listings. The Read-Only file attribute prevents accidental erasure of these important files.

> Do not remove the file attributes of the DBLSPACE.BIN or DBLSPACE.INI files. Deleting or modifying either file could make your compressed volumes temporarily or permanently unavailable.

Changes to CONFIG.SYS and AUTOEXEC.BAT

Because DoubleSpace is closely integrated with DOS 6, you need not add commands to your CONFIG.SYS and AUTOEXEC.BAT files to load DoubleSpace. If the DBLSPACE.BIN file is in the root directory of your boot disk when your computer starts, DOS 6 automatically loads the device driver into memory.

As your computer starts, DOS first loads the DBLSPACE.BIN device driver into conventional memory, where the device driver uses approximately 44K. Because users often want to keep as much conventional memory available as possible, DoubleSpace provides a way to relocate the DBLSPACE.BIN device driver into upper memory. If DoubleSpace Setup detects XMS memory, it adds a line to your CONFIG.SYS file, similar to the following line, that relocates the DBLSPACE.BIN device driver into upper memory.

```
DEVICEHIGH=C:\DOS\DBLSPACE.SYS /MOVE
```

Normally, you need not concern yourself about this addition to your CONFIG.SYS file. DoubleSpace makes the correct change automatically. DBLSPACE.SYS is discussed more fully in Chapter 4, "Configuring and Optimizing DoubleSpace."

DoubleSpace makes no permanent changes to your AUTOEXEC.BAT file.

Compressed Volume Files

As discussed in Chapter 1, "Understanding and Using Disk Compression," your disk compression software works by creating a large file on your hard disk and then treating this file as a logical disk drive. All data on the compressed disk is actually stored in this large file, which is located on the uncompressed part of your original disk drive or partition. Each time you create a new compressed drive, DoubleSpace creates a new compressed volume file for the compressed drive. DoubleSpace gives the file Hidden, System, and Read-Only file attributes so that you are unaware of the file and cannot accidentally delete it.

DoubleSpace names the first compressed volume file it creates on an uncompressed disk DBLSPACE.000. If you create additional compressed drives on the same uncompressed host drive, DoubleSpace gives every additional compressed volume file the DBLSPACE

> **NOTE:**
> Do not confuse DBLSPACE.SYS with DBLSPACE.BIN. DBLSPACE.BIN is the device driver that provides access to your compressed volumes and is automatically loaded into memory by DOS. DBLSPACE.SYS is used only to control the final memory location of DBLSPACE.BIN.

> ⚠ Do not change file attributes or alter compressed volume files in any way. If you erase or damage a compressed volume file, all data on the compressed drive may be permanently lost or corrupted.

name plus a sequential extension number. The second compressed volume file created on the same host drive is DBLSPACE.001, the third is DBLSPACE.002, and so on. DoubleSpace creates and maintains the compressed volume file automatically. Troubleshooting your compressed drive is described in Chapter 7, "Troubleshooting DoubleSpace."

How DoubleSpace Exchanges Drive Letters and Volume Labels

DoubleSpace creates the DBLSPACE.INI file in the uncompressed root directory of your boot disk. DoubleSpace uses the information in DBLSPACE.INI for instructions on exchanging drive letters between compressed drives and uncompressed host drives. (Remember that the host drive is the uncompressed drive containing the compressed volume file.) Each time you create a compressed drive, DoubleSpace modifies the contents of DBLSPACE.INI to include the new compressed drive and its host. This section describes in detail how DoubleSpace chooses and exchanges drive letters.

Drive Letters

Before you compress any drives, your computer system includes a certain number of physical hard disks. A certain number of physical partitions also may be present on one or more hard disks, configured as logical disk drives. DOS assigns drive letters to these physical disks and partitions on a first-come, first-served basis. As you create a compressed disk by using DoubleSpace, you create a logical disk drive, and DOS assigns it the next available drive letter. If the highest drive letter in your system before compression is drive E, for example, DOS assigns the drive letter F to the first compressed volume you create. DOS drive letters and drive letter assignments are described in more detail in Chapter 1, "Understanding and Using Disk Compression."

For your convenience, the DoubleSpace device driver exchanges drive letters between the compressed volume and its host drive. If you compress drive C, for example, DoubleSpace reassigns drive letters so that all data on the new compressed volume is still accessible to you as drive C. DoubleSpace gives the uncompressed disk (formerly accessible as drive C) another drive letter.

When you create your first compressed volume, DoubleSpace assigns drive letters by skipping four letters higher than the current highest drive letter. DoubleSpace then uses the fifth drive letter for the host drive of the new compressed volume file. Suppose that, before you add DoubleSpace, your computer has two disk drives, C and D. The highest drive letter in your system is drive D. If you compress drive C, DoubleSpace skips four drive letters—E, F, G, and H—from the current highest drive letter and assigns the fifth drive letter—drive I—as the host drive for the new compressed volume C.

DoubleSpace reserves the four skipped drive letters for its own future use. As you create additional compressed drives, DoubleSpace assigns drive letters by working backward (from highest to lowest) through the list of reserved drive letters. In the preceding example, if you compress drive D after compressing drive C, DoubleSpace assigns drive letter H to the host drive for the new compressed volume D. If you continue to create compressed volumes, drive letters G, F, and E are assigned in that order to the new host drives. DoubleSpace reserves drive letters this way to ensure that other drives—such as network drives or drives created by other device drivers—do not conflict with DoubleSpace's assignment of drive letters.

Occasionally, you may need to alter how DoubleSpace assigns drive letters. Altering DoubleSpace's drive letter assignments is described in Chapter 4, "Configuring and Optimizing DoubleSpace." If you create more than four or five compressed volumes, DoubleSpace runs out of drive letters. Increasing the number of DoubleSpace drive letters is described in Chapter 6, "Using the DoubleSpace Utilities."

Volume Labels

A volume label provides a means of identifying a disk drive apart from its drive letter. You give disks a volume name as you format them or by using the DOS LABEL command. (Refer to your DOS documentation for information on the LABEL command.) As you create a new compressed volume, DoubleSpace may assign a volume label to the compressed volume and alter the volume label on the uncompressed volume. If the drive you compress already has a volume label, DoubleSpace transfers that volume label to the new compressed volume. The uncompressed volume is assigned a new volume label, indicating which compressed drive it hosts.

Assume, for example, that you have a drive C with the volume label DRIVE_1. If you use DoubleSpace to compress this drive C, DoubleSpace labels the new compressed volume DRIVE_1 and labels the uncompressed drive HOST_FOR_C. The reassignment of drive labels ensures that drive C has the same volume label to which you are accustomed and provides an easy way to determine the uncompressed host drive for each compressed volume.

If you create a compressed volume on an uncompressed volume that has no volume label, DoubleSpace does not assign a volume label to either the newly compressed volume or the new uncompressed volume. If you create a new compressed volume from the free space on a drive, DoubleSpace assigns to this new compressed volume the label COMPRESSED.

Preparing To Install DoubleSpace

In general, installing DoubleSpace is a straightforward and trouble-free operation. Installing DoubleSpace does represent a major change in your computer's configuration, however, so you need to make some preparations before you attempt the installation.

NOTE: DoubleSpace cannot be easily removed from your system after installation.

Installing DoubleSpace

⚠ After you install the DOS 6 upgrade, make sure that all your DOS programs work correctly before you install DoubleSpace. After you install DoubleSpace, you cannot use the Uninstall disk created by the DOS 6 Setup program to revert to an earlier DOS version.

NOTE: Compressing all files on your hard disk or partition may require anywhere from a few minutes to a few hours, depending on the number of files you need to compress. Begin the DoubleSpace Setup only if your computer can be left free for several hours—for example, at the end of a working day or on the weekend.

STOP If you do not uninstall your copy-protected software before compressing your disk, you cannot use that software after compression.

Follow these guidelines to prepare for DoubleSpace installation:
- *Upgrade DOS.* Upgrade to DOS 6 if you have not already done so. You cannot use DoubleSpace unless you first install DOS 6.
- *Back up.* Back up all files on the disks you plan to compress. Problems installing DoubleSpace are rare, but a recent backup of your files is the most secure protection for your data. If you experience a problem while installing DoubleSpace, a current backup of your data can make the difference between an inconvenience and a tragedy.
- *Make a bootable floppy disk.* Again, problems installing DoubleSpace are rare, but if you do experience a problem, you may need to start your computer from a floppy disk. Make sure that you have available a bootable floppy disk containing DOS 6. Refer to your DOS documentation for information on creating a bootable floppy disk. If you use a third-party utility such as Central Point's PC Backup or 5th Generation's Fastback to perform your backup, make sure also that you have copies of your backup utilities on a floppy disk.
- *Preserve your CONFIG.SYS and AUTOEXEC.BAT.* For safety, keep copies of your current configuration files on a floppy disk in case you experience any difficulty. Although DoubleSpace does not make permanent changes to AUTOEXEC.BAT, it does make temporary changes while performing its setup routines. If your computer experiences a problem (such as a power failure) as DoubleSpace changes CONFIG.SYS and AUTOEXEC.BAT, those files can be lost or damaged. If you made copies of these files, you may be able to regain access to your entire system by restoring only the configuration files, without needing to restore an entire backup or reinstall software.
- *Uninstall copy-protected software.* Some software programs use copy-protection schemes that rely on finding certain data in certain areas of the disk. Compressing your disk moves this special data. As a result, the copy-protection scheme no longer recognizes your software as a legitimate copy, and you cannot use your program. Refer to your program's documentation if you are unsure whether it uses this type of copy-protection scheme; the documentation also includes instructions for uninstalling the software. After you compress your drive, you can reinstall the copy-protected program.
- *Use the DOS CHKDSK command.* The DOS CHKDSK command checks the integrity of your disk drive. Use this command on each of your disks before you compress them. Resolve any problems that CHKDSK reveals before you begin the DoubleSpace setup. Refer to your DOS documentation for instructions on using the DOS CHKDSK command. CHKDSK also is discussed in Chapter 7, "Troubleshooting DoubleSpace."
- *Connect to the network.* If your computer connects to a network, make sure that your network software is running before you install DoubleSpace. DoubleSpace automatically considers the network drive letters as it assigns and exchanges drive letters for your new compressed volumes.

- *Disable disk cache programs loaded in CONFIG.SYS.* Disable any disk cache programs loaded as device drivers in your CONFIG.SYS file. To disable these device drivers, use a text editor such as the DOS EDIT program to change your CONFIG.SYS file. Add REM (for *remark*) at the beginning of the line in your CONFIG.SYS file that loads the disk cache device driver. Refer to your DOS documentation for more information on CONFIG.SYS; refer also to the documentation for your disk cache program to identify the disk cache device driver line.

After you complete all the steps in the preceding checklist, you are ready to install DoubleSpace. As you install DoubleSpace, remember to read all on-screen instructions for each step of the compression process. Avoid shortcuts, even if you are an experienced computer user. In areas involving the safety and integrity of your disk data, the adage "It is better to err on the side of caution" is particularly true.

Use the DoubleSpace Express Setup to automatically compress your drive C and create the largest possible compressed volume. Use Custom Setup to compress a drive other than drive C or if you want to leave more than the minimum amount of working space uncompressed.

> You also can disable device drivers in your CONFIG.SYS file by using the DOS 6 capability to conditionally process lines in your CONFIG.SYS file. Press F8 to have DOS prompt you before loading each device driver. Do not load the disk cache device drivers. Refer to your DOS documentation for more information.

Running Express Setup

The DoubleSpace Express Setup automatically compresses your drive C. To start Express Setup, follow these steps:

1. Make sure that you are at the DOS prompt. If you use Windows, DESQview, GEM, or GEOworks, you must exit to DOS before starting DoubleSpace. You also need to exit from any shell program you may use, such as the DOS Shell, XTree, or Norton Desktop for DOS.

2. At the DOS prompt, type **DBLSPACE** and then press Enter. DoubleSpace Setup starts and displays the greeting screen shown in figure 3.1.

   If your screen is similar to that shown in figure 3.2 (instead of in fig. 3.1), DoubleSpace is already installed, and you cannot use DoubleSpace Setup. Instead, refer to the section "Creating Additional Compressed Drives," in Chapter 6, to create a new compressed drive.

3. Press Enter to continue DoubleSpace Setup. DoubleSpace displays the Express or Custom Setup menu, as shown in figure 3.3.

   If you were referred to these steps from the section "Custom Setup," go now to step 2 in that section. The remaining instructions in this section cover Express Setup only.

   If you decide not to install DoubleSpace at this time, press F3 to exit DoubleSpace Setup without compressing any drives. To use the DoubleSpace on-line Help system, press F1.

4. Choose Express Setup. DoubleSpace displays a screen showing the estimated time required to compress all files on drive C. The actual time may vary slightly, depending on the speed of your computer's disk drive and CPU.

> After you install DoubleSpace, you can enable your disk cache device drivers again by removing the REM prefix from those lines in your CONFIG.SYS file.

> The DoubleSpace Setup program restarts your computer twice. If you have data on a RAM disk or in TSR programs, save it *before* you begin the DoubleSpace Setup.

Installing DoubleSpace

> **NOTE:** If a Windows permanent swap file is located on your hard disk, DoubleSpace Setup automatically leaves enough uncompressed space on the drive to accommodate the permanent swap file and then moves the permanent swap file to the uncompressed portion of the drive. DoubleSpace alters your Windows configuration to search for the permanent swap file by using the new drive letter of the uncompressed drive.

If you continue, you are committed to compressing drive C; you cannot cancel the operation. If you choose not to install DoubleSpace now, press F3 to exit DoubleSpace Setup without compressing any drives.

5. To continue, remove all disks from your floppy drives and press C.

Installing DoubleSpace may take several hours. After DoubleSpace begins the disk compression process, it cannot be interrupted. If you must use your computer before the estimated completion time, press F3 to end DoubleSpace Setup. DoubleSpace asks you to confirm ending the Setup process; press F3 again to return to the DOS command line.

After you press C, DoubleSpace runs the DOS CHKDSK command. Your computer screen clears and remains blank momentarily as the CHKDSK program examines the disk drive. After CHKDSK finishes, its report appears briefly on-screen. If CHKDSK finds any errors, DoubleSpace Setup reports the errors and stops running. Fix the problems and restart DoubleSpace Setup. Refer to your DOS documentation and Chapter 7, "Troubleshooting DoubleSpace," for more information about CHKDSK and how to correct these errors.

DoubleSpace now displays a message that it is checking your system. If DoubleSpace finds a floppy disk in drive A, an error message appears (see fig. 3.4). Remove the floppy disk from drive A, and choose the **R**etry button to recheck your system. If you decide not to install DoubleSpace at this time, choose the **C**ancel button instead. If you choose **C**ancel, DoubleSpace restarts your computer but does not compress any drives.

After DoubleSpace ensures the integrity of the drive and that drive A is empty, the program briefly displays a message that it is about to restart your computer. This message remains on-screen while DoubleSpace adds the DBLSPACE.BIN file to the boot disk root directory and makes temporary changes in your AUTOEXEC.BAT that ensure that DoubleSpace resumes operation after your computer restarts. A few moments after DoubleSpace restarts your computer, the message `Starting MS-DOS...` appears on-screen. DOS loads into your computer's memory, loads the DBLSPACE.BIN device driver, and begins processing CONFIG.SYS.

Fig. 3.1

The DoubleSpace Setup greeting.

If you use the DOS 6 feature to create multiple start-up configurations in your CONFIG.SYS, choose the same start-up configuration from the CONFIG.SYS menu that was in effect when you started DoubleSpace Setup. (Refer to your DOS documentation for more information on multiple start-up configurations.)

DOS now processes the rest of your CONFIG.SYS file and starts processing AUTOEXEC.BAT. If you pressed F8 to conditionally process lines in CONFIG.SYS, make sure that you process your AUTOEXEC.BAT file. (Refer to your DOS documentation for information on conditional execution CONFIG.SYS.) You should now see the message Continuing with DoubleSpace as DoubleSpace Setup loads into memory and resumes operation where it left off.

In rare cases, your computer may not respond correctly to the method that DoubleSpace Setup uses to restart your computer. If your computer does not restart, turn your computer's power off and back on, or press your computer's reset button if it has one. Your computer should now restart as described.

DoubleSpace displays various messages as it verifies your computer's status; DoubleSpace then displays a screen similar to that shown in figure 3.5. The exact contents of this screen vary, depending on your computer's specific disk drive and number of files. This screen indicates DoubleSpace's progress as it compresses the drive. The progress display shows at what time the compression started, the current time, the estimated finish time, and the time remaining to compress the drive. The progress report also indicates the name of the file DoubleSpace currently is compressing and displays a horizontal bar graph representing the percentage of completion for the entire job. After DoubleSpace displays its progress report screen, it can complete the compression process unattended.

After all files on the drive are compressed and added to the compressed volume, DoubleSpace runs the DOS DEFRAG program to defragment the compressed volume file. DEFRAG displays a screen similar to that shown in figure 3.6. (For more information about the DOS DEFRAG command, consult your DOS documentation.)

A beep signals that DEFRAG is complete, and a screen similar to that shown in figure 3.7 appears. DoubleSpace is finished compressing the drive.

The final report displays the results of compressing the drive. The report shows the amount of your drive's free space before and after compression. Usually, the free space after compression is much higher than before compression. The actual amount of free space after compression depends on how full the drive was before compression and how well the files on it compressed. The final report from DoubleSpace Setup also lists the actual compression ratio of the files on the drive and the total time required to compress

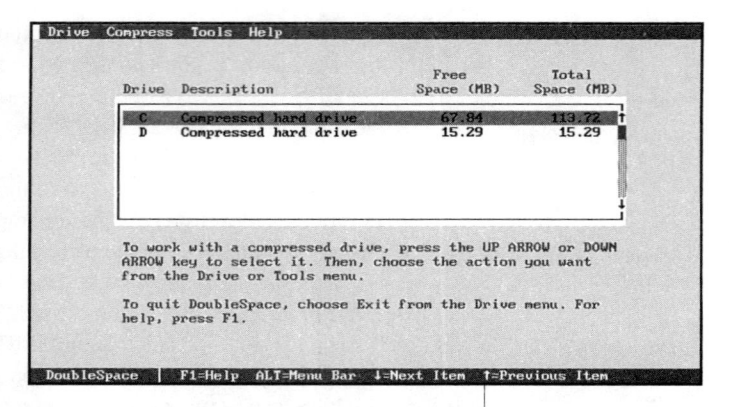

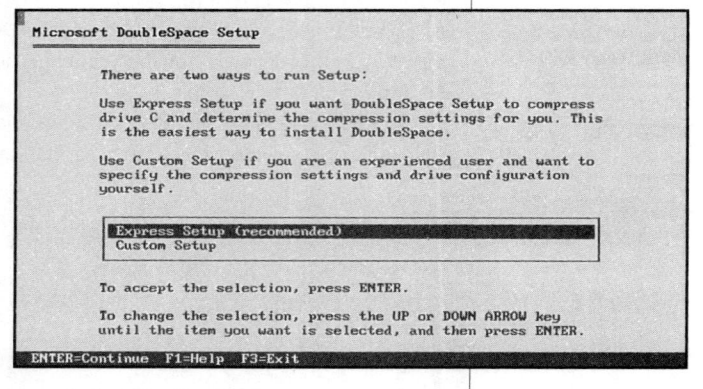

Fig. 3.2, top

The standard DoubleSpace program screen, displayed if DoubleSpace is already installed.

Fig. 3.3, bottom

The DoubleSpace Express or Custom Setup menu.

Installing DoubleSpace

the files. The report names the drive letter for the compressed volume's host drive and the amount of free space on the host drive. The host drive is referred to on-screen as a *new drive* (refer to fig. 3.7).

After reviewing information in the compression report screen, press Enter. DoubleSpace now displays the message that it is making final adjustments to AUTOEXEC.BAT and CONFIG.SYS. DoubleSpace removes the temporary changes made earlier. DoubleSpace checks your system to ensure that drive A is empty. If a floppy disk is in drive A, DoubleSpace displays the error message shown earlier (refer to fig. 3.4). Remove the disk from drive A and choose **R**etry. DoubleSpace briefly displays a message that it is about to restart your computer. DoubleSpace then restarts your computer. If your computer does not restart, turn it off and on, or press the reset button if it has one.

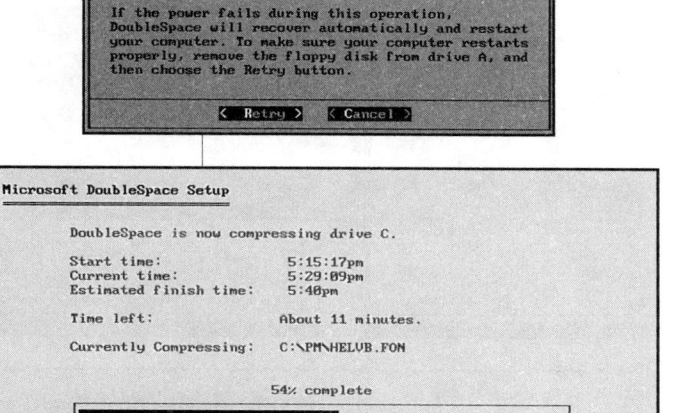

Fig. 3.4, top

The DoubleSpace error message for a disk in drive A.

Fig. 3.5, bottom

The DoubleSpace compression progress report.

Your DoubleSpace Setup is now complete. After your computer restarts, you can use the compressed drive just as you did compression. Now, however, much more storage space is available to you.

If you uninstalled copy-protected software before beginning the DoubleSpace Express Setup, you can reinstall that software now. If you need to compress additional disk drives or partitions, or if you want to create a compressed volume from the free space on an uncompressed disk, see Chapter 6, "Using the DoubleSpace Utilities."

Running Custom Setup

After following the recommendations in "Preparing to Install DoubleSpace," earlier in this chapter, you are ready to begin your DoubleSpace Custom Setup. Use Custom Setup instead of Express Setup if you want your first compressed disk to be a drive other than drive C. Custom Setup configures DoubleSpace and enables you to choose not only which drive to compress, but also whether to compress a drive and all its files or to create a drive from only the free space on the disk. You also can choose how much free space is to remain on your drive after compression, and you can specify which drive letter DoubleSpace assigns to the new uncompressed drive.

To start the Custom Setup, follow these steps:

1. Follow steps 1 through 3 in the procedure for using DoubleSpace Express Setup. (Refer to the section, "Running Express Setup," earlier in this chapter.)
2. Choose Custom Setup (refer to fig. 3.3). DoubleSpace now displays the screen shown in figure 3.8. This menu enables you to choose between compressing an existing drive or creating a new compressed drive.

se this is the first
pace drive on your com-
you can choose any avail-
drive letter. The list starts with
next available drive letter and
ends with the last available drive
letter. If, for example, your computer has drives C and D, the next available drive letter is E. The last available drive letter is Z, unless a LASTDRIVE statement is in your CONFIG.SYS file; in this case, the last available drive letter is the same as that specified by LASTDRIVE. (Refer to your DOS documentation for information about LASTDRIVE.)

The drive letter you select is the drive letter to be assigned to the uncompressed host drive, not to the compressed drive. Double-Space always exchanges drive letters so that the new compressed drive has the same drive letter as the original uncompressed drive.

5. Select the drive letter you want assigned to the new uncompressed host drive, and press Enter. DoubleSpace returns to the screen shown in figure 3.10, which now lists the new host drive letter you selected.
6. To compress the drive, select Continue, and press Enter (refer to fig. 3.10). (If you chose not to change the free space or drive letter for the uncompressed drive, Continue is already selected; you need only press Enter.) DoubleSpace now displays a screen indicating the estimated time required to compress all files on the drive. The actual time may vary, depending on the speed of your computer's disk drive and CPU.

If you continue, you are committed to compressing the drive and you cannot cancel the operation. If you must use your computer before the estimated completion time, press F3 to end DoubleSpace Setup and compress your disk some other time. DoubleSpace asks you to confirm ending Setup; press F3 again to return to the DOS prompt.
7. To continue, remove all disks from your floppy drives and press C. The remaining actions performed by DoubleSpace Custom Setup are the same as performed during Express Setup. Refer now to the text description beginning on page 57 for a description of the remaining procedures performed by DoubleSpace Setup.

Fig. 3.9, top

The DoubleSpace Custom Setup list of compressible drives.

Fig. 3.10, bottom

The DoubleSpace compression options screen.

Your DoubleSpace Custom Setup is complete. After DoubleSpace creates the compressed volume and restarts your computer (as described beginning on page 57), you can use your compressed drive the same way you did before compressing it.

If you need to compress additional disk drives or partitions, or if you want to create a compressed volume out of the free space on an uncompressed disk, see Chapter 6, "Using the Double-Space Utilities."

Creating a New Empty Compressed Drive

If you choose Create a New Empty Compressed Drive (from the menu shown in fig. 3.8), DoubleSpace displays a list of drives similar to the one already shown in figure 3.9. DoubleSpace lists all the disk drives on your computer that hold sufficient free space to create a compressed drive. The list shows the drive's current free space and the projected size of the new compressed drive. The actual drives listed on your display depend on the number of hard disks in your computer and the number of partitions on each hard disk. DoubleSpace includes in the list any removable media drives—such as floppy disks—that have a disk inserted.

DoubleSpace does not list drives with insufficient working room. DoubleSpace also does not list RAM drives, network drives, CD-ROM drives, or drives connected by using the DOS INTERLNK program or the DOS SUBST command. Refer to your DOS documentation for information about INTERLNK and SUBST. To compress a RAM drive, refer to Chapter 4, "Configuring and Optimizing DoubleSpace."

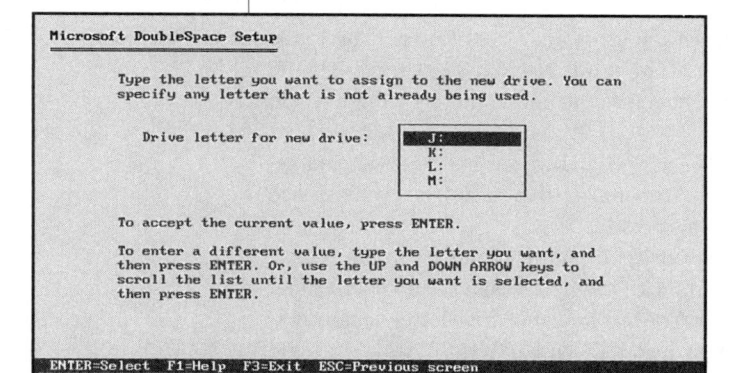

Fig. 3.11, top

The DoubleSpace screen for changing uncompressed free space.

Fig. 3.12, bottom

The DoubleSpace screen for changing the drive letter for the new uncompressed host drive.

To create a free space compressed volume, follow these steps:

1. Select the drive on which you want to create the free space compressed volume, and press Enter. DoubleSpace displays the screen shown in figure 3.13.

    DoubleSpace shows the amount of free space to remain on the uncompressed host drive, the estimated compression ratio for the new compressed volume, and the drive letter for the new compressed volume. Unless you specify otherwise, DoubleSpace leaves 2M of uncompressed space free on the uncompressed host drive, uses an estimated compression ratio of 2:1, and assigns to the new compressed volume the drive letter obtained by using the rules explained in the section "How DoubleSpace Exchanges Drive Letters and Volume Labels," earlier in this chapter.

Increase the amount of uncompressed free space left on the host drive if you need more than 2M uncompressed storage; decrease the amount of uncompressed free space if you are certain you need less than 2M uncompressed storage. Increasing the amount of uncompressed space on the host drive makes the compressed volume smaller; decreasing the amount of uncompressed space makes the compressed volume larger.

Change the estimated compression ratio if you are certain the files you intend to store on the new compressed volume will consistently compress with a ratio higher or lower than 2:1.

2. To change the uncompressed free space left on the host drive, select that line and press Enter; otherwise, skip to step 4. DoubleSpace displays the screen shown in figure 3.14.
3. Type the amount of uncompressed free space to leave on the uncompressed host drive in megabytes (M) and decimal fractions of a megabyte. (To leave 3,500,000 bytes free on your uncompressed host drive, for example, type **3.5**.) Then press Enter. DoubleSpace returns to the screen in figure 3.13, which now shows your changes to the free space.
4. To change the estimated compression ratio for the new compressed drive, select the compression ratio and press Enter; otherwise, skip to step 6. DoubleSpace displays the screen shown in figure 3.15.
5. Select your desired estimated compression ratio, and press Enter. (The ratios increase from 1:1 to 16:1, in increments of one-tenth.) DoubleSpace returns to the screen displayed in figure 3.13, which now lists the new estimated compression ratio.
6. To change the drive letter DoubleSpace assigns to the new compressed volume, select the drive letter, and press Enter; otherwise, skip to step 8. DoubleSpace displays the screen already shown in figure 3.12.

Because this is the first DoubleSpace drive on your computer, you can choose any available drive letter. The list starts with the next available drive letter and ends with the last available drive letter. The last available drive letter usually is Z, unless there is a LASTDRIVE statement in your CONFIG.SYS file; in that case, the last available drive letter is the same as that specified by LASTDRIVE. (Refer to your DOS documentation for more information about LASTDRIVE.)

7. Select the drive letter you want for the new compressed drive, and press Enter. DoubleSpace returns to the screen in figure 3.13, which now shows the new drive letter you selected.
8. To create the new compressed drive, select Continue, and press Enter (refer to fig. 3.13). (If you chose not to change the free space, estimated compression ratio, or drive letter for the uncompressed drive, Continue is already selected; you need only press Enter.) DoubleSpace displays a screen showing the drive letter for the new compressed drive and the estimated time required to create the compressed volume from the drive's free space. The actual time may vary slightly, depending on the speed of your computer's disk drive and CPU.

> **NOTE:**
> Change the estimated compression ratio only if you are certain the files stored on the new compressed drive will consistently compress higher or lower than the standard estimated compression ratio of 2:1.

> **NOTE:**
> The drive letter you select in step 7 is assigned to the new drive created from free space. After the new compressed volume is created, you access it through the drive letter you choose here.

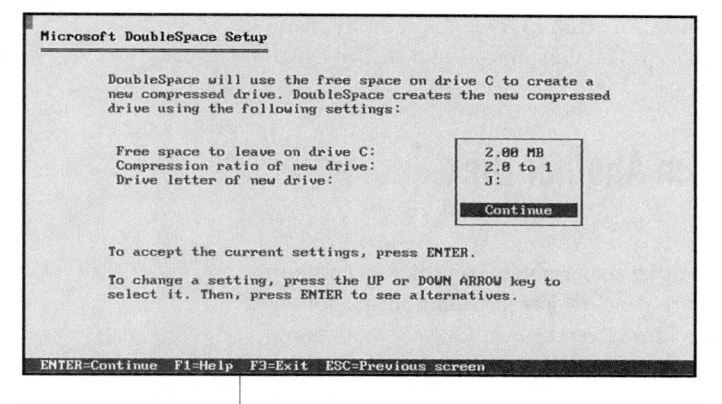

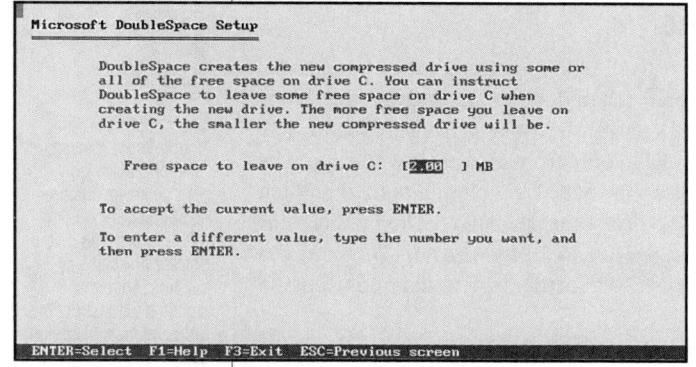

Fig. 3.13, top
The DoubleSpace free space compression options.

Fig. 3.14, bottom
The DoubleSpace screen for changing the amount of uncompressed free space.

If you continue, you are committed to creating the compressed drive, and you cannot cancel the operation. If you decide not to install DoubleSpace at this time, press F3 to exit DoubleSpace Custom Setup.

9. To continue, remove all disks from your floppy drives and press C. The remaining actions performed by DoubleSpace Custom Setup are the same as performed during Express Setup, with a few differences described in the remaining part of this section. Refer now to the text description beginning on page 57 and to the following text for a description of the remaining procedures performed by DoubleSpace Setup.

Because a compressed volume created from free space on a disk contains no files, DoubleSpace does not need to restart your computer before making the new compressed volume available. As soon as DoubleSpace finishes creating the new compressed volume, DoubleSpace displays a message that it is mounting the new compressed drive.

The report that DoubleSpace displays after it creates the new compressed drive is somewhat different from the report DoubleSpace displays after compressing an existing drive. Figure 3.16 shows the final report for a compressed volume created from free space.

The final report displays the results of creating the new compressed drive from free space. The report shows the new compressed volume's drive letter and names the host drive for the compressed volume. The report shows the amount of free space used from the host drive and the amount of free space on the new compressed drive. (The amount of free space reported for the new compressed drive is an estimate based on your specified estimated compression ratio.) DoubleSpace also reports the total amount of time required to create the new compressed volume. Finally, DoubleSpace reports the amount of free space still remaining on the uncompressed host drive.

After reviewing the compression report, press Enter. DoubleSpace removes the temporary changes made earlier to your AUTOEXEC.BAT file and restarts your computer, as described at the end of the section "Running Express Setup," earlier in this chapter.

Your DoubleSpace Custom Setup is completed. After DoubleSpace restarts your computer, you can use your new compressed drive just as if you added another physical disk drive to your computer.

If you need to compress additional disk drives or partitions, or if you want to create another compressed volume using the free space on an uncompressed disk, see Chapter 6, "Using the Double-Space Utilities."

Converting to DoubleSpace from Another Disk Compression Program

If you already use a disk compression program other than DoubleSpace, but you want to switch to DoubleSpace, you must first convert your compressed data into a format DoubleSpace can use. This section describes how to convert from other disk compression programs to DoubleSpace.

Converting from Stacker to DoubleSpace

If you currently use Stacker and want to convert to DoubleSpace, you have two options. The first option is to use the manual conversion method described in this section. Your second option is to use the special conversion disk currently available from Microsoft. The Stacker to DoubleSpace conversion disk is available only from Microsoft while supplies last or through March 31, 1994. Microsoft charges a fee of $5 U.S., plus shipping/handling and applicable sales tax—a total of about $10 U.S. To obtain this disk, contact Microsoft Sales and Service in the United States at (800) 426-9400. Refer to Appendix B, "Using the Microsoft Stacker to DoubleSpace Conversion Disk," for further instructions on using the conversion disk.

If you cannot use the conversion disk—or do not want to order it—you still can convert your Stacker compressed drives to DoubleSpace by following the steps in the following section. The instructions in the following section also can be used to convert any disk compression scheme to DoubleSpace.

NOTE: You can use the DoubleSpace conversion disk for Stacker only if your disks are compressed by Stacker version 2.0 or higher and if your Stacker disks use 8K clusters. Appendix B contains full instructions for using the conversion disk.

Converting from Other Disk Compression Programs

Converting your data to DoubleSpace compression format is a fairly demanding task, requiring more than a little familiarity with DOS. Carefully follow the procedures in this section, and observe all precautions and warnings. Do not attempt to perform the conversion to DoubleSpace if you are pressed for time. In this procedure, you perform actions that fundamentally affect your computer and the data stored on it; patience and attention to procedural detail are important if you are to successfully complete the conversion. Read through the following instructions *before* you begin the actual conversion, and make sure that you understand all the steps involved. If you have any doubts, consult a more experienced individual for advice and assistance (such as your company's computer support person).

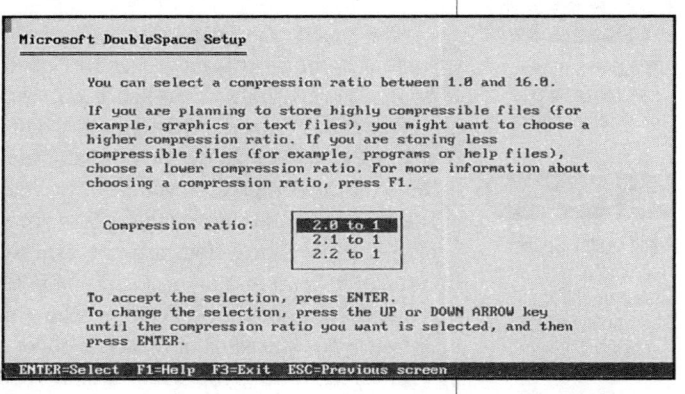

Fig. 3.15

The DoubleSpace screen for changing the estimated compression ratio.

Installing DoubleSpace 67

> **NOTE:** Using your disk compression's uninstall utility may not work on your system. If your compressed disk is nearly full, an uncompressed disk may not have sufficient room to store all your data.

> **STOP** If you do not uninstall your copy-protected software before performing the conversion to Stacker, you cannot use those programs after the conversion is completed.

Before attempting to convert your compressed data to DoubleSpace, install your DOS 6 upgrade if you have not already done so. If you recently installed your DOS 6 upgrade, or if you install it now, make sure that all your programs work correctly before adding DoubleSpace.

The manual conversion method described here essentially involves backing up all disk data, reformatting your hard disk, installing DoubleSpace, and then restoring your data to the hard disk from the backup.

If your disk compression program provides a means of uncompressing your disk files and uninstalling itself, you may benefit from using that method instead of reformatting your disk drive. Stacker and IIT's XtraDrive, for example, include a utility to decompress all of a disk's files and then remove the compressed volumes.

To convert your disk compression software to DoubleSpace, follow these steps:

1. Uninstall any copy-protected software you may have on your disk. Refer to the guidelines in the section "Preparing To Install DoubleSpace," earlier in this chapter, for more information about removing copy-protected software. After you convert your disk to DoubleSpace, you can reinstall any copy-protected programs.

2. Back up all the files on your compressed and uncompressed disks.

Almost all disk compression schemes, including DoubleSpace, use the same basic approach: The compressed data is stored in a file on an uncompressed host drive and accessed as a logical disk drive. Every compressed disk on your computer, therefore, has a matching uncompressed host drive. As you back up the files on the uncompressed host disk, do not back up the compressed volume files. The compressed volume file that contains all your compressed data usually has System, Hidden, and Read-Only file attributes. If your compressed drive is drive C, for example, and its host drive is drive D, you back up all files on drives C and D except for the compressed volume file. Refer to your backup program's documentation for information on how to exclude certain files from a backup. Refer to your disk compression software's documentation for information on how to identify the compressed volume file.

```
Microsoft DoubleSpace Setup

    DoubleSpace has created drive J by converting free space
    from drive C.

        Space used from drive C:        25.1 MB
        Free space on new drive:        50.3 MB
        Compression ratio:              2.0 to 1
        Total time to create:           1 minute.

    Drive C still contains 2.0 MB of free uncompressed space.


    To quit DoubleSpace and restart your computer, press ENTER.


ENTER=Continue
```

Fig. 3.16

The DoubleSpace final report for a free space compressed drive.

Backing up the compressed volume files is not useful. Only the original disk compression software can read data in the compressed volume files. You must back up the files from the compressed drive to transfer them to DoubleSpace. If you do not back up the files from the compressed volume individually, you cannot transfer the files to DoubleSpace. Instead, you lose all your data. Refer to Chapter 1, "Understanding and Using Disk Compression," for information about compressed volume files.

3. Notice how much space is required on the uncompressed disk to hold all the files you back up from that disk. Notice also how much total space is required for the files you back up from each compressed disk. This information is useful when you create your DoubleSpace compressed disks.
4. Keep track of which uncompressed disk is your boot disk. You must make sure that you restore files from this disk to the correct disk or disk partition.
5. Create a bootable floppy disk for DOS 6 if you do not already have one. Refer to your DOS documentation for instructions on creating a bootable floppy disk.
6. Make sure that you also have a floppy disk (or disks) that contain the following files:
    - The DOS FDISK utility.
    - The DOS FORMAT utility.
    - Any device drivers or TSRs your system needs to operate, except for your old disk compression software. These device driver files must go on your bootable floppy disk.
    - CONFIG.SYS and AUTOEXEC.BAT files to start your computer and load any needed device drivers or other configuration information. These files must go on your bootable floppy disk.
    - Your backup and restore software.
7. Edit your CONFIG.SYS and AUTOEXEC.BAT files so that they no longer load the device drivers or TSR programs needed for your old disk compression software. Refer to your disk compression software's documentation for information on identifying the device drivers and TSR programs used with the old disk compression program.
8. Edit your CONFIG.SYS and AUTOEXEC.BAT files so that any disk caching programs are disabled.
9. Reboot your computer by using the bootable floppy disk you created for step 5.
    At this point, your compressed disks are unavailable. You are working directly with the actual physical disk drives and disk partitions in your computer. No drive letters are exchanged; your first hard disk or hard disk partition is drive C, the next is drive D, and so on.
10. Double-check to make sure that your floppy disks have all the utility programs and other software you need to complete the conversion (see the checklist in step 6).
11. If you want to change the way your hard disk or disks are physically partitioned, use the DOS FDISK utility to repartition your disk at this time. Refer to your DOS documentation for information about the FDISK utility. If you want only to convert from your old disk compression software to DoubleSpace, you do not need to use FDISK.
12. Use the DOS FORMAT utility to format each of your disk's partitions. As you format your hard disk partitions, use the /U switch option. Using this option prevents the FORMAT utility from creating information necessary to unformat the disk. (This information is not useful to you.) The following example shows the syntax to use with the FORMAT command to format the second partition on a hard disk:

    FORMAT D: /U

> **NOTE:**
> The procedure described in step 11 is optional. Perform that step only if you previously contemplated rearranging how your hard disk or disks are currently partitioned. Because you must reformat your hard disk and restore all your data anyway, this is a good time to repartition your disks.

> ⚠ Step 11 through the end of this procedure effectively wipes out *all* data on your compressed or uncompressed hard disks. *Make absolutely sure* that you have a complete, valid backup of all your files from all your hard disks, whether compressed or uncompressed; otherwise, you are certain to lose data.

As you format the C partition of your hard disk, make sure that you use the /S switch to transfer the system files to the hard disk so that the C partition is bootable. If your hard disk has only one partition, that partition is drive C; otherwise, the first partition on your hard disk is drive C. Use the following syntax with the FORMAT command to format your drive C:

FORMAT C: /S /U

13. After you format your disk partitions, verify that drive C is bootable. Remove all floppy disks from your drives, and press Ctrl+Alt+Del to restart your computer. Your computer should start, load DOS, and leave you at the C prompt.
14. From the floppy disks you prepared in step 6, copy your CONFIG.SYS, AUTOEXEC.BAT, and any required device drivers to your C drive.
15. Copy your backup software program from the floppy disks you prepared in step 6, or reinstall the backup software from its distribution disks. Refer to the documentation for your backup software for information on setting up the backup and restore programs.
16. Restore *only* your DOS 6 program files from the backup you made in step 2. Alternatively, you can run the DOS 6 Setup program again to reinstall the DOS 6 program files.
17. Restart your computer again. Remove any floppy disks from the drives, and press Ctrl+Alt+Del. Your computer should restart, load DOS, and leave you at the DOS prompt.
18. Follow the instructions in the section "Running Express Setup," earlier in this chapter, to compress your drive C. If you need more than 2M of space on the uncompressed boot drive, follow the instructions in the section "Running Custom Setup," earlier in this chapter. If you have other drives or partitions to compress, follow the instructions in the section "Creating Additional Compressed Drives," in Chapter 6. (If you follow the instructions in Chapter 6 to create additional compressed drives, make sure that you compress all disks and partitions by using the Compress an Existing Drive option, even if no data currently exists on the drive.)
19. Restore all remaining data from your backup to your hard disks. As you restore your data from the backup, configure your backup and restore program so that files from the backup do *not* replace files already on the hard disk.
20. To complete the restoration of your data, reinstall any copy-protected software you uninstalled earlier.

You have completed the conversion to DoubleSpace disk compression. Your computer should now work as it did before, although you may need to make a few additional adjustments before you are truly finished. You also may find a few differences in your system. As explained at the beginning of this chapter, DoubleSpace has specific rules for how it assigns drive letters. DoubleSpace's rules for assigning drive letters may be different from the rules that your previous disk compression software used.

Some of your drive letters are likely to be different after you convert to DoubleSpace. Your compressed volumes should all have the same drive they did before, but the drive letters for your uncompressed drives may be different. With a single disk partition on a

---

NOTE:
You must restore DOS 6 files from your backup or reinstall DOS 6 files from the DOS setup disks. The DOS directory contains the DoubleSpace program files needed to compress your disks with DoubleSpace.

STOP
If your restore program replaces files that already exist on your hard disk, you inadvertently replace your modified CONFIG.SYS and AUTOEXEC.BAT files with the old versions that still load your former disk compression device drivers. If these device drivers load into memory, your DoubleSpace drives may become inaccessible or corrupted, and you must change CONFIG.SYS and AUTOEXEC.BAT again.

drive using Stacker, for example, the host drive for compressed drive C is usually drive D. Under DoubleSpace, however, the host drive for the compressed drive C is usually H. The drive letter for the compressed drive is the same in both cases, but the host drive is different.

Usually, having different drive letters for the uncompressed drives does not affect your computer's operation. You simply may need to adjust to the new drive letters in your computer system. In a few situations, however, different drive letters may make a difference. If your DOS PATH statement (in AUTOEXEC.BAT) refers to directories on your uncompressed drives, you may need to change the path statement to reflect the new drive letters. You also may need to reconfigure any software programs that refer to directories on an uncompressed drive.

In particular, Windows users may need to make some minor changes. As discussed in Chapter 1, "Understanding and Using Disk Compression," Windows permanent swap files do not work on a compressed drive; you must put the permanent swap file on an uncompressed drive. To get the best speed from Windows, many people also place temporary swap files on an uncompressed drive. (Refer to your Windows documentation for more information about Windows swap files.) Because drive letters for your uncompressed drives are likely to change, Windows may report that it cannot open the swap file. If you have a permanent swap file, Windows may report that the swap file is corrupted. Refer to Chapter 7, "Troubleshooting DoubleSpace," for information on correcting problems with the Windows swap file.

Summary

In this chapter, you learned about the changes DoubleSpace makes to your computer system. You learned which files DoubleSpace adds or changes on your boot disk, and how DoubleSpace exchanges drive letters and volume labels. You also learned how to prepare for DoubleSpace installation and were guided step-by-step through the procedures for both Express and Custom Setup for DoubleSpace. Finally, you learned how to convert from another disk compression program to DoubleSpace.

The next chapter provides information on how to configure and optimize DoubleSpace for your system.

CHAPTER 4

Configuring and Optimizing DoubleSpace

You can make the most of your computer's resources by optimizing DoubleSpace after installation. If you change your computer's configuration after installing DoubleSpace—by adding or removing a disk drive, for example, or by adding network software—you may need to change the way DoubleSpace configures and assigns drive letters.

This chapter describes how to configure DoubleSpace to make the most conventional memory available and then discusses ways to use the MS-DOS SMARTDRV disk cache program to increase the speed of DoubleSpace compressed drives. This chapter also describes when and how to change the estimated compression ratio for a DoubleSpace compressed drive. The chapter then explains how to alter the way DoubleSpace assigns drive letters and how to change the number of removable media drives DoubleSpace can accommodate. This chapter concludes by describing how to set up a DoubleSpace compressed RAM drive.

> **NOTE:** Memory management is a complex subject, and this book cannot adequately cover all the issues involved. This book describes only the information needed to load the DoubleSpace device driver into upper memory. For more information about DOS memory management, consult *Using MS-DOS 6*, also published by Que.

Relocating DoubleSpace in Memory

This section explains how to relocate the DoubleSpace device driver in conventional memory to avoid potential conflicts with other programs and also explains how to free more conventional memory by loading the DoubleSpace device driver into upper memory.

Many DOS programs require substantial amounts of conventional memory. If enough conventional memory is not available for your application, it may display `insufficient memory` error messages. DOS may even tell you that you do not have enough memory to load the program at all. You may be able to load DOS and many of your device drivers—including the DoubleSpace device driver—into upper memory, making more conventional memory available for your applications. To load DOS and device drivers into upper memory, you must use a *memory manager*—a program that helps DOS control access to upper memory and all memory beyond 1M in your computer.

The following section explains the mechanism DoubleSpace uses to control its placement in memory and then describes the procedure for loading the DoubleSpace device driver in upper memory.

Using DBLSPACE.SYS and DBLSPACE.BIN

You load device drivers into conventional memory by using the DEVICE command in your CONFIG.SYS file. Your CONFIG.SYS file, for example, may already contain a line similar to the following, which loads a mouse device driver:

```
DEVICE=MOUSE.SYS
```

Similarly, you load device drivers into upper memory by using the DEVICEHIGH command in CONFIG.SYS. The DEVICEHIGH command tells DOS to use the memory manager to load the device driver into upper memory. (Refer to your DOS documentation for more information about the DEVICE and DEVICEHIGH commands.)

The device driver for DoubleSpace compressed disk drives is the DLBSPACE.BIN file, which is placed in your boot disk root directory as you install DoubleSpace (refer to Chapter 3, "Installing DoubleSpace," for details of this process). DOS loads DBLSPACE.BIN into memory before processing CONFIG.SYS. DOS, therefore, must always load DBLSPACE.BIN into conventional memory as your computer first starts—DOS has no way of knowing where you want the device driver to ultimately reside.

Commands in CONFIG.SYS cannot apply directly to DBLSPACE.BIN, because the device driver is already loaded in memory at the time DOS processes CONFIG.SYS. Instead, you indirectly control the memory location of DBLSPACE.BIN by using commands in CONFIG.SYS that refer to DBLSPACE.SYS. DBLSPACE.SYS is not really a device driver; it contains only instructions that move the DBLSPACE.BIN device driver to another location in memory. After DBLSPACE.SYS moves the DBLSPACE.BIN device driver, DBLSPACE.SYS unloads itself from memory. As DOS processes the DBLSPACE.SYS statement in CONFIG.SYS, the DBLSPACE.BIN device driver is moved to a new location in memory. The specific memory location depends on whether you use the /MOVE switch and the DEVICE or DEVICEHIGH command. The specific effects of these commands are described in the following section.

Using DBLSPACE.SYS To Relocate the DoubleSpace Device Driver

To load any device driver into upper memory, you must use a memory manager program. Although many memory manager programs are available, this book describes only the memory manager software supplied with DOS. If you use another memory manager, such as QEMM or 386MAX, refer to the documentation for that program for details. Regardless of which memory management software you use, the CONFIG.SYS commands you use to control the DoubleSpace device driver's location in memory are the same.

If you load disk drive device drivers that make logical disk drives available to DOS (such as a RAM disk or network software), adding DBLSPACE.SYS to your CONFIG.SYS file may affect how DOS and DoubleSpace assign drive letters to these other drives. So that DBLSPACE.SYS does not affect these drive letters, make sure that the DBLSPACE.SYS statement in CONFIG.SYS comes *after* all other statements that load disk drive device drivers. You may even want DBLSPACE.SYS as the last line in your CONFIG.SYS file.

If you use the new DOS 6 feature to create start-up menus by using CONFIG.SYS, make sure that you put the statements for DBLSPACE.SYS in the common area of your configuration menu. Refer to your DOS documentation for information on creating CONFIG.SYS start-up menus.

Using the DBLSPACE.SYS /MOVE Switch

DBLSPACE.SYS enables you to specify two different types of memory location for the DoubleSpace device driver. The first of these is specified by using the /MOVE switch. DOS first loads DBLSPACE.BIN into the highest possible location in conventional memory. Some DOS programs, however, conflict with the DoubleSpace device driver if it is loaded at the top of conventional memory. To avoid such conflicts, DBLSPACE.SYS provides the /MOVE switch; this switch relocates the DBLSPACE.BIN device driver to the bottom of conventional memory. Although the /MOVE switch controls the final location of DBLSPACE.BIN in conventional memory, it does not relocate the DoubleSpace device driver into upper memory.

To avoid potential problems with programs that may conflict with DBLSPACE.BIN at the top of conventional memory, always add the DBLSPACE.SYS /MOVE switch to your CONFIG.SYS file.

Follow these steps to relocate DBLSPACE.BIN to the bottom of conventional memory:

1. Use a text editor (such as DOS EDIT) to edit CONFIG.SYS.
2. Add the following line at the end of the CONFIG.SYS file, if it is not already present:\
   DEVICE=C:\DOS\DBLSPACE.SYS /MOVE
   This line assumes that the directory containing your DOS files is on drive C and is named DOS. If the DOS files are in a different directory or drive, substitute that directory name for C:\DOS.
3. Save CONFIG.SYS with its new line, and exit the text editor.
4. Press Ctrl+Alt+Del to restart your computer. You must restart your computer for changes in CONFIG.SYS to take effect; DOS processes CONFIG.SYS only during start-up.

Before editing CONFIG.SYS, copy the original CONFIG.SYS file to a floppy disk so you can restore your original configuration if you make a mistake or experience other problems.

DOS is now configured to relocate the DBLSPACE.BIN device driver to the bottom of conventional memory. The following section describes how to load DBLSPACE.BIN in upper memory.

Using DEVICEHIGH with DBLSPACE.SYS

NOTE: *A DBLSPACE.SYS /MOVE statement may already be in your CONFIG.SYS file. DoubleSpace adds this statement to CONFIG.SYS if it detects an active memory manager during DoubleSpace Setup.*

To control the upper memory area, DOS requires the additional services provided by an expanded memory manager. To load any device driver (including DBLSPACE.BIN) into upper memory, you must use an expanded memory manager such as EMM386 (supplied with DOS) or a third-party memory manager such as QEMM or 386MAX. To use the DOS EMM386 memory manager, you must have an 80386 or higher CPU, and you also must load the DOS HIMEM.SYS extended memory manager.

To add instructions to CONFIG.SYS that relocate DBLSPACE.BIN into upper memory, follow these steps:

1. Use a text editor (such as DOS EDIT) to edit your CONFIG.SYS file.
2. Add the following line to the beginning of the CONFIG.SYS file, if not already present:
   DEVICE=C:\DOS\HIMEM.SYS
   This line installs the HIMEM.SYS extended memory manager when you restart your computer.

Before editing CONFIG.SYS, always copy the original file to a floppy disk.

3. Immediately following the HIMEM.SYS line, add a line for the DOS EMM memory manager, EMM386. The EMM386 line follows the HIMEM.SYS line because EMM386 uses services provided by HIMEM.SYS.

   To make upper memory available for device drivers, you must use one of two switches with EMM386. The first switch—/RAM—enables both upper memory and expanded memory. The second switch—/NOEMS—enables only upper memory.

   To make upper memory available for DOS and device drivers and also to provide expanded memory for other programs, add the following line to CONFIG.SYS:

   DEVICE=C:\DOS\EMM386.EXE /RAM

   To make upper memory available only for DOS and device drivers, add the following line to CONFIG.SYS:

   DEVICE=C:\DOS\EMM386.EXE /NOEMS

4. Following the HIMEM.SYS and EMM386 statements, add the following line (if not already present):

   DOS=UMB

   DOS needs this statement to access upper memory. No device driver can load in upper memory without this statement.

   Alternatively, you may use the following line:

   DOS=UMB,HIGH

   This statement enables DOS to access upper memory and also loads parts of DOS into upper memory.

   So far, you have added only the memory management device drivers required to enable upper memory for use. Now you must add the statement that actually loads DBLSPACE.BIN into upper memory.

5. Add the following line at the end of the CONFIG.SYS file, if not already present:

   DEVICEHIGH=C:\DOS\DBLSPACE.SYS /MOVE

   The DEVICEHIGH statement causes DOS to relocate the DoubleSpace device driver into upper memory.

6. Save CONFIG.SYS with its newly added lines, and exit the text editor.
7. Press Ctrl+Alt+Del to restart your computer and make the changes in CONFIG.SYS take effect.

DOS is now configured to relocate the DBLSPACE.BIN device driver into upper memory. The following section describes how to verify whether DBLSPACE.BIN is loaded into upper memory.

Verifying that DoubleSpace Is Using Upper Memory

If your computer has insufficient room in upper memory to load a device driver, DOS instead loads the device driver into conventional memory without displaying any error messages or other notices. To determine which device drivers are loaded into upper memory, you must

---

If a DEVICE statement for DBLSPACE.SYS already is in your CONFIG.SYS file, you can use the DOS MEMMAKER command to change the statements in CONFIG.SYS to load the device driver into upper memory. Refer to your DOS documentation for more information on using DOS MEMMAKER.

All lines given for CONFIG.SYS in these steps assume that your DOS files are on drive C in a directory named DOS. If your DOS files are in a different directory or drive, substitute the correct drive and directory name for C:\DOS.

DEVICE statements for HIMEM.SYS and EMM386 may already be in your CONFIG.SYS file. The EMM386 line in CONFIG.SYS may have other switches, especially if you used the DOS MEMMAKER command. Do not alter these switches; doing so may cause your computer to become inoperable or may cause a memory conflict.

Configuring and Optimizing DoubleSpace 75

Upper Memory Conflicts

If you already use upper memory, and you load the DoubleSpace device driver into upper memory, you may begin to receive disk drive read error messages from DOS, similar to the following example:

    Error reading drive C:

Read errors may result from conflicts between DoubleSpace and other software that uses the upper memory area. If the upper memory area becomes too crowded, device drivers may interfere with one another's data areas. Another cause of read errors may be a conflict between DoubleSpace and a feature called *shadow RAM*. Computers using shadow RAM copy the BIOS software from their ROM chips into RAM. This "shadow" copy of the BIOS ROM enables your computer to operate faster, because RAM typically operates faster than ROM. If you experience disk read errors after loading the DoubleSpace device driver into upper memory, remove the DEVICEHIGH command for DoubleSpace from CONFIG.SYS. If you think the errors result from a conflict with shadow RAM, try turning off the shadow RAM instead of removing DoubleSpace from upper memory. Refer to your computer's hardware documentation to determine whether your computer uses shadow RAM and how to disable it.

use the DOS MEM command to display a report describing how your computer's memory is used by DOS and other programs. (Refer to your DOS documentation for full information about MEM.)

To determine whether the DoubleSpace device driver is loaded into upper memory, type the following command at the DOS prompt, and press Enter:

MEM /C /P

The /C switch for the MEM command instructs it to classify memory usage by the program using the memory. The /P switch tells MEM to pause after each screenful of information. After you issue the MEM command with the specified switches, a display similar to the following appears:

> **NOTE:**
> Your CONFIG.SYS may already contain a DEVICEHIGH statement for DBLSPACE.SYS. DoubleSpace adds this statement to CONFIG.SYS if it detects an active memory manager during setup. DoubleSpace Setup does not add statements for HIMEM.SYS and EMM386.EXE.

```
Modules using memory below 1 MB:
  Name           Total        =   Conventional    +    Upper Memory
  ----           -----            ------------         ------------
  MSDOS          75245  (73K)     75245   (73K)        0       (0K)
  HIMEM           3792   (4K)      3792    (4K)        0       (0K)
  EMM386          3120   (3K)      3120    (3K)        0       (0K)
  COMMAND         4992   (5K)      4992    (5K)        0       (0K)
  DBLSPACE       45232  (44K)         0    (0K)    45232      (44K)
  SMARTDRV       27280  (27K)         0    (0K)    27280      (27K)
  Free          588832 (575K)    568048  (555K)    20784      (20K)

Memory Summary:
  Type of Memory          Total      =      Used       +      Free
  --------------          -----             ----              ----
  Conventional           655360 (640K)     87312   (85K)   568048  (555K)
  Upper                   93296  (91K)     72512   (71K)    20784   (20K)
  Adapter RAM/ROM        131072 (128K)    131072  (128K)        0    (0K)
  Extended  (XMS)*      3314576 (3237K)  1545104 (1509K)  1769472 (1728K)
                        -------          -------          -------
  Total memory          4194304 (4096K)  1836000 (1793K)  2358304 (2303K)

  Total under 1 MB       748656 (731K)    159824  (156K)   588832  (575K)
  Total Expanded (EMS)                   3735552 (3648K)
  Free Expanded (EMS)*                   2015232 (1968K)
 * EMM386 is using XMS memory to simulate EMS memory as needed.
   Free EMS memory may change as free XMS memory changes.
  Largest executable program size         567952  (555K)
  Largest free upper memory block          15072   (15K)
  The high memory area is available.
```

The first section of the MEM report, under the heading Modules using memory below 1MB, indicates where the device driver is located in memory. The first column shows the name of the device driver or program, and the remaining columns show the total memory used and how much conventional and upper memory is consumed. Notice in the DBLSPACE entry (first section, fifth entry) that 0K of conventional memory and 44K of upper memory are used. This indicates that the DoubleSpace device driver, DBLSPACE.BIN, is loaded into upper memory. (If a report shows instead that DBLSPACE uses 44K of conventional memory and 0K of upper memory, the device driver is not loaded into upper memory.)

The specific contents of your report vary depending on the configuration of your computer system. If the report shows that the DoubleSpace device driver is not loaded into upper memory, carefully review the configuration steps in the preceding section of this chapter. Make sure especially that you included either the /RAM or /NOEMS switch with EMM386 and that you also included the DOS=UMB statement. If you performed the procedures correctly but also are loading many device drivers into upper memory, you simply may not have sufficient upper memory to accommodate the DoubleSpace device driver.

Improving DoubleSpace Performance by Using SMARTDRV.EXE

SMARTDRV.EXE is the disk cache program supplied with DOS 6 to speed disk reading and writing operations. Chapter 1 describes the general principles on which disk caching is based.

If you want to use a disk cache with DoubleSpace, you must use the SMARTDRV version 4.1 supplied with DOS 6 (or a later version). Although versions of SMARTDRV are supplied with Windows 3.1 and with DOS 5, only the DOS 6 version is compatible with DoubleSpace. If you try to use an older version of SMARTDRV, you receive an error message as SMARTDRV loads into memory, which appears similar to the following example:

```
Cannot run SMARTDrive 4.0 with DoubleSpace
```

DoubleSpace is unaware of the disk cache and relies on SMARTDRV being aware of DoubleSpace. For this reason, DoubleSpace may not work with other disk cache programs, especially if they perform write-delay caching.

SMARTDRV is a TSR program; it is loaded through AUTOEXEC.BAT instead of CONFIG.SYS. You should load SMARTDRV near the beginning of AUTOEXEC.BAT so that the benefit of the cache is available as early as possible. Load SMARTDRV by adding to your AUTOEXEC.BAT file a line similar to the following:

C:\DOS\SMARTDRV

(This example assumes that your DOS files are in the DOS subdirectory on drive C; if they are located in another directory or on another drive, substitute the correct name or names for C:\DOS in this line.)

NOTE:
This section discusses only those aspects of SMARTDRV relevant to using DoubleSpace. For more information, refer to either your DOS documentation or to *Using MS-DOS 6,* also published by Que.

SMARTDRV 4.1 automatically caches all your disk drives, using write-delay caching for all hard disks. SMARTDRV does not normally use write-delay caching for removable media drives, because it cannot tell when the disk may be removed from the drive.

Using a disk cache on a logical disk drive is not effective. Disk caching works only if you cache the physical disk drive or a physical disk partition. Because SMARTDRV is aware of DoubleSpace, it automatically caches any compressed drives through their physical host drives.

For information about how SMARTDRV currently is operating, type **SMARTDRV /S** at the DOS prompt and press Enter. This command tells SMARTDRV to display a status report similar to that of the following example:

```
Microsoft SMARTDrive Disk Cache version 4.1
Copyright 1991,1993 Microsoft Corp.

Room for     128 elements of    8,192 bytes each
There have been      724 cache hits
      and      543 cache misses
Cache size:  1,048,576 bytes
Cache size while running Windows:   524,288 bytes
              Disk Caching Status
  drive    read cache    write cache    buffering
  ---------------------------------------------
   A:         yes           no             no
   B:         yes           no             no
   C:*        yes           yes            no
   D:*        yes           yes            no
   E:*        yes           yes            no
   F:         yes           yes            no
   G:         yes           yes            no
   H:         yes           yes            no
 * DoubleSpace drive cached via host drive.

For help, type "Smartdrv /?".
```

This report is for a computer with three physical disk partitions, each of which hosts a compressed volume file. The compressed volumes are drives C, D, and E. Their respective host disks are H, G, and F. Notice the asterisk (*) next to each of the compressed drive letters. SMARTDRV recognizes these drives as DoubleSpace compressed volumes and caches them by caching their host drives. For more information about the SMARTDRV report, refer to your DOS documentation.

The write-delay caching used by SMARTDRV 4.1 requires careful consideration. Although the write-delay cache, along with the regular read cache, increases the speed of disk operations, it has an inherent danger. Because the write-delay cache holds information in memory before writing it to the disk, some data may be lost if your computer experiences a power failure or a problem that requires you to restart the computer by turning it off instead of using Ctrl+Alt+Del. (SMARTDRV does write all its write-delay data to the disk if you use Ctrl+Alt+Del to restart your computer.) Although the risk of data loss from a write-delay cache may be small, it does exist, and the consequences can be serious. If data loss occurs, and the lost data is part of a compressed volume's structural information, the compressed volume may become corrupted. A corrupted compressed volume file may result in the loss of all files on the compressed volume.

> If you use a disk cache other than SMARTDRV, configure the disk cache so that caching for compressed volumes is disabled. Refer to the documentation for your cache program to determine how to correctly disable the cache for particular drives.

Because of the increased risk of data loss, turning off the write-delay cache for disk drives that contain compressed volume files is recommended. If you have an 80386 or higher computer running at 33Mhz or greater, you may not even notice the speed difference when the write cache is off.

In the SMARTDRV sample status report, notice that the write cache is active for all hard disk drives. SMARTDRV 4.1 uses write caching for all hard disk drives and partitions unless you specify otherwise.

To turn off the SMARTDRV 4.1 write cache for one or more disk drives, follow these steps:

1. Type **DBLSPACE /LIST** at the DOS prompt, and press Enter. DoubleSpace displays a report similar to that of the following example, listing all compressed and uncompressed disk drives and the name and location for each compressed volume file:

```
Drive  Type                   Total Free  Total Size  CVF Filename
 --    --------------         ----------  ----------  ------------
  A    Removable-media drive  No disk in drive
  B    Floppy drive              1.25 MB     1.39 MB
  C    Compressed hard drive    71.04 MB   119.62 MB  H:\DBLSPACE.000
  H    Local hard drive          0.90 MB    69.96 MB
```

In this sample report, drive C is compressed, and the compressed volume file—shown in the last column—is on drive H; therefore, you want to disable write-delay caching for drive H.

2. Use a text editor (such as DOS EDIT) to edit your AUTOEXEC.BAT file. If your AUTOEXEC.BAT does not already contain a line to load SMARTDRV, add the following line (assuming that SMARTDRV is in your DOS directory on drive C):

    C:\DOS\SMARTDRV

3. Now add to the SMARTDRV line the drive letters for which you want to disable write caching. To disable write caching for drive H, for example, leave a space at the end of the line and then type **H** so that the resulting line in AUTOEXEC.BAT appears as follows:

    `C:\DOS\SMARTDRV H`

If your computer had compressed drives C, D, and E, hosted by drives H, G, and F, respectively, this line in AUTOEXEC.BAT must appear as follows, after all changes, to disable write caching for all drives:

    `C:\DOS\SMARTDRV H G F`

4. Save your changes to AUTOEXEC.BAT, and exit the text editor.
5. Restart your computer. After your computer restarts, SMARTDRV is reconfigured so that write caching for the selected drives is disabled.
6. To check your work, type **SMARTDRV /S** at the DOS prompt and press Enter to display the SMARTDRV status report. SMARTDRV displays a status report similar to the one already shown, except that all drives should display "no" in the write cache column of the report.

> **NOTE:**
> If you are concerned about problems with the SMARTDRV write-delay cache, you may want to know that SMARTDRV version 4.2 is now available from Microsoft. SMARTDRV 4.2 does not automatically use write-delay caching; instead, write-delay caching is off for all drives unless you explicitly turn it on. You can obtain SMARTDRV 4.2 through the Microsoft Software Library on CompuServe Information Services, or contact Microsoft Customer Service directly. The DOS 6 Upgrade will continue to include SMARTDRV version 4.1.

If the write cache is still turned on for any of your drives, carefully work your way through these steps again. Make sure especially that you use the correct drive letters in the SMARTDRV line of AUTOEXEC.BAT.

You have successfully configured SMARTDRV to work with maximum safety for your DoubleSpace drives.

> **NOTE:**
> Remember that you must control disk caching for compressed drives through their host drives. If you accidentally specify the drive letter for a compressed drive, SMARTDRV displays the following error message:
>
>   You must
>   specify the
>   host drive for
>   a Double-Space
>   drive.

Changing the Estimated Compression Ratio

The reported free space on your compressed disk drive is based on the estimated compression ratio, which usually is set at the presumed 2:1 compression. If you have 10M physically available on the drive and the estimated compression ratio is 2:1, for example, the reported free space is 20M. If the files on your compressed disk consistently compress with an actual compression ratio greater or less than 2:1, however, the free space reported on your disk may be inaccurate.

If you store many files that compress well, and your overall actual compression ratio is greater than 2:1, the free space reported by using the standard estimated compression of 2:1 is less than the amount of data that can be stored on the compressed disk. This situation may lead you to believe that you have less available storage than you really have. If, however, you store many files that do not compress well, and your overall actual compression ratio is less than 2:1, the free space reported by using the standard estimated compression of 2:1 is greater than the amount of data that can be stored on the compressed disk. This situation is even more annoying, because it may lead you to believe that you have more available storage than you really do.

You may want to change the estimated compression ratio so that the reported free space for your compressed disk more accurately reflects the actual storage available. If you raise the estimated compression ratio, DoubleSpace reports more space available on the compressed disk. If you lower the estimated compression ratio, DoubleSpace reports less available space on the compressed disk. You normally change the estimated compression ratio to match the actual overall compression ratio, although you may specify any value for the estimated compression ratio. Setting the estimated compression ratio to match the actual overall compression ratio generally provides the best free space reports.

Changing the Estimated Compression Ratio at the Command Line

You can change the estimated compression ratio by using DoubleSpace command line switches—especially to change the estimated compression ratio for one or more compressed drives from a DOS batch file. You can, for example, use one of these commands in AUTOEXEC.BAT to update the estimated compression ratio each time your computer starts.

DoubleSpace provides two command line switches for changing the estimated compression ratio: /RATIO and /RATIO=. The /RATIO switch causes DoubleSpace to change the estimated compression ratio to match the actual average compression ratio. Using /RATIO= causes DoubleSpace to change the estimated compression ratio to a specific compression ratio specified after the equals sign. You can specify any compression ratio from 1.0 to 16.0. You also can use the /ALL switch with either form of the /RATIO switch to simultaneously set the estimated compression ratio for all compressed drives. Instead of using the /ALL switch, however, you can specify a single disk drive by letter. If you do not use the /ALL switch or specify a drive letter, DoubleSpace changes the estimated compression ratio for the current compressed disk drive.

To set the estimated compression ratio for all compressed disk drives to match the actual compression ratio for each drive, use the following command:

DBLSPACE /RATIO /ALL

To set the estimated compression ratio for only the current compressed drive to match the actual compression ratio for this drive, use the following command instead:

DBLSPACE /RATIO

To set the estimated compression ratio for a specific compressed drive to match the actual compression ratio for that drive, use the following command:

DBLSPACE /RATIO C:

This line sets the compression ratio for drive C. Substitute the drive letter of any drive you want to change.

To set the estimated compression ratio to a value you specify, use any of the preceding forms and add the equals sign (=) and the desired estimated compression ratio to the end of the /RATIO switch. The following command, for example, sets the estimated compression ratio for the current drive at 1.8:1:

DBLSPACE /RATIO=1.8

Changing the Estimated Compression Ratio by Using the DoubleSpace Menus

If you use the menu system in the DoubleSpace utility to change the estimated compression ratio, you must set the estimated compression ratio for each compressed drive separately; the DoubleSpace menus have no selection equivalent to the /ALL command line switch.

To use DoubleSpace menus to change the estimated compression ratio, follow these steps:

1. To start the DoubleSpace utility, type **DBLSPACE** at the DOS prompt and press Enter. The DoubleSpace program starts and displays the screen shown in figure 4.1. The exact list of drives varies, depending on the number and size of your compressed drives.
2. Highlight the compressed drive for which you want to change the estimated compression ratio.
3. Open the **D**rive menu, and choose Change **R**atio. DoubleSpace displays the Change Compression Ratio dialog box, which shows the current estimated compression ratio for the selected drive, the actual average compression ratio for all files stored on the drive, and a text box for the new estimated compression ratio (see fig. 4.2).

Configuring and Optimizing DoubleSpace 81

DoubleSpace suggests making the new estimated compression ratio the same as the actual compression ratio by entering that value in the text box for you. To accept DoubleSpace's suggested new compression ratio, skip to step 5.

4. To change the estimated compression ratio, type a new value in the text box, using only one decimal place.

   DoubleSpace restricts the range of values you may enter to ensure that you do not set the estimated compression ratio unreasonably high or low. In figure 4.2, for example, DoubleSpace restricts the new estimated compression ratio to a number from 1.0 to 4.2.

5. Choose **OK** to accept the new estimated compression ratio. DoubleSpace returns to the main menu (refer to fig. 4.1).

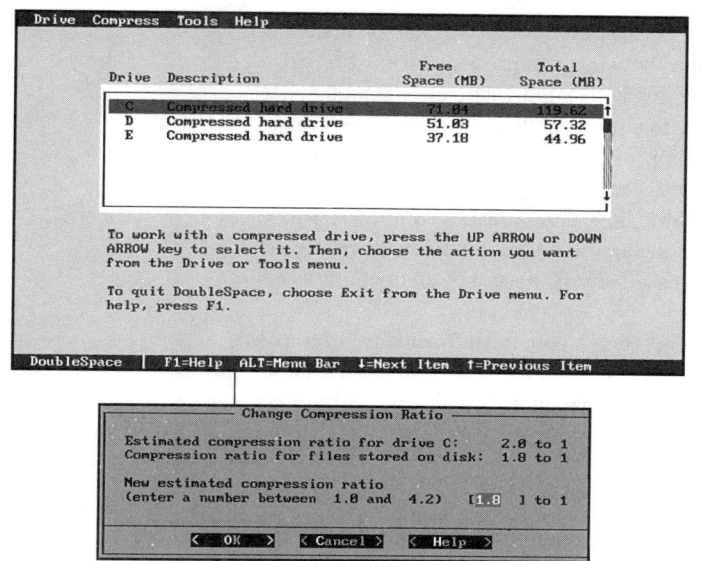

Fig. 4.1, top

The DoubleSpace main menu and drive list display.

Fig. 4.2, bottom

The DoubleSpace Change Compression Ratio dialog box.

If you decide not to change the estimated compression ratio, choose **C**ancel instead. The estimated compression ratio is now changed for the drive selected in step 2. To change the estimated compression ratio for additional compressed drives, follow steps 2 through 5 for each drive.

6. To leave DoubleSpace, choose E**x**it from the **D**rive menu. DoubleSpace returns to the DOS prompt.

Changing DoubleSpace Drive Letter Assignments

As you create your first compressed drive, DoubleSpace reserves four drive letters for its use, in addition to the drive letter used for the uncompressed host drive (as explained in Chapter 3, "Installing DoubleSpace"). Usually, you need not be concerned with drive letter assignments made by DoubleSpace. In a few circumstances, however, you may need to alter DoubleSpace's drive letter assignments.

One such circumstance occurs if you need to create more than five compressed drives. In this case, you must increase the number of drive letters that DoubleSpace reserves by raising the drive letter for the last drive DoubleSpace uses. Another circumstance requiring you to alter DoubleSpace drive letter assignments is if you add a network to your computer after installing DoubleSpace or if you install DoubleSpace while your network is not running. In this case, you may have a conflict between drive letters used by DoubleSpace and your network log-in drive letters. If, for example, drive C is your only physical drive, and you compress it, DoubleSpace reserves drive letters D, E, F, G, and H for its own use. You cannot use the typical network log-in drive letter F, because drive letter F is now reserved by DoubleSpace.

You also may want to change DoubleSpace's drive letter assignments if, on installing DoubleSpace, you misunderstood the difference between compressing an existing drive and creating a new compressed drive. (Compressing an existing drive causes DoubleSpace to create a compressed volume corresponding to a physical disk drive and to exchange drive letters accordingly. Creating a new compressed drive causes DoubleSpace to create a compressed volume from free space on a physical disk drive and assign it a new drive letter, without reassigning other drive letters.) If you create a new compressed drive and your computer has only one disk drive, you end up with an uncompressed drive C and a new compressed drive D rather than a compressed drive C hosted by an uncompressed drive.

To change DoubleSpace drive letter assignments, you must manually alter the DBLSPACE.INI file in the boot disk's root directory. The following section describes the information contained in DBLSPACE.INI and how changing this information affects DoubleSpace.

Understanding the DBLSPACE.INI File

During setup, DoubleSpace places the DBLSPACE.INI file in the root directory of your uncompressed boot drive. DBLSPACE.INI is a plain DOS text file, similar to other files on your disk drive. DBLSPACE.INI contains information used by the DoubleSpace device driver to configure itself and determine drive letter assignments. DBLSPACE.INI has the Hidden file attribute, because you normally need not be aware of this file, as well as System and Read-Only attributes to prevent accidental deletion. The following example shows the contents of a DBLSPACE.INI file for a computer with three physical drive partitions. All drive partitions are compressed, and one partition also contains a compressed volume created from free space.

```
MaxRemovableDrives=2
FirstDrive=F
LastDrive=J
MaxFileFragments=127
ActivateDrive=J,C0
ActivateDrive=I,D0
ActivateDrive=H,E0
ActivateDrive=G,D1
```

DBLSPACE.INI provides the DoubleSpace device driver with all necessary operating information, including the following elements:

MaxRemovableDrives= This line in DBLSPACE.INI tells DoubleSpace how many removable media drives to accommodate, indicated by the number to the right of the equals sign (=). Normally, this number corresponds to the physical number of removable media drives in your computer, although it need not do so. The example shows two removable media drives. DoubleSpace can mount only the number of removable drives specified by this line. You must change this number if you add another removable drive to your computer, such as a second floppy drive or a Bernoulli drive. The best way to change the maximum number of removable media drives is through the DoubleSpace menus, as described in the section "Adjusting the Number of Removable Media Drives," later in this chapter.

> ⚠️ If you change the DoubleSpace first drive specification, you also must make changes in two other areas. First, you must change all DoubleSpace drive letter assignments for compressed drives so that these drives are assigned only drive letters reserved by DoubleSpace. Second, you also must raise the last drive specification an equivalent number of drive letters so that DoubleSpace has the same number of drive letters reserved for its use. (If, for example, the last drive letter is H, and you raise the DoubleSpace first drive letter from D to E, you also must raise the last drive letter from H to I.) If you do not make sure that all drive letters assigned by DoubleSpace are between the specified first and last drives, and that the number of drive letters reserved by DoubleSpace remains constant, DoubleSpace does not work correctly.

> 📝 NOTE: Remember that DoubleSpace normally exchanges drive letters by starting with the specified last drive and working back down to the specified first drive.

FirstDrive= This line instructs DoubleSpace to use the drive letter to the right of the equals sign (=) as the first drive letter in the group of drive letters DoubleSpace reserves. This line, therefore, sets the lower boundary for the group of DoubleSpace reserved drive letters. Normally, this drive letter is the same as the next available drive letter from DOS *before* DoubleSpace mounts any compressed volumes or exchanges any drive letters. In the example DBLSPACE.INI file, the computer has three physical disk partitions, C, D, and E. The first drive letter reserved by DoubleSpace is drive letter F, which also is the next available DOS drive letter. Raising the first drive letter from F to G leaves drive letter F available to DOS—and also available for use as a network log-in drive.

LastDrive= This line instructs DoubleSpace to use the drive letter to the right of the equals sign (=) as the last drive letter in the group of drive letters DoubleSpace reserves. This line, therefore, sets the upper boundary for the group of DoubleSpace reserved drive letters. In the example file, the first compressed drive is drive C. DoubleSpace (using the rules described in Chapter 3) skips four drive letters beyond the first available drive letter—F— and uses the fifth drive letter as host for the compressed drive C. Drive letter J is now the highest drive letter available to DoubleSpace. If all the DoubleSpace reserved drive letters between the first drive and the last drive are already assigned, you must raise the specification for the last drive to a higher drive letter to create and mount additional compressed volumes. The best way to change the last drive specification is to use the DoubleSpace menus, as described in the section "Adjusting the Last Drive Letter," later in this chapter.

MaxFileFragments= This line tells DoubleSpace how much memory is required for the file fragment list. A whole number—with a maximum of four digits—follows the equals sign (=). This number changes occasionally as DoubleSpace performs various internal housekeeping functions. You should never change the maximum file fragments specification. Altering the maximum file fragments specification may cause DoubleSpace to operate incorrectly.

ActivateDrive= This line instructs DoubleSpace to mount the specified compressed volume file when your computer starts. DoubleSpace adds an Activate Drive line to DBLSPACE.INI every time you create a DoubleSpace compressed drive (except for removable media drives). You should have one Activate Drive line in DBLSPACE.INI for *each* compressed volume on your system. The Activate Drive statements control DoubleSpace's drive letter assignments and are the lines in DBLSPACE.INI you are most likely to alter. Each Activate Drive line in DBLSPACE.INI uses the following syntax:

```
ActivateDrive=h,dn
```

The Activate Drive line specifies the following information for DoubleSpace:

- *n* represents the number of the compressed volume file to mount. As discussed in Chapter 3, the first compressed volume file DoubleSpace creates on a disk drive or partition is DBLSPACE.000. The second compressed volume file created on the same disk drive or partition is DBLSPACE.001, and so on. The following example mounts the DBLSPACE.000 compressed volume file. The 0 at the end of the line tells DoubleSpace to use the file DBLSPACE.000.

```
ActivateDrive=J,C0
```

- *d* represents the drive letter of the host disk drive or partition that contains the compressed volume file to mount. As DoubleSpace exchanges drive letters, this drive letter is assigned to the mounted compressed volume file. In the preceding example, the DBLSPACE.000 compressed volume file is mounted from drive C. As drive letters are exchanged, DoubleSpace assigns drive letter C to this compressed volume file.
- *h* usually represents the drive letter assigned to the uncompressed host drive as DoubleSpace exchanges drive letters with the compressed volume. If the compressed volume is one created from free space on a drive, *h* represents the drive letter DoubleSpace assigns to the compressed volume.

The first Activate Drive line in the following example mounts the DBLSPACE.000 compressed volume file located on host drive D. As the compressed volume is mounted, DoubleSpace exchanges drive letters so that the uncompressed host drive now is referred to as I and the compressed volume is referred to as D.

```
ActivateDrive=I,D0
ActivateDrive=G,D1
```

The second Activate Drive line in this example mounts the DBLSPACE.001 compressed volume file that also is hosted on drive D. This compressed volume is created from free space on drive D. As DoubleSpace exchanges drive letters, this compressed volume is assigned drive letter G. The uncompressed host for this drive is the same as the host for DBLSPACE.000—drive I. Normally, you need to change only the host drive letter in the Activate Drive lines. You should not change the uncompressed drive or compressed volume parts of the Activate Drive lines.

The following example shows Activate Drive statements for a computer with two physical disk drives:

```
ActivateDrive=I,C0
ActivateDrive=H,D0
ActivateDrive=G,D1
```

The first line in this example mounts the DBLSPACE.000 file from the original uncompressed drive C. DoubleSpace assigns drive letter I to the uncompressed host drive and mounts the compressed volume as drive C at the time drive letters are exchanged. The second line mounts the DBLSPACE.000 file from the original uncompressed drive D. DoubleSpace assigns drive letter H to the uncompressed host drive and mounts the compressed volume as drive D at the time drive letters are exchanged. The third line mounts the DBLSPACE.001 file, also from the original uncompressed drive D. (DBLSPACE.001 is a compressed volume created from free space on the uncompressed drive.) DoubleSpace assigns drive letter G to the compressed volume; the host drive is H.

The Activate Drive statements in this example set up DoubleSpace so that the compressed drives are C, D, and G. The uncompressed host drive letters are H and I. You may find this arrangement inconvenient and may prefer to have drive letters arranged so that all compressed drive letters are contiguous—C, D, and E, instead of C, D, and G. To change the drive letter assignments, you edit DBLSPACE.INI, changing the Activate Drive statements to look like those in the following example:

```
ActivateDrive=I,C0
ActivateDrive=H,D0
ActivateDrive=E,D1
```

Only the third Activate Drive statement is different (the assigned drive letter is changed from G to E). DoubleSpace now assigns drive letter E to the DBLSPACE.001 compressed volume file as it is mounted, and all the compressed drive letters are contiguous: C, D, E.

To change drive letter assignments so that *all* drive letters are contiguous, with compressed drives first and uncompressed drives last, you edit the Activate Drive statements to look like those in the following example:

```
ActivateDrive=G,C0
ActivateDrive=F,D0
ActivateDrive=E,D1
```

With the preceding Activate Drive statements in DBLSPACE.INI, DoubleSpace assigns drive letters so that the available drives are C, D, E, F, and G, rather than C, D, G, I, and H. Drives C, D, and E are compressed volumes; drive F is the host drive for both compressed drives D and E; and drive G is the host for drive C.

Editing DBLSPACE.INI

Never delete statements in DBLSPACE.INI, although you can *cautiously* modify them. Deleting statements from DBLSPACE.INI may make one or more of your compressed volumes temporarily unavailable or may cause DoubleSpace to operate incorrectly.

Before making changes in DBLSPACE.INI, always make a bootable floppy disk. You may need to reboot your computer from a floppy disk if you experience a problem after making changes in DBLSPACE.INI. (Refer to your DOS documentation for information on making a bootable floppy disk.) Make sure also that you have a copy of the DOS ATTRIB utility on your bootable floppy disk. If you experience problems that require booting your computer from a floppy disk after changing DBLSPACE.INI, you need the ATTRIB program to make DBLSPACE.INI accessible.

Follow these steps to edit DBLSPACE.INI:

1. To identify the uncompressed disk drive that is your boot drive *before* DoubleSpace exchanges any drive letters, type **DBLSPACE /LIST** at the DOS prompt and press Enter.

    DoubleSpace displays a report similar to the following example, listing all compressed and uncompressed disk drives and the file name and location of the compressed volume files.

    ```
    Drive  Type                   Total Free  Total Size  CVF Filename
    ─ ─    ─ ─ ─ ─ ─ ─ ─ ─ ─ ─    ─ ─ ─ ─ ─   ─ ─ ─ ─ ─   ─ ─ ─ ─ ─ ─
      A    Removable-media drive  No disk in drive
      B    Floppy drive              1.25 MB     1.39 MB
      C    Compressed hard drive    71.04 MB   119.62 MB  H:\DBLSPACE.000
      H    Local hard drive          0.90 MB    69.96 MB
    ```

    If drive C is compressed, the uncompressed boot drive is the host drive for C. In this example, drive C is compressed and its host is H; therefore, DBLSPACE.INI is in the root directory of drive H. If drive C is uncompressed, your boot drive is C and is listed as a `Local hard drive`.

2. Make the uncompressed boot drive the current disk drive, and make the root directory the current directory.

3. Use the DOS directory command to verify the presence of DBLSPACE.INI by typing the following at the DOS prompt and pressing Enter:
   DIR DBLSPACE.INI /AH
   If you correctly identified the uncompressed boot drive, DOS displays a directory list showing only one file—the DBLSPACE.INI file. If you are in the wrong drive or directory, DOS displays the message `No files found`.
   If you are in the directory containing the DBLSPACE.INI file, go to step 4; otherwise, try again from step 1.
4. To alter DBLSPACE.INI, you must first remove its protective file attributes by typing the following at the DOS prompt and pressing Enter:
   ATTRIB –S –H –R DBLSPACE.INI
   This command removes the System, Hidden, and Read-Only file attributes of DBLSPACE.INI. DBLSPACE.INI now appears in regular directory displays and can be modified or deleted.
5. Copy DBLSPACE.INI to a floppy disk. If you experience a problem after modifying DBLSPACE.INI, you can use this copy to restore DBLSPACE.INI to its original condition.
6. Use a text editor (such as DOS EDIT) to edit DBLSPACE.INI. Use information in the preceding section of this chapter for guidance on the changes to make.
7. Save the DBLSPACE.INI file, and exit from your text editor after completing the desired changes.
8. Restore the protective file attributes for DBLSPACE.INI by typing the following at the DOS prompt and pressing Enter:
   ATTRIB +S +H +R DBLSPACE.INI
9. To make your changes take effect, restart your computer by pressing Ctrl+Alt+Del.

If your changes to DBLSPACE.INI do not work as you anticipated, restore your original DBLSPACE.INI file and try the editing process again. Assuming that you made a copy of the original DBLSPACE.INI file (refer to step 5), use the following procedure to restore the original DBLSPACE.INI file:

1. On the uncompressed boot disk, type the following command to remove the DBLSPACE.INI file attributes:
   ATTRIB –S –H –R DBLSPACE.INI
2. Copy the original DBLSPACE.INI file from the floppy disk to your uncompressed boot disk.
3. Restore the protective file attributes by typing the following at the DOS prompt:
   ATTRIB +S +H +R DBLSPACE.INI
4. Restart your computer to restore the original drive assignments.

After your computer restarts, you should have the original drive assignments that were in place before editing DBLSPACE.INI. You can now try editing DBLSPACE.INI again.

Adjusting the Last Drive Letter

You can adjust the last drive letter if you want DoubleSpace to reserve fewer drive letters or if you use all drive letters reserved by DoubleSpace. On rare occasions, you may need

STOP

If you reduce the number of drive letters DoubleSpace reserves by lowering the last drive specification, you also must change the Activate Drive statements so that none uses a drive letter higher than the last drive. Failure to make sure that all Activate Drive statements use only drive letters within the boundaries established by the first and last drive specifications may cause your computer to stop functioning.

NOTE:

Changes made in DBLSPACE.INI do not take effect until you restart your computer. DoubleSpace processes DBLSPACE.INI only as the DBLSPACE.BIN device driver first loads into memory.

To change drive letters assigned by DoubleSpace, you need change only the Activate Drive statements. Remember that you should change only the drive letter represented by *h* in the following syntax:
`ActivateDrive=h,dn`

to lower the last drive letter used by DoubleSpace so that DoubleSpace reserves fewer drive letters. This situation may occur, for example, if you need to make a specific drive letter available to a network. You can lower the last drive letter only by editing DBLSPACE.INI and changing the Last Drive statement. The preceding section describes how to edit DBLSPACE.INI.

More often, if you create several compressed drives from free space, you may use all the drive letters reserved by DoubleSpace. You then must raise the last drive letter so that DoubleSpace reserves more drive letters for additional compressed drives. Although you can raise the last drive setting by editing DBLSPACE.INI, the DoubleSpace utility provides an easy way to make this change, as described in the following steps:

1. To start the DoubleSpace utility, type **DBLSPACE** at the DOS prompt and then press Enter. DoubleSpace displays its opening menu and list of compressed drives (refer to fig. 4.1).
2. Open the **T**ools menu, and choose **O**ptions. DoubleSpace displays the DoubleSpace Options dialog box, as shown in figure 4.3.
3. In the top of the DoubleSpace Options dialog box is a list of drive letters you can select as the new last drive letter. The list starts at the current last drive letter and ends with the last drive letter available to DOS (usually drive Z).
4. Select the drive letter you want to assign as the new last drive.
5. Choose **O**K to confirm your choice of the new last drive letter. If you decide not to set the last drive letter, choose **C**ancel to close the dialog box without making any changes. DoubleSpace returns to its main menu.
6. From the **D**rive menu, choose E**x**it to exit from the DoubleSpace utility. DoubleSpace returns to the DOS prompt.

The last drive letter for DoubleSpace is now changed to the letter you designated in the DoubleSpace Options dialog box.

Adjusting the Number of Removable Media Drives

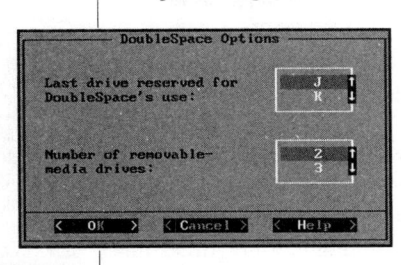

Fig. 4.3

The DoubleSpace Options dialog box.

DoubleSpace can mount only a specified maximum number of removable media drives at one time. If you have more physical removable media drives than DoubleSpace can mount, you may have to unmount one compressed volume before you can mount another. This situation may occur if you add a floppy disk, Bernoulli, Floptical, Syquest, or other removable media drive to your computer. Although you can change the maximum number of removable media drives by editing DBLSPACE.INI, the DoubleSpace utility provides an easy way to change the maximum number of removable media drives, as described in the following steps:

1. Follow steps 1 and 2 of the procedure for adjusting the last drive letter, as described in the preceding section. DoubleSpace displays the DoubleSpace Options dialog box (refer to fig. 4.3).

The bottom of the DoubleSpace Options dialog box lists the values DoubleSpace accepts for the maximum number of removable media drives (from 1 to 26).
2. Select the correct value for the number of removable media drives.
3. Choose **OK** to confirm the new number of removable media drives. If you decide not to set the maximum number of removable media drives, choose **C**ancel instead. DoubleSpace returns to its main menu.
4. From the **D**rive menu, choose E**x**it to leave the DoubleSpace utility. DoubleSpace returns to the DOS prompt.

The maximum number of removable media drives that DoubleSpace can mount at one time is now changed to the value you set in the DoubleSpace Options dialog box.

Creating a DoubleSpace RAM Disk

A *RAM disk* is an area of computer memory set aside by a device driver and configured to be used like a disk drive. Like the DoubleSpace device driver, the RAM disk device driver makes a logical disk drive available to DOS. Because the RAM disk's data is stored in computer memory, access to a RAM disk is extremely fast. RAM disks often are used to hold temporary files or files that must be read frequently. Many users, for example, set the DOS TEMP environment variable to use a RAM disk, thus speeding up the operation of programs that use the TEMP environment variable to specify the location of their temporary files.

RAM disks have limitations and drawbacks, however. Apart from the fact that a RAM disk's data is lost whenever you turn your computer off (unless you copy the data to one of your hard disks), a RAM disk takes up computer memory. A RAM disk usually must be about 1M to 2M in size to be useful. On many computers, this represents 25, 50, or 100 percent of total available memory. You can somewhat compensate for a RAM disk's heavy memory use by compressing the RAM disk. A RAM disk 1M in size, for example, yields about 2M of storage when compressed.

You may use either of two methods to compress a RAM disk by using DoubleSpace. The first method involves placing DoubleSpace commands in AUTOEXEC.BAT to compress the RAM disk. This method is not preferred, because it makes your computer's start-up process slower and much more awkward. If you compress a disk by using a DoubleSpace command line parameter—such as DBLSPACE /COMPRESS—DoubleSpace goes to its main menu after compressing the drive. You must manually return to the DOS command line, making your computer's start-up inconvenient. The second method involves copying the compressed volume file for the RAM disk onto one of your uncompressed drives and then copying it back to the RAM disk whenever your computer starts. After the compressed volume file is copied to the RAM disk, you use DoubleSpace to mount the drive. This method, though more difficult to set up, does not slow your computer's start-up as much as the first method and does not delay the execution of AUTOEXEC.BAT in any way.

> **NOTE:**
> Whether you use the RAMDRIVE.SYS provided with DOS or another RAM disk, make sure that the RAM disk device driver loads *before* any references to DBLSPACE.SYS are read in CONFIG.SYS. DoubleSpace assigns drive letters differently depending on whether the RAM disk device driver—or other disk device drivers—load before or after DBLSPACE.SYS. If your computer has, for example, two physical drives (C and D), and the RAM disk device driver loads before DBLSPACE.SYS, the RAM disk is assigned drive letter E. If the RAM disk device driver loads after DBLSPACE.SYS, the RAM disk is assigned the next available DOS drive letter after all the DoubleSpace drives are assigned drive letters.

Configuring and Optimizing DoubleSpace

Using a RAM disk with some programs, such as Windows, maybe counterproductive. The RAM disk may leave other programs "starved" for memory and force them to access the disk more often, slowing them down. You may get better results by using a disk cache program such as SMARTDRV to speed up disk operations for many of your programs.

The following sections describe both methods of compressing your RAM disk. Choose the method that suits you best.

Compressing the RAM Disk by Using AUTOEXEC.BAT

To compress a RAM disk by adding commands to your AUTOEXEC.BAT file, follow these steps:

1. Create a RAM disk, if you do not already have one. Refer to your DOS documentation or the documentation supplied with your RAM disk software. (Remember that 1280K is the smallest RAM disk you can compress by using DoubleSpace.)
2. Determine the drive letter assigned to the RAM disk after CONFIG.SYS is processed by typing **DBLSPACE /LIST** at the DOS prompt and pressing Enter. DoubleSpace prints a report similar to that of the following example:

```
Drive  Type                      Total Free   Total Size   CVF Filename
--     ----------------------    ----------   ----------   ------------
A      Removable-media drive     No disk in drive
B      Removable-media drive     No disk in drive
C      Compressed hard drive      80.31 MB    128.90 MB    J:\DBLSPACE.000
D      Compressed hard drive      25.89 MB     32.18 MB    I:\DBLSPACE.000
E      Compressed hard drive      37.18 MB     44.96 MB    H:\DBLSPACE.000
F      Local RAMDrive              1.24 MB      1.24 MB
G      Available for DoubleSpace
H      Local hard drive            0.13 MB     23.97 MB
I      Local hard drive            8.01 MB     29.93 MB
J      Local hard drive            1.02 MB     69.96 MB
K      Available for DoubleSpace
```

NOTE: Because DoubleSpace treats a RAM disk as a hard disk, 1280K is the smallest RAM disk you can compress; otherwise, DoubleSpace does not have enough working space.

DoubleSpace shows an uncompressed RAM disk using drive letter F. Your report and drive letter depend on your specific computer.

3. Use a text editor (such as DOS EDIT) to add the following line to AUTOEXEC.BAT:
   DBLSPACE /CREATE F: /RESERVE=.13

Substitute the drive letter of your RAM disk (determined in step 2) for F in the preceding line. This command tells DoubleSpace to compress the existing disk drive and leave only .13M (about 130K) of uncompressed space free. The number .13M is the smallest amount of uncompressed space DoubleSpace permits.

To check your work, restart your computer. After your computer starts, DoubleSpace compresses the RAM disk and mounts the compressed drive (as it now does every time you start your computer). You must choose **Ex**it from the **D**rive menu to return to the DOS prompt so that any remaining commands in your AUTOEXEC.BAT file can execute.

Type the following command at the DOS prompt, and press Enter:
   DBLSPACE /LIST

You should receive a report similar to the one already shown in step 2 of this procedure, except that the drive formerly listed as a `Local RAMDrive` is now listed as a `Compressed RAMDrive`. The uncompressed host drive for the compressed RAM disk is still listed as a `Local RAMDrive` but has a new drive letter.

NOTE: You also may create a compressed drive from free space on the RAM disk by adding the following as line to AUTOEXEC.BAT (remembering to use the drive letter for your RAM disk instead of the letter F used in the example):

DBLSPACE /COMPRESS F: /RESERVE=.13

If you use this method to create a new compressed drive from free space on the RAM disk, the new compressed drive does not exchange its drive letter with its host drive.

Compressing the RAM Disk by Copying the Compressed Volume

To compress a RAM disk by copying the compressed volume file and then mounting the drive, you first must create a compressed volume on the RAM disk.

To prepare the compressed volume on your RAM disk, follow these steps:

1. Create a RAM disk, if you do not already have one. Refer to your DOS documentation or the documentation supplied with your RAM disk software. (Remember that 1280K is the smallest RAM disk you can compress by using DoubleSpace.)
2. Determine the drive letter assigned to the RAM disk after CONFIG.SYS is processed by typing **DBLSPACE /LIST** at the DOS prompt and pressing Enter. DoubleSpace prints a report similar to that of the following example:

```
Drive  Type                      Total Free   Total Size   CVF Filename
--     --------------            ----------   ----------   ------------
  A    Removable-media drive     No disk in drive
  B    Removable-media drive     No disk in drive
  C    Compressed hard drive       80.31 MB     128.90 MB   J:\DBLSPACE.000
  D    Compressed hard drive       25.89 MB      32.18 MB   I:\DBLSPACE.000
  E    Compressed hard drive       37.18 MB      44.96 MB   H:\DBLSPACE.000
  F    Local RAMDrive               1.24 MB       1.24 MB
  G    Available for DoubleSpace
  H    Local hard drive             0.13 MB      23.97 MB
  I    Local hard drive             8.01 MB      29.93 MB
  J    Local hard drive             1.02 MB      69.96 MB
  K    Available for DoubleSpace
```

   DoubleSpace reports an uncompressed RAM drive using drive letter F. Your report and drive letter depend on your specific computer.

3. Compress the RAM disk by typing the following command at the DOS prompt (using your RAM disk drive letter, as determined in step 2, instead of F):

    DBLSPACE /CREATE F: /RESERVE=.13

    This command tells DoubleSpace to compress the existing disk drive, leaving only .13M (about 130K) of uncompressed space free. .13M is the smallest amount of uncompressed space DoubleSpace permits.

    DoubleSpace compresses the RAM disk and mounts the compressed drive, returning to the DoubleSpace main menu and drive list after it finishes.

4. Open the **D**rive menu, and choose E**x**it. DoubleSpace returns to the DOS prompt.
5. Unmount the compressed RAM drive you just created by typing the following command at the DOS prompt and pressing Enter (remembering to use your RAM disk drive letter instead of F):

    DBLSPACE /UNMOUNT F:

6. Make the RAM disk the current disk drive, and make the root directory the current directory.
7. Remove the protective file attributes from the compressed volume file by typing the following at the DOS prompt and pressing Enter:

    ATTRIB –S –H –R DBLSPACE.000

> **NOTE:**
> As DoubleSpace creates the new compressed drive, it displays messages on-screen stating that your computer is going to restart. The computer does not actually restart, however, unless this is the first time you run DoubleSpace.

The compressed volume file from the RAM disk requires about as much uncompressed hard disk space as the size of the RAM disk in memory. If you allocate 1M of memory to a RAM disk, for example, the compressed volume file for that RAM disk requires about 1M of disk space. If your uncompressed drive does not have enough room for the compressed volume file from the RAM disk, you may be able to resize one of your compressed volumes to free enough space on its uncompressed host drive. See Chapter 6, "Using the DoubleSpace Utilities," for information on changing the size of DoubleSpace compressed drives.

To preserve all the data on the compressed RAM disk before you turn off or restart your computer, first unmount the RAM disk compressed volume and then remove the Read-Only attribute from your previous hard disk copy of the RAM disk's compressed volume file. Finally, repeat steps 6 through 10 of the above procedure to again copy the RAM disk's compressed volume file to your uncompressed hard disk. Unmounting compressed volumes is described in Chapter 5, "Using DoubleSpace."

8. Copy the compressed volume file to an uncompressed hard disk, renaming the file to avoid interfering with other compressed volume files on the uncompressed hard disk, by typing the following command at the DOS prompt and pressing Enter:

   COPY DBLSPACE.000 H:\RAMVOL.CVF

   Remember to use your uncompressed drive letter if it is not H, as used in the example. You also can use a name other than RAMVOL.CVF for the copy of the compressed volume file.

9. To protect the copied compressed volume file from accidental deletion, assign it the Read-Only file attribute by typing the following at the DOS prompt and pressing Enter (remembering to use your file name if you chose one other than that used in the example):

   ATTRIB +R RAMVOL.CVF

   The preparation necessary to set up your compressed RAM disk is complete. You must now make changes in your AUTOEXEC.BAT file.

10. Use a text editor to add the following two lines to AUTOEXEC.BAT:

    COPY H:\RAMVOL.CVF F:\DBLSPACE.000
    DBLSPACE /MOUNT F:

    (Remember to substitute your RAM disk drive letter for F in the example and to substitute your uncompressed drive letter for H. Substitute your file name, too, if it is different than the name used in this example.)

The next time you start your computer, the new commands in AUTOEXEC.BAT copy the compressed volume file onto the RAM disk and then mount the DoubleSpace compressed volume. Your computer's start-up is delayed only by the amount of time required to copy the compressed volume file and to mount the compressed volume. After the compressed volume is mounted, control returns to DOS and all other commands in AUTOEXEC.BAT are carried out without further delay.

To verify the presence of the new compressed volume, type the following command at the DOS prompt and press Enter:

DBLSPACE /LIST

You should receive a report similar to the one already shown in step 2 of this procedure, except that the drive formerly listed as a `Local RAMDrive` is now listed as a `Compressed RAMDrive`. The uncompressed host drive for the compressed RAM disk is still listed as a `Local RAMDrive`, but has a new drive letter.

You have now configured your RAM disk by copying the compressed volume file.

Summary

In this chapter, you learned how to control the final location of the DoubleSpace device driver in memory, and how to make available more conventional memory by relocating the DoubleSpace device driver to upper memory. You also learned how to safely improve the speed of your computer's disk accesses with SMARTDRV. This chapter explained how to improve the accuracy of DoubleSpace's estimate of free space on your compressed drives by changing the estimated compression ratio and showed you when and how to adjust the last drive letter used by DoubleSpace, as well as how to adjust the maximum number of removable media drives DoubleSpace can mount at one time.

You also learned how DoubleSpace uses DBLSPACE.INI to configure itself, and how to change drive letter assignments by safely editing DBLSPACE.INI. Finally, you learned two methods of compressing a RAM disk by using DoubleSpace—by adding commands to AUTOEXEC.BAT or by copying the compressed volume. You also learned how to preserve the RAM disk's compressed volume file and how to restore it after your computer restarts.

The next chapter describes how to use DoubleSpace in your day-to-day operations.

CHAPTER 5

Using DoubleSpace

This chapter provides the information you need to use DoubleSpace successfully on a day-to-day basis. The chapter assumes you have already installed and configured DoubleSpace. (Installing DoubleSpace is described in Chapter 3; configuring DoubleSpace is discussed in Chapter 4.)

This chapter begins with a general discussion of file management on your DoubleSpace compressed drives and then describes the DOS commands that work differently with your compressed drives. The chapter also explains how to get information about your DoubleSpace compressed drives and discusses how to mount and unmount compressed volumes. This chapter gives special attention to using DoubleSpace with removable media drives. You learn how to compress removable media disks, how to mount and unmount them, and how to solve the most common problems encountered with removable media. You then learn the correct methods for backing up compressed and uncompressed drives as well as which files not to back up. This chapter also discusses various issues involved in using third-party disk-maintenance utility programs and concludes by describing how to use DoubleSpace's Help system.

Performing File Management on Compressed Drives

Because DoubleSpace disk compression is transparent—that is, not noticeable to the user—you manage your files the same as you did before you installed DoubleSpace. The DOS commands for creating directories, copying files, and displaying directory listings work the same with your DoubleSpace compressed disks as with uncompressed disks.

Whenever DOS reads information from a disk, DoubleSpace determines whether the disk is compressed. If the disk is compressed, DoubleSpace uncompresses the information before making it available to DOS. Similarly, whenever DOS writes information to a disk, DoubleSpace determines whether the disk is compressed and compresses the information if necessary.

If you save a file on an uncompressed disk, DoubleSpace does not compress the data, and the file is stored in standard DOS format. With DoubleSpace, you never need to be concerned about translating your data if you copy a file from a compressed disk to an uncompressed disk or vice versa. DoubleSpace handles all the work behind the scenes, reading or writing the disk information with or without compression, as appropriate for that disk. The main difference you notice after adding DoubleSpace to your computer system is that your computer system has more disk drive letters. These additional drive letters are the host drives for your compressed volumes or are the compressed volumes themselves.

Keeping track of these additional drive letters may seem tricky at first. Usually, though, you need not be concerned about the host drives for your compressed volumes. Because DoubleSpace exchanges drive letters, your compressed volumes replace your original uncompressed hard drives. Normally, you use your compressed volumes as if they are the only disk drives in your computer. You need be concerned about the host drives for your compressed volumes only if you perform maintenance on your disk drives or alter your DoubleSpace configuration. The section "Getting Information about Your Compressed Drives," later in this chapter, shows you how to obtain information about your compressed volumes and their host drives.

The host drive letters for your compressed volumes may shift in some cases. Each time you mount a compressed drive, DoubleSpace assigns it the next available host drive letter from a list of reserved drive letters. Each time you unmount a compressed drive, its host drive letter becomes available for use as the host drive of a different compressed volume. If you mount and unmount several compressed volumes, their host drive letters may end up being different than they were when you first started your computer.

As you mount a compressed floppy disk in drive A, for example, DoubleSpace assigns drive letter A to the compressed volume and assigns the next available drive letter from DoubleSpace's reserved list to be the host drive for the compressed floppy disk. If you have a system with a single compressed drive C, the next available DoubleSpace drive letter is G (remember, H is the host for C). If you then mount a compressed floppy disk in drive B, DoubleSpace assigns drive letter B to the compressed volume and assigns the next available DoubleSpace drive letter as the host drive. In this example, the host drive letter for the compressed volume in drive B is F. If you mount the compressed floppy in drive B first, however, the host drive letter for that floppy disk is G instead of F. In this case, a compressed floppy disk mounted later in drive A is assigned host drive letter F.

You can see that the assignment of host drive letters for your compressed drives depends on the order in which the compressed drives are mounted. Don't worry too much about the host drive letters for your hard disks; these are assigned according to the information in your DBLSPACE.INI file as your computer starts up. The host drive letters for your hard disks change only if you manually unmount and mount your compressed hard disks while working. (For a more thorough explanation of drive letter assignments, refer to Chapter 3, "Installing DoubleSpace.")

Using the DIR Command on DoubleSpace Drives

Among the first DOS commands any computer user becomes familiar with is the DIR command. The DIR command in DOS 6 adds a special command line switch—/C—for compressed drives. The /C switch instructs DOS to display the actual compression ratio for each file that appears in the directory listing and the average compression ratio for all files on the compressed disk. Occasionally viewing the actual compression ratios for files on your compressed volumes can be useful. To view a listing of all the DoubleSpace program files in your DOS directory, for example, and to show their actual compression ratios, enter the following command at the DOS prompt and press Enter:

DIR C:\DOS\DBLSPACE.* /C

This command produces a listing similar to that of the following example:

```
Volume in drive C is D1_P1
Volume Serial Number is 1BE6-1437
Directory of C:\DOS
DBLSPACE BIN      51214 03-10-93   6:00a    2.5 to 1.0
DBLSPACE EXE     274484 03-10-93   6:00a    1.3 to 1.0
DBLSPACE HLP      72169 03-10-93   6:00a    1.9 to 1.0
DBLSPACE INF       2178 03-10-93   6:00a    4.0 to 1.0
DBLSPACE SYS        339 03-10-93   6:00a   16.0 to 1.0
                  1.6 to 1.0 average compression ratio
        5 file(s)        400384 bytes
                       84197376 bytes free
```

The /C switch adds the following information to a standard directory listing: The actual compression ratio of each individual file appears to the right of the file listing, in a column after the file size, date, and time. The DBLSPACE.SYS file shown in this listing, for example, has a compression ratio of 16:1. The average compression ratio for all listed files appears on a new line, right above the two lines that show the number of files listed and the number of bytes free. In this example, all the DoubleSpace program files compressed at an average ratio of 1.6:1.

The /C switch shows the compression ratio for the files in the directory listing based on the 8K cluster size DoubleSpace uses. You can instead use the /CH switch to show the compression ratio for files based on the actual cluster size of the uncompressed disk. To display the same listing as the previous example, therefore, but using the actual cluster size of the uncompressed disk, type the following command:

DIR C:\DOS\DBLSPACE.* /CH

This command produces a listing similar to that of the following example:

```
Volume in drive C is D1_P1
Volume Serial Number is 1BE6-1437
Directory of C:\DOS
DBLSPACE BIN      51214 03-10-93   6:00a    2.4 to 1.0
DBLSPACE EXE     274484 03-10-93   6:00a    1.3 to 1.0
DBLSPACE HLP      72169 03-10-93   6:00a    1.9 to 1.0
DBLSPACE INF       2178 03-10-93   6:00a    2.0 to 1.0
DBLSPACE SYS        339 03-10-93   6:00a    4.0 to 1.0
                  1.5 to 1.0 average compression ratio
        5 file(s)        400384 bytes
                       84197376 bytes free
```

Notice that some of the reported compression ratios are different—the compression ratio for DBLSPACE.SYS, for example, is now shown as 4:1. The average compression ratio also is lower than the compression ratio reported if you use the /C switch. The calculation of the compression ratio in this listing is now based on how many clusters the compressed data occupies on the physical disk instead of how many clusters the uncompressed data would occupy.

Computing the compression ratio by using the actual cluster size of the uncompressed disk produces different results than does using the cluster size of the compressed volume. If the actual cluster size on your disk is smaller than 8K, you may see slightly lower reported compression ratios. If the actual cluster size on your uncompressed disk is greater than 8K, you may see slightly higher reported compression ratios.

For most purposes, use the information provided by the /C switch instead of that provided by the /CH switch.

Using the CHKDSK Command on DoubleSpace Drives

CHKDSK is the basic disk troubleshooting and repair program supplied with DOS. CHKDSK tests the logical integrity of a disk drive. Most users are familiar with the standard report displayed by using the DOS CHKDSK command on an uncompressed disk. (Chapter 7, "Troubleshooting DoubleSpace," contains detailed information on using CHKDSK to locate and correct errors on your disks.) The CHKDSK command performs the same logical integrity checks on your compressed drives as it does on your uncompressed drives. CHKDSK recognizes compressed volumes, however, and performs one extra task as it checks them.

If you use CHKDSK on a compressed disk, it first performs the standard DOS integrity checks and displays the usual report. CHKDSK then executes the DoubleSpace /CHKDSK command, which performs additional integrity checks on the compressed volume. If you use CHKDSK on a compressed disk, the resulting report is similar to that shown in the following example:

```
Volume D1_P1        created 05-14-1993 1:08p
Volume Serial Number is 1BE6-1437

 135159808 bytes total disk space
     81920 bytes in 2 hidden files
    229376 bytes in 28 directories
  50651136 bytes in 993 user files
  84197376 bytes available on disk

      8192 bytes in each allocation unit
     17234 total allocation units on disk
     11013 available allocation units on disk

    655360 total bytes memory
    619904 bytes free
DoubleSpace is checking drive C.

DoubleSpace found no errors on drive C.
```

DoubleSpace produces the last two lines of this report as it checks the compressed drive's integrity. Your actual report depends on the specific condition of your compressed drive. Chapter 7, "Troubleshooting DoubleSpace," provides more information on using the DBLSPACE /CHKDSK command.

Getting Information about Your Compressed Drives

As you work, you often need to obtain information about your compressed drives. In addition to finding out how much free space remains on a compressed drive (which you can determine by using the DOS DIR command), you may want to know the overall compression ratio for a disk, which drive is the host drive for a compressed volume, how much free space remains on the host drive, or other information about your compressed and uncompressed drives. DoubleSpace enables you to obtain information about your compressed and uncompressed drives directly at the DOS prompt, from menu commands in the DoubleSpace utility, or, if you use Windows, from the Tools menu in the Windows File Manager.

Obtaining Information at the DOS Prompt

The simplest way to get information about your drives is to obtain the information directly at the DOS prompt, using command line switches as you start DoubleSpace to display information about your drives. If you use the command line switches, DoubleSpace displays its reports on-screen without going into the DoubleSpace menus. DoubleSpace simply carries out the particular task associated with the command line switch you use. Think of the command line switches as shortcuts for obtaining the information you want.

You also can use the DoubleSpace command line switches in a DOS batch file to display information about your compressed and uncompressed drives. The DoubleSpace command line switches are ideal for batch files, because DoubleSpace carries out the action specified by the command line switches without requiring any intervention from the user. You can add a line to your AUTOEXEC.BAT file, for example, to display a list of all your compressed and uncompressed drives so that you can see what drives are available each time your computer starts.

The first DoubleSpace command line switch—/INFO—displays detailed information about a single drive at a time. To use the /INFO switch with DoubleSpace, use the following syntax:

DBLSPACE /INFO *d*:

The *d* stands for the drive letter of the compressed drive about which you want to obtain information. To obtain information about compressed drive E, for example, type this command as follows:

DBLSPACE /INFO E:

If you do not specify a drive letter, DoubleSpace displays information about the current disk drive. You can save a few keystrokes by omitting the /INFO switch if you do specify a drive letter. If only a drive letter is specified, DoubleSpace assumes that you want information about that drive. The following command, therefore, provides the same information as does the previous example, which included the /INFO switch:

DBLSPACE E:

The command **DBLSPACE C:**, for example, produces a report that contains information about your drive C, similar to that shown in the following sample:

```
DoubleSpace is examining drive C.

Compressed drive C is stored on uncompressed drive J in the file
J:\DBLSPACE.000.

        Space used:                 48.60 MB
        Compression ratio:          1.8 to 1

        Space free:                 80.30 MB
        Est. compression ratio:     2.0 to 1

        Total space:               128.90 MB
```

Because it takes a few moments for DoubleSpace to generate the information report, the program first displays a message stating that it is examining your drive (and telling you which drive it is examining). DoubleSpace next lists the amount of space already in use on the compressed volume and the average compression ratio for the existing files. DoubleSpace then lists the amount of free space still available on the compressed volume and the estimated compression ratio. (Remember that the amount of free space is calculated by using this estimated compression ratio.) Finally, DoubleSpace adds a line showing the total space on the compressed volume.

The second DoubleSpace command line switch—/LIST—displays summary information about all your compressed and uncompressed disk drives at once. Because the /LIST switch displays information about all your drives, you need not specify any drive letters if you use this switch. Use the /LIST switch as shown in the following example:

DBLSPACE /LIST

This command produces a report similar to that of the following sample:

```
Drive  Type                        Total Free   Total Size   CVF Filename
-----  --------------------------  ----------   ----------   --------------
  A    Removable-media drive       No disk in drive
  B    Floppy drive                  1.13 MB      1.39 MB
  C    Compressed hard drive        80.30 MB    128.90 MB    J:\DBLSPACE.000
  D    Compressed hard drive        25.89 MB     32.18 MB    I:\DBLSPACE.000
  E    Compressed hard drive        37.18 MB     44.96 MB    H:\DBLSPACE.000
  F    Available for DoubleSpace
  G    Available for DoubleSpace
  H    Local hard drive              0.13 MB     23.97 MB
  I    Local hard drive              8.01 MB     29.93 MB
  J    Local hard drive              1.02 MB     69.96 MB
```

> **NOTE:**
> If you try to obtain information about a drive that is not a DoubleSpace compressed drive, DoubleSpace displays an error message.

> You can use the standard DOS output redirection command to send the DoubleSpace information report to a printer or a disk file. (Refer to your DOS documentation for more information about redirection commands.) The following command, for example, uses the output redirection command (>) to send the information report to your printer:
>
> **DBLSPACE /INFO C: > PRN**

The /LIST report includes all your drives, compressed or uncompressed, and provides five columns of information. The first column lists the drive letter DOS uses to access the drive, and the second column notes the drive type. The first drive listed in the sample report, for example, is drive A, a removable media drive. The third drive listed in the report is drive C, identified as a compressed hard disk. The third column in the /LIST report shows the total amount of free space available on the drive. If the drive is compressed, the figure for free space is calculated by using the estimated compression ratio. The fourth column in the report shows the total size of the drive. Both the free space and total space figures are given in megabytes (M). In the fifth and last column of the report, DoubleSpace lists the drive location and file name of the compressed volume file. If the drive is uncompressed, this last column is empty.

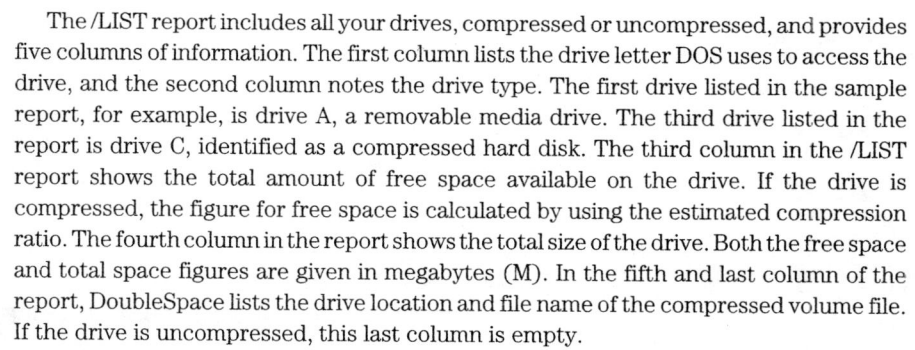

For removable media drives containing disks, DoubleSpace reports the specific type of removable media, the free space, and the total disk space available. If no disk is currently in the drive, DoubleSpace places a message to that effect in the free space column of the report. In the sample report, no disk is in drive A, so DoubleSpace identifies the removable media drive generically and reports that it does not contain a disk. Removable media drive B does contain a disk, so DoubleSpace identifies it as a floppy disk drive and reports the free space and total space available for that disk.

Compare the /LIST sample report with the /INFO sample report provided earlier in this section. To obtain information about compression ratios, use the /INFO switch. To learn which drives are compressed or to discover which removable drives contain mounted compressed volumes, use the /LIST switch.

Obtaining Information by Using the DoubleSpace Menus

You can obtain the same information you get by using the /INFO command line switch from inside the DoubleSpace utility program. If you use the DoubleSpace utility to perform other tasks (such as resizing or defragmenting a compressed drive), you may also want to use it to obtain information about your compressed drives.

To obtain information about a compressed drive by using the DoubleSpace menu system, follow these steps:

1. To start the DoubleSpace utility program, type **DBLSPACE** at the DOS prompt, and then press Enter. DoubleSpace starts and displays its main menu and list of compressed drives (see fig. 5.1).
2. In the list of mounted compressed drives at the center of the screen, highlight the drive about which you want information.
3. Open the **D**rive menu, and choose **I**nfo. DoubleSpace displays the Compressed Drive Information dialog box, as shown in figure 5.2.
   The Compressed Drive Information dialog box shows the host drive letter and the compressed volume file name at the top of the dialog box. It also lists the space used, the average compression ratio, estimated free space, estimated compression ratio, and total space for the selected compressed drive.
4. After you finish viewing the compressed drive information, choose **OK** to close the dialog box. DoubleSpace returns to the main menu and list of compressed drives.

As is true with the /INFO command line switch, you can send the /LIST report to a printer or disk file by using the standard DOS output redirection command. The following command, for example, uses the output redirection command (>) to send the information generated by /LIST to your printer:

DBLSPACE /LIST > PRN

You also can display the Compressed Drive Information dialog box simply by highlighting the drive about which you want information (as described in step 2 of this procedure) and pressing Enter.

100   The Disk Compression Book

The Compressed Drive Information dialog box provides you with shortcuts to perform two other tasks involving the compressed volume you select. The **S**ize and **R**atio command buttons at the bottom of the dialog box enable you to change the size of the compressed volume or change the estimated compression ratio for the compressed drive. See Chapter 6, "Using the DoubleSpace Utilities," for information on changing the size of a compressed drive; see Chapter 4, "Configuring and Optimizing DoubleSpace," for details concerning the estimated compression ratio.

Obtaining Information from the Windows File Manager

DOS 6 adds a new menu—Too**l**s—to the Windows File Manager's main menu. You can use the Too**l**s menu in the File Manager to obtain information about compressed drives without exiting Windows. (Remember that the DoubleSpace utility program itself cannot run from inside Windows.)

DOS 6 adds the Too**l**s menu to File Manager *only* if you chose to install the Windows version of either the Microsoft Backup or Microsoft Anti-Virus utilities when you install DOS 6. You can run the DOS 6 Setup program at any time to install these utilities and add the Too**l**s menu to the Windows File Manager. Refer to your DOS manual for specific instructions on using DOS Setup.

Fig. 5.1

The DoubleSpace main menu and list of compressed drives.

To obtain information about your compressed drives in Windows, follow these steps:

1. Open the Windows File Manager (if it is not already running), and open a file list window for the drive about which you want information.
2. In the file list window, select any files about which you want information.
3. From the File Manager Too**l**s menu, choose **D**oubleSpace Info. File Manager displays the DoubleSpace Info dialog box, as shown in figure 5.3.

If the current file list window is not for a compressed drive, an error dialog box containing a message that the drive is not compressed appears instead. Click OK, and choose a different drive.

As shown in figure 5.3, the DoubleSpace Info dialog box lists the host drive and file name for the compressed volume file, displays a graphic representation of the used and free space on the compressed volume, and shows both the average compression ratio of the space used and the estimated compression ratio used to calculate free space.

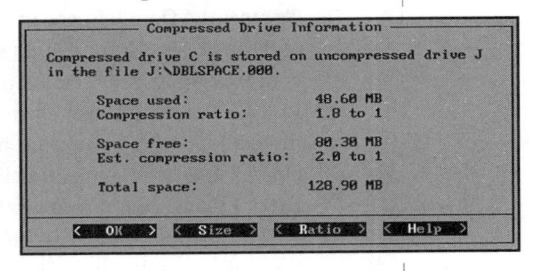

Fig. 5.2

The Compressed Drive Information dialog box.

4. To display specific information about any selected files, choose the Show **D**etails command button. The DoubleSpace Info dialog box changes in appearance to display additional details about the selected files, as shown in figure 5.4. The compression ratio for each selected file and the average compression ratio for all the selected files now appear at the bottom of the dialog box.

   Only files you select *before* displaying the DoubleSpace Info dialog box appear in the detailed file list. If no files are selected, this file list is empty.

5. If you do not want to display the detailed file information, choose the Hide **D**etails command button that replaces Show **D**etails in the expanded dialog box. The dialog box returns to the appearance shown in figure 5.3.

6. To close the DoubleSpace Info dialog box, choose Close. If you need help with the DoubleSpace Info dialog box, choose **H**elp.

The DoubleSpace Info dialog box does not offer any shortcuts to other tasks. You cannot run DoubleSpace from within Windows, so you cannot change the size of a drive or the estimated compression ratio while you are inside Windows.

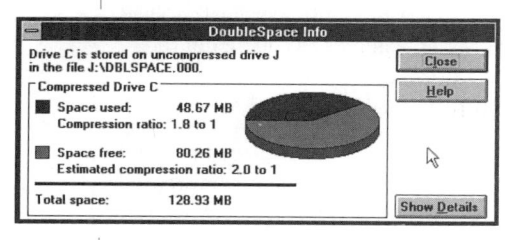

Mounting and Unmounting Compressed Drives

Fig. 5.3

The DoubleSpace Info dialog box in the Windows File Manager.

Except for compressed removable media disks, you usually need not be concerned about mounting or unmounting your compressed disks. Your compressed hard disks are automatically mounted when your computer starts. (Chapter 4, "Configuring and Optimizing DoubleSpace," describes how DoubleSpace uses the DBLSPACE.INI file to mount your compressed hard disks and to exchange drive letters as your computer starts.) You may, however, need to unmount a compressed hard disk for safety if you perform disk diagnostic or repair procedures. (Chapter 7, "Troubleshooting DoubleSpace," discusses such procedures.) The section "Using Disk Utilities with DoubleSpace," later in this chapter, discusses considerations you must observe when using various disk optimization and repair utilities.

Keep in mind that you cannot use DoubleSpace or any of the DoubleSpace commands while you are running Windows, DESQview, GEM, or GEOworks. You can mount or unmount compressed drives by using DoubleSpace only if you are at the DOS prompt.

Fig. 5.4

The DoubleSpace Info dialog box with file details displayed.

You can run DoubleSpace or use DoubleSpace commands from inside shell programs such as the DOS Shell, Norton Commander, or XTree Pro. You should not, however, run

DoubleSpace or use DoubleSpace commands from a DOS prompt you open from Windows, DESQview, GEM, or GEOworks. You must exit Windows (or the other programs) completely before using DoubleSpace.

Each time you mount or unmount a compressed volume from a hard disk, DoubleSpace modifies DBLSPACE.INI to reflect the new status of DoubleSpace's configuration. DoubleSpace makes these changes regardless of the method used to mount or unmount the compressed drive. If you unmount a compressed volume stored on your hard disk, therefore, it is *not* mounted automatically the next time your computer starts; similarly, if you mount a compressed volume stored on your hard disk, it *is* mounted automatically the next time your computer starts. If you mount and unmount compressed volume files on your hard disks in different orders, the drive letters assigned to their host drives may shift. These shifts can require you to make changes to SMARTDRV or other program configurations. To avoid this problem, use the DBLSPACE /MOUNT /NEWDRIVE command described in the following section, "Mounting and Unmounting from the DOS Prompt," to assign specific drive letters to your compressed volumes as you mount them.

Mounting and Unmounting from the DOS Prompt

Command line switches offer a direct, simple way to mount or unmount compressed drives. Switches also enable you to use DOS batch files to mount or unmount compressed drives. (Refer to your DOS manual for information on writing DOS batch files.)

You use two command line switches to mount a compressed drive: /MOUNT and /NEWDRIVE. The /MOUNT switch is required; it tells DoubleSpace you want to mount a compressed drive. The /NEWDRIVE switch is optional.

To use the /MOUNT switch with DoubleSpace, use the following syntax:

DBLSPACE /MOUNT=*nnn d1*: /NEWDRIVE=*d2*:

Except for the /MOUNT switch itself, all other switches and drive letters in this example are optional. In this syntax example, *nnn* stands for the number of the compressed volume file to mount; *d1* stands for the drive letter of the drive that contains the compressed volume file to mount; and *d2* stands for a new drive letter for DoubleSpace to use as it mounts the drive.

The number of the compressed volume file is the three character extension in the compressed volume file's name. The compressed volume file that has its drive letter exchanged with the host drive, for example, is always named DBLSPACE.000. Additional compressed drives created from free space on an uncompressed drive have their compressed volume file names numbered sequentially: DBLSPACE.001, DBLSPACE.002, and so on. If you do not specify the compressed volume file number, DoubleSpace tries to mount the DBLSPACE.000 compressed volume file. To mount a compressed volume file other than the DBLSPACE.000 file, you must specify the compressed volume file number.

The following command, for example, mounts the DBLSPACE.001 file on the current disk drive:

DBLSPACE /MOUNT=001

If the compressed volume file you want to mount does not reside on the current disk drive, you can specify the correct disk drive by adding the disk drive letter to the /MOUNT switch. The following command, for example, mounts the DBLSPACE.000 compressed volume stored on uncompressed drive E:

DBLSPACE /MOUNT E:

The results produced by the /NEWDRIVE switch depend on which compressed volume file you mount. If you mount the DBLSPACE.000 file, the /NEWDRIVE switch controls the host drive letter assignment for the compressed volume. The following command, for example, mounts the DBLSPACE.000 file on drive A and assigns host drive letter F to the disk in drive A:

DBLSPACE /MOUNT A: /NEWDRIVE=F:

If you mount a compressed volume file with a number of 001 or greater, however, the /NEWDRIVE switch controls the drive letter assigned to the compressed volume as it is mounted. Compressed volumes from files with a number 001 or greater do not have their drive letters exchanged with the host drive. The following command mounts the DBLSPACE.001 compressed volume file on drive E and assigns it drive letter G:

DBLSPACE /MOUNT=001 E: /NEWDRIVE=G:

A couple error messages you may encounter while mounting compressed volume files require special discussion. If you created several compressed volumes and you also have several removable media compressed volumes mounted, DoubleSpace may run out of drive letters. If you try to mount another drive after DoubleSpace runs out of drive letters, the following error message appears on-screen:

```
There are no more drive letters reserved for DoubleSpace to use. To add more
drive letters, choose the Options command from the Tools menu.
```

To correct this problem, follow the instructions in Chapter 4, "Configuring and Optimizing DoubleSpace," for raising the last drive letter DoubleSpace uses. Raising the last drive letter increases the number of drive letters reserved by DoubleSpace. After you make this change, you must restart your computer for the change to go into effect.

Another problem you may experience occurs only while using removable media drives. If you try to mount more compressed volumes in removable media drives than DoubleSpace is configured to handle, the following error message appears:

```
DoubleSpace has used all the memory reserved by the settings in the Options
dialog box. To enable DoubleSpace to allocate more memory, you should restart
your computer now.
```

You may find this error message confusing because the text of the message is not quite correct; simply restarting your computer does not alleviate this problem. Instead, you must follow the instructions in Chapter 4, "Configuring and Optimizing DoubleSpace," for increasing the number of removable media drives DoubleSpace can handle at one time. Restart your computer only *after* you complete these procedures, not before.

The /UNMOUNT switch tells DoubleSpace that you want to unmount a compressed drive. To use /UNMOUNT, use the following syntax:

DBLSPACE /UNMOUNT *d*:

In this example, *d* stands for the drive letter of the compressed volume you want to unmount. You are not required to specify the drive letter; if you do not specify the drive letter, the current drive is unmounted. The following command, for example, unmounts the compressed drive mounted in floppy disk drive A:

NOTE:

Each drive letter you assign by using the /NEWDRIVE switch must be from the group of drive letters Double-Space reserves for its own use. If you use a drive letter outside that group, you receive an error message stating that the drive letter is already in use. Use the /LIST switch discussed earlier in this chapter to determine which DoubleSpace reserved drive letters are still available.

DBLSPACE /UNMOUNT A:

Using the /UNMOUNT switch is, as you can see, very simple. A couple error messages you may encounter as you unmount compressed drives, however, do deserve additional discussion.

DOS requires continuous access to the COMMAND.COM file (which interprets the commands you type at the DOS prompt), because DOS occasionally needs to reload the command interpreter into memory. The COMMAND.COM file is usually stored on your boot disk. DoubleSpace, therefore, does not permit you to unmount your boot disk. If your computer boots from a hard disk, your boot disk is always drive C. If your drive C is compressed, and you try to unmount it, you receive the following error message:

```
Drive C is your startup disk drive and should not be unmounted.
```

If you need to work on your computer with the compressed volume on drive C unmounted, you must start your computer from a floppy disk.

Occasionally, you may accidentally use the DBLSPACE /UNMOUNT command on a drive that is not compressed. If you use compressed removable media, for example, you may forget that you have already unmounted a disk before removing it from the drive. As a result, you may issue the DBLSPACE /UNMOUNT command twice. If you try to unmount a drive that is not a compressed volume, DoubleSpace displays the following error message (the drive letter listed in the error message depending on which drive you tried to unmount):

```
DoubleSpace cannot unmount drive B because it is not a compressed drive.
```

Mounting and Unmounting by Using the DoubleSpace Menus

You also can mount or unmount compressed drives from within the DoubleSpace utility. If you currently are using the DoubleSpace menu system to perform other tasks, you may also want to use it to mount or unmount a compressed drive.

To mount a compressed drive by using the DoubleSpace utility, follow these steps:

1. To start the DoubleSpace utility, type **DBLSPACE** at the DOS prompt and press Enter. DoubleSpace starts and displays its main menu and list of compressed drives (refer to fig. 5.1).
2. Open the **D**rive menu and choose **M**ount. DoubleSpace scans all the hard disks and removable media disks currently on your system, searching for unmounted compressed volume files. DoubleSpace displays a status message on-screen as it performs the scan.

   After DoubleSpace locates all the unmounted compressed volumes on your system, it displays the Mount a Compressed Drive dialog box, as shown in figure 5.5. The exact drives listed depend on your computer's configuration.

   If no unmounted compressed volumes are on your system, DoubleSpace displays an error dialog box stating this. Press Enter or click OK; DoubleSpace closes the error dialog box and returns to the main menu.

To mount a compressed removable disk, insert the disk in the drive before you open the **D**rive menu and choose **M**ount. After you choose **M**ount, DoubleSpace scans your drives for unmounted volumes; you cannot mount a volume that DoubleSpace does not detect during this scan.

The Mount a Compressed Drive dialog box lists all the unmounted compressed volume files DoubleSpace locates. Each line in the list shows the drive letter of the disk drive that contains the unmounted compressed volume, the compressed volume's file name, the volume label of the host disk (if any), and the size of the host disk.

3. Highlight the compressed volume file you want to mount, and choose **O**K. DoubleSpace mounts the compressed volume and returns you to the main menu and list of compressed drives.

If you change your mind about mounting a compressed volume, choose **C**ancel. To use the DoubleSpace Help system, choose **H**elp.

As when mounting compressed volumes from the DOS prompt, you may encounter a few error messages that require special discussion. These error messages are described under the procedures in the preceding section, "Mounting and Unmounting from the DOS Prompt." (These error messages appear in dialog boxes, however, if you are working in the DoubleSpace utility.) Follow the instructions given in that section to correct these errors.

To unmount a compressed drive by using the DoubleSpace utility, follow these steps:

1. To start the DoubleSpace utility, type **DBLSPACE** at the DOS prompt and press Enter. DoubleSpace starts and displays its main menu and compressed drive list (refer to fig. 5.1).
2. Highlight the compressed drive you want to unmount.
3. From the **D**rive menu, choose **U**nmount. DoubleSpace displays the Unmount Confirmation dialog box, as shown in figure 5.6.
4. Choose **O**K to unmount the drive. DoubleSpace unmounts the compressed drive.

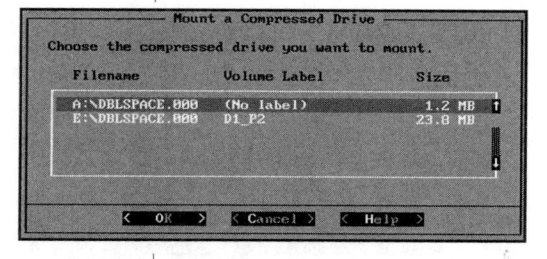

If you change your mind about unmounting the compressed volume, choose **C**ancel. To use the DoubleSpace help system, choose **H**elp.

As when you unmount compressed drives from the DOS prompt, an error message appears if you attempt to unmount your boot disk. This is the same error message described for the unmount procedures in the preceding section, "Mounting and Unmounting from the DOS Prompt," except that the error message now appears in a dialog box.

Fig. 5.5

The DoubleSpace Mount a Compressed Drive dialog box.

Using DoubleSpace with Removable Media

This section describes how to use DoubleSpace with removable media. You mount and unmount compressed removable media drives the same way you mount and unmount compressed volumes on your hard disks. (Mounting and unmounting compressed volumes is described in the preceding sections of this chapter.)

Compressing Removable Media

Compressing removable media disks is slightly different from compressing hard disks. Normally, you compress a hard disk only once, and you compress hard disks only if you add another hard disk to your computer or get a new computer. You are much more likely to compress removable media disks on a day-to-day basis.

As you compress a removable disk, DoubleSpace creates a compressed volume file named DBLSPACE.000 in the uncompressed root directory of the removable disk and assigns that file Hidden, System, and Read-Only file attributes. After creating the compressed volume file, DoubleSpace adds an information file to the uncompressed root directory of the removable disk. This DOS text file, called READTHIS.TXT, informs you that the disk is DoubleSpace compressed. READTHIS.TXT also includes brief instructions on how to mount the disk or how to determine whether the disk is already mounted. The READTHIS.TXT file appears as follows:

```
This disk has been compressed by MS-DOS 6 DoubleSpace.

To make this disk's contents accessible, change to the drive that contains it,
and then type the following at the command prompt:

   DBLSPACE/MOUNT

(If this file is located on a drive other than the drive that contains the
compressed disk, then the disk has already been mounted.)
```

NOTE: Remember that you cannot compress a 360K floppy disk by using DoubleSpace, because DoubleSpace requires more than 360K of available working space to compress a disk.

You can compress removable media drives by using either the DOS command line or the DoubleSpace menu system. Both methods are described in the following sections.

Compressing Removable Media Disks from the DOS Prompt

DoubleSpace uses several command line switches to compress removable media drives. Those described in this section are the most commonly used. (See Chapter 6, "Using the DoubleSpace Utilities," for the full syntax of other command line switches used to compress disk drives.)

To compress a removable media drive, the following command line syntax is recommended:

DBLSPACE /COMPRESS *d1*: /RESERVE=*n.nn*

This command instructs DoubleSpace to compress a drive specified by drive letter *d1* and to reserve *n.nn* megabytes of uncompressed space. The following command, for example, compresses the floppy disk in drive A and reserves .13 M of uncompressed space—the minimum that DoubleSpace accepts:

DBLSPACE /COMPRESS A: /RESERVE=.13

You should normally specify a reserve of only .13 M so that your compressed volume file is as large as possible. Except for READTHIS.TXT, you rarely store files on the uncompressed part of a removable disk.

To compress a removable disk from the DOS command line, type a command at the DOS prompt similar to the one that follows (using the recommended syntax), and press

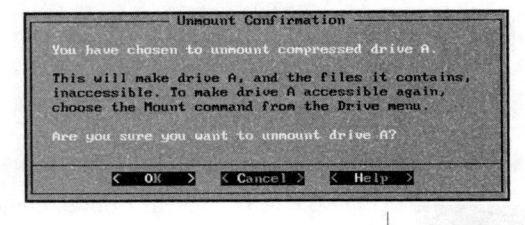

Fig. 5.6

The DoubleSpace Unmount Confirmation dialog box.

Enter. Replace *d* with the drive letter for the removable media drive that contains the disk you want to compress.

DBLSPACE /COMPRESS *d*: /RESERVE=.13

DoubleSpace compresses the removable disk in the specified drive.

If you intend to compress a removable disk in a drive other than drive A, first ensure that drive A is empty. If a mounted compressed volume is in drive A, unmount the volume before removing the disk. Clearing drive A makes the compression process go more smoothly.

You cannot uncompress a removable media disk. If you want to use the removable disk without DoubleSpace compression at some future time, you must remove the compressed volume file by formatting the disk or by following the procedure for deleting compressed volume files described in Chapter 6, "Using the DoubleSpace Utilities."

Before compressing a removable disk, DoubleSpace runs the DOS CHKDSK utility on that disk. If CHKDSK finds anything wrong, you must correct the errors before you can compress the disk. See Chapter 7, "Troubleshooting DoubleSpace," for instructions about correcting errors found by CHKDSK. If CHKDSK does not find any problems, DoubleSpace makes a system check to ensure that enough drive letters are available and that enough removable drives are allocated so that the new compressed removable drive can be mounted. If not enough memory or drive letters are reserved for removable drives, DoubleSpace displays an error message. Refer to the section "Mounting and Unmounting from the DOS Prompt," earlier in this chapter, for instructions on dealing with these errors.

After these checks, DoubleSpace begins to compress the removable disk. As DoubleSpace compresses the disk, it displays a status report to indicate its progress.

If you compress a removable disk in a drive other than drive A, and a disk is in drive A at the same time, DoubleSpace displays the error dialog box shown in figure 5.7. DoubleSpace really does not need to restart your computer; in fact, it does not do so. To proceed, you must remove the disk in drive A and then choose **R**etry.

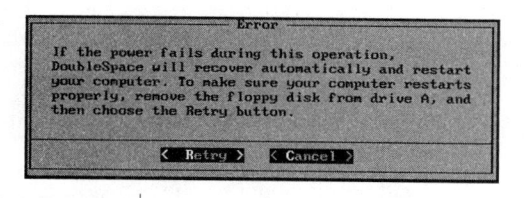

If drive A is empty and DoubleSpace still displays the error message shown in figure 5.7, do not be alarmed. You probably had a mounted compressed volume in drive A last. If you removed the disk without unmounting the compressed volume, DoubleSpace responds as if a disk is still in drive A, even if one is not. Choose **R**etry; DoubleSpace checks the drive again and proceeds with the compression.

The version of DoubleSpace supplied with DOS 6.00 Revision A displays the anomalous behavior described here. Microsoft probably will correct this behavior in upcoming DOS revisions, so if you own a later revision, you may not experience these difficulties. To find out which version of DOS you have, including the revision letter, enter the following command at the DOS prompt:

VER /R

As DoubleSpace finishes compressing the removable disk, it displays messages telling you that it is examining your system and scanning for compressed drives. Finally, DoubleSpace

---

To save keystrokes, create a DOS batch file called COMPRESS.BAT that contains the following command line:

DBLSPACE /COMPRESS %1 /RESERVE=.13

(The command in the file must be on a single line with a space between elements.) DOS replaces the %1 symbol with the first entry that appears on the DOS command line after the name of the batch file. The following command, for example, uses the batch file to compress the floppy disk in drive B:

COMPRESS B:

Refer to your DOS documentation for more information on DOS batch files and replaceable parameters.

Fig. 5.7

The error message displayed if a disk is in drive A.

mounts the new compressed drive and returns you to the DOS prompt. To compress more than one removable disk in the same drive, you need not unmount the disk. Just put in the next disk you want to compress and issue the DBLSPACE /COMPRESS command again. After you finish, the last removable disk you compressed is mounted.

Compressing Removable Media Disks by Using the DoubleSpace Menus

You also can compress removable disks by using the DoubleSpace menu system. To do so, simply follow these steps:

1. To start the DoubleSpace utility program, type **DBLSPACE** and then press Enter. DoubleSpace starts and displays its main menu and list of compressed drives (refer to fig. 5.1).
2. Insert in a disk drive the removable disk you want to compress.
3. Open the **C**ompress menu, and Choose **E**xisting Drive. DoubleSpace scans your computer system for disks that can be compressed and then displays a list of choices on-screen (see fig. 5.8).
4. Select the drive containing the disk to be compressed, and press Enter. DoubleSpace displays a confirmation screen showing the estimated time required to compress the disk.
5. To begin compressing the disk, press C. DoubleSpace displays a progress chart as it compresses the disk.

DoubleSpace now performs the same operations described in the preceding section of this chapter, "Compressing Removable Media Disks from the DOS Prompt." Refer to that section for a discussion that includes important Notes and Tips to help you avoid or solve problems. After DoubleSpace finishes compressing the removable disk, it mounts the new compressed drive and returns to the main menu list of compressed drives. The removable disk you just compressed is now mounted and displayed in that list.

If you compress removable disks by using the DoubleSpace menus, you should unmount the new compressed drive before compressing another disk (unlike when using command line switches). After the removable disk is compressed and mounted, the physical removable media disk is accessible only through the host drive of the mounted compressed volume. In the DoubleSpace menus, this condition makes it impossible to compress another removable disk in the same physical drive without unmounting the previous compressed volume.

Using Removable Media

This section describes several issues involved in using removable media on a day-to-day basis: changing disks, using write-protected disks, and transporting disks to another computer.

Changing Disks

Before you can access the files on a compressed removable disk, you must mount the disk. After mounting the compressed volume on one removable disk, however, you may need to insert a different disk in the drive to access a different group of files. If you replace a mounted compressed removable disk with an uncompressed disk, DoubleSpace automatically unmounts the compressed volume. As you access the new disk, DoubleSpace

STOP

If you choose **C**ancel in the error dialog box shown in figure 5.7, DoubleSpace *does* restart your computer. This may have unfortunate consequences if you use a RAM disk or TSR programs.

Remember to make sure that drive A is empty if you are compressing disks in another drive. Clearing drive A makes the compression process go more smoothly, as explained in the discussions on compressing from the DOS prompt.

STOP

The usual general precautions for using removable disks also apply to compressed removable disks. Never remove a disk while data is being written to it or while it is still in use by an application. Doing so may result in loss of data. Remove or change disks only if the disk drive activity light is off and you are sure that the disk is not being used by an application.

Using DoubleSpace 109

> **NOTE:**
> If the drive containing the removable disk you want to compress is not listed on the screen shown in figure 5.8, make sure that the drive actually contains a disk. If a disk is present, make sure that it contains at least .65M of free space.

recognizes that it is not compressed and unmounts the previous drive. If you later insert another compressed removable disk, you must mount its compressed volume before you can access its files. If, however, you replace a mounted compressed removable disk with another compressed disk, DoubleSpace keeps the removable drive mounted. The new removable disk is immediately available; it does not need to be mounted.

Using Write-Protected Removable Media

You cannot use a write-protected removable disk with DoubleSpace. If you attempt to mount a write-protected removable disk, DoubleSpace displays the following message (the exact drive letter and compressed volume file in the message depending on the drive you are mounting):

```
DoubleSpace cannot mount drive B because the file B:\DBLSPACE.000 is not a
valid compressed volume file.
```

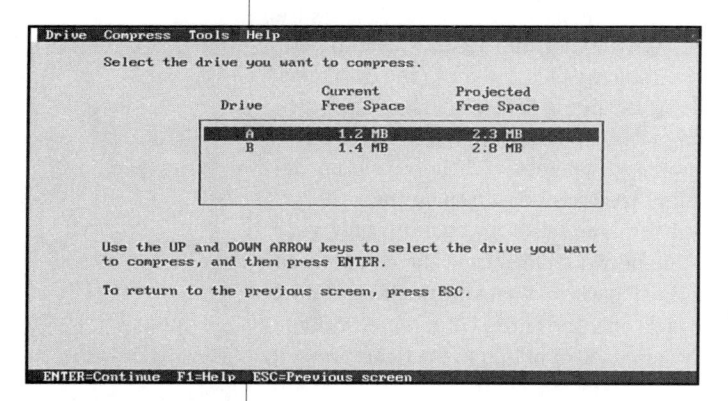

Fig. 5.8

The DoubleSpace list of compressible drives.

If you attempt to mount the removable disk at the DOS prompt, DoubleSpace displays this message on your screen; if you are using the DoubleSpace menus, the same error message appears in a dialog box. If you receive this error message on a write-protected removable disk, do not be alarmed. Nothing is really wrong with your compressed volume file; DoubleSpace is just informing you that it cannot mount the compressed volume.

As discussed earlier in this book, DoubleSpace safeguards a compressed volume file by giving it System, Hidden, and Read-Only file attributes. As DoubleSpace updates information in the compressed volume, it first removes the special attributes from the compressed volume file so that it can make the necessary changes. After updating the compressed volume file, DoubleSpace restores the protective attributes. To manipulate the compressed volume file, therefore, DoubleSpace must be able to write to the removable disk. The write-protect devices for removable media disks operate at a hardware level, protecting the entire disk. DoubleSpace cannot make the file attribute changes, so it cannot mount the compressed volume. As a result, it reports that the compressed volume file is not valid.

If you encounter this error, simply remove the write-protection from the compressed removable disk and try mounting it again. DoubleSpace should then be able to mount the compressed volume without any problems.

Using DoubleSpace Compressed Removable Media in Other Computers

You can use your DoubleSpace compressed removable disks on any computer that has DoubleSpace installed. These disks cannot be read by computers that do not use DoubleSpace. To make files from a compressed removable disk available on a computer that does not have DoubleSpace, you must copy the files from that disk to an uncompressed removable disk on a computer that *does* have DoubleSpace.

If you expect to frequently need to make data on DoubleSpace compressed removable disks available on computers that do not use DoubleSpace, you may want to consider using the SPACEMANager add-in utility. See Chapter 8, "Beyond DoubleSpace: Using SPACEMANager," for details.

Backing Up Your Compressed Drives

You can back up your compressed volumes the same way you backed up your uncompressed drives before you installed DoubleSpace. The main difference is that you now have more drives to back up. As your compressed volumes fill up, you also need to use more floppy disks or tape cartridges to perform your backup, because you have effectively doubled your disk storage by installing DoubleSpace. Whenever you perform a backup, make sure that you back up all the files on your compressed volumes and all the files on your uncompressed drives, except for your compressed volume files. (Refer to the documentation for your backup program for information on excluding files from a backup.)

Although backing up your compressed volume files is possible, doing so is pointless. If you back up individual files from your compressed volumes and then back up the compressed volume file itself, you are duplicating your effort and using many more floppy disks or tapes than necessary. Especially avoid the temptation to back up only your compressed volume file instead of backing up the individual files from the compressed volume. If you back up only the compressed volume file without backing up its individual files, you cannot restore single files. You can restore only the entire compressed volume file, which results in the loss of any files you have changed or added to your compressed volume since your last backup.

For information on a comprehensive and cost-effective backup technique that enables you to restore any file for a period of up to three months past, refer to Appendix C, "The 'Grandfather' Backup Technique."

Using Disk Utilities with DoubleSpace

Most hard disk utilities are compatible with your DoubleSpace compressed volumes, as long as they also are compatible with your version of DOS and your specific hardware. In general, always use the most current version of your disk utilities available. If you have any doubts about the compatibility of a particular disk utility, consult its manufacturer or your vendor for information on the product's compatibility with DOS 6 and DoubleSpace.

Among the most frequently used disk utilities are those categorized as *disk optimizers*, or *defragmentation programs*. Many software publishers offer disk optimization programs; DOS 6 even supplies its own version of a disk optimization utility, called DEFRAG. Disk optimization programs improve your hard disk's performance by *defragmenting* the files on the disk. As discussed in Chapter 1, "Understanding and Using Disk Compression," DOS divides your disk into small chunks called clusters (also referred to as allocation units). DOS stores files on your disk by dividing the information in the file into several different clusters; the actual number of clusters used by a file depends on the size of the file and the size of the clusters.

DOS uses whatever unused clusters it finds as it writes new information to the disk. Files that change frequently usually are stored in clusters scattered all across the surface of your hard disk. If the clusters used by a file are scattered widely over the surface of the disk, the disk's read/write heads must move farther and more often to retrieve all the information in the file. A disk that contains many files consisting of clusters that are physically separated is said to be fragmented. Disk optimization, or defragmenting, programs rearrange the file clusters on your disk so that all clusters in use by a particular file are contiguous. Making the clusters for a file contiguous can speed up disk access, because the disk's read/write heads need not move around as much to retrieve the entire file.

Unlike when defragmenting a physical disk, using an optimization program on a DoubleSpace compressed volume does not necessarily speed up access to that volume, because your compressed volume file already is arranged in contiguous clusters on the physical disk. Defragmenting your compressed volume is normally useful only if you need to change its size. Chapter 6, "Using the DoubleSpace Utilities," describes how to change the size of a compressed volume. Most defragmentation programs do not move files that are marked with the System, Hidden, or Read-Only attributes—such as the compressed volume files. Your compressed volume file, therefore, should not be affected by running defragmentation programs on your uncompressed hard disk.

> Do not run a defragmentation program on your uncompressed disk if you have altered the Hidden, System, or Read-Only attributes on your compressed volume file. You may lose data from the compressed volume if you defragment the uncompressed host drive while the compressed volume file is unprotected. If the host drive's cluster size is different than DoubleSpace's cluster size—which is usually the case—the DoubleSpace clusters may be corrupted if they are moved by the defragmentation program.

Using the DoubleSpace Help System

DoubleSpace provides a fairly comprehensive Help system. You can obtain help from DoubleSpace as you use the DoubleSpace command line switches or the DoubleSpace menu system. You also can use the DOS Help system to obtain information about DoubleSpace. To use the DOS Help system for information about DoubleSpace, type the following command at the DOS prompt, and press Enter:

HELP DBLSPACE

Refer to your DOS documentation for more information about the DOS Help system. This section concentrates on DoubleSpace Help.

If you use the DoubleSpace command line switches frequently, you may occasionally need a short reminder about the switch names and their effects. To obtain such a reminder, type the following command at the DOS prompt, and press Enter:

DBLSPACE /?

DoubleSpace displays a list of all its command line switches and their options, along with a brief description of the action or effect associated with each switch.

DoubleSpace also provides several ways to access Help from within the DoubleSpace menu system.

Context-Sensitive Help

To access *context-sensitive help*—that is, help that relates to the immediate task on which you are working (the context)—press the F1 key at any time while you are in the

DoubleSpace utility. DoubleSpace displays a Help screen related to your current activity. DoubleSpace uses the currently highlighted menu choice, the currently open dialog box, and other cues to determine your operating context and display the appropriate Help screen. Figure 5.9, for example, shows the Help screen DoubleSpace displays if you press F1 while the **M**ount choice on the **D**rive menu is highlighted.

You also can obtain context-sensitive help by using the **H**elp button that appears in most DoubleSpace dialog boxes. Tab to the button and press Enter, or click the button with the mouse. The same Help screen appears whether you use the Help button or press F1.

The DoubleSpace Help Menu

You can invoke DoubleSpace's Help system from the DoubleSpace main menu. You can access the **H**elp menu whenever the DoubleSpace main menu and compressed drive list are shown on-screen. To activate the **H**elp menu, press Alt+H, or click **H**elp. The **H**elp menu offers you three choices: **C**ontents, **I**ndex, and **A**bout.

If you choose **A**bout, DoubleSpace displays a dialog box that provides information about DoubleSpace. Choose **O**K to clear this dialog box from your screen.

If you choose **C**ontents, DoubleSpace displays the screen shown in figure 5.10. (This screen also appears if you press F1 while at the main menu and compressed drive list.) Help Contents provides an overview of the topics covered by the DoubleSpace Help system. Use the up- and down-arrow keys to scroll through the Help Contents text.

If you choose **I**ndex from the **H**elp menu, DoubleSpace displays the screen shown in figure 5.11. The DoubleSpace Help Index provides a list of topics covered by the DoubleSpace Help system, organized by task.

Navigating the Help System

In most cases, more than a single screen of text is required to cover a Help topic. Use the up- and down-arrow keys, the PgUp and PgDn keys, or the scroll bar to move forward or backward through the text.

The DoubleSpace Help system connects certain words and topics with other topics by way of *hot links*. As shown in figure 5.12, hot links appear in a lighter color than the rest

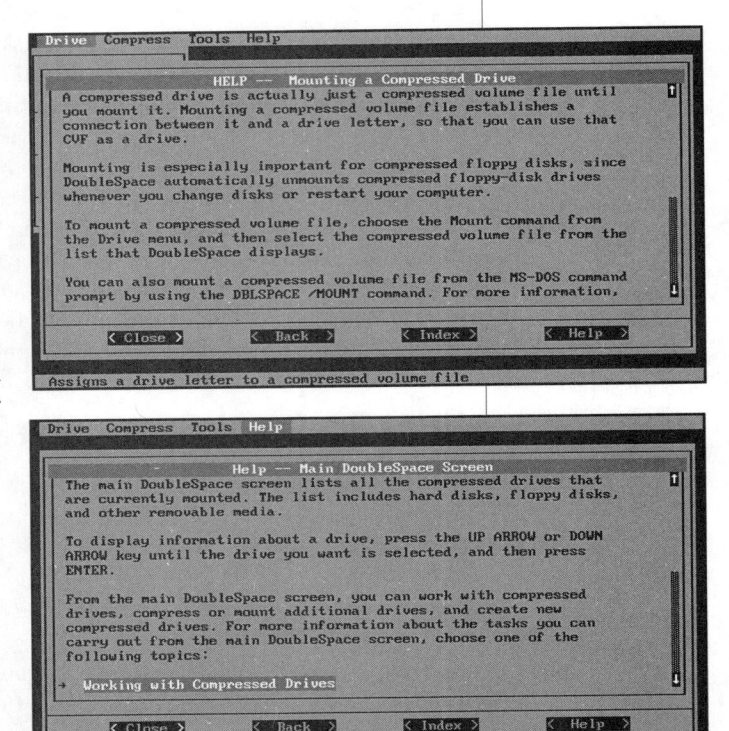

Fig. 5.9, top

DoubleSpace's context-sensitive Help for the Mount choice on the Drive menu.

Fig. 5.10, bottom

The DoubleSpace Help Contents screen.

of the Help screen's text. Use the Tab key or a mouse to highlight a hot link topic of interest, and then press Enter. The DoubleSpace Help system displays additional text on the chosen topic.

If you use the Tab key to move the highlight from one hot link to another, notice that, after the highlight hits the last hot link on-screen, it jumps to the row of command buttons at the bottom of the screen. A hot link word or phrase must be displayed on-screen before you can highlight it. Press the Tab key repeatedly to highlight each of the command buttons in turn; the highlight eventually returns to the first hot link word or phrase on-screen. You can move the highlight in the opposite direction by pressing Shift+Tab.

Every Help screen has four command buttons across the bottom of the screen. **C**lose clears the Help system display from your screen and returns you to whatever you were doing before you invoked DoubleSpace Help. **B**ack returns you to the previous DoubleSpace Help topic you displayed. **I**ndex displays the same index screen that appears if you choose **I**ndex from the **H**elp menu. The fourth and final command button, **H**elp, causes DoubleSpace to display a Help screen that explains the use of DoubleSpace Help and its menus.

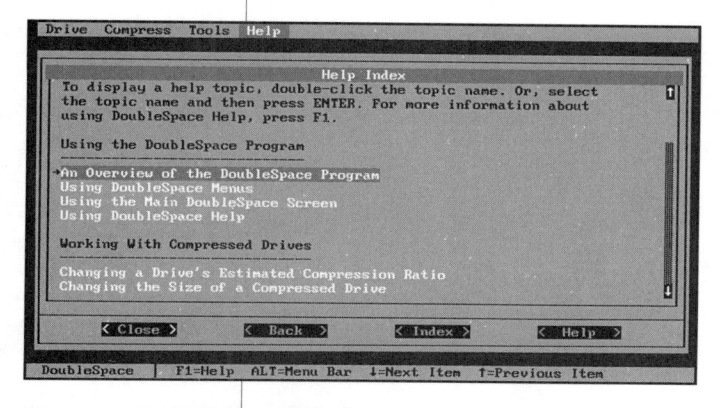

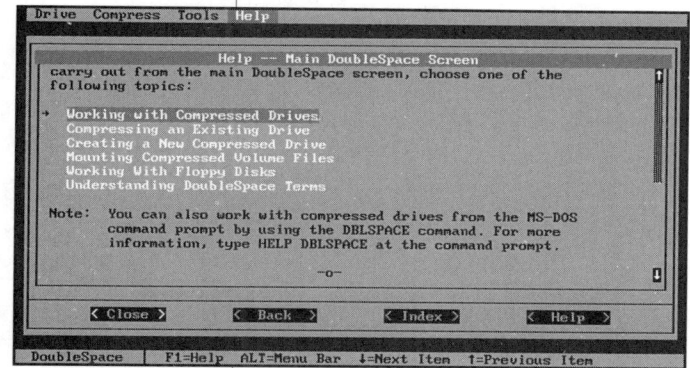

Fig. 5.11, top

The DoubleSpace Help Index screen.

Fig. 5.12, bottom

A page of the Help Contents screen, showing several hot links.

Summary

This chapter covered issues affecting your day-to-day work with your compressed drives. The chapter gave you information about managing files on DoubleSpace compressed drives and discussed the DOS commands that have been enhanced to work with those drives. The chapter also explained how to get information about your compressed drives from the DOS prompt or from the DoubleSpace menus.

You learned from this chapter how to mount and unmount compressed drives and how to compress removable media drives. You also learned about the special concerns associated with using compressed removable media. This chapter also provided brief descriptions of how to back up your compressed drives and how to use disk utilities safely with DoubleSpace. Finally, you learned how to use the DoubleSpace Help system.

The next chapter explains how to use DoubleSpace to perform some less common tasks.

CHAPTER 6

Using the DoubleSpace Utilities

This chapter discusses tasks you do not need to perform on a daily basis, although you probably must perform some of them eventually. Some tasks, such as creating a new compressed volume, you are likely to perform only once for each of your compressed drives. You learn how to use the DoubleSpace utility to create additional compressed drives, change the size of an existing compressed drive, and check the integrity of your compressed drives. The chapter also describes how to defragment a compressed drive and tells you when defragmenting is necessary. You also learn how to delete or format a compressed drive.

> **NOTE:**
> This section focuses on creating compressed drives on your hard disks. To compress a removable disk, such as a floppy disk, refer to Chapter 5, "Using DoubleSpace."

Creating Additional Compressed Drives

DoubleSpace enables you to create compressed drives either by compressing an existing uncompressed disk (and all files on it) or by using only the free space on an uncompressed disk. Both types of compressed drive are discussed in this section.

If you followed the instructions in Chapter 3, "Installing DoubleSpace," you may have been referred to this chapter to compress all your hard disk drives or partitions. DoubleSpace Express or Custom Setup can compress only one drive for you. If you have more than one physical hard disk or partition, you must compress the additional disks or partitions by using one of the procedures described in this chapter. After you create at least one compressed drive, DoubleSpace Setup does not run. Instead, it displays the menu for the DoubleSpace utilities.

If you add another disk drive to your computer, or if you decide to repartition your physical hard disk, you may need to perform some of the procedures in this section to create or re-create new compressed drives. After you create a compressed drive, you do not usually need these procedures again. If, after you create a compressed drive, you decide that the drive is too large or small, you can change the size of the compressed drive. Changing the size of a compressed drive is described later in this chapter.

Compressing an Existing Drive

If you compress an existing uncompressed drive, DoubleSpace compresses all files on the drive and puts those files on the new compressed volume. DoubleSpace then exchanges drive letters between the new compressed volume and the original uncompressed drive so that the new compressed volume has the same drive letter you formerly used for the original uncompressed drive. You can use either the DoubleSpace menus or the DBLSPACE command with command line switches to compress an existing drive.

Compressing an Existing Drive from the DOS Prompt

You can add command line switches to the DBLSPACE command to compress an existing drive from the DOS prompt. The DoubleSpace command line you use to compress an existing drive, with its switches, has the following syntax:

DBLSPACE /COMPRESS *d1*: /NEWDRIVE=*d2*: /RESERVE=*n.nn*

The /NEWDRIVE and /RESERVE switches are optional. You can use them alone or together. The /NEWDRIVE switch enables you to select the drive letter DoubleSpace assigns to the uncompressed host drive. The /RESERVE switch enables you to specify how much space to reserve on the uncompressed host drive.

In this syntax example, *d1* represents the letter of the drive you want to compress. To compress drive D, for example, you use the following command:

DBLSPACE /COMPRESS D:

DoubleSpace compresses drive D, mounts the new compressed drive, and then exchanges drive letters between the compressed drive and its host. Because /RESERVE was not specified, DoubleSpace also reserves 2M of free space on the uncompressed host drive.

Without the /NEWDRIVE switch in this command, DoubleSpace determines which drive letter to use for the uncompressed host drive. By default, DoubleSpace chooses the highest available letter from the group of drive letters DoubleSpace has reserved for its own use. To specify the drive letter for the host drive yourself, add the /NEWDRIVE switch. To compress drive D and assign drive letter G to the uncompressed host drive, for example, you use the following command:

DBLSPACE /COMPRESS D: /NEWDRIVE=G:

The drive letter you specify by adding the /NEWDRIVE switch must be one of the drive letters reserved by DoubleSpace for its own use and must not already be in use. Refer to Chapter 3, "Installing DoubleSpace," for information on how DoubleSpace reserves drive letters. Refer to Chapter 5, "Using DoubleSpace," for information on determining which drive letters are available.

Whenever you compress a hard disk—whether or not you use the /NEWDRIVE switch—DoubleSpace changes the DBLSPACE.INI file so that the new compressed drive

---

Some programs—such as early versions of Lotus 1-2-3 and most contemporary DOS-based music programs such as Voyetra Sequencer Plus—use copy-protection schemes that rely on finding certain data in certain areas of the disk. Compressing a disk moves the data for which the copy-protection scheme searches. You must uninstall any software that uses this type of copy protection before compressing a disk; otherwise, the copy-protection scheme no longer recognizes your software as a legitimate copy, and you cannot use it. Refer to your program's documentation to determine whether it uses this type of copy-protection scheme and for instructions on uninstalling the software. After you compress the drive, you can re-install the copy-protected program.

Never compress a drive from the DOS prompt without first using DOS CHKDSK on the disk you intend to compress. If DOS CHKDSK finds any errors, correct them before compressing the disk. Failure to correct errors detected by DOS CHKDSK before compressing a disk may result in lost data.

is mounted whenever you start your computer. DoubleSpace also records the drive letter for the new uncompressed host drive. If you use the /NEWDRIVE switch, the drive letter you specified for the uncompressed host drive is used every time the new compressed drive is mounted. Refer to Chapter 4, "Configuring and Optimizing DoubleSpace," for more information about the DBLSPACE.INI file.

To instruct DoubleSpace to reserve more or less than 2M free space for the uncompressed host drive, use the /RESERVE switch. You do not, for example, want to reserve as much free space on the uncompressed host drive if you do not expect to store any files on the uncompressed host drive. If you do expect to store files on an uncompressed drive, however, you may want to reserve more space for that drive.

The following example compresses drive D and reserves .13M free space on the uncompressed host drive (the smallest amount of space DoubleSpace accepts):

DBLSPACE /COMPRESS D: /RESERVE=.13

The following example also compresses drive D, but reserves 20M space on the uncompressed host drive and instructs DoubleSpace to assign drive letter G to the new uncompressed host drive:

DBLSPACE /COMPRESS D: /NEWDRIVE=G: /RESERVE=20

As discussed in Chapter 3, "Installing DoubleSpace," you cannot compress a disk drive that does not contain DoubleSpace's minimum amount of working space (about 1.2M). If you try to use the command line switches to compress a disk drive with insufficient working space, DoubleSpace displays the following error message:

```
Drive D does not have enough free space to enable it to be compressed.
Compressing a drive requires 1.13 MB of free space.
```

Compressing an Existing Drive by Using the DoubleSpace Menus

To compress an existing drive by using the DoubleSpace menus, follow these steps:

1. If necessary, start the DoubleSpace program by typing **DBLSPACE** at the DOS prompt and pressing Enter. DoubleSpace starts and displays its main menu and list of compressed drives (see fig. 6.1).

2. From the **C**ompress menu, choose **E**xisting Drive. DoubleSpace searches your system for drives it can compress. After DoubleSpace finishes searching, it ists the drives that can be compressed, their current free space, and their projected free space after compression. A screen appears, similar to the one shown in figure 6.2.

If DoubleSpace does not find any drives it can compress, it displays an error dialog box. Choose **O**K to close the error dialog box and return to the DoubleSpace main menu and list of compressed drives.

DoubleSpace does not list drives that do not contain enough working room or that are already compressed. DoubleSpace also does not list RAM drives, network drives, CD-ROM drives, drives connected by DOS INTERLNK, or drives created by using DOS SUBST. Refer to your DOS documentation for information about INTERLNK and SUBST. To compress a RAM drive, refer to Chapter 4, "Configuring and Optimizing DoubleSpace."

NOTE:
If you are a Windows user, you must exit from Windows before using DoubleSpace or any of the DoubleSpace commands.

STOP
If you use the DoubleSpace menus to compress an existing drive, DoubleSpace restarts your computer near the end of the process. If you have a RAM disk, preserve any data on it that you want to keep *before* you begin this procedure. Similarly, any TSR programs you use may have open files or unsaved data in memory. Make sure that all files used by TSR programs are closed and all data saved.

If the drive you want to compress is not listed, the drive probably does not have enough free space on it for DoubleSpace's working room. Exit DoubleSpace and use the DOS DIR command to determine how much free space is on the drive you want to compress. If free space is less than 1.2M, make more space available on the drive, and then follow these instructions again.

3. Select the drive you want to compress, and then press Enter. DoubleSpace displays the screen shown in figure 6.3.

   DoubleSpace displays its settings for compressing the drive you selected. Unless you specify otherwise, DoubleSpace leaves 2M uncompressed space free on the uncompressed host drive. DoubleSpace also lists the drive letter to be assigned to the uncompressed host drive, unless you specify otherwise.

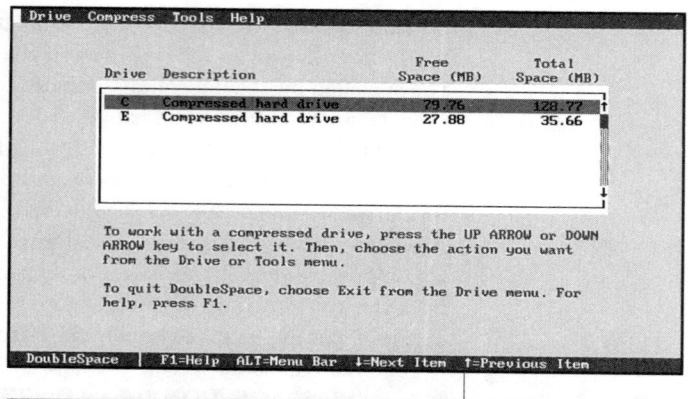

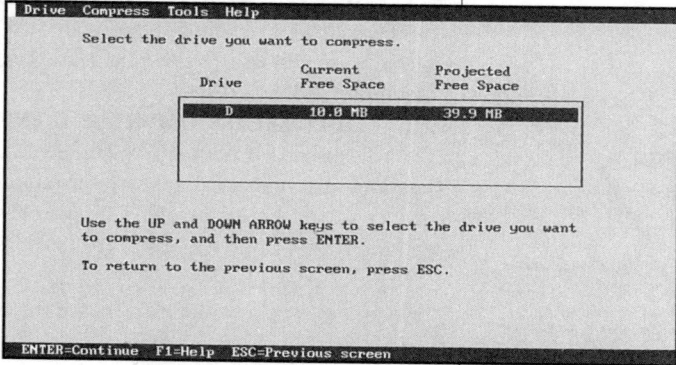

4. To change the amount of uncompressed free space DoubleSpace leaves on the host drive, highlight that line and press Enter; otherwise, skip to step 6. DoubleSpace displays the screen shown in figure 6.4.

   The amount of uncompressed free space DoubleSpace leaves on the uncompressed drive is *in addition to* any files that must remain uncompressed. If, for example, you compress a drive containing a 5M Windows permanent swap file, DoubleSpace moves the swap file to the uncompressed drive, allocating 5M for it. If the uncompressed free space is set to 2M, the new uncompressed drive is actually about 7M—5M occupied by the Windows swap file and 2M of empty space.

5. Type the amount of uncompressed free space you want to leave on the uncompressed drive as a number in megabytes (M) and decimal fractions of a megabyte, and press Enter. (If, for example, you want 3,500,000 bytes free on your uncompressed drive, type **3.5**.) DoubleSpace returns to the screen shown in figure 6.3, with your changes in the free space displayed.

6. To change the drive letter that DoubleSpace assigns to the uncompressed host drive, select that line, and press Enter; otherwise, skip to step 8. DoubleSpace displays the screen shown in figure 6.5.

Fig. 6.1, top

The DoubleSpace main menu and list of compressed drives.

Fig. 6.2, bottom

The DoubleSpace list of compressible drives.

Using the DoubleSpace Utilities   **119**

> **NOTE:**
> The drive letter you select in step 7 is assigned to the uncompressed host drive, not to the new compressed drive. If you compress an existing drive, DoubleSpace always exchanges drive letters so that the compressed drive you create has the same drive letter it did before you compressed it.

> **NOTE:**
> Compressing an existing drive may take from several minutes to several hours. Notice the amount of time DoubleSpace estimates it requires to compress your drive. (The time estimate is listed in the first line of text at the top of the confirmation screen.) After DoubleSpace begins compressing the disk, it cannot be interrupted until it is finished. If you cannot do without your computer for the length of time required to compress the drive, you should compress your disk some other time. To avoid compressing the disk, press Esc repeatedly until you are back at the DoubleSpace main menu.

The list of drives displayed on this screen starts with the first available drive letter and ends with the last available drive letter in the group of drive letters DoubleSpace has reserved for its own use.

7. Select the drive letter you want to use for the new uncompressed host drive, and press Enter. DoubleSpace returns to the screen shown in figure 6.3, showing the drive letter you just selected.

After you set the free space and drive letter, you are ready to compress the drive.

8. To begin compressing the drive, choose Continue. DoubleSpace displays a confirmation screen, telling you the estimated time required to compress the drive. The actual time may vary slightly, depending on the speed of your computer's disk drive and CPU.

If you continue from this point, you are committed to compressing the drive; you cannot cancel the operation. If you change your mind, press Esc to return to the previous screen.

9. Make sure that drive A is empty. (DoubleSpace restarts your computer; if a disk is in drive A, however, your computer does not restart correctly.)

10. Press C to compress the drive. DoubleSpace begins compressing your disk.

DoubleSpace runs the DOS CHKDSK command on the drive it is compressing. Your computer screen clears and remains blank for a few moments as the CHKDSK program examines the drive. After CHKDSK is done, the results display on your screen for a few seconds. If CHKDSK finds any errors, DoubleSpace tells you what those errors are and then returns to the DoubleSpace main menu. To compress the disk, fix the problems that CHKDSK found, and start the compression procedure from step 1 again. Refer to your DOS documentation and Chapter 7, "Troubleshooting DoubleSpace," for more information about CHKDSK and correcting errors that it finds.

DoubleSpace displays various messages as it checks your system. If DoubleSpace detects a floppy disk in drive A, it displays the error dialog box shown in figure 6.6.

Remove the floppy disk from drive A. Choose **R**etry to have DoubleSpace check your system again. If you decide not to compress the drive, choose **C**ancel. If you choose **C**ancel, DoubleSpace restarts your computer and does not compress any drives. DoubleSpace displays various messages as it verifies your computer's status, and then displays a screen showing DoubleSpace's progress as it compresses the drive.

After DoubleSpace displays the progress screen, it can finish compressing the drive unattended. You do not need to make additional choices or perform any other actions at this point. The progress display shows the time that compression started, the current time, the estimated finish time, and the time remaining to compress the drive. The progress display also indicates the name of the file DoubleSpace is currently compressing and displays a horizontal bar graph representing the percentage of completion for the entire job of compressing the selected drive.

After all files on the drive have been compressed and added to the compressed volume, DoubleSpace runs the DOS DEFRAG program to defragment the compressed volume file.

DEFRAG displays a map of the disk's clusters as it optimizes the disk. DEFRAG beeps after it finishes, and DoubleSpace displays a compression completion report. This report shows the results of compressing your drive; it lists the amount of free space on the drive before you compressed it and the amount of free space on the drive after compression. Usually, the free space after compression is much higher than the free space before compression, but the actual amount depends on how full the drive was before you compressed it and how well the files compressed. The report then lists the compression ratio of the files on your drive and the total time it took to compress the files. Finally, the report names the drive letter for the compressed volume's host drive and the amount of free space on the host drive. (The host drive is called the *new drive* on-screen.)

After you finish reviewing the information in the compression report, press Enter to continue. DoubleSpace checks your system to make sure that drive A is empty. If a disk is in drive A, DoubleSpace displays an error message similar to the one already shown in figure 6.6. Remove the disk from drive A, and choose **R**etry. DoubleSpace restarts your computer. If your computer does not restart, turn it off and back on, or press the reset button if your computer has one. After DoubleSpace restarts your computer, you can use your compressed drive the same as you did before it was compressed.

If you uninstalled any copy-protected software before compressing the drive, reinstall that software now.

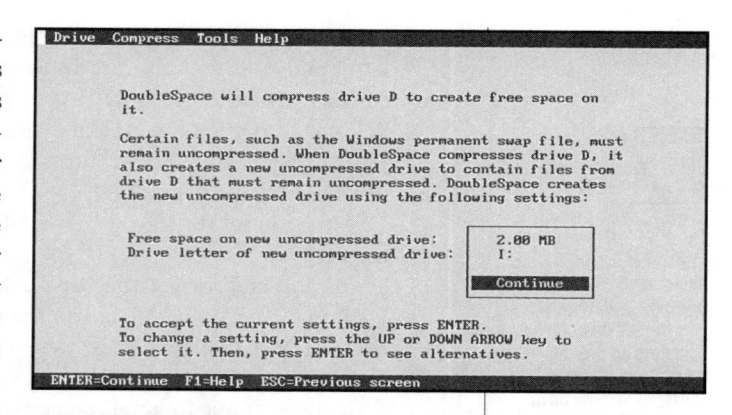

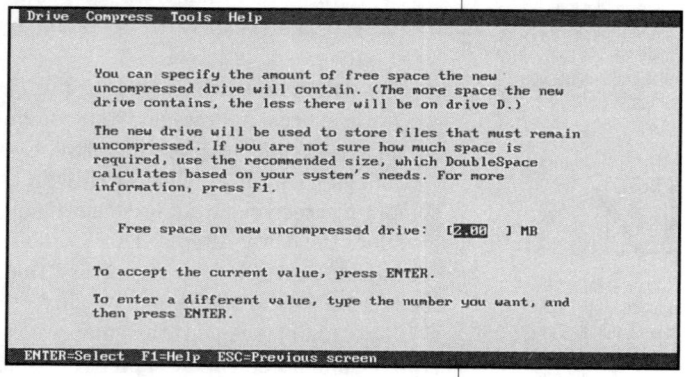

Fig. 6.3, top

The DoubleSpace compression options screen.

Fig. 6.4, bottom

The DoubleSpace screen for changing the amount of uncompressed free space on a drive.

Creating a New Compressed Drive from Free Space

If you create a new compressed drive from the free space on an uncompressed drive, DoubleSpace creates a new compressed volume without compressing any files or exchanging any drive letters. Instead, DoubleSpace uses the free space on the uncompressed drive to create an empty compressed volume. DoubleSpace assigns this new compressed volume the next available drive letter, but does not exchange the drive letter with the host drive.

You create new compressed drives from free space for several reasons. You may want to increase the available storage on your hard disk but want to leave your existing files uncompressed, or you may want to compress a physical disk drive that is larger than DoubleSpace's limit of 512M for a compressed drive. If, for example, you have a disk drive

Fig. 6.5, top

The DoubleSpace screen for changing the host drive letter.

Fig. 6.6, bottom

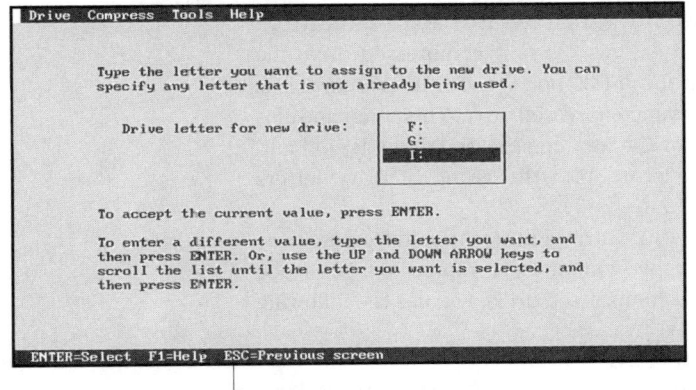

The DoubleSpace disk in drive A error message.

STOP

Never create a new compressed drive from the DOS prompt without first using the DOS CHKDSK command on the drive the free space of which you intend to compress. Failure to correct errors detected by DOS CHKDSK before creating a new compressed drive can result in lost data.

with an uncompressed capacity of 500M, you must create at least two compressed volumes to compress all the space on the drive. If the 500M drive is the only drive in your computer and is all one partition, it is drive C. If you create the first compressed volume by compressing an existing drive, DoubleSpace creates a 512M compressed volume and exchanges drive letters so that the compressed volume is now drive C.

The uncompressed host drive is drive H and still contains about 244M uncompressed free space. To apply compression to this additional space, you must create a new compressed volume from free space on drive H. DoubleSpace creates a new compressed volume of about 488M and assigns the new compressed volume the next available drive letter. In this example, the new drive letter is G, because DoubleSpace works backward as it assigns drive letters. In effect, if you create a new compressed drive, the DoubleSpace compressed drive is added to your system as if it were a new disk drive.

You can use either the DoubleSpace menus to create a new compressed drive or the DBLSPACE command with command line switches.

Creating a New Compressed Drive from the DOS Prompt

You can use command line switches with the DBLSPACE command to create a new compressed drive. Think of using the command line switches as a shortcut to compressing a drive.

The DoubleSpace command line switches you use to compress an existing drive are entered with the following syntax:

DBLSPACE /CREATE *d1*: /NEWDRIVE=*d2*: /SIZE=*n.nn* /RESERVE=*n.nn*

The /NEWDRIVE, /SIZE, and /RESERVE switches are optional. You can use the /NEWDRIVE switch with any of the other switches, but the /SIZE and /RESERVE switches are mutually exclusive and cannot both be used at the same time. The /NEWDRIVE switch enables you to select which drive letter DoubleSpace uses for the uncompressed host drive. The /SIZE switch enables you to specify the size of the new compressed drive, and the /RESERVE switch enables you to specify how much space to reserve for the uncompressed host drive. You can use either the /SIZE or the /RESERVE switch to specify the resulting size of the new compressed volume, but not both.

In the preceding syntax example, *d1* represents the letter of the drive the free space of which you want to compress. To compress the free space on drive H, for example, you use the following command:

DBLSPACE /CREATE H:

DoubleSpace creates the new compressed drive from the free space on drive H, mounts the new compressed drive, and then assigns the new compressed drive the next available drive letter. Because neither the /SIZE nor the /RESERVE switch is used, DoubleSpace reserves 1M of space on the uncompressed drive. This command also has DoubleSpace determine the drive letter for the new compressed drive. By default, DoubleSpace chooses the highest available letter from the group of drive letters that DoubleSpace has reserved for its own use.

You can use the /NEWDRIVE switch to specify the drive letter you want DoubleSpace to use for the new compressed drive. If, for example, you want to compress the free space on drive H and assign drive letter G to the new compressed drive, you use the following syntax:

DBLSPACE /CREATE H: /NEWDRIVE=G:

The letter you specify by using the /NEWDRIVE switch must be one of the drive letters reserved by DoubleSpace for its own use and must not already be in use. Refer to Chapter 3, "Installing DoubleSpace," for information on how DoubleSpace reserves drive letters. Refer to Chapter 5, "Using DoubleSpace," for information on determining which drive letters are available.

Whenever you create a new compressed drive on a hard disk (whether or not you use the /NEWDRIVE switch), DoubleSpace changes the DBLSPACE.INI file so that the new compressed drive is mounted whenever you start your computer. DoubleSpace also records the drive letter for the new compressed drive. If you use the /NEWDRIVE switch, the drive letter you specified for the new compressed drive is used every time the new compressed drive is mounted during your computer's start-up. If you want more or less than the 1M free space DoubleSpace reserves for the uncompressed host drive, use either the /SIZE or the /RESERVE switch.

The following example uses the /RESERVE switch to create a new compressed drive from the free space on H and reserves 0M of space on the uncompressed host drive:

DBLSPACE /CREATE H: /RESERVE=0

You may find specifying the size of your new compressed drive easier than specifying the reserve on the uncompressed host drive. The following example uses the /SIZE switch to create a new compressed drive from the free space on H:

DBLSPACE /CREATE H: /SIZE=20

This command causes DoubleSpace to create a compressed volume file that uses 20M of the free space on drive H, resulting in a compressed drive with a capacity of about 40M.

Creating a New Compressed Drive by Using the DoubleSpace Menus

To create a new compressed drive by using the DoubleSpace menus, follow these steps:

1. If necessary, start the DoubleSpace program by typing **DBLSPACE** at the DOS prompt and pressing Enter. The DoubleSpace utility starts and displays the main menu and its list of compressed drives (refer to fig. 6.1).
2. From the **C**ompress menu, choose **C**reate New Drive. DoubleSpace searches your system for drives with enough free space to create a new compressed drive

> **NOTE:**
> Creating a new compressed drive from free space is one of only two special cases in which DoubleSpace enables you to specify a reserve of less than .13M. If you reserve 0M, DoubleSpace uses all the free space on the uncompressed drive except for about 1K.

> **NOTE:**
> You must exit from Windows before using DoubleSpace or any of the DoubleSpace commands.

Using the DoubleSpace Utilities **123**

and then displays the resulting list of drives (see fig. 6.7). The list shows each drive's current free space and the projected size of the new compressed drive.

If DoubleSpace finds no drives with enough free space to compress, it displays an error dialog box instead. Choose **OK** to close the error dialog box and return to the DoubleSpace main menu.

If DoubleSpace does not have a drive letter available for the new compressed drive (because all DoubleSpace's reserved drive letters are already in use), DoubleSpace also displays an error dialog box. Choose **OK** to close the error dialog box and return to the DoubleSpace main menu. To increase the number of drive letters that DoubleSpace reserves, follow the instructions in Chapter 4, "Configuring and Optimizing DoubleSpace," for raising the last drive letter DoubleSpace uses.

3. Select from the list the drive containing the free space you want to use for the new compressed drive, and press Enter.

    DoubleSpace displays the screen shown in figure 6.8, showing the settings that are to be used as it creates the new compressed volume from the free space on the drive you selected.

    Unless you specify otherwise, DoubleSpace leaves 2M uncompressed space free on the uncompressed host drive and uses an estimated compression ratio of 2:1. DoubleSpace also shows the drive letter it gives to the new compressed drive unless you specify otherwise.

4. To change the amount of uncompressed free space DoubleSpace leaves on the host drive, highlight that line and press Enter; otherwise, skip to step 6. DoubleSpace displays a screen containing a text box for changing the reserved space value.

5. Type the new amount of uncompressed free space you want to leave on the uncompressed host drive as a number in megabytes (M) and decimal fractions of a megabyte, and then press Enter. DoubleSpace returns to the screen shown in figure 6.8, now showing your changes in the free space.

6. To change the estimated compression ratio for the new compressed drive, highlight that line and press Enter; otherwise, skip to step 8. DoubleSpace displays the screen shown in figure 6.9.

    The list of estimated compression ratios displayed on this screen ranges from 1:1 to 16:1, in increments of one-tenth.

7. Highlight the estimated compression ratio you want to use, and press Enter. DoubleSpace returns to the display shown in figure 6.8, now showing your new estimated compression ratio.

8. To change the drive letter DoubleSpace assigns to the new compressed volume, highlight that line, and press Enter; otherwise, skip to step 10. DoubleSpace displays a screen showing a list of available drive letters.

    The drive letter you select in step 9 of this procedure is the drive letter assigned to the new drive you create from free space. After the new compressed volume is created, you access it through the drive letter you choose in this step.

> **NOTE:**
> DoubleSpace does not list drives with insufficient working room to create a new compressed drive; DoubleSpace also does not list RAM drives, network drives, CD-ROM drives, drives connected with DOS INTERLNK, or drives created by using DOS SUBST. To compress a RAM drive, refer to Chapter 4.

> Change the estimated compression ratio only if you know that the files you are going to store on the new compressed drive consistently compress higher or lower than the standard estimated compression ratio of 2:1.

9. Highlight the drive letter you want to use for the new compressed drive, and press Enter. (You can choose any available drive letter in the group of drive letters DoubleSpace has reserved for its own use.) DoubleSpace returns to the screen shown in figure 6.8, now showing the drive letter you just selected.
10. Choose Continue to create the new compressed drive. DoubleSpace now displays a confirmation screen showing the drive letter for the new compressed drive and the estimated time required to create the compressed volume from the free space on the drive. The actual time may vary slightly, depending on the speed of your computer's disk drive and CPU.

    At this point, you are committed to creating the compressed drive; you cannot cancel the operation. If you change your mind, press Esc repeatedly until DoubleSpace returns to the main menu.
11. Make sure that drive A is empty. (After you perform the following step, DoubleSpace checks your floppy drive as if it intends to restart your computer. DoubleSpace does not actually restart your computer, but displays an error message if a floppy disk is in drive A.)
12. Press C to create the compressed drive.

    DoubleSpace now runs the DOS CHKDSK command for you and tells you it is checking your system. If DoubleSpace finds a floppy disk in drive A, it displays an error dialog box. Remove the floppy disk from drive A, and choose **R**etry to have DoubleSpace check your system again. If you decide not to create the new compressed drive, choose **C**ancel.

    If you choose **C**ancel after receiving the error dialog box about a disk in drive A, DoubleSpace restarts your computer. This may have unfortunate consequences if you use a RAM disk and is inconvenient at best.

After CHKDSK finishes checking your system, the results of the check appear on-screen for a few seconds. If CHKDSK finds any errors, DoubleSpace tells you what those errors are and returns to the main menu. Fix the problems that CHKDSK found, and start this procedure again from step 1.

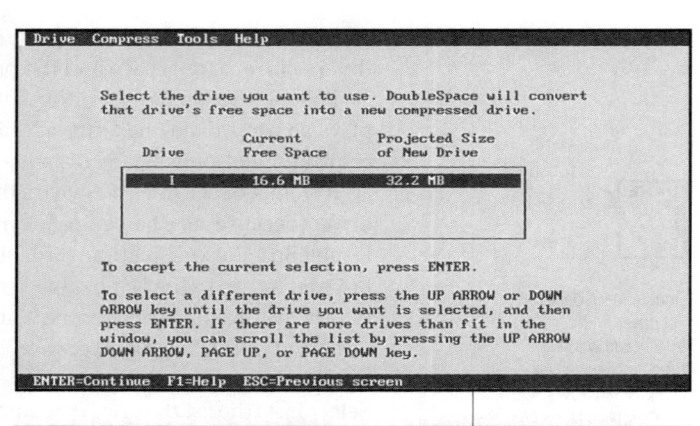

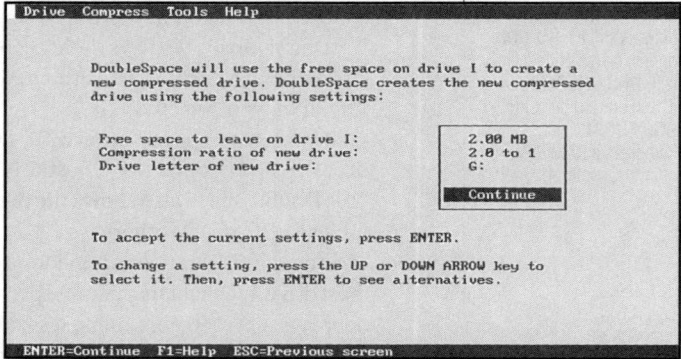

Fig. 6.7, top

The DoubleSpace list of drives with free space to compress.

Fig. 6.8, bottom

The DoubleSpace free space compression options screen.

> **NOTE:**
>
> The version of DoubleSpace supplied with DOS 6.00 Revision A displays the anomalous behavior described in step 12. Microsoft probably will correct this behavior in upcoming DOS revisions, so if you own a more recent revision, you may not experience these difficulties. To determine which version of DOS you have, including the revision letter, enter the following command at the DOS prompt:
>
> **VER /R**

After DoubleSpace ensures the integrity of the drive to be compressed and ensures that drive A is empty, it creates the new compressed drive. DoubleSpace displays various messages as it verifies your computer's status and creates the new compressed drive. Because a compressed volume created from the free space on a disk contains no files, DoubleSpace does not have to restart your computer before making the new compressed volume available. After DoubleSpace finishes creating the new compressed volume, it mounts the drive and returns to the main menu and list of compressed drives.

Changing the Size of a Compressed Drive

You may find at some point that you want to change the size of your compressed volumes. If a compressed volume begins to fill up, and you still have free space on the uncompressed host drive, you may want to increase the size of a compressed volume so that you can store more data on it. If, however, you need more room on the uncompressed host drive, you may want to make a compressed volume smaller to create more free space on the host drive. You may, for example, decide to create or enlarge a Windows permanent swap file, which must be stored on an uncompressed drive. If so, you may need to make more space available on the uncompressed drive by changing the size of a compressed volume.

Normally, you should be able to make a compressed volume file smaller by approximately half as much free space as is on the compressed volume—depending on the estimated compression ratio. If, for example, a compressed volume has about 20M free and has an estimated compression ratio of 2:1, you should be able to reduce the physical size of the compressed volume file by about 10M.

Sometimes, however, even if the compressed volume contains sufficient free space on it, DoubleSpace does not permit you to make the compressed volume file any smaller. This happens because most of the free space on the compressed volume is near the beginning. The files at the end of the compressed volume prevent DoubleSpace from making the compressed volume file any smaller. You also may have difficulty making a compressed volume larger, even if free space is on the uncompressed drive. You may even receive an error message to the effect that the drive is too fragmented to resize. The solution to both these problems is to use the various defragmenting utilities provided with DOS and DoubleSpace. (Refer to Chapter 7, "Troubleshooting DoubleSpace," for more information.)

Normally, however, you can easily change the size of a compressed drive, either from the DOS prompt or by using the DoubleSpace menus.

Fig. 6.9

The DoubleSpace screen for changing the estimated compression ratio.

Changing Drive Size from the DOS Prompt

You can use command line switches with the DBLSPACE command to change the size of a compressed drive. The DoubleSpace command line switches used to change the size of a compressed drive take one of the following three forms:

DBLSPACE /SIZE=*n.nn d*:
DBLSPACE /SIZE /RESERVE=*n.nn d*:
DBLSPACE /SIZE *d*:

In these syntax examples, *d* stands for the letter of the compressed drive the size of which you want to change; *n.nn* stands for a number of megabytes. If you omit the drive letter, the size of the current drive—if it is a compressed volume—is changed.

In the first example of the syntax used for the /SIZE switches, the specified compressed drive has its compressed volume file changed to match the specified size in megabytes. The value you specify is the physical size of the compressed volume file. The following command, for example, changes the size of the compressed volume file for drive C to 60M in size. (If the compression ratio is 2:1, this is 120M on the compressed drive.)

DBLSPACE /SIZE=60 C:

In the second form of the /SIZE switches, the /RESERVE switch is added. You use the /RESERVE switch to determine the new size of the compressed volume file by telling DoubleSpace how much free space on the uncompressed drive you want to keep. The following command, for example, changes the size of the compressed volume file for drive D by reserving 10M of space on the uncompressed host drive:

DBLSPACE /SIZE /RESERVE=10 D:

In this example, if the host drive for compressed volume D has a physical capacity of 40M, 10M of space—in addition to the space required by any files on the uncompressed drive—is reserved, leaving approximately 30M available for the compressed volume. The compressed volume's new size of 30M produces a 60M compressed volume (if the estimated compression ratio is 2:1).

The third and final form of the /SIZE switch has a special purpose. It causes DoubleSpace to make the compressed volume file as small as possible. The following command, for example changes the size of drive D, making the compressed volume file as small as possible:

DBLSPACE /SIZE D:

The amount of free space remaining on the compressed drive varies, depending on the amount of free space originally on the compressed volume and its location. If most of the compressed volume's free space is near the beginning of the compressed volume file, the compressed volume file may not be very much smaller after you issue the preceding command than it was originally. If most of the free space is near the end of the compressed volume file, however, the compressed volume may have only about 1K left on it.

Changing Drive Size by Using the DoubleSpace Menus

To change the size of a compressed volume by using the DoubleSpace menus, follow these steps:

The /SIZE switch is another of DoubleSpace's special cases concerning the minimum amount of space you can reserve. If used with the /SIZE switch, the /RESERVE switch enables you to reserve 0M on the uncompressed host drive. This leaves only about 1K of uncompressed space on the host drive. Use /RESERVE=0 to make a compressed volume as large as possible.

1. If necessary, start the DoubleSpace program by typing **DBLSPACE** at the DOS prompt and pressing Enter. The DoubleSpace utility starts and displays the main menu and its list of compressed drives (refer to fig. 6.1).
2. Highlight the drive the size of which you want to change.
3. From the **D**rive menu, choose Change **S**ize. DoubleSpace displays the Change Size dialog box, as shown in figure 6.10.
4. To make the compressed volume larger, type a number smaller than the current free space of the uncompressed drive in the New Free Space text box. DoubleSpace does not accept a number smaller than the minimum free space for the uncompressed drive.

    To make the compressed volume smaller, type a number larger than the current free space of the uncompressed drive in the New Free Space text box. DoubleSpace does not accept a number larger than the maximum free space for the uncompressed drive.
5. Choose **OK** after you are satisfied with the new amount of free space for the uncompressed drive. DoubleSpace closes the Change Size dialog box and displays a status message as it changes the compressed drive's size.

DoubleSpace changes the size of the compressed volume you selected and remounts it. DoubleSpace then returns to the main menu.

Deleting a Compressed Drive

> If you delete a compressed volume, you also delete all files stored on the compressed volume. After a compressed volume has been deleted, no way exists to recover the individual files on the compressed volume. In some cases, however, it may be possible to recover the compressed volume file. Refer to Chapter 7, "Troubleshooting DoubleSpace," for information on recovering a deleted compressed volume file.

You may occasionally decide that you no longer need a particular compressed volume. Be very careful, however, if you do decide to delete one of your compressed volumes. Deleting a compressed drive also deletes all the information on the drive. If you have any doubts about whether you need any of the information on the compressed drive, run a backup before deleting the drive.

You can delete a compressed drive either from the DOS prompt or through the DoubleSpace menus.

Deleting a Compressed Drive from the DOS Prompt

As is possible with all the other DoubleSpace utility functions, you can delete a compressed volume from the DOS prompt by using DoubleSpace command line switches. Only one command line switch exists for deleting a compressed volume. The syntax used for the command to delete a compressed volume is as follows:

> **DBLSPACE /DELETE *d*:**

The *d* stands for the drive letter of the compressed drive you want to delete. If, for example, you want to delete the compressed drive G, you use the following command:

DBLSPACE /DELETE G:

DoubleSpace displays the following message, asking that you confirm your command to delete the compressed volume:

```
Deleting drive G will permanently erase it and all the files it contains.
Are you sure you want to delete drive G?
```

If you are certain you want to delete the compressed volume, press **Y**. DoubleSpace immediately begins to delete the compressed drive. If you are not certain you want to delete the compressed volume, press **N**. DoubleSpace returns you to the DOS prompt without performing any further actions.

DoubleSpace does not permit you to delete your start-up drive (the disk drive DOS uses to load itself into memory).

Deleting a Compressed Drive by Using the DoubleSpace Menus

To delete a compressed volume by using the DoubleSpace menus, follow these steps:

1. If necessary, start DoubleSpace by typing **DBLSPACE** at the DOS prompt and pressing Enter. The DoubleSpace utility starts and displays the main menu and its list of compressed drives (refer to fig. 6.1).
2. Highlight in the list of compressed drives the compressed drive you want to delete.
3. From the **D**rive menu, choose **D**elete. DoubleSpace displays the Delete a Compressed Drive dialog box, as shown in figure 6.11.

    The Delete a Compressed Drive dialog box lists the drive letter of the compressed volume you selected for deletion and cautions you that deleting it permanently erases the drive and any data it contains.
4. Carefully check the drive letter displayed in the Delete a Compressed Drive dialog box; make sure that it is the correct drive letter for the compressed volume you want to delete.
5. Choose **OK** to confirm deleting the compressed volume. If you change your mind, choose **C**ancel.

    DoubleSpace now requests a second confirmation to delete the compressed volume by displaying a Delete Confirmation dialog box.
6. To confirm that you really do want to delete the compressed volume, choose **Y**es. If you change your mind, choose **N**o. DoubleSpace returns to the main menu.

    If your start-up (boot) disk drive is compressed, DoubleSpace does not permit you to delete that compressed volume. If you attempt to delete the compressed volume that is your start-up disk, DoubleSpace displays an error dialog box. Choose **OK** to clear this error dialog box and return to the DoubleSpace main menu.

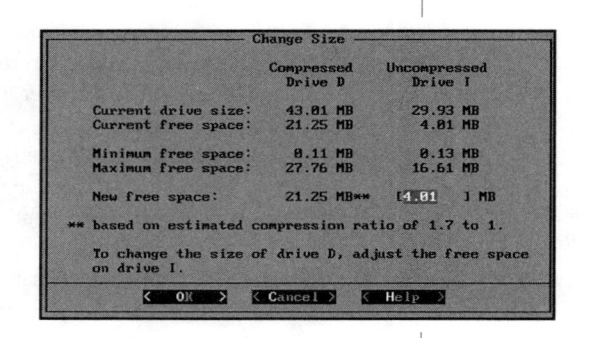

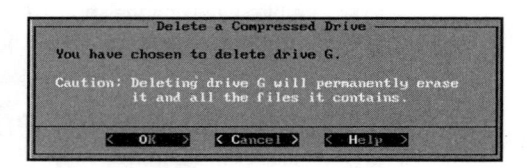

Fig. 6.10, top

The Change Size dialog box.

Fig. 6.11, bottom

The Delete a Compressed Drive dialog box.

After you confirm the deletion of the compressed volume a second time, DoubleSpace deletes the compressed volume file and returns you to the main menu and list of compressed drives. The drive you deleted is no longer shown in the list of compressed drives.

Defragmenting a Compressed Drive

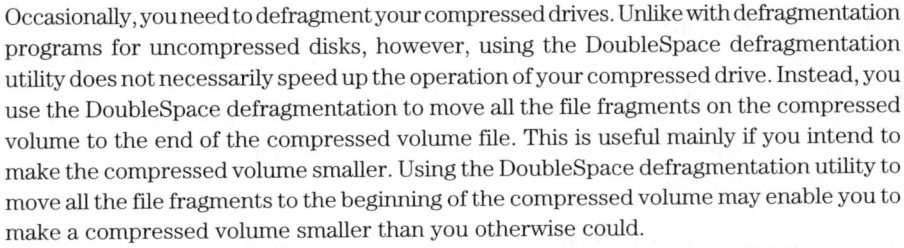

Occasionally, you need to defragment your compressed drives. Unlike with defragmentation programs for uncompressed disks, however, using the DoubleSpace defragmentation utility does not necessarily speed up the operation of your compressed drive. Instead, you use the DoubleSpace defragmentation to move all the file fragments on the compressed volume to the end of the compressed volume file. This is useful mainly if you intend to make the compressed volume smaller. Using the DoubleSpace defragmentation utility to move all the file fragments to the beginning of the compressed volume may enable you to make a compressed volume smaller than you otherwise could.

You can run the DoubleSpace defragmentation utility from either the DOS prompt or by using the DoubleSpace menus.

Defragmenting a compressed volume may take from several minutes to several hours, depending on how many files are on the compressed drive and how badly the files are fragmented. DoubleSpace does not provide any estimates on how long the defragmentation may take. You may want to use the DoubleSpace defragmentation utility only at the end of a work day or on a Friday evening so that you are not inconvenienced by a long defragmentation process. If necessary, you can interrupt the defragmentation process to can use your computer for some other task.

If you use the DOS DEFRAG program on a DoubleSpace compressed drive, DEFRAG recognizes that the drive is compressed by DoubleSpace and runs the DoubleSpace defragmentation utility after performing the defragmentation at the DOS level. Refer to your DOS documentation for more information about the DEFRAG utility.

Defragmenting a Drive from the DOS Prompt

You use two command line switches to defragment a compressed volume. The syntax used to defragment a compressed volume is as follows:

DBLSPACE /DEFRAGMENT /F *d*:

The /F switch is optional; it causes DoubleSpace to fully defragment the compressed volume. Without the /F switch, DoubleSpace defragments the drive but may leave some areas of free space between the files on the compressed volume. If you use the /F switch, DoubleSpace defragments all the files and moves them to the end of the compressed volume so that all the free space on the compressed volume is in one contiguous area at beginning the of the compressed volume.

The *d* stands for the drive letter of the compressed drive you want to defragment. If you omit the drive letter specification, DoubleSpace defragments the current drive. If, for example, you want to defragment the compressed drive C, use the following command:

DBLSPACE /DEFRAGMENT C:

In this command, DoubleSpace moves the clusters on the compressed volume so that each file's clusters are contiguous. Some free space may be left between the files on the compressed volume, however.

To fully defragment a drive, add the /F switch. The following example defragments compressed volume D and arranges the clusters on the compressed volume so that the clusters for each file are contiguous and all the files are moved to the end of the compressed volume file:

DBLSPACE /DEFRAGMENT /F D:

As DoubleSpace defragments your compressed volume, it displays a simple progress report showing the percentage of completion. After DoubleSpace finishes defragmenting the compressed volume, it remounts the compressed volume and displays a message indicating that it is done. If you need to interrupt the defragmentation process, press Esc. DoubleSpace displays a message asking for confirmation to interrupt the defragmenting process. Press **Y** to stop defragmenting, or press **N** to continue defragmenting.

If you interrupt the defragmenting, no harm is done, but your compressed volume is not completely defragmented. DoubleSpace restarts the defragmenting process from the beginning the next time you defragment your drive.

Defragmenting a Drive by Using the DoubleSpace Menus

To defragment a compressed volume by using the DoubleSpace menus, follow these steps:

1. If necessary, start DoubleSpace by typing **DBLSPACE** at the DOS prompt, and pressing Enter. The DoubleSpace utility starts and displays the main menu and its list of compressed drives (refer to fig. 6.1).
2. Highlight in the list of compressed drives the compressed drive you want to defragment.
3. From the **T**ools menu, choose **D**efragment. DoubleSpace displays the Defragment dialog box, as shown in figure 6.12.
    The Defragment dialog box lists the drive letter of the compressed volume you selected and offers a brief explanation of what defragmenting does.
4. To confirm that you want to defragment the compressed volume, choose **Y**es. If you change your mind, choose **N**o. DoubleSpace returns to the main menu.
    DoubleSpace displays a progress report as it defragments the drive.

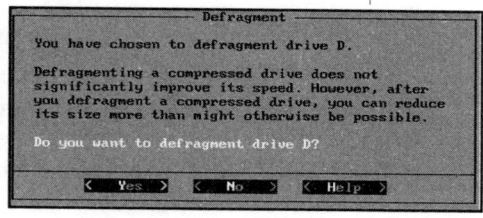

Fig. 6.12

The DoubleSpace Defragment dialog box.

If you need to interrupt DoubleSpace at any time while it is defragmenting a compressed volume, press Esc. DoubleSpace displays a dialog box asking you to confirm the interruption of the defragmenting process. To stop defragmenting the compressed drive, choose **C**ancel. To continue defragmenting the compressed drive, choose **R**etry.

After DoubleSpace finishes defragmenting the compressed volume, it remounts the compressed volume and returns to the main menu.

Checking the Integrity of a Compressed Drive

Periodically checking the logical integrity of your disk drives is always a good idea, whether or not they are compressed. Checking the logical integrity of a drive ensures that all the clusters on the drive are correctly allocated and accounted for and that all the file chains on the disk are intact and correctly linked. Just as you use the DOS CHKDSK command to check the integrity of an uncompressed disk, you use DoubleSpace CHKDSK to check the integrity of DoubleSpace drives.

For some operations (such as changing the size of a compressed drive), using both DOS and DoubleSpace CHKDSK utilities is necessary to ensure that no problems exist on the compressed drive before you perform the operation. If problems do exist on the compressed drive, you must correct them as soon as possible; otherwise, you risk losing data.

Using the DOS CHKDSK and the DoubleSpace CHKDSK utilities to solve specific problems is discussed in Chapter 7, "Troubleshooting DoubleSpace." This section describes how to operate the DoubleSpace CHKDSK utility and how to use it so that it attempts to correct any problems it finds.

The DoubleSpace CHKDSK utility is designed to identify two types of problems: *lost clusters* and *cross-linked files*. Repairing lost clusters is explained in the following section, along with instructions for starting the DoubleSpace CHKDSK utility. Repairing cross-linked files is described in Chapter 7, "Troubleshooting DoubleSpace."

Whenever you use DOS CHKDSK on a DoubleSpace compressed drive, DOS CHKDSK automatically recognizes the compressed drive and runs DoubleSpace CHKDSK after it finishes.

Keep in mind that DoubleSpace CHKDSK may detect problems on a compressed drive that are not detected by DOS CHKDSK. This is why DOS CHKDSK automatically runs DoubleSpace CHKDSK. Just because DOS CHKDSK and DoubleSpace CHKDSK do not find any problems on the compressed volume, however, do not assume that no problems exist on the uncompressed host drive. Use DOS CHKDSK on the uncompressed host drive to check its integrity, too.

Using DoubleSpace CHKDSK from the DOS Prompt

You use two command line switches to check the integrity of a compressed volume. The syntax used to start DoubleSpace CHKDSK for a compressed volume is as follows:

DBLSPACE /CHKDSK /F *d*:

The /F switch is optional; it causes DoubleSpace to fix any lost clusters it finds on the compressed volume. Without the /F switch, DoubleSpace reports the errors it finds but does not repair them. If you use the /F switch, DoubleSpace repairs any lost clusters it finds and reports all errors.

The *d* in the syntax example stands for the letter of the compressed drive you want to check. If you omit the drive letter specification, DoubleSpace checks the current drive. If, for example, you want to check compressed drive D, use the following command:

DBLSPACE /CHKDSK D:

In this command, DoubleSpace checks for lost clusters, cross-linked files, and any other errors on compressed volume C. The /F switch is not included, so these errors are only reported.

If DoubleSpace finds any errors on the compressed volume it is checking, it displays a report similar to the one shown in figure 6.13. The report lists the number of lost clusters, cross-linked files, or other problems that DoubleSpace CHKDSK found.

To instruct DoubleSpace to repair any lost clusters it finds as it checks your compressed volume, include the /F switch. To check the integrity of compressed volume D, for example, and to have DoubleSpace fix any lost clusters it finds, you use the following command:

DBLSPACE /CHKDSK /F D:

This command produces the same report as that of the example in figure 6.13, but the lost clusters are repaired.

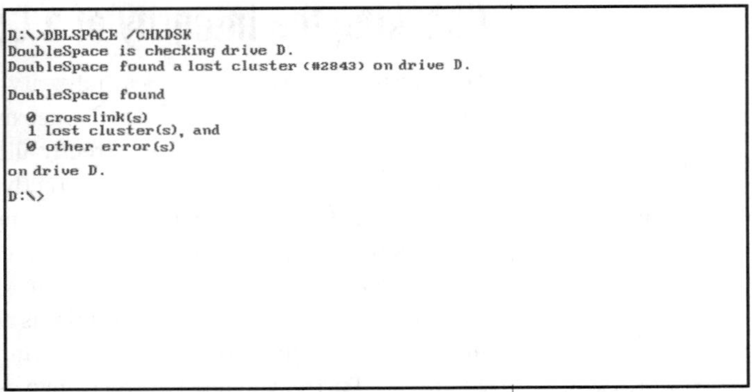

```
D:\>DBLSPACE /CHKDSK
DoubleSpace is checking drive D.
DoubleSpace found a lost cluster (#2843) on drive D.

DoubleSpace found
  0 crosslink(s)
  1 lost cluster(s), and
  0 other error(s)
on drive D.
D:\>
```

Fig. 6.13

DoubleSpace CHKDSK's error report.

Running DoubleSpace CHKDSK by Using the DoubleSpace Menus

To start the DoubleSpace CHKDSK utility from the DoubleSpace menus, follow these steps:

1. If necessary, start DoubleSpace by typing **DBLSPACE** at the DOS prompt and pressing Enter. The DoubleSpace utility starts and displays the main menu and its list of compressed drives (refer to fig. 6.1).
2. Highlight in the list of compressed drives the compressed drive you want to check.
3. From the **T**ools menu, choose **C**hkdsk. DoubleSpace displays the Chkdsk dialog box, as shown in figure 6.14.

    The Chkdsk dialog box lists the drive letter of the compressed volume you selected to check and enables you to choose whether DoubleSpace repairs any lost clusters it finds.
4. To instruct DoubleSpace to check the selected compressed volume and fix any errors it can, choose **F**ix. DoubleSpace begins checking your compressed drive. To instruct DoubleSpace check the selected compressed volume and display a report only, choose **Ch**eck. If you change your mind about checking the drive, choose **C**ancel.

    DoubleSpace displays a status message as it checks the drive. After DoubleSpace finishes checking the drive, it displays another dialog box showing the results of the check. If DoubleSpace found no errors, the dialog box simply contains a message to that effect. If DoubleSpace does find errors, however, it displays a dialog box similar to the one shown in figure 6.15. In this example, no cross-linked files were found, one lost cluster was found, and no other errors were detected.

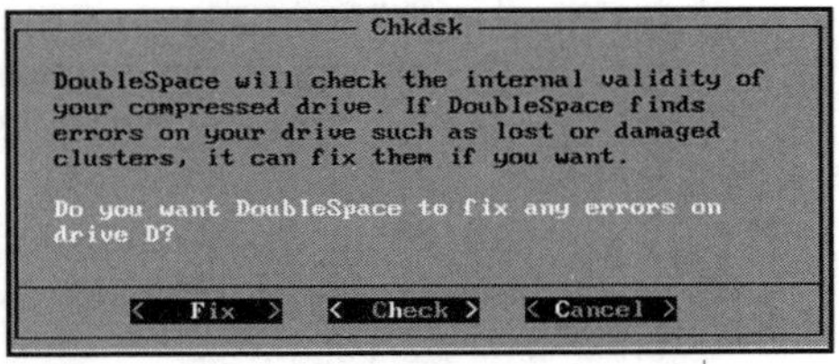

    If you chose **F**ix, DoubleSpace has repaired the lost cluster errors; you need take no further action. For information on repairing cross-linked files, refer to Chapter 7, "Troubleshooting DoubleSpace."
5. Choose **OK**. DoubleSpace returns to the main menu.

Fig. 6.14

The DoubleSpace Chkdsk dialog box.

Formatting a Compressed Drive

In general, you never need to format a compressed volume. Although you need to format physical disks before you can use them with DOS, you need not format a compressed volume before you can use it. You normally format a compressed volume only to make sure that no confidential data remains on the drive.

You must format a physical disk to create the logical structures DOS uses to access the disk (such as the FAT and the root directory). As DoubleSpace creates a compressed volume, however, it also creates the internal logical structures of the compressed volume so that a separate formatting operation is not necessary. Formatting a compressed volume manually merely writes a regular pattern of bytes over the entire compressed volume. This erases all the data on the compressed volume and writes over any data formerly on the used or unused portions of the compressed volume file.

You can format a compressed volume either from the DOS prompt or by using the DoubleSpace menus.

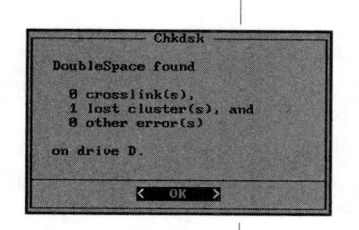

Fig. 6.15

The DoubleSpace Chkdsk dialog box for reporting errors.

Formatting a Compressed Drive from the DOS Prompt

Formatting a compressed drive from the DOS prompt is easy. The syntax used for the DoubleSpace command line switch is as follows:

DBLSPACE /FORMAT *d*:

In this syntax, *d* stands for the drive letter of the compressed volume you want to format. DoubleSpace asks for confirmation before actually formatting the drive. If you are formatting drive G, for example, DoubleSpace displays this message:

```
Formatting drive G will permanently erase all the files it contains.
Are you sure you want to format drive G?
```

To go ahead and format the compressed drive, press **Y**. DoubleSpace formats the compressed drive. If you change your mind about formatting the compressed volume, press **N**.

Because formatting your compressed start-up disk prevents you from restarting your computer, DoubleSpace does not permit you to format your start-up disk. If you specify the start-up disk, DoubleSpace displays the following error message:

```
Drive C is your startup disk drive and should not be formatted.
```

Formatting a compressed volume permanently deletes all files on the drive. If you format a compressed volume, no way exists to recover any of its files.

Formatting a Compressed Drive by Using the DoubleSpace Menus

To format a compressed volume by using the DoubleSpace menus, follow these steps:

1. If necessary, start DoubleSpace by typing **DBLSPACE** at the DOS prompt, and pressing Enter. The DoubleSpace utility starts and displays the main menu and its list of compressed drives (refer to fig. 6.1).

2. Highlight in the list of compressed drives the compressed drive you want to format.
3. From the **D**rive menu, choose **F**ormat. DoubleSpace displays the Format a Compressed Drive dialog box, as shown in figure 6.16.

    The Format a Compressed Drive dialog box lists the drive letter of the compressed volume you selected to format and cautions you that formatting the compressed drive permanently erases any data it contains.
4. Check the drive letter displayed in the dialog box carefully to make sure that it is the correct drive letter.
5. To confirm that you want to format the compressed volume, choose **OK**. DoubleSpace displays a second dialog box asking for a second confirmation to format the compressed volume.
6. To confirm that you really do want to format the compressed volume, choose **Y**es. If you change your mind about formatting the compressed volume, choose **N**o.

    DoubleSpace does not permit you to format your start-up disk drive (if it is compressed). If you attempt to format a compressed start-up disk, DoubleSpace displays an error dialog box. Choose **OK** to clear the error dialog box and return to the DoubleSpace main menu.

After you confirm the format of the compressed volume a second time, DoubleSpace formats the compressed volume file and returns you to the main menu and list of compressed drives.

If you format a compressed volume, all files on the compressed volume are erased. After a compressed volume is formatted, no way exists to recover the files on the compressed volume.

Summary

In this chapter, you learned why and how to use the DoubleSpace utilities to perform a variety of tasks. You learned how to compress an existing disk drive, and how to create a new compressed drive from free space on an uncompressed drive. This chapter showed you how to change the size of a compressed drive, delete a compressed drive, and format a compressed drive. The chapter also explained how to defragment a compressed drive. Most important, you learned how to use the DoubleSpace CHKDSK utility to test the integrity of your DoubleSpace compressed drives.

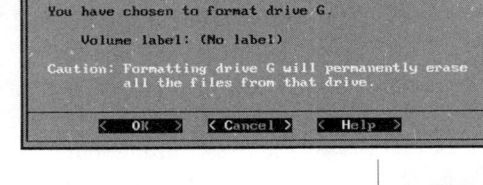

The next chapter deals with solving specific problems you may encounter while using DoubleSpace. Many of the techniques in the next chapter refer you to this chapter for instructions on using the utilities.

Fig. 6.16

The Format a Compressed Drive dialog box.

CHAPTER 7

Troubleshooting DoubleSpace

In this chapter, you learn the causes of and solutions for many problems DoubleSpace users encounter. The chapter begins with a discussion of measures you can take to prevent common errors and then explores some of the most common problems you may encounter—as well as some that are more rare.

Preventing Problems

The best way to solve problems is to prevent them. You can take several actions to prevent the most common problems that occur with DoubleSpace. A few of these actions can save you from severe data loss or the corruption of your compressed volume files.

Memory Manager and Upper Memory Conflicts

Conflict with device drivers and programs in upper memory can cause a variety of problems, from relatively harmless disk read errors to corrupted data files or even a corrupted compressed volume file. By giving up memory needed only for loading, or by taking over more memory for data, device drivers and TSR programs often change their size. Thus DOS cannot always tell whether a program or device driver can fit into upper memory. Occasionally, programs in upper memory inadvertently use memory locations that overlap. If overlap occurs, each program can corrupt the other's data or program instructions.

Corrupted data in memory results in corrupted data in your disk files. If corrupted data is part of the disk's File Allocation Table, serious data loss may result. If overlap results in corrupted program instructions, your computer can stop operating or may operate erratically, requiring you to restart it. Restarting your computer while programs run can often result in lost clusters on your disk.

Memory manager programs usually provide command line switches that enable you to explicitly include or exclude areas of upper memory. If you include an area of memory already in use by a hardware device, any program or data the memory manager places in that memory area also is likely to be corrupted.

To prevent programs from conflicting with each other or from being corrupted by incorrect inclusions with your memory manager, follow these guidelines:

- *Update your memory manager configuration whenever your system changes.* Whenever you install a new device driver or a new piece of hardware, run your memory manager's configuration program again. By rerunning its configuration program—such as DOS MEMMAKER or QEMM's Optimize—you ensure that your memory manager is adjusted to the system revisions. If you add a new video board to your computer, for example, and you use HIMEM.SYS and EMM386 (supplied with DOS) as your memory managers, run the DOS MEMMAKER utility. Consult the documentation supplied with your memory management software for information about its configuration program and how to use it.
- *Use conservative settings.* The more aggressively you configure your memory manager to use all the nooks and crannies of upper memory, the more likely you are to inadvertently create a situation in which programs using upper memory interfere with each other or with your computer's hardware. If you use the DOS MEMMAKER utility, for example, do not use its aggressive scanning at first. If you use EMM386 and suspect problems caused by memory conflicts, do not use the HIGHSCAN switch. Refer to your DOS documentation for more information about MEMMAKER and about EMM386.
- *Add only one device driver or program to upper memory at a time.* Load a single device driver into upper memory and then use your system for a while to make sure that everything operates correctly. If you do not experience any difficulties, add the next device driver or program to upper memory, and so on.

For more details on configuring your specific memory manager, refer to your DOS documentation and the documentation provided with your memory management program.

STACKS Statement in CONFIG.SYS

DOS provides a command for use in your CONFIG.SYS file to tell DOS how much memory to allocate for stacks. (A *stack* is an area of memory set aside for use by DOS or other programs as a temporary working area.) The STACKS= command in CONFIG.SYS tells DOS how many stacks to create and the number of bytes to allot each stack.

If DOS or a device driver attached to DOS needs a stack to perform a requested service, DOS usually exchanges the current stack for a new stack, leaving the contents of the original stack unaffected. After DOS or the device driver has completed the requested service, DOS restores the original stack that was in use at the time the service request was performed. Whatever program was running before the service request now continues with its original stack as if it had never been interrupted. Because specific services are often performed by different layers of software (refer to Chapter 1), several different parts of DOS and/or a device driver may need space on a stack at the same time.

The line containing the STACKS command in CONFIG.SYS is usually similar to the following, although the numbers may differ:

```
STACKS=9,256
```

Because the number and size of the stacks you allocate affects how much memory DOS uses, some computers are configured to include the following statement in the CONFIG.SYS file:

```
STACKS=0,0
```

The preceding statement tells DOS not to reserve any memory for stacks. With the number and size of the stacks set to zero, DOS does not exchange stacks whenever a new working space is needed. Instead, DOS permits the service that needs the working space to use the current stack.

If all the service requests in your computer use the same working stack, the stack may grow too large and the information in the stack may overwrite or corrupt other information in memory. If the information that is overwritten or corrupted includes the disk's File Allocation Table or other data waiting to be written to the disk, a damaged file or corrupted compressed volume can result. To avoid this problem, examine your CONFIG.SYS file. If the file contains a STACKS=0,0 command, remove it. You can replace STACKS=0,0 with the standard STACKS=9,256 or remove the STACKS= command entirely. Refer to your DOS documentation for more information on CONFIG.SYS and the STACKS command.

Write-Delay Disk Cache

A disk cache program with a write-delay cache may cause some of the greatest problems with DoubleSpace. Many difficulties users experience with corrupted data or corrupted compressed volume files are traceable to a write-delay cache program. You can learn more about disk cache programs in Chapter 1, "Understanding and Using Disk Compression," and Chapter 4, "Configuring and Optimizing DoubleSpace." As described in these chapters, a write-delay cache involves holding some disk data in memory before physically writing it to the disk to speed up your computer's disk operations. DoubleSpace requires you to use Microsoft's SMARTDRV version 4.1 (supplied with DOS 6), which uses a write-delay cache.

Some specific problems occur with write-delay cache programs. If your computer experiences a power failure, if you turn the computer off, or if the computer is restarted by using its Reset switch, any data in the cache that has not been written to the disk is lost. The result may be lost clusters, lost or damaged files, or a corrupted compressed volume file.

Among the first things novice users learn is that turning off the computer while the cursor is at the DOS prompt is safe. This statement usually is true—but not if a write-delay cache is in use. Unwritten data still can be in the cache, even if the DOS prompt is visible.

Although SMARTDRV writes the write-delay data to disk after about five seconds of inactivity, a vulnerable period still exists after the DOS prompt is visible but before the data is written to the disk. Thus you may think turning off the computer is safe when, in fact, turning off the computer results in data loss.

To avoid problems caused by cache programs that use a write-delay cache, take one of the following approaches:

- *Disable the write-delay cache.* This approach is the most highly recommended. Disable write-delay caching for the host drives of your compressed volumes, because they are more likely to be severely affected by a write-delay cache problem. Follow the instructions in Chapter 4, "Configuring and Optimizing DoubleSpace," to disable write-delay caching with SMARTDRV. Read caching is still active even if write-delay caching is turned off, so you still obtain a speed benefit from using the cache program.
- *Clear the cache buffers before turning the computer off.* SMARTDRV provides a command line switch that forces it to write to disk any data currently held in memory. Use the following command to force SMARTDRV to clear the write-delay cache:

    SMARTDRV /C

    After the cache is cleared, you can safely turn off the computer.
- *Wait before turning off your computer.* Make sure that you wait at the DOS prompt a couple minutes before turning off your computer. Waiting gives the cache program time to write data to the disk. Most write-delay cache programs clear the write cache after a period of inactivity.

Other Precautions

In general, never use software that rearranges the data in a compressed volume unless the program is compatible with DoubleSpace. This restriction includes almost all disk repair and optimization utilities, such as Norton Disk Doctor and Central Point PC Tools. Check with your vendor or the publisher of your utility to determine whether your utilities are compatible with DoubleSpace.

In particular, never use the SETVER program to enable a disk or any other system utility that reports whether you are using an incorrect DOS version. Doing so invites disaster; if the disk utility is incompatible with your version of DOS, using it is likely to result in lost data and corrupted disks. Refer to your DOS documentation for more information on the SETVER program.

Passive disk utilities, such as surface scan utilities, are safe to use, however, because they read data from the disk without changing or moving the data.

For the cache-clearing technique to be successful, you must always clear the write-delay cache yourself or clear it through a DOS batch file. If you forget and turn your computer off before the write-delay cache writes to the disk, you can lose data.

If you load Windows, the DOS Shell, or another shell program from your AUTOEXEC.BAT file, add the SMARTDRV /C command to AUTOEXEC.BAT after the line that calls Windows or the shell program. If the last line in your AUTOEXEC.BAT starts Windows, for example, add the SMARTDRV /C command to the next line, so that it appears as in the following example:

    WIN
    SMARTDRV /C

With this line in your AUTOEXEC.BAT file, the SMARTDRV write-delay cache automatically clears after you exit Windows or your shell program. You now can turn your computer off right away.

Solving Drive Letter Problems

Occasionally, you may experience difficulty with some of DoubleSpace's drive letter assignments. Drive letter problems are most likely to occur immediately after you install DoubleSpace, add a network, or add additional disk drives to your computer system.

Local Drive Letter Problems

If you use a RAM disk or a disk drive that requires a device driver loaded in CONFIG.SYS, you may notice that your drives are assigned unusual drive letters. If so, check your CONFIG.SYS file for a line that refers to DBLSPACE.SYS. If you find such a line, make sure that it comes after those of any other device drivers that make disk drives available to DOS. Chapter 4, "Configuring and Optimizing DoubleSpace," describes DBLSPACE.SYS and the use of RAM disks with DoubleSpace.

If the DBLSPACE.SYS line in CONFIG.SYS already comes after those of all other device drivers that make disk drives available to DOS, you may need to change the DBLSPACE.INI file to alter how DoubleSpace assigns drive letters. Chapter 4 also explains how to edit DBLSPACE.INI.

Edit the DBLSPACE.INI file very carefully. If you make a mistake while altering DBLSPACE.INI, you can make your compressed volumes inaccessible.

Network Drive Letter Problems

Problems with network drive letters generally occur only if you already have a network and you install DoubleSpace while the network is not running. If you install DoubleSpace with the network running, DoubleSpace tries to accommodate the network drives, leaving those drive letters available.

To resolve problems with network drive letters, try one of the following solutions:
- *Change the network drive letter.* If possible, change the drive letter you use for the network drive.
- *Change how DoubleSpace assigns drive letters.* If changing the network drive letter is inconvenient, you can edit the DBLSPACE.INI file to change the drive letters DoubleSpace uses. Editing DBLSPACE.INI is described in Chapter 4.
  You may be able to make the usual network drive letter, F, available by shifting the entire group of drive letters that DoubleSpace uses upward by several letters. Remember to change the host drive letters so that they remain within the range of drive letters reserved by DoubleSpace.

Solving Windows Swap File Problems

If you use Windows, you already know that a swap file enables Windows to work much faster. (Programs use a *swap file* on a hard disk to store data from the computer's memory. Programs access data in the swap file as if the swap file is actually part of the computer's memory.) Windows enables you to set up either temporary or permanent swap files, but you can use only one type at a time.

The *temporary swap file* uses regular DOS file services. You can put a temporary swap file on any disk, whether compressed or uncompressed. Windows provides better performance, however, if the temporary swap file is on an uncompressed disk, because the data in the temporary swap file does not compress well and the compression time may slow Windows down. Although temporary Windows swap files pose no problems for your DoubleSpace compressed drives, the Windows *permanent swap file* does not work correctly if installed on a compressed drive. Windows does not use DOS disk services to manipulate the permanent swap file. For maximum speed, Windows instead uses BIOS services to access the permanent swap file or directly accesses the disk hardware itself. Because Windows bypasses DOS to access its permanent swap file, it also bypasses the DoubleSpace device driver. The Windows permanent swap file is therefore incompatible with a compressed drive and must be placed on an uncompressed drive.

You need not worry about problems with the Windows permanent swap file when you install DoubleSpace. If Windows is already installed on your computer before you add DoubleSpace, and you use a permanent swap file, DoubleSpace automatically moves the permanent swap file to an uncompressed drive. DoubleSpace also changes the Windows configuration information so that Windows uses the new uncompressed drive letter to search for the permanent swap file. If you install Windows after you install DoubleSpace, however, or you later change your swap file configuration, you may inadvertently install the permanent swap file on a compressed volume. If so, the next time you start Windows, a message appears indicating that the permanent swap file is corrupted.

If Windows cannot find the temporary or permanent swap file, the DoubleSpace drive letter assignments for your uncompressed host drives have probably changed. This change usually occurs after you edit the DBLSPACE.INI file to change DoubleSpace's drive letter assignments or after you add another disk drive to your computer. To correct this problem, follow these steps:

1. If Windows displays the message that it cannot open the swap file, press any key to continue. Windows should finish loading.
2. After Windows finishes loading, exit immediately.
3. Use the DBLSPACE /LIST command (described in Chapter 5, "Using DoubleSpace") to determine which drives are uncompressed. Notice which uncompressed drive has enough room for your temporary or permanent swap file.
4. Restart Windows. You may again see the message that Windows cannot open the swap file. Press any key to continue; Windows should finish loading.
5. After Windows is loaded, use the Control Panel to change the swap file location to match the drive letter you determined in Step 3. Refer to your Windows documentation for information on using the Windows Control Panel and setting Virtual Memory options.

If Windows reports that your permanent swap file is corrupted, you probably inadvertently configured Windows to put a permanent swap file on a compressed volume. To correct this problem, follow these steps:

1. After Windows displays the message that the permanent swap file is corrupted and asks whether you want to delete the permanent swap file, press **Y** to answer **Y**es. Windows should finish loading into memory.

> **NOTE:**
> If you use Windows with a permanent or temporary swap file, you may receive an error message from Windows after you change the DoubleSpace drive letter assignments. Windows may report that it cannot open the swap file or that the permanent swap file is corrupted. These messages simply mean that the disk drive on which Windows was configured to use a swap file now has a different drive letter. If necessary, follow the procedures in this section.

2. After Windows finishes loading, exit immediately.
3. Use the DBLSPACE /LIST command (described in Chapter 5) to determine which drives are uncompressed. Notice which uncompressed drive has enough room for your temporary or permanent swap file.
4. Restart Windows. The message that the permanent swap file is corrupted may appear again. Press **Y** to answer **Y**es to delete the permanent swap file. Windows should finish loading into memory.
5. After Windows is loaded, use the Windows Control Panel to change the permanent swap file location.
6. After Windows asks if you want the corrupted permanent swap file set to zero length, press **Y** to answer **Y**es.

    If your corrupted permanent swap file results from a change in DoubleSpace drive letters, Windows may report that it has found a permanent swap file not created by your Windows installation.
7. After Windows asks if this permanent swap file should be deleted, press **Y** to answer **Y**es.
8. You can now set the permanent swap file location to the uncompressed drive letter you determined in Step 3. Refer to your Windows documentation for information on using the Windows Control Panel and setting Virtual Memory options.

Examining Lost Clusters

A *lost cluster*, or *lost allocation unit*, is any disk cluster that is marked as in use but is not actually part of a file chain legitimately connected to an entry in your disk's file directory. Lost clusters usually do not cause problems. They do, however, occupy disk space, because the cluster is marked as in use and is not available to store new data. The only way to detect lost clusters is to use the DOS CHKDSK or DoubleSpace CHKDSK utilities.

What Causes Lost Clusters?

Lost clusters result from several causes. Usually, lost clusters result from power failures or from restarting your computer before all information in a file is written to disk. Lost clusters also result from incorrect use of disk optimization utilities on compressed volumes and from the use of incompatible versions of optimization or repair utilities on compressed volumes. Using a version of Norton Utilities prior to version 7 to defragment a compressed volume, for example, usually results in a large number of lost clusters on the compressed volume, particularly if the Clear Space option is used. Similar problems with lost clusters may occur if you use the Compress program in PC Tools version 5.5 and 6.0 with the Clear Unused Disk Space option. If you use a disk cache program with a write-delay cache, lost clusters may occur if you turn your computer off before the write cache has been physically written to the disk.

To avoid problems with lost clusters, make sure that any disk optimization utilities you use are compatible with DoubleSpace and DOS 6. Especially avoid restarting or turning off your computer while Windows or another program is running. Refer also to the section "Write-Delay Disk Cache," earlier in this chapter, for more information on difficulties with disk cache programs and write-delay caches.

Repairing Lost Clusters

To detect and repair lost clusters on your compressed volumes, use both the DOS CHKDSK and the DoubleSpace CHKDSK utilities. You can use DOS CHKDSK to repair lost clusters on both compressed and uncompressed drives; use the DoubleSpace CHKDSK utility only to repair lost clusters on compressed drives.

To repair lost clusters on a compressed or uncompressed drive by using the DOS CHKDSK utility, use the following command:

CHKDSK /F *d*:

Substitute the drive letter of the drive you want to check and repair for the *d* in this command. If DOS CHKDSK finds any lost clusters, it gathers the clusters into legitimate file chains and places each file chain in the root directory of the disk drive you check. The files that DOS CHKDSK creates from the lost clusters all have file names that end with an extension of CHK. For more information about the DOS CHKDSK command and the CHK files it produces, refer to your DOS documentation. For information on using the DoubleSpace CHKDSK utility, refer to Chapter 6, "Using the DoubleSpace Utilities."

Examining Cross-Linked Files

Cross-linked files occur if two file chains include the same cluster or clusters. File chains should never share clusters. Because subdirectories on your disk are actually special files that point to other files, two subdirectories can be cross-linked, and a subdirectory can be cross-linked with a file. Cross-linked files can cause additional problems. Because the files that are cross linked have one or more clusters in common, updating one cross-linked file can cause data in a cluster belonging to the second file to be overwritten.

You must repair cross-linked files as quickly as possible. The only way to detect cross-linked files is by using the DOS CHKDSK and the DoubleSpace CHKDSK utilities.

What Causes Cross-Linked Files?

Cross-linked files are not as common as lost clusters. Both, however, can be caused by power failures and by incorrectly restarting your computer. Cross-linked files also can result from conflicts among programs in upper memory or from overly aggressive use of upper memory. Having a STACKS=0,0 statement in your CONFIG.SYS file, using the HIGHSCAN switch with EMM386, or using a disk cache program with a write-delay cache all may cause programs in memory to corrupt each other's data, resulting in cross-linked files. Refer to the section "Preventing Problems," earlier in this chapter, for information on dealing with upper memory conflicts, problems with the STACKS command in CONFIG.SYS, and write-delay disk caches.

Repairing Cross-Linked Files

To detect cross-linked files on an uncompressed drive, you must use the DOS CHKDSK utility. To detect cross-linked files on a compressed drive, you can use either the DOS or the DoubleSpace CHKDSK utility. If many cross-linked files exist, or if other problems are present on a compressed drive, DoubleSpace reports the situation after the compressed drive is mounted. Neither the DOS CHKDSK nor the DoubleSpace CHKDSK utilities, however, can repair cross-linked files. You must repair cross-linked files manually.

Cross-linked files almost always involve some lost data from one or both of the files. Because the two files share one or more clusters, one or both files may contain invalid data in one or several clusters.

You often can retrieve one of the two cross-linked files; successfully retrieving both cross-linked files, however, is rare. Often, you cannot retrieve either file, and your only recourse is to restore the files from backup. Refer to Appendix C, "The 'Grandfather' Backup Technique," for information on a backup method that enables you to restore any file up to three months past.

To repair cross-linked files and attempt to retrieve the affected files, follow these steps:

1. Run DOS CHKDSK for either a compressed or uncompressed drive. Refer to your DOS documentation for more information on DOS CHKDSK.
2. Record the names of any files or directories reported as cross-linked. You do not need to note the specific cluster numbers.
3. If the cross-links are for files only—that is, they do not include a subdirectory name—copy each cross-linked file to a separate directory, preferably on a separate disk.. (Skip to step 4 if a subdirectory name appears as part of the cross-link.) Assume, for example, that two cross-linked files, FILE1.DOC and FILE2.DOC, are located in the root directory of drive C. You can copy FILE1.DOC and FILE2.DOC to a floppy disk in drive A or to a directory other than the root directory on drive C.
4. If any cross-linked files involve subdirectories—two subdirectories linked together or a subdirectory cross-linked with a file—you must copy all the files in each affected subdirectory to another subdirectory or disk. If DIR1 and DIR2 are cross-linked subdirectories, for example, copy all the files and subdirectories in DIR1 to drive A or to any subdirectory other than DIR2. Then copy all the files and subdirectories in DIR2 to drive B or to any subdirectory other than DIR1.
5. After copying the cross-linked files, delete the originals. If the cross-linked files include any subdirectories, use the DOS DELTREE command to delete the directory and all its files. Deleting the files or removing the subdirectory marks all clusters in both chains as unused, eliminating the cross-link.
6. Check each file you copied to determine whether the files are damaged or have lost data, and delete any damaged files.
7. If the files are undamaged, move them back to their original directory. If you deleted a directory, re-create the directory and copy or move the files back into it.
8. Use DOS CHKDSK again to make sure that all cross-linked files are eliminated and that no lost clusters are present.

> **NOTE:** Even if you do not expect to recover the data in any of your cross-linked files, you must perform one of the repair methods described in this section to remove the cross-linked files from your disk.

> **NOTE:** The compressed volume file itself can become cross-linked to files on the uncompressed host drive. The only way to detect this condition is to use DOS CHKDSK on the uncompressed host drive. If the compressed volume file becomes cross-linked with one or more files on the uncom-pressed host drive, you can try to recover the files from the uncompressed host drive as described in this section. You then must delete and recreate your compressed volume.

> **NOTE:** Make sure that you *copy* the files to another directory; do not use the DOS RENAME or MOVE commands or the Windows File Manager to simply move the files into another directory. Copying the files forces DOS to allocate an entirely new file chain for each copy of each file. Moving or renaming a file simply relocates the directory entry for the file without affecting the clusters in the file chain.

The procedure just described can be time-consuming. If you have a current backup and you do not need to retrieve the cross-linked files or directories, use the following alternative:

1. Follow steps 1 and 2 from the preceding procedure.
2. Delete all cross-linked files. If a subdirectory is cross-linked, use the DOS DELTREE command to delete the subdirectory and its contents.
3. Restore the affected files and directories from your backup. Refer to the documentation for your backup program for information on restoring selected files or subdirectories. If you deleted a directory, make sure that you restore all the directory's subdirectories and files.

> **STOP**
> If you repair cross-links that involve a subdirectory, make sure that you copy not only all the files in the affected subdirectory, but also all the subdirectories farther down the directory tree—and all their files, too. If you do not copy all the files and subdirectories, you can lose even more data than just that in the immediately affected files.

Solving Problems in Changing a Compressed Volume's Size

You may experience difficulty changing the size of a compressed drive, particularly if you try to make the drive smaller. You normally have difficulty enlarging a compressed volume only if the uncompressed host drive does not have enough space. Chapter 6, "Using the DoubleSpace Utilities," describes how to change the size of a compressed volume.

Difficulty reducing the size of a compressed volume may manifest in one of two ways. You may receive a DoubleSpace error message that a disk is too fragmented to resize. In this case, the error message contains instructions for correcting the problem. If, after following these instructions, you get the same error message, use the second problem-solving procedure described in this section. Instead of receiving an error message, you may notice that the compressed volume contains a large amount of free space, but you cannot decrease the size of the compressed volume by more than a small fraction of the free space.

In either case, the root causes are similar. As DoubleSpace makes a compressed volume smaller, it discards unused space at the end of the compressed volume file. The discarded space then becomes available on the uncompressed host drive. If clusters near the end of the compressed volume file are in use, DoubleSpace cannot discard space from the end of the compressed volume file without losing disk clusters. DoubleSpace simply refuses to make the compressed volume file any smaller to avoid losing any clusters.

If you do not receive an error message but cannot make the compressed volume as small as you think it should become, you may be able to resolve the problem by using the following procedure:

1. Run DOS DEFRAG on the compressed drive you want to resize. Use the DEFRAG command with the /F and /H command line switches, substituting the drive letter of the drive you want to resize for the *d* in the following example:

    DEFRAG *d*: /F /H

    DOS DEFRAG defragments the compressed drive. The /F switch causes DEFRAG to fully defragment the drive, and the /H switch tells DEFRAG to move Hidden

> **STOP**
> Make sure *before* you delete them that you have current backups for the files or subdirectories you delete.

> **NOTE:**
> Defragmenting your drive may take some time. If you need to interrupt the defragmenting process, press Esc.

files (System files are not affected). Refer to your DOS documentation for more information on DOS DEFRAG.

After DOS DEFRAG finishes defragmenting the disk, it runs the DoubleSpace defragmenting utility, which packs all the file clusters at the beginning of the compressed volume. After the DoubleSpace defragment utility is done, DoubleSpace returns to the DOS prompt.

2. Attempt to change the size of the compressed volume again, as described in Chapter 6. DoubleSpace should now enable you to reduce the compressed volume's size by about half the amount of free space on the compressed volume, depending on the compression ratio.

If, after following this procedure, you still cannot make the compressed volume any smaller, even though it contains a fairly large amount of free space, try the following procedure.

The DOS DEFRAG program and the DoubleSpace defragment utility do not move file clusters that belong to files assigned the System file attribute. Several different types of programs create System files on your drive. Many delete-protection programs—including the DOS UNDELETE utility (at maximum protection) and programs such as Norton SMARTCAN—create System files. Many format-protection programs, such as MIRROR, also create System files.

Because DOS DEFRAG and the DoubleSpace defragment utility do not move clusters that belong to files with the System attribute, these files may remain at the end of the compressed volume file even after the defragmenting processes, preventing you from changing the compressed volume's size. To circumvent this problem, you must locate the System files on your compressed disk, temporarily remove the System attribute, and then defragment the compressed disk. To do so, follow these steps:

1. Locate on the compressed volume all files with the System attribute by issuing the following command at the DOS prompt, substituting the letter of the drive you want to resize for the *d* in the example:

    DIR *d*:\ /A:S /S /P

    This command causes DOS to list all the files on the specified drive that have the System attribute, beginning at the root directory and continuing through all the subdirectories. DOS pauses the list after every full screen.

2. Write down the name and full directory path of every file with a System attribute. This list is very important; you must use it again at the end of this procedure.

3. Use the DOS ATTRIB command to remove the System attribute for each file on your compressed volume that has a System attribute. To remove the System attribute, use the following command:

    ATTRIB –S *filename*

    Substitute the name of the file (including the full directory path) from which you want to remove the System attribute for *filename*. To remove the System

---

You can send the list of System files directly to your printer by using the following command, substituting the letter of your drive for the *d* in the example:

DIR d:\ /A:S /S > PRN

Refer to your DOS documentation for more information on redirecting output from DOS commands.

attribute from a file named FILE1.DOC in the DOCUMENTS subdirectory, for example, you use the following command:

ATTRIB −S \DOCUMENTS\FILE1.DOC

Refer to your DOS documentation for more information on the ATTRIB utility.

4. Run DOS DEFRAG on the compressed drive you want to resize. Use DEFRAG with the /F and /H command line switches, substituting the drive letter of the drive you want to resize for the *d* in the following example:

DEFRAG *d*: /F /H

DOS DEFRAG defragments the compressed drive. The /F switch causes DEFRAG to fully defragment the drive. The /H switch causes DEFRAG to move Hidden files.

After DOS DEFRAG finishes defragmenting the disk, it runs the DoubleSpace defragmenting utility, which moves all the file clusters to the beginning of the compressed volume. After the DoubleSpace defragment utility is done, DoubleSpace returns to the DOS prompt.

5. Using the list of file names you created in Step 2, add the System attribute back to each file from which you removed it in Step 3. To restore the System attribute, use the following command:

ATTRIB +S *filename*

6. Attempt to change the size of the compressed volume again, as described in Chapter 6. DoubleSpace should now enable you to reduce the compressed volume's size by about half the amount of free space on the compressed volume, depending on the compression ratio.

> **STOP**
> Do not confuse your compressed volume with its uncompressed host. You are looking for System files on your compressed volume. If you remove the System attribute from your compressed volume file and then use the DOS DEFRAG program or another disk defragmenting program, you may lose data on your compressed volume. *Never* remove the System attribute from any file named DBLSPACE.nnn, where *nnn* stands for a three-digit number (usually 000).

Recovering a Deleted Compressed Volume File

From time to time, all computer users accidentally delete something they really want to keep. The proliferation of delete-protection utilities clearly testifies to this problem. (DOS, in fact, even includes its own UNDELETE program.) Accidentally deleting a compressed volume file from the DOS prompt is difficult; DoubleSpace protects the compressed volume file by giving it the System, Hidden, and Read-Only file attributes. Nevertheless, the Windows File Manager—and some shell and menu programs—enable you to delete Hidden, System, and Read-Only files, although they usually ask for confirmation before doing so. You also can use the DoubleSpace command line switch or the DoubleSpace menus to delete a compressed volume file and then realize that you deleted the wrong compressed volume. Whatever the cause, you may still be able to recover the compressed volume file.

You must attempt to recover the compressed volume file as soon as you realize you deleted it. The sooner you attempt recovery, the more likely is your success. If any new data has been written to the uncompressed drive that hosted the compressed volume file, a strong possibility exists that disk clusters that were part of the compressed volume file are now being use by other files. If so, you cannot recover the compressed volume file.

Instead, you must re-create the compressed volume file and restore your files from backup.

To recover your deleted compressed volume file, follow these steps:

1. Make the current disk drive the uncompressed drive that hosted the compressed volume you are trying to recover.

   The uncompressed host drive usually now has its original drive letter, which is the same letter as the deleted drive. If you accidentally deleted compressed volume D, for example, its uncompressed host drive is probably drive D now.

2. Make sure that you are in the root directory of the uncompressed drive. If necessary, use the DOS change directory (CD or CHDIR) command.

3. Type **UNDELETE** at the DOS prompt, and press Enter.

   UNDELETE displays the first part of the screen shown in figure 7.1. The number and names of files UNDELETE finds depends on the specific files and recent deletions on your computer's hard disk.

4. After UNDELETE asks whether to delete a file, press N to answer No for all files except those with the file name ?BLSPACE and a three-digit number for the extension.

```
UNDELETE - A delete protection facility
Copyright (C) 1987-1993 Central Point Software, Inc.
All rights reserved.

Directory: D:\
File Specifications: *.*

    Delete Sentry control file not found.

    Deletion-tracking file not found.

    MS-DOS directory contains    1 deleted files.
    Of those,    1 files may be recovered.

Using the MS-DOS directory method.

    ?BLSPACE 000  23742464  5-26-93  9:49p  ....  Undelete (Y/N)?Y
    Please type the first character for ?BLSPACE.000: D

File successfully undeleted.
```

Fig. 7.1

The DOS UNDELETE display as it recovers deleted compressed volume files.

5. Where UNDELETE asks for the first letter of the file name, type D.

   UNDELETE undeletes the compressed volume file. Because the compressed volume file usually is quite large, the undeleting process may take several seconds, depending on the speed of your computer. After UNDELETE finishes undeleting the compressed volume file, it returns to the DOS prompt.

6. Use the DoubleSpace command line switch or the DoubleSpace menus to mount the compressed volume file you just recovered.

7. If the compressed volume mounts, check its integrity by using the DoubleSpace CHKDSK utility. (Refer to Chapter 12, "Using the DoubleSpace Utilities.")

The deleted compressed volume file is now recovered.

Correcting Corrupt CVF or Damaged CVF Error Messages

If problems in the structure of your compressed volume file occur, DoubleSpace may report that the compressed volume file (*CVF*) is damaged or corrupted when DoubleSpace mounts the compressed drive. These problems usually result from cross-linked files. Refer to the section "Examining Cross-Linked Files," earlier in this chapter for the possible causes of the damage to the compressed volume file. That section also contains instructions on using CHKDSK to find and repair cross-linked files. After you finish repairing any errors CHKDSK finds on the compressed drive, restart your computer. If you have corrected all the errors, DoubleSpace should mount your compressed drives without error messages.

Correcting Chronic Disk Read Errors

If you receive frequent error messages as DOS or your applications read data from your disk drives, try to identify the cause immediately. Frequent `Error reading drive...` messages indicate potentially serious problems in your computer's hardware or in your software. Chronic read errors from *all* of your disk drives, both compressed and uncompressed, are probably caused by a problem in your computer's hardware. You should seek assistance from your vendor or a qualified hardware technician to determine the specific cause of the problem.

If the read errors occur *only* on your compressed drives, a memory conflict of some kind is the probable cause of the errors. If you use EMM386 with the HIGHSCAN switch, try removing the HIGHSCAN switch to see if the read errors cease. If the DoubleSpace device driver is loaded into upper memory, relocate the device driver to the conventional memory area; the read errors should cease.

Summary

This chapter serves as a troubleshooting guide for DoubleSpace users. It began by acquainting you with measures you can take to head off many common problems associated with using DoubleSpace. The chapter then described ways to solve problems involving DoubleSpace drive letter assignments and Windows swap files. The chapter next described typical causes of lost clusters and cross-linked files and offered techniques for repairing them.

You also learned how to resolve problems in changing the size of a compressed drive and how to recover an accidentally deleted compressed volume file. The chapter concluded with a discussion of causes and possible remedies for chronic disk read errors.

The next chapter describes a special enhancement product for DoubleSpace, called SPACEMANager.

CHAPTER 8

Beyond DoubleSpace: Using SPACEMANager

This chapter describes the SPACEMANager add-in for DoubleSpace. (An *add-in* is a program that works only with another specific program to add special features to the original program.) SPACEMANager is published by Vertisoft Systems, Inc., the developers of DoubleSpace. SPACEMANager can be an important addition to your DoubleSpace system. SPACEMANager adds several important capabilities to DoubleSpace. If you use compressed removable media regularly or primarily use Microsoft Windows, you may want to consider adding SPACEMANager to your DoubleSpace system.

This chapter describes SPACEMANager and briefly explains how it works. The chapter also includes how-to information for installing and using SPACEMANager. A thorough discussion of SPACEMANager is not possible here, but this chapter offers an overview of SPACEMANager's functions and operations, along with some practical tips and instructions.

What is SPACEMANager?

SPACEMANager consists of a group of programs that enhance the performance and capabilities of DoubleSpace. SPACEMANager itself, however, does not provide disk compression. You must have DoubleSpace to use SPACEMANager and the utility programs provided with SPACEMANager. SPACEMANager adds to DoubleSpace the capabilities to automatically mount removable media disks, to use multiple levels of compression, and to use your DoubleSpace-compressed removable disks even on computers that do not have DoubleSpace installed. SPACEMANager also integrates better with Windows than does DoubleSpace alone. The following sections describe each of these features.

Multiple Compression Levels

All compression schemes make a trade-off between maximum compression of data and the time required to compress the data. The more you compress the data, the longer it takes to compress. By using SPACEMANager, you can choose one of four compression levels for your files. SPACEMANager applies the compression levels you select based on each file's extension, so you can control the type of compression applied to each file, based on the file's type.

SPACEMANager includes a feature—called *SelectCompress*—that enables you to choose a level of compression appropriate for each type of file on your disk. Because higher compression levels require proportionally more time to compress data, you should choose a high level of compression for files that do not change often and use a lower level of compression for files that do change often. Program files, for example, are candidates for a high level of compression, because the file is not changed often and, therefore, not compressed often; you do not suffer from the extra time needed to compress the files, yet you benefit from the smaller amount of disk space the more highly compressed files use. Database files, as another example, are candidates for a moderate level of compression, because these files change frequently and, therefore, are compressed often; you are more likely to notice the additional time required if you use a high level of compression on these files.

SPACEMANager provides the following four levels of compression:

- **None.** No compression is used. The file is stored on the compressed volume, but SPACEMANager makes no attempt to compress the file. This compression level is intended for use with files that are already compressed, such as the ZIP files produced by PKZIP or some already-compressed graphic file formats, such as GIF.
- **DOS.** This is the standard compression level used by DoubleSpace alone.
- **Ultra I.** This compression level is the first step beyond standard DoubleSpace compression. This level takes longer to compress data but compresses the data more than does DoubleSpace alone.
- **Ultra II.** This level offers the highest compression available in SPACEMANager. Ultra II compression takes the greatest amount of time, but the data occupies the smallest amount of disk space possible.

You select which compression level to apply to each of four file categories. SPACEMANager uses a table of file name extensions to classify the files on your disk into one of the following four categories:

- **Text.** This category is for files that predominantly contain text information, including any file created by using a text editor or a word processor. This category also can include some types of database files. Typical file name extensions for text files are BAT, DOC, and TXT.
- **Binary.** This category is for files that predominantly contain binary information, including program files, Windows DLL files, device driver files, and some types of data files, such as database or spreadsheet files. Typical file name extensions for binary files are EXE, COM, SYS, DLL, OVL, and BIN.

> **NOTE:**
> DoubleSpace can read both the Ultra I and Ultra II compression levels even without SPACEMANager. If you use an Ultra I- or Ultra II-compressed removable disk in another computer that has DoubleSpace (but not SPACEMANager), that computer still can read all the files on the compressed removable disk.

- **Compressed.** This category is for files containing data that already is compressed and includes files produced by archiving programs such as PKZIP, some types of graphics files, and some types of audio and video files. (Many digital sound and video sampling boards compress data in hardware as it is sampled.) Typical file name extensions for compressed files are ZIP and ARC.
- **Other.** SPACEMANager uses this category for any file it cannot fit into one of the other categories by matching the file name extension with one in SPACEMANager's table of file extensions and file types.

SPACEMANager enables you to add new file extensions to the table it uses to determine the type of a file. If you write Paradox database programs, for example, you may add the SC extension—the file extension for Paradox program files—to the file extension table so that SPACEMANager groups your Paradox program files in the Text file category. You cannot add new file categories.

SPACEMANager provides multiple levels of compression by loading a special TSR program from your AUTOEXEC.BAT file whenever your computer starts. To use the selective compression in SPACEMANager, your computer must have an 80286 or higher CPU and at least 250K XMS extended memory. The SelectCompress TSR loads into extended memory. SelectCompress takes advantage of the capabilities of the 80286, 80386, and higher CPUs to accommodate more than one active program in memory at a time. If you have an 80286 CPU, SPACEMANager must use a special program, called a DPMI (*D*OS *P*rotected-*M*ode *I*nterface) loader, to run correctly. Some 80286 computers with older BIOS programs may not be compatible with DPMI.

Automatic Mounting of Removable Media

SPACEMANager also incorporates a feature called *SuperMount*, which makes your computer capable of mounting a compressed removable disk automatically. If you use SuperMount, you need not mount a compressed removable drive manually before using it. Whenever you (or one of your programs) access a removable drive, SuperMount checks the disk. If the disk in the drive is a DoubleSpace compressed disk, SuperMount mounts the compressed volume for you.

SuperMount is extremely useful if you frequently use compressed removable disks. SuperMount enables you to access these disks without exiting Windows or a DOS application. Like SelectCompress, SuperMount loads into your computer's memory from your AUTOEXEC.BAT file as a TSR program every time your computer starts.

Transportable Removable Media

Removable disks compressed by DoubleSpace are readable only by other computers that also have DoubleSpace installed. Occasionally, however, you may need to use a computer without DoubleSpace to access files on a compressed removable disk. By using SPACEMANager's *SuperExchange* program, you can use DoubleSpace compressed removable disks on computers that do not have DoubleSpace. SPACEMANager provides a utility for adding the SuperExchange program to your compressed removable disks so that these disks can be used by computers without DoubleSpace. SuperExchange cannot actually compress removable disks; it can only make the compressed disks usable on computers without DoubleSpace.

SuperExchange is a TSR program that, after it is loaded on a computer that does not have DoubleSpace installed, enables that computer to read data from and write data to compressed removable disks. After you finish using the compressed removable drive on the computer without DoubleSpace, you can remove SuperExchange from that computer's memory.

How to add SuperExchange to a compressed removable disk is described in the section "Making Removable Media Usable on Computers without DoubleSpace," later in this chapter. How to use SuperExchange is described in the section "Using SUPERX Exchangeable Removable Disks," also later in this chapter.

NOTE: The SuperExchange program requires DOS version 3.31 or higher. You cannot use SuperExchange to read or write compressed removable disks on computers that use versions of DOS earlier than 3.31.

Improved Windows Integration

SPACEMANager significantly improves DoubleSpace's integration with Windows. If you use SuperMount, you can access your DoubleSpace-compressed floppy disks without needing to exit Windows to mount them; SuperMount mounts the disks automatically.

The Windows version of SPACEMANager provides information about your compressed volumes and enables you to control SPACEMANager's configuration, compression levels, and file extension table, just as does the DOS version of SPACEMANager. The Windows version of SPACEMANager also improves your capability to use compressed removable media with Windows and enables you to compress a floppy disk or to add SuperExchange to the disk without leaving Windows. The SPACEMANager installation program creates a Windows program group for SPACEMANager. You use the SPACEMANager Windows utility the same as you do any other Windows application.

Improved Free Space Reporting

SPACEMANager provides a final component to enhance DoubleSpace's performance: the *FortuneTeller* free-space estimator. FortuneTeller improves the accuracy of the free-space estimates DoubleSpace makes for your compressed volumes. FortuneTeller assumes that the types of files you intend to store are similar to files you already have stored on your compressed volume. FortuneTeller uses the compression ratios of files already on your compressed volume to calculate a more accurate report of the free space on your compressed volume than DoubleSpace alone can calculate. Like other SPACEMANager components, FortuneTeller loads into your computer's memory from your AUTOEXEC.BAT file as a TSR program every time your computer starts.

How SPACEMANager Works

SPACEMANager consists of several separate programs. SelectCompress selective compression, SuperMount automatic removable drive mounting, and FortuneTeller free-space reporting each are contained in separate program files. Each SPACEMANager component loads into your computer's memory as a TSR program. After loading into memory, SPACEMANager's component programs function much like device drivers, extending the capabilities of DOS and DoubleSpace. The FortuneTeller free-space reporting program, for example, attaches itself to the DOS service that reports free space on a disk.

You can load the SPACEMANager programs in any combination. If you do not use compressed removable disks, for example, you do not need the SuperMount program. To keep more memory in your computer free, simply disable the loading of the SuperMount program. You can use SPACEMANager to enable or disable SelectCompress, SuperMount, and FortuneTeller program loading. To avoid editing your AUTOEXEC.BAT file repeatedly, SPACEMANager uses a special initialization file.

Each line in your AUTOEXEC.BAT file that invokes one of the SPACEMANager programs uses a command line switch that tells the program to search the SPACEMANager initialization file. Only if the initialization file indicates that this particular SPACEMANager feature is enabled does that SPACEMANager program remain in memory. Suppose, for example, that you disabled SuperMount. As SuperMount loads from your AUTOEXEC.BAT file, it searches the SPACEMANager initialization file and sees that it is disabled. The SuperMount program does not stay in memory; it simply stops running without installing itself.

Installing SPACEMANager

This section describes the changes SPACEMANager makes to your computer system as you install it and then describes the installation process itself. This section also offers pointers on preparing for SPACEMANager's installation.

Changes Made by SPACEMANager Installation

The SPACEMANager installation program installs the SPACEMANager files on your hard disk and, optionally, modifies your AUTOEXEC.BAT file and your Windows PROGMAN.INI and SYSTEM.INI files (if Windows is installed on your computer). Refer to your DOS documentation for more information on AUTOEXEC.BAT. Refer to your Windows documentation for more information on PROGMAN.INI and SYSTEM.INI.

SPACEMANager adds the directory containing the SPACEMANager program files to your DOS PATH statement. If your AUTOEXEC.BAT file does not already have a PATH statement, SPACEMANager adds one. (Refer to your DOS documentation for more information on the PATH statement.) SPACEMANager changes your AUTOEXEC.BAT file so that the SPACEMANager programs load into memory whenever you start your computer. SPACEMANager changes your Windows PROGMAN.INI file to create a program group for SPACEMANager. If you have an 80386 or higher CPU, SPACEMANager also adds a device driver to your Windows SYSTEM.INI file so that the SelectCompress feature works correctly.

> **NOTE:** Whenever you enable or disable a SPACEMANager feature, your change does not take effect until the next time you restart your computeer.

SPACEMANager adds the following lines to your AUTOEXEC.BAT file:

```
SET SPACEMAN=C:\SPACEMAN\
.
.(existing commands in your batch file)
.
ECHO.
REM *** SPACEMANager STARTUP ***
REM The /B option will prevent startup of a module unless the SPACEMAN.INI
REM file contains a line that says Load=1 for that module.
CALL C:\SPACEMAN\SELECTC /B
C:\SPACEMAN\SMOUNT /B
C:\SPACEMAN\FORTUNE /B
```

The first line SPACEMANager adds to your AUTOEXEC.BAT file is the SET command, which sets a DOS environment variable for SPACEMANager, indicating the directory that contains the SPACEMANager program files. (If you install SPACEMANager on a drive other than C or in a directory other than \SPACEMAN, the actual drive and directory appear in your AUTOEXEC.BAT file instead of the C:\SPACEMAN drive and directory shown in the example.) SPACEMANager adds the SET command immediately after the existing PATH statement in your AUTOEXEC.BAT file.

The remaining lines SPACEMANager adds to your AUTOEXEC.BAT file are placed at the very end of the file. These lines actually load the SPACEMANager programs into memory. Because each program checks the SPACEMANager initialization file to see whether it should install itself, you must leave all three lines in your AUTOEXEC.BAT file.

Table 8.1 lists all the files the SPACEMANager installation program puts on your disk and briefly explains the purpose of each file.

Table 8.1 SPACEMANager Files

SPACEMANager File	Purpose
README	A text file containing last-minute information about SPACEMANager.
ADDX.EXE	Adds SuperExchange to a floppy disk.
BADDX.BAT	Batch file used by SPACEMANager Windows to add SuperExchange to a floppy disk.
DBLFLOP.EXE	Compresses floppy disks and optionally adds SuperExchange at the same time.
BDBLFLOP.BAT	Batch file used by SPACEMANager Windows to compress floppy disks and optionally add SuperExchange at the same time.
FORTUNE.EXE	The FortuneTeller free-space estimating TSR program.
SMOUNT.EXE	The SuperMount removable media mounting TSR program.
SELECTC.BAT	Batch file called from AUTOEXEC.BAT to load the SelectCompress TSR program into memory.

Beyond DoubleSpace: Using SPACEMANager   **155**

SPACEMANager File	Purpose
SPACEMAN.INI	The SPACEMANager initialization file; contains information about which SPACEMANager features are enabled.
SPACEMAN.EXE	The DOS version of the SPACEMANager utility.
SPACMANW.EXE	The Windows version of the SPACEMANager utility.
SPACEMAN.GRP	Windows Program Group file for SPACEMANager.
PROTTSR.EXE	SPACEMANager SelectCompress program, protected mode portion; loads into extended memory.
REALTSR.EXE	SPACEMANager SelectCompress program, conventional-memory portion.
BWCC.DLL	Windows Dynamic Link Library file used by the SPACEMANager Windows utility.
EDPMI.OVL	DPMI file used by SPACEMANager for 80286 computers.
SMVERS.ION	Text file, listing the version of SPACEMANager on your disk.
SPACEMAN.386	Windows protected-mode device driver; used by SPACEMANager Windows utility and SelectCompress.

Preparing To Install SPACEMANager

You need not make any special preparations to install SPACEMANager. Installing SPACEMANager is much like installing any other program. (Unlike DoubleSpace, SPACEMANager does not compress your disks or make major alterations in your computer on installation.) You mainly need only to make sure that your system meets the following system requirements for SPACEMANager:

- **Hardware.** You must have an MS-DOS compatible computer with at least 640K conventional memory. An 80286 or higher CPU and 250K XMS memory are required to use SelectCompress. SPACEMANager requires approximately 1.5M of disk space—that is, 1.5M *before* any of SPACEMANager's files are compressed.
- **Software.** You must have DOS 6 or higher to use SPACEMANager. You must have Windows 3.1 or higher to use SPACEMANager with Windows. You also must have DoubleSpace installed to use any of SPACEMANager's capabilities.

As noted, SPACEMANager does alter your AUTOEXEC.BAT file. If you have Windows, SPACEMANager also alters your PROGMAN.INI and SYSTEM.INI files. Although

> **NOTE:**
> You cannot use SPACEMANager in an OS/2 compatibility box or with Windows NT.

SPACEMANager makes backup copies of your original files before changing them, you may want to make your own copies of these files for additional safety. If you have such copies, you can always restore your system to its condition before you installed SPACEMANager.

Performing the Installation

After you are sure you have enough disk space and conventional memory available to install SPACEMANager, you can begin the installation. This section provides step-by-step instructions on installing SPACEMANager.

To start the SPACEMANager installation program, follow these steps:

1. Insert the SPACEMANager installation disk into floppy drive A or B (whichever drive can accommodate the SPACEMANager installation disk).
2. Make the floppy disk drive containing the SPACEMANager installation disk the current disk drive. (If you insert the SPACEMANager disk into drive A, for example, type **A:** at the DOS prompt, and press Enter.)
3. Type **install** at the DOS prompt (now set for drive A), and press Enter.

The SPACEMANager installation program displays a copyright message and takes a few moments to load into memory. As the installation program loads, it prints a series of solid blocks on-screen so that you know it is working. After the installation program loads into memory, it asks whether you are installing SPACEMANager on a system with a color monitor.

To complete the installation, follow these steps:

1. Choose **Y** if your computer has a color monitor; otherwise, choose **N**. (If you change your mind about installing SPACEMANager, press Ctrl+X to exit the SPACEMANager installation program and return to DOS.)

    The installation program then asks you to confirm its identification of your start-up disk drive (usually drive C).

2. Press Enter to confirm SPACEMANager's identification of your start-up disk drive; otherwise, type the letter of the drive from which your computer starts, and press Enter. SPACEMANager displays the screen shown in figure 8.1, asking whether you want to install both the DOS and Windows versions of the SPACEMANager utility or only the DOS version.

3. Select the installation you prefer, and press Enter. Choose Install SPACEMANager for Both DOS and Windows if you have Windows 3.1 and want to use SPACEMANager from Windows. Choose Install SPACEMANager for DOS Only if you do not have Windows or are sure you do not want to use SPACEMANager from Windows. (If you have Windows 3.1, installing SPACEMANager for both DOS and Windows is recommended.)

    If you change your mind about installing SPACEMANager now, choose Exit to DOS.

    SPACEMANager displays the screen shown in figure 8.2, asking you to select the disk drive on which to install its files. SPACEMANager also displays a list of hard disk drives on your computer system, showing the free space on each drive.

The SPACEMANager installation program requires at least 505K conventional memory. Use the DOS MEM command to determine whether you have enough conventional memory. (Refer to your DOS documentation for information on using the MEM command.) If you do not have enough conventional memory, you may need to make a special CONFIG.SYS file that does not load any device drivers other than those needed to access your hard disk. You also may need to edit your AUTOEXEC.BAT file and temporarily disable any TSR programs that load into memory as your computer starts.

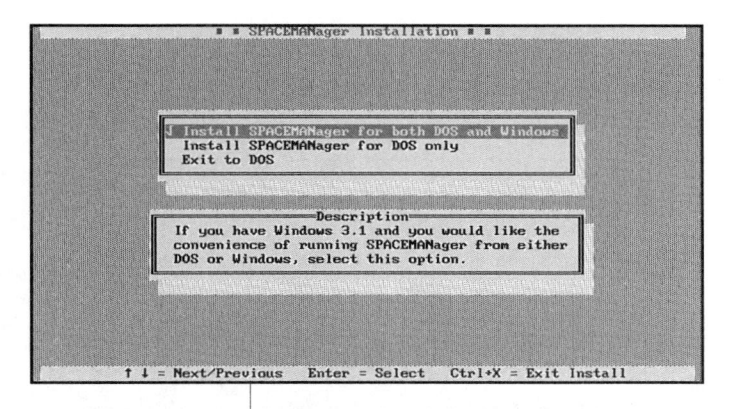

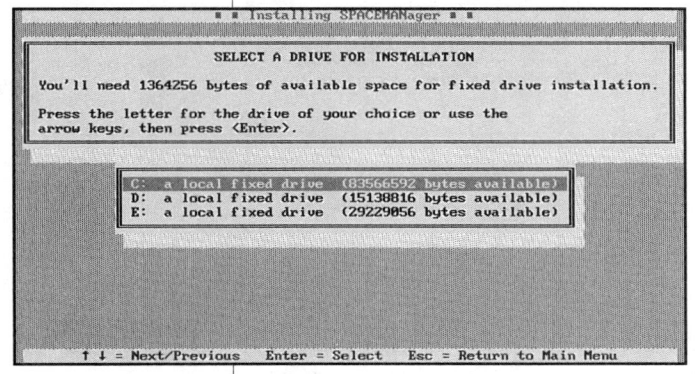

Fig. 8.1, top

The screen for selecting which SPACEMANager files to install.

Fig. 8.2, bottom

The screen for selecting the drive on which to install SPACEMANager.

4. Select the drive on which you want to install SPACEMANager, and press Enter. (Alternatively, just type the letter for the drive you want.) Make sure that you select a drive with enough free space to accommodate the SPACEMANager files.

The amount of free disk space required for the installation configuration you choose in step 4 appears in the Select a Drive for Installation box at the top of the screen.

SPACEMANager now displays the message shown in figure 8.3, asking for the name of the directory in which to install the SPACEMANager files.

5. Press Enter to accept the \SPACEMAN directory suggested by the installation program, or type in a different directory name and then press Enter.

SPACEMANager now searches your system directory on which Windows appears to be installed, SPACEMANager displays the message shown in figure 8.4, asking you to confirm that this directory is the correct directory containing Windows.

If you do not have Windows installed on your computer, the SPACEMANager installation program immediately begins copying files as described after step 6.

6. Press Enter to confirm the Windows directory name. If the directory name is not the correct directory for your Windows files, type the correct directory name, and then press Enter.

SPACEMANager begins copying files to your hard disk. A screen similar to the one shown in figure 8.5 appears, indicating the progress of the installation process. After SPACEMANager transfers all its files onto your hard disk, it asks whether you want to read the SPACEMANager README file.

7. Choose Y to view the README file or N to skip the README file for now. If you choose Y, the README file is displayed on-screen. Use the arrow keys to move through the README file. Press Esc after you finish with the README file.

8. If you did not install the Windows version of SPACEMANager, skip to step 12. If you installed the Windows version of SPACEMANager, the screen shown in

figure 8.6 appears, asking whether you want SPACEMANager to make changes to your Windows PROGMAN.INI file. (The Windows Program Manager uses the PROGMAN.INI file to locate all the program groups it displays.)

9. Select the action you want SPACEMANager to take, and press Enter.

    Choose Go Ahead and Modify if you want SPACEMANager to modify the file. This choice is recommended. If you make this choice, SPACEMANager makes a backup of the original PROGMAN.INI file and makes its changes to PROGMAN.INI. SPACEMANager displays a message listing the name of the backup file for PROGMAN.INI.

    Choose Create Example Files if you want to change your PROGMAN.INI file yourself, using an example supplied by SPACEMANager.

    Choose Bypass These Changes if you do not want SPACEMANager to change PROGMAN.INI and you do not want to create an example file. This choice is not recommended.

10. Press any key to continue. SPACEMANager asks whether to change your Windows SYSTEM.INI file. (Windows uses the SYSTEM.INI file to locate and load all the Windows device drivers.)

11. Select the action you want SPACEMANager to take, and press Enter. The choices are the same as those described in step 9. If you choose for SPACEMANager to make the changes, SPACEMANager makes a backup of the original SYSTEM.INI file and changes SYSTEM.INI. SPACEMANager displays a message listing the name of the backup file for SYSTEM.INI.

12. Press any key to continue (unless you skipped from step 8 to this step). SPACEMANager asks whether to change your AUTOEXEC.BAT file. (The screen that appears is similar to that shown in fig. 8.6, but C:\AUTOEXEC.BAT appears in place of the C:\WINDOW\PROGMAN.INI shown in that figure.)

13. Select the action you want SPACEMANager to take, and then press enter. The choices are the same as those described in step 9. If you choose for SPACEMANager to make the changes, SPACEMANager makes a backup of the original AUTOEXEC.BAT file and then changes it. SPACEMANager displays a message listing the name of the backup file for AUTOEXEC.BAT.

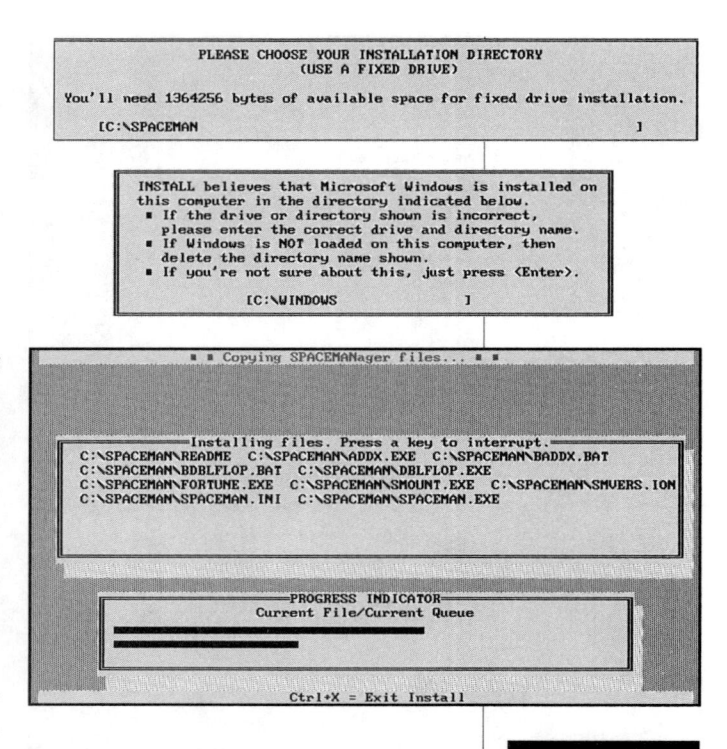

Fig. 8.3, top

Choosing the SPACEMANager directory.

Fig. 8.4, middle

Confirming the Windows directory.

Fig. 8.5, bottom

SPACEMANager's installation progress report.

Fig. 8.6
SPACEMANager's request for confirmation to modify the PROGMAN.INI file.

> As SPACEMANager modifies your AUTOEXEC.BAT file, it places the commands that load the SPACEMANager programs at the end of the AUTOEXEC.BAT file, before any commands that load Windows or a shell program. If you use the DOS CHOICE command (or a similar utility, such as Norton ASK) or use IF...GOTO commands to select different configurations in your AUTOEXEC.BAT file, the SPACEMANager lines may not be correctly positioned. Check your AUTOEXEC.BAT file to make sure that the SPACEMANager program lines are positioned before any of the branching statements in your AUTOEXEC.BAT file.

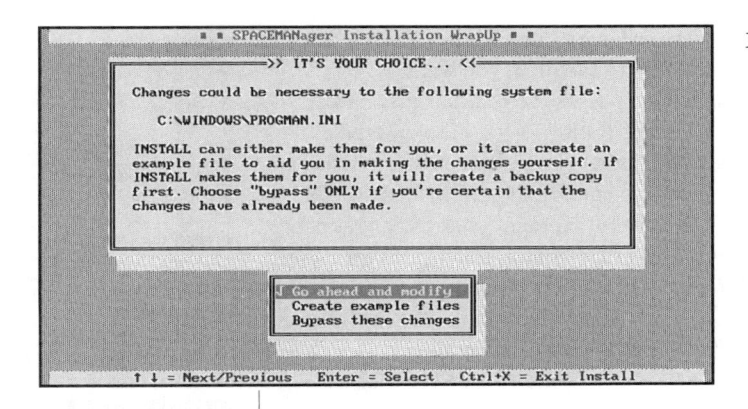

14. Press any key to continue. If you are installing SPACEMANager on an 80386 or higher computer, the installation program now returns to the DOS prompt. If you install SPACEMANager on an 80286 computer, however, SPACE-MAN-ager runs a special test program to test the DPMI loader. Follow the on-screen instructions to complete the DPMI test. SPACEMANager does not perform this test if you install SPACEMANager on an 80386 or higher computer.

You are now finished installing SPACEMANager. To load the SPACEMANager TSR programs, however, you must restart your computer. Press Ctrl+Alt+Del to reboot your computer. (*See also the Tips on the following page.*)

Using SPACEMANager

This section describes SPACEMANager's basic operations, covering the most important activities you can perform with either SPACEMANager in DOS or SPACEMANager in Windows.

Starting SPACEMANager

The SelectCompress, SuperMount, and FortuneTeller features of SPACEMANager are loaded into memory (if enabled) whenever your computer starts. SPACEMANager also provides a utility that enables you to obtain information about your compressed drives and to control the SPACEMANager settings for compression levels and file extensions.

Starting SPACEMANager from DOS

To start the DOS version of SPACEMANager, type the following command at the DOS prompt and press Enter:

SPACEMAN

SPACEMANager starts and displays the statistics report and main menu (see fig. 8.7). The statistics report consists of four sections, plus the main menu. The SPACEMANager main menu appears along the top of the screen, offering **F**ile, **V**iew, and **O**ptions menus. (To select a menu, press Alt plus the highlighted letter of the menu choice. To select the **F**ile menu, for example, press Alt+F. If you use a mouse, just click the name of the menu you want.)

The first section of the SPACEMANager statistics screen is the **D**rives section, which lists all the disk drives in your computer, compressed or uncompressed. The drive letter with the diamond-shaped bullet inside the parentheses located to the left of the letter is the currently selected drive. The statistics and information shown elsewhere on-screen relate to this drive. (To change the currently selected drive, press Alt+D to select the

Drives section, and then use the left- and right-arrow keys to change the selected drive. If you use a mouse, click inside the parentheses next to the drive you want.)

The second section of the statistics display encompasses the four bar graphs at the center left of the display and is titled Compression Ratio. These graphs depict the compression ratios of files on the selected disk and do not appear if the selected disk is not compressed. The first bar graph shows the average compression ratio for all the files on the selected disk. In figure 8.7, for example, the overall average compression ratio for drive C is 1.6:1. The next three graphs show the average compression ratio for three different types of file extensions. Figure 8.7, for example, shows statistics for EXE, DOC, and BAT files—the three extensions SPACEMANager displays by default. You can use the **V**iew menu to select other file extensions to be shown for these bar graphs.

Underneath the compression ratio graphs lies the third section of the SPACEMANager display. This section shows which SPACEMANager features are currently enabled. Each feature is listed with a pair of brackets (a check box) to the left of each feature's name. If an X appears in the brackets, the feature is enabled. (Unlike most such check boxes, these are not actually used to enable or disable these features; they merely show these features' status.) How to enable and disable these features is described later in this chapter.

The fourth section of the display is the large bar graph at the right side of the screen. This graph shows how much space on the selected disk drive is used and how much is free. The percentage value of the selected drive's used space appears below the graph, along with the actual value of the free space remaining. Also underneath the free-space bar graph appears information indicating whether the selected drive is compressed. If so, the host drive letter also appears.

An **Ex**i**t** command button appears near the top of the right-hand edge of the screen. Choose this button to leave SPACEMANager and return to DOS. (You also can press Alt+X to leave SPACEMANager and return to DOS, or choose E**x**it from the SPACEMANager **F**ile menu.)

Starting SPACEMANager from Windows

You start the Windows version of the SPACEMANager utility the same as you start any other Windows application. As you installed the SPACEMANager Windows files, SPACEMANager created a program group in the Windows Program Manager. The SPACEMANager program group window and program icon are shown in figure 8.8.

To start the Windows SPACEMANager utility, double-click the SPACEMANager icon. SPACEMANager starts and displays the statistics report and main menu (see fig. 8.9). Like the DOS SPACEMANager utility, the Windows SPACEMANager statistics report consists of four main regions, plus the main menu. The main menu is a typical Windows menu across the top of the application window. You make menu choices just as you do for any other Windows program. This section and others in this chapter that discuss the Windows SPACEMANager program assume you are familiar with operating Windows programs.

The drives section of the SPACEMANager statistics screen is at the top of the SPACEMANager window, near the center. The drives section displays an icon and a diamond-shaped radio button for each drive letter in your computer, compressed or uncompressed. The drive icon indicates the type of the drive. In figure 8.9, for example,

---

Immediately after you install SPACEMANager and restart your computer, you may want to check the compression levels assigned to various file types. The default compression level that SPACEMANager uses for the Other category is None. This means that any files that do not have an extension listed in the SPACEMANager table of file extensions may not be compressed. You should change this setting to apply at least standard DOS compression to Other type files. How to set the compression levels and types is described in the section "Setting Compression Levels," later in this chapter.

After SPACEMANager is first installed, SelectCompress is disabled. To make multiple compression levels available, follow the instructions in this section to enable the SelectCompress feature immediately after you install SPACEMANager.

To update the SPACEMANager free-space display, click the radio button for the selected drive again.

Beyond DoubleSpace: Using SPACEMANager 161

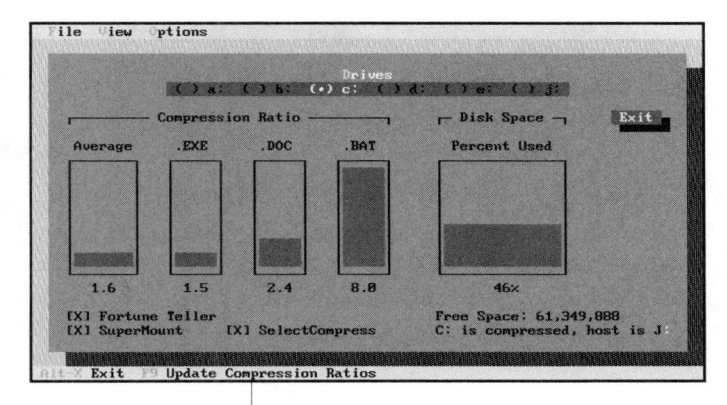

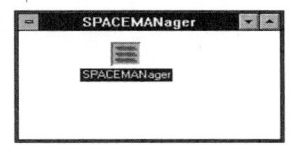

Fig. 8.7, top

The SPACEMANager statistics report and main menu.

Fig. 8.8, bottom

The SPACEMANager program group window and program icon in Windows.

If you expect to use SPACEMANager extensively in Windows, you may want to copy the SPACEMANager icon to your Startup program group so that SPACE-MANager starts whenever you start Windows. Refer to your Windows documentation for information on copying program icons and on the Start-up program group.

drives A and B are floppy drives, and drives C, D, and E are hard disks. Drive G is the host drive for a compressed volume in one of the floppy drives. The drive letter displaying a diamond-shaped bullet in the radio button below the drive icon is the currently selected drive. To change the currently selected drive, click the diamond-shaped button below the drive icon; do not click the drive icon itself. Clicking the drive icon does not change the selected drive. The statistics and information shown on the rest of the screen relate to this currently selected drive.

If you have more disk drives than can fit in the drives section of the display, the two command buttons at the right of the drive icons become enabled—that is, they become solid black arrows instead of gray arrows. Click these buttons to scroll the list of drive icons to the right or left.

Four bar graphs in the left portion of the statistics display are titled Compression Ratio. These graphs depict the compression ratios of files on the selected disk and do not appear if the selected disk is not compressed. The first bar graph shows the overall average compression ratio for all the files on the selected disk. In figure 8.9, for example, the overall compression ratio for drive C is 1.8:1. The next three graphs show the average compression ratio for three different types of file extensions. Figure 8.9, for example, shows statistics for EXE, DOC, and BAT files—the three extensions SPACEMANager shows by default. Use the **V**iew menu to select other file extensions for these bar graphs.

The **U**pdate command button at the top left of the SPACEMANager window updates the Compression Ratio statistical display. You must click this button to make sure that you view the most current statistics for the selected drive.

Beneath the Compression Ratio graphs lies the third section of the SPACEMANager display, which tells you which SPACEMANager features currently are enabled. To the left of each feature's name is a check box. If a check mark appears inside the box, the feature is enabled. How to enable and disable these features is described later in this chapter.

The curved bar graph in the right-hand area of the statistics display, labeled Disk Space Usage, shows how much space on the selected disk drive is occupied and how much is free. The percentage value of the selected drive's used space appears below the graph, along with the actual value of the free space remaining. As your disk becomes increasingly full, the bar graph advances, gradually turning from green to red, indicating low disk space. Also below the free-space bar graph appears information indicating whether the selected drive is compressed. If the selected drive is compressed, the host drive letter is displayed.

An OK command button appears in the upper-right corner of the SPACEMANager window. Click the command button to close the SPACEMANager utility. You also can choose E**x**it from the SPACEMANager **F**ile menu.

Enabling SelectCompress

To enable the SelectCompress feature, follow these steps:

1. Start the DOS or Windows version of the SPACEMANager utility, if not already running. SPACEMANager displays the appropriate statistical report and main menu.
2. Access the **O**ptions menu of the SPACEMANager main menu, and then choose Compression **L**evels from the **O**ptions menu. DOS SPACEMANager displays the SelectCompress Options dialog box shown in figure 8.10. Windows SPACEMANager displays the SelectCompress Options dialog box shown in figure 8.11.

    Near the bottom of the SelectCompress dialog box, in both DOS and Windows versions, is the **L**oad SelectCompress TSR on System Startup option. To the left of this phrase is a check box. If the check box contains an X or a check mark, SelectCompress already is enabled, so skip to step 4.

3. Press Alt+L, and then press the spacebar to enable the SelectCompress TSR (or use the mouse to click the check box).

    If the SelectCompress check box is already enabled, this step clears the mark from the check box, and SelectCompress becomes *disabled*.

4. Press Enter or click OK to close the SelectCompress Options dialog box.

The SPACEMANager SelectCompress feature is now enabled. SelectCompress is not actually installed in memory, however, until the next time you start your computer.

Setting Compression Levels

To change the compression level SPACEMANager applies to each of the four file categories, follow these steps:

1. Start the SPACEMANager utility, if not already running. SPACEMANager displays the statistical report and main menu.
2. Access the **O**ptions menu, and then choose Compression **L**evels. The appropriate SelectCompressOptions dialog box appears (refer to fig. 8.10 or fig. 8.11).
3. In the Disk Drive(s) area, select the disk drive for which you want to set compression levels. (Select the disk drive the same way you select a drive for the main statistics display.)

    After selecting the drive, you must select the compression level to apply to each type of file on the drive.

4. Press Alt plus the highlighted (or underlined) letter in the name of the file category to select that file category. To select the **T**ext file category, for example, press Alt+T.
5. After selecting a file category, use the appropriate arrow keys to move the diamond-shaped mark from the radio button of one compression level to that of

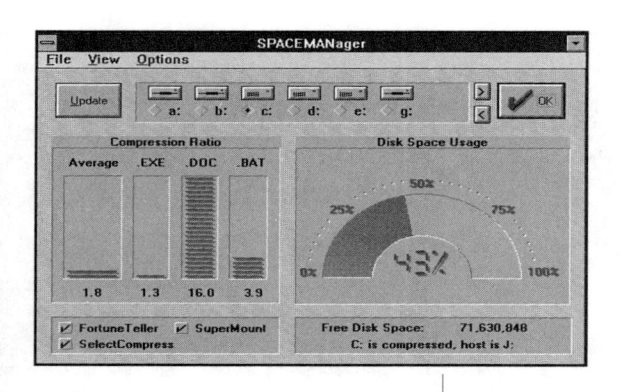

Fig. 8.9

The Windows SPACEMANager statistics report and main menu.

If you decide to restart your computer now, make sure that you have saved all your data and exited from Windows or any other programs before you do so.

Your changes to compression levels take effect immediately if the SelectCompress feature is enabled. The new compression levels affect only data written to your disk *after* you make the changes. Files already on your disk are not affected by changes in the compression levels unless you copy or edit these files.

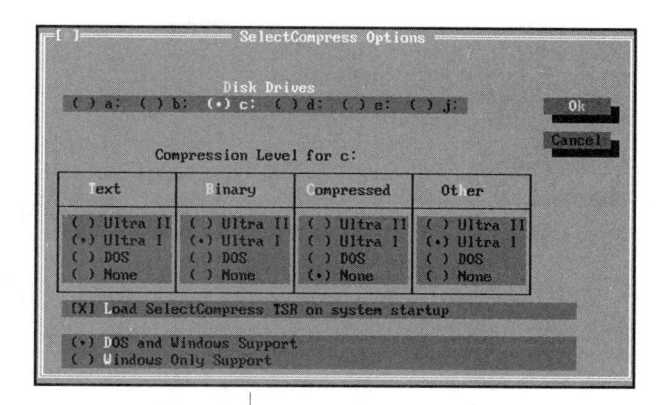

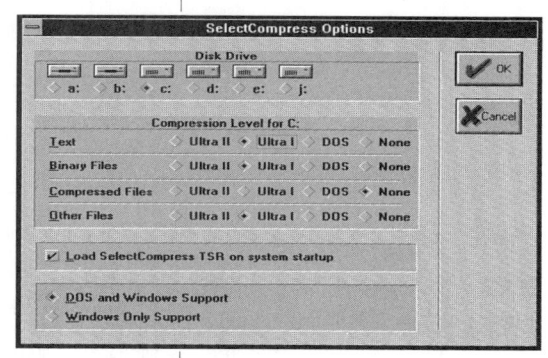

Fig. 8.10, top

The SelectCompress Options dialog box in DOS.

Fig. 8.11, bottom

The SelectCompress Options dialog box in Windows.

the next level. (Use the up and down arrows in the DOS dialog box; use the right and left arrows in the Windows version.) If the mark is in the radio button of the compression level you want for that category, that level is selected.

To set the compression level for Ot**h**er files to standard DOS compression in the DOS SelectCompress options dialog box, for example, press Alt+H to select the Ot**h**er category, and then press the left- or up-arrow once to move the diamond-shaped mark to the DOS compression level radio button.

If using a mouse, simply click the radio button next to the desired compression level in the appropriate line or column for the file category you want. This inserts the diamond-shaped mark in that compression level's radio button without the need for first choosing a file category.

6. Continue selecting disk drives and setting compression levels until you are satisfied with your selections.

7. To confirm the changes you have made, press Enter or click OK.

   If you change your mind about making changes to the compression levels, press Esc or click Cancel.

Making Removable Media Usable on Computers without DoubleSpace

SPACEMANager's SuperExchange program enables you to use DoubleSpace compressed removable disks on computers on which DoubleSpace is not installed. This section describes how to add SuperExchange to a removable media disk and how to use SuperExchange to read the compressed data on a computer lacking DoubleSpace.

Adding SuperExchange to a Compressed Removable Disk

You can add SuperExchange to an already-compressed removable disk from either DOS or Windows. To add SuperExchange to a compressed removable disk from DOS, you use the ADDX utility supplied with SPACEMANager. Use the following syntax with this command:

   ADDX *d***:**

In this example, *d* stands for the letter of the drive containing the compressed removable disk to which you want to add SuperExchange. To add SuperExchange to a compressed floppy disk in drive B, for example, enter the following command at the DOS prompt:

ADDX B:

As ADDX puts SuperExchange on a compressed removable disk, it first unmounts the disk (if mounted) and adds the file SUPERX.EXE to the root directory of the uncompressed portion of the compressed removable disk. Then ADDX mounts the compressed removable disk and adds the file SUPERX–.EXE to the root directory of the compressed volume on the removable disk. (The SUPERX and SUPERX– programs are described in the section "Using SUPERX Exchangeable Removable Disks," later in this chapter.)

To add SuperExchange to a compressed removable disk by using the SPACEMANager Windows utility, follow these steps:

1. Start the Windows SPACEMANager utility, if not already running.
2. Access the **F**ile menu, and then choose Make Floppy **E**xchangeable. SPACEMANager displays the Add SuperExchange to a Diskette dialog box, as shown in figure 8.12.
3. Click the radio button below the drive icon to select the drive containing the removable disk to which you want to add SuperExchange.
4. Click OK to add SuperExchange to the disk in the selected drive.

Compressing a Removable Disk and Adding SuperExchange

Compressing a removable disk and adding SuperExchange at the same time is usually more convenient than is compressing a removable disk and adding SuperExchange separately. You can compress a floppy and add SuperExchange simultaneously from either DOS or Windows.

To simultaneously compress a removable disk and add SuperExchange from DOS, use the DBLFLOP utility supplied with SPACEMANager. Use the following syntax with the DBLFLOP utility command:

DBLFLOP *d*: /X

In this example, *d* stands for the letter of the drive that contains the disk you want to compress. The /X switch is optional and instructs DBLFLOP to add SuperExchange to the disk without asking you whether to do so.

To compress a disk in drive B and add SuperExchange at the same time, for example, enter the following command at the DOS prompt:

DBLFLOP B:

This example does not use the /X switch. Before compressing the removable disk, therefore, DBLFLOP asks whether you want to add SuperExchange. Press Enter to add SuperExchange, or press N and then press Enter to compress the removable disk without adding SuperExchange. If you decide not to compress the disk at all, type a minus sign (–) and press Enter.

In this example, the following command compresses the floppy disk in drive B and adds SuperExchange without pausing to ask permission:

DBLFLOP B: /X

> **STOP**
>
> If you have obtained the DOS 6 supplemental disks from Microsoft, do not confuse the SPACEMANager DBLFLOP.EXE program with the DBLFLOP.BAT batch file contained on these supplemental disks. The SPACEMANager DBLFLOP.EXE program compresses a removable disk and optionally adds SuperExchange to it. The DOS supplemental DBLFLOP.BAT creates a bootable compressed floppy disk. If the directory that contains DBLFLOP.BAT is listed in your PATH statement before the directory that contains SPACEMANager, the DBLFLOP.BAT may execute instead of the SPACEMANager DBLFLOP.EXE. To correct this problem, change your PATH statement, or remove DBLFLOP.BAT from your hard disk or put it in a directory that is not on the path.

> **NOTE:**
> Any removable disk you want to compress—whether it is a floppy disk, a Floptical disk, a Bernoulli cartridge, a Syquest cartridge, or other removable media—must already be formatted so that the disk is usable by DOS.

If you want to compress the removable disk without adding SuperExchange and do not want DBLFLOP to ask whether to add SuperExchange, add a minus sign after the /X switch. The following example compresses the disk in drive B but does not add SuperExchange to the disk:

DBLFLOP B: /X–

If you use DBLFLOP to add SuperExchange, DBLFLOP first compresses the removable disk and adds the SUPERX program to the root directory of the uncompressed portion of the disk. DBLFLOP then mounts the compressed removable disk and adds the SUPERX– program to the root directory of the compressed volume.

The SUPERX and SUPERX– programs are described in the section "Using SUPERX Exchangeable Removable Disks," later in this chapter.

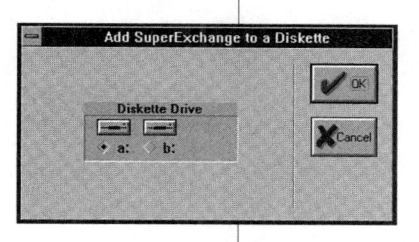

Compressing a Floppy Disk from Windows

Among SPACEMANager's important additions to DoubleSpace is its capability to compress a floppy disk without leaving Windows. You also can add SuperExchange to the floppy disk while you compress it from Windows.

To compress a floppy disk by using the SPACEMANager Windows utility, follow these steps:

1. Start the Windows SPACEMANager utility, if it is not already running.
2. Access the **F**ile menu, and then choose **C**ompress a Floppy. SPACEMANager displays the Compress a Formatted Diskette dialog box, as shown in figure 8.13.
3. Click the radio button below the drive icons to select the drive containing the removable disk you want to compress.
4. To add SuperExchange to the floppy disk at the same time you compress it, select the **A**dd SuperExchange to Diskette check box.

   If a check mark appears in the check box to the left of **A**dd SuperExchange to Diskette, the option is enabled and SPACEMANager adds SuperExchange to the disk after it finishes compressing the disk.

5. After you are satisfied with your settings, click OK or press Enter to begin compressing the disk.

   If you change your mind about compressing the disk, press Esc or click Cancel.

   After SPACEMANager finishes compressing the disk and adding SuperExchange to it, it closes the dialog box and returns to the statistical display and main menu.

Fig. 8.12

The Windows SPACEMANager Add SuperExchange to a Diskette dialog box.

> **NOTE:**
> As Windows SPACEMANager adds SuperExchange to your compressed removable disk, it uses the same method as the ADDX utility does in DOS.

Using SUPERX Exchangeable Removable Disks

Whenever you add SuperExchange to a removable disk—whether at the same time you compress the disk or afterward—SPACEMANager adds a special file named READTHIS.TXT to the root directory of the uncompressed portion of the removable disk. The READTHIS.TXT file is a DOS text file that contains text explaining that the disk is compressed for DoubleSpace. The file also gives brief instructions for accessing the information on the compressed volume by using either DoubleSpace or SUPERX.

166 The Disk Compression Book

On a computer with DoubleSpace installed, you simply mount the compressed volume by using either DoubleSpace or SPACEMANager. The purpose of an exchangeable removable disk, however, is to enable the disk to be used on a computer that does not have DoubleSpace installed.

To mount the compressed volume on a computer that does not have DoubleSpace, follow these steps:

1. Insert the compressed removable disk in a drive.
2. To access the compressed volume on the removable disk, type **A:SUPERX** at the DOS prompt (substituting the appropriate letter for your drive, if not A), and press Enter.

   The SUPERX program loads into memory and mounts the compressed volume. SUPERX operates similarly to DoubleSpace, but only for the disk from which SUPERX is loaded. SUPERX creates a new drive letter for DOS and exchanges it with the drive letter of the drive containing the compressed disk. If you use SUPERX to mount a compressed volume in drive A, for example, the compressed volume is accessible as drive A, and the uncompressed portion of the disk is accessible as another drive letter.
3. Use the compressed volume as you do any other disk drive. Observe the usual precautions against removing the disk while it is in use by a program or while the drive's activity light is on.
4. After you no longer need to access the compressed volume, type **A:SUPERX–** at the DOS prompt (substituting the appropriate letter for your drive, if not A), and press Enter.

   SUPERX– unmounts the compressed volume and removes SuperExchange from memory. The compressed volume is no longer accessible.

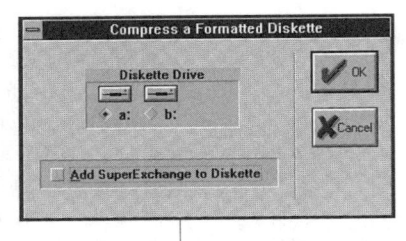

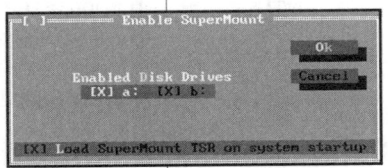

Fig. 8.13

The Windows SPACEMANager Compress a Formatted Diskette dialog box.

Fig. 8.14

The Enable SuperMount dialog box in DOS.

Enabling and Disabling Automatic Mounting of Removable Disks

You can enable or disable the SPACEMANager SuperMount feature individually for each removable media drive, as well as enable or disable SuperMount for your entire system. You usually want the SuperMount feature activated so that compressed removable drives are mounted automatically. You especially want SuperMount active if you use compressed removable media with Windows. If you do not use compressed removable media at all, however, you may want to disable the SuperMount feature to make more memory available for other uses.

This section describes how to enable or disable SuperMount for each removable media drive and how to enable or disable SuperMount for your entire system. These instructions cover both the DOS and Windows SPACEMANager utilities.

NOTE:

SPACEMANager SUPERX requires DOS 3.31 or higher to work. You cannot use SUPERX on a computer with an earlier version of DOS. If you try, SUPERX displays an error message and does not mount the compressed volume.

Enabling or Disabling SuperMount for Individual Drives

To enable or disable the SuperMount feature for individual drives in SPACEMANager, follow these steps (the procedure is the same whether you use SPACEMANager for DOS or Windows):

Beyond DoubleSpace: Using SPACEMANager   **167**

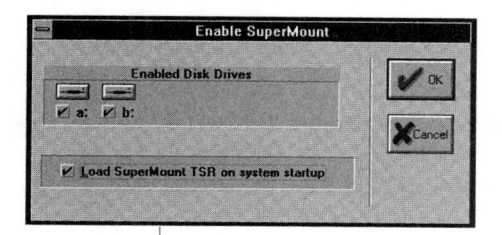

Fig. 8.15

The Enable SuperMount dialog box in Windows.

1. Start SPACEMANager, if not already running. The SPACEMANager statistical report and main menu appears.
2. Access the **O**ptions menu, and then choose Automatic Floppy **M**ount. DOS SPACEMANager displays the Enable SuperMount dialog box, as shown in figure 8.14. Windows SPACEMANager displays the Enable SuperMount dialog box, as shown in figure 8.15.

   Near the center of each dialog box is a list of removable media disk drives. In DOS SPACEMANager, each drive has a check box to its left; in Windows SPACEMANager, each drive icon displays a check box below it. If the check box contains an X or a check mark, SuperMount is enabled for that drive; compressed removable disks in those drives are mounted automatically.
3. Select the drive you want to enable. If using DOS SPACEMANager, press Alt+D to activate the Enabled **D**isk Drives list. Use the arrow keys to highlight the drive you want to enable or disable, and then press the spacebar to change the contents of the check box. If using Windows SPACEMANager, simply click the check box for the drive you want to enable or disable.

   If SuperMount was enabled for the drive, it is now disabled. If SuperMount was disabled for the drive, it is now enabled.
4. To close the Enable SuperMount dialog box, press Enter or click OK. SPACEMANager saves your changes and closes the dialog box.

   If you change your mind, press Esc or click Cancel. SPACEMANager closes the Enable SuperMount dialog box without saving any of your changes.

Enabling or Disabling SuperMount for Your Entire System

To enable or disable the SuperMount feature for your entire system, follow these steps:

1. Start SPACEMANager, if not already running. The SPACEMANager statistical report and main menu appears.
2. Access the **O**ptions menu, and then choose Automatic Floppy **M**ount. Both DOS and Windows versions of SPACEMANager display the appropriate Enable SuperMount dialog box (refer to fig. 8.14 [DOS] or fig. 8.15 [Windows]). At the bottom of the Enable SuperMount dialog box in both versions is the **L**oad SuperMount TSR on System Startup option. To the left of the option name is a check box. If the check box contains an X or a check mark, SuperMount is installed whenever you start your computer. If the check box is empty, you must enable this option.
3. Press Alt+L to select the **L**oad SuperMount TSR on System Startup check box, and then press the spacebar to enable or disable the SuperMount TSR. If you use a mouse, click the check box to enable or disable the SuperMount TSR.

   If the SuperMount TSR was enabled, it is now disabled. If the SuperMount TSR was disabled, it is now enabled.

4. To close the Enable SuperMount dialog box, press Enter or click OK. SPACEMANager saves your changes and closes the dialog box.

   If you change your mind, press Esc or click Cancel. SPACEMANager closes the Enable SuperMount dialog box without saving any of your changes.

If you disable the SuperMount TSR, the TSR is not loaded into memory the next time you start your computer and none of your compressed removable disks are mounted automatically. If you enable the SuperMount TSR, the TSR is loaded into memory the next time you start your computer and those removable media drives for which you have individually enabled SuperMount automatically mount their compressed disks.

Summary

In this chapter, you learned about the features SPACEMANager adds to DoubleSpace and how SPACEMANager works. The chapter described the changes SPACEMANager makes to your system and then walked you through the SPACEMANager installation process. Next, the chapter described how to start SPACEMANager and how to interpret the information SPACEMANager displays. The final section of the chapter included specific instructions for several common or important tasks that you can perform by using SPACEMANager.

The next chapter begins Part III, "Using Stacker," which describes how to prepare and install the Stacker disk compression program.

> **STOP**
>
> If you decide to restart your computer now, make sure that you save all your data and exit from Windows or any other programs before you actually restart the computer.

PART III

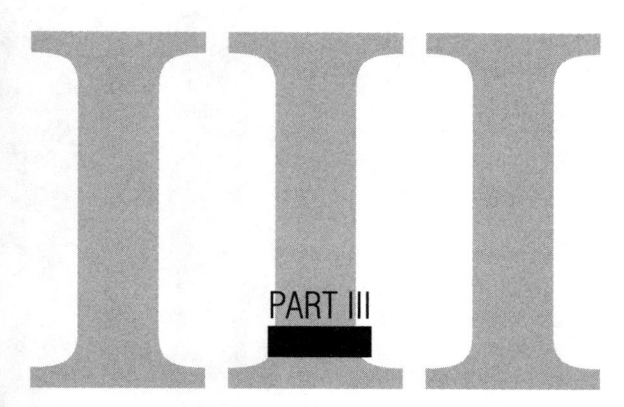

Using Stacker

9. Installing Stacker
10. Configuring and Optimizing Stacker
11. Using Stacker
12. Using the Stacker Utilities
13. Troubleshooting Stacker

CHAPTER 9

Installing Stacker

This chapter describes how to set up Stacker 3.1 on your computer. To use Stacker 3.1, you must have DOS 6 or a later version. You use Stacker's Setup program to install Stacker. The Stacker Setup program copies Stacker's program files to your hard disk and makes any necessary changes in your computer's configuration. If you have already installed DoubleSpace on your computer, the Stacker Setup program converts your DoubleSpace compressed drives to Stacker compressed drives.

You can install Stacker from either DOS or Windows. The Stacker Setup program also enables you to choose between two installation methods: Express Setup and Custom Setup. Express Setup automatically compresses all the disk drives on your computer. Custom Setup enables you to choose specific drives for compression and to control other aspects of the Stacker installation.

This chapter begins by describing how Stacker alters your computer's setup, assigns drive letters, and alters the disk volume labels. The chapter then describes how to prepare to add Stacker to your computer system. This chapter also provides step-by-step instructions for both Express Setup and Custom Setup. The final section of this chapter describes how to convert from DoubleSpace or another disk compression program to Stacker.

Changes Made by Stacker Setup

Stacker Setup must make changes in your computer's configuration so that Stacker can operate. This section describes those configuration changes and how they affect your computer.

Files Added to Boot Disk Root Directory

In addition to any compressed volume files you create, Stacker adds two files—DBLSPACE.BIN and STACKER.INI—to the root directory of your boot disk. Stacker puts these files in the uncompressed part of your boot disk, because DOS and Stacker must be able to read them at a time when your compressed volumes are not accessible. The DBLSPACE.BIN file is the Stacker device driver; it provides access to your compressed drives. Whenever DOS starts up, DOS looks for the DBLSPACE.BIN file in the root directory of your boot disk and, if found, loads it into memory. The STACKER.INI file contains information the Stacker device driver needs as it loads into memory during start-up. STACKER.INI tells the Stacker device driver how to mount the compressed drives, how to swap drive letters, whether to use EMS memory, and other configuration information. Chapter 10, "Configuring and Optimizing Stacker," describes the options you can set in STACKER.INI.

As Stacker places the DBLSPACE.BIN and STACKER.INI files on your boot disk, it assigns them Hidden, System, and Read-Only file attributes. Normally, you are not aware of these files, because the Hidden attribute prevents them from appearing in most directory listings. The Read-Only file attribute prevents you from accidentally erasing these important files.

Stacker adds a third file, STACKER.LOG, to the root directory of every disk containing a Stacker-compressed volume. STACKER.LOG contains information about when your Stacker volumes were created and about any errors that occurred during their creation. The STACKER.LOG file's Read-Only attribute prevents its accidental deletion.

Stacker also places some of the Stacker program files and a couple DOS files in the root directory of your uncompressed boot disk. Stacker moves all other data and program files to the compressed portion of the boot disk. If a problem ever prevents Stacker from mounting the compressed drive after your computer starts, you can use the Stacker and DOS files on the uncompressed root directory of your start-up drive to troubleshoot the problem.

Changes to CONFIG.SYS and AUTOEXEC.BAT

Stacker takes advantage of the DOS 6 device driver preload feature to load itself into memory; consequently, you need not add commands to your CONFIG.SYS or AUTOEXEC.BAT files to load Stacker. If the Stacker DBLSPACE.BIN file is in the root directory of your boot disk as your computer starts, DOS 6 automatically loads the device driver into memory. Although additions to CONFIG.SYS and AUTOEXEC.BAT are not required for Stacker to operate, Stacker does add a line to your CONFIG.SYS that enables optional Stacker features. Stacker also adds commands to your AUTOEXEC.BAT file to increase the safety and convenience of Stacker's operation. Each of these changes is described in this section.

As you run the Stacker Setup program, it adds the following line to your CONFIG.SYS file:

```
DEVICE=C:\STACKER\STACHIGH.SYS
```

> **STOP**
>
> Do not confuse the DBLSPACE.BIN file provided with Stacker with the DBLSPACE.BIN file provided with DOS 6. Although both files have the same name, only the Stacker version can read Stacker compressed drives. DOS 6 can preload only a device driver with the exact name DBLSPACE.BIN. The Stacker device driver, therefore, must have the same name as the DoubleSpace device driver supplied with DOS 6. Make sure that you delete the DoubleSpace files listed in the preparation guidelines in this chapter before you install Stacker so that the DoubleSpace version of DBLSPACE.BIN is removed. Take care also to follow the instructions in the section "Making a DOS 6 Start-up Disk Containing Stacker," later in this chapter, to make a DOS 6 start-up floppy disk that includes the Stacker device driver.

> **!**
>
> Do not remove the file attributes of either the DBLSPACE.BIN or STACKER.INI files. Deleting or modifying either of these files can disable your compressed volumes.

Installing Stacker 173

> **NOTE:**
> Do not confuse Stacker's STACHIGH.SYS with Stacker's DBLSPACE.BIN. DBLSPACE.BIN is the device driver that provides access to your Stacker compressed volumes and is automatically loaded into memory by DOS. STACHIGH.SYS is a special program you use to control the final memory location of DBLSPACE.BIN and to provide redirection of DOS commands to their Stacker equivalents.

The STACHIGH.SYS device driver enables you to relocate the Stacker device driver to upper memory, thus freeing about 48K of conventional memory. (Refer to Chapter 10, "Configuring and Optimizing Stacker" for instructions on how to relocate the Stacker device driver to upper memory.) STACHIGH.SYS also contains the instructions necessary to redirect several DOS disk commands to the Stacker equivalent commands. If Stacker command redirection is loaded and you use the DOS DIR command, for example, the Stacker SDIR command is executed instead. Stacker equivalent commands are described in Chapter 11, "Using Stacker," and Chapter 12, "Using the Stacker Utilities." Controlling Stacker command redirection is described in Chapter 10, "Configuring and Optimizing Stacker."

Stacker also makes a minor change in your AUTOEXEC.BAT file by adding the following lines during Stacker Setup:

```
REM  THE CHECK LINE BELOW PROVIDES ADDITIONAL SAFETY FOR STACKER DRIVES.
REM  PLEASE DO NOT REMOVE IT.
C:\STACKER\CHECK /WP
```

The first two lines are explanatory comments. The third (and most important) line runs the Stacker program that checks the internal integrity of Stacker compressed volume files. With this line in your AUTOEXEC.BAT, Stacker checks the integrity of your drives every time your computer starts.

Finally, Stacker adds the Stacker directory to your PATH statement in AUTOEXEC.BAT. If you choose Express Setup, Stacker automatically adds the Stacker directory to the PATH statement. If you choose Custom Setup, you decide whether to add the Stacker directory to the PATH statement.

Stacker Volumes

As discussed in Chapter 1, "Understanding and Using Disk Compression," your disk compression software works by creating a large file on your hard disk and then treating this large file as a logical disk drive. The data stored on your compressed disk is actually stored in this large file, which is located on the uncompressed part of your original disk drive or partition. Each time you create a new compressed drive, Stacker creates a new compressed volume file for the compressed drive. Stacker assigns the file Hidden, System, and Read-Only file attributes so that you are unaware of the file and cannot accidentally delete it.

> ⚠ Do not change the file attributes for the compressed volume files or attempt to alter them in any way. If you accidentally erase or damage the compressed volume file, you may lose or corrupt all data on the compressed drive.

Stacker names the first compressed volume file it creates on an uncompressed disk STACVOL.DSK. Stacker gives every additional compressed volume file on the same physical host drive the STACVOL name plus a sequential extension number (STACVOL.001, STACVOL.002, and so on). Stacker creates and maintains the compressed volume file automatically. Troubleshooting your compressed drive is described in Chapter 13, "Troubleshooting Stacker."

How Stacker Assigns Drive Letters and Volume Labels

As described earlier, Stacker creates the STACKER.INI file in the root directory of your uncompressed boot disk. Stacker uses the information in the STACKER.INI file as instructions on how to exchange drive letters between the compressed drives and the uncompressed host drives. (Remember that the host drive is the uncompressed drive that contains the compressed volume file.) Each time you create another compressed drive, Stacker modifies the contents of the STACKER.INI file to include the new compressed drive and its host. The information in this section describes in detail how Stacker chooses drive letters. It also describes the rules Stacker uses for assigning these letters.

Assigning Drive Letters

Before you compress any of its drives, your computer system includes a certain number of physical hard disks. A certain number of physical partitions also may be present on one or more hard disks, configured as logical disk drives. DOS assigns drive letters to these physical disks and partitions on a first-come, first-served basis.

As you create a compressed hard disk by using Stacker, you create another logical disk drive, and DOS assigns it the next available drive letter. If the highest drive letter in your system before compression is drive E, for example, DOS assigns the drive letter F to the first compressed volume you create. (DOS drive letters and drive letter assignment are described in more detail in Chapter 1, "Understanding and Using Disk Compression.") For your convenience, the Stacker device driver exchanges drive letters between the compressed volumes and their host drives. If you compress drive C, for example, Stacker reassigns drive letters so that all your data on the new compressed volume is still accessible to you as drive C. Stacker gives the uncompressed disk (formerly accessible as drive C) another drive letter. When you create the first compressed volume, Stacker assigns the next available DOS drive letter as the drive letter for the host drive of the new compressed volume file.

To understand the assignment process, assume that, before you add Stacker, your computer has two physical disk drives, C and D. The highest drive letter in your system is drive D. If you compress drive C, Stacker assigns the next available DOS drive letter, drive E, as the host drive for the new compressed volume C. Stacker continues assigning the next available DOS drive letter as the host drive letter for each new compressed drive. If you use Express Setup, Stacker creates compressed drives by compressing the physical drive with the highest drive letter first. On a system with the two drives C and D, for example, Stacker first compresses drive D and assigns drive letter E to the host drive for the new compressed volume D. Stacker next compresses drive C and assigns drive letter F to the host drive for the compressed volume C.

Creating Stacker drives from free space on a disk creates a special case in drive letter assignments. (A *free space* compressed drive is a Stacker compressed drive created from only the free space on an uncompressed drive.) If you create a free space drive on an uncompressed disk that contains no files, Stacker exchanges drive letters as already described. If you create a Stacker free space drive on an uncompressed drive that contains

> **NOTE:** If you convert from DoubleSpace to Stacker, Stacker does not change how drive letters are exchanged. Your drive letters are exchanged just as they were in DoubleSpace.

even one file, however, Stacker does not exchange drive letters at all. Instead, Stacker assigns the new free space drive the next available drive letter.

Occasionally, you may need to alter how Stacker assigns drive letters. Altering the drive letters assigned by Stacker is described in Chapter 10, "Configuring and Optimizing Stacker."

Assigning Volume Labels

A volume label provides a means of identifying a disk drive apart from its drive letter. You give disks a volume name as you format them or by using the DOS LABEL command. (Refer to your DOS documentation for information on the LABEL command.)

Stacker assigns the volume label STACVOL_DSK to each compressed drive as the drive is created but does not alter the volume label of the original, uncompressed host drive. Assume, for example, that you have a drive C with the volume label DRIVE_1. If you use Stacker to compress this drive C, Stacker labels the new compressed volume STACVOL_DSK. The uncompressed drive retains its original label of DRIVE_1. The STACVOL_DSK label identifies the compressed drives on your system.

Preparing To Install Stacker

In general, installing Stacker is a straightforward and trouble-free operation. Installing Stacker does represent a major change in your computer's configuration, however, so you need to make some preparations before you attempt the installation.

Follow these guidelines to prepare for Stacker installation:

- *Upgrade DOS.* To use Stacker 3.1 with DOS 6, you must install your DOS 6 upgrade before you install Stacker. This book covers only Stacker 3.1 used with DOS 6.
- *Back up.* Back up all files on the disks you intend to compress. Problems installing Stacker are rare, but a recent backup of your files is the most secure protection for your data. If you experience a problem while installing Stacker, a current backup of your data can make the difference between an inconvenience and a tragedy.
- *Make a bootable floppy disk.* Again, problems installing Stacker are rare, but if you do experience a problem, you may need to start your computer from a floppy disk. Make sure that you have available a bootable floppy disk containing DOS 6. Refer to your DOS documentation for information on creating a bootable floppy disk. If you use a third-party utility such as Central Point's PC Backup or 5th Generation's Fastback to perform your backup, make sure that you also have copies of your backup utilities on a floppy disk.
- *Preserve your CONFIG.SYS and AUTOEXEC.BAT.* For safety, keep copies of your current configuration files on a floppy disk in case you experience any difficulty during setup. Along with the file changes already discussed, Stacker makes other, temporary, changes in AUTOEXEC.BAT while performing its setup routines. If your computer experiences a problem (such as a power failure) as

---

NOTE: If you convert from DoubleSpace to Stacker, Stacker does not change any of your volume labels.

You can use the DOS LABEL command to change the volume label of a Stacker compressed drive at any time. Refer to your DOS documentation for information on using the LABEL command.

After you install the DOS 6 upgrade, make sure that all your DOS programs work correctly before you install Stacker. After you install Stacker, you cannot use the Uninstall disk created by the DOS 6 Setup program to revert to an earlier DOS version.

Stacker changes CONFIG.SYS and AUTOEXEC.BAT, those files can be lost or damaged. If you made copies of these files, you may be able to regain access to your entire system by restoring only the configuration files, without needing to restore an entire backup or reinstall software.

- *Uninstall copy-protected software.* Some software programs use copy-protection schemes that rely on finding certain data in certain areas of the disk. Compressing your disk moves this special data. As a result, the copy-protection scheme no longer recognizes your software as a legitimate copy, and you cannot use your program. Refer to your program's documentation if you are unsure whether it uses this type of copy-protection scheme; the documentation also includes instructions for uninstalling the software. After you compress your drive, you can re-install the copy-protected program.

- *Use the DOS CHKDSK command.* The DOS CHKDSK command checks the integrity of your disk drive. Use this command on each of your disks before you compress them. Resolve any problems that CHKDSK reveals before you begin the Stacker setup. Refer to your DOS documentation for instructions on using the DOS CHKDSK command. CHKDSK also is discussed in Chapter 13, "Troubleshooting Stacker."

- *Disconnect from a network.* If your computer connects to a network, make sure that your network software is not running before you install Stacker.

- *Disable disk cache programs loaded in CONFIG.SYS.* If you have any disk cache programs loaded as device drivers in your CONFIG.SYS file, disable them. To disable the device drivers, use a text editor such as the DOS EDIT program to change your CONFIG.SYS file. Add REM (for *remark*) to the beginning of the line in your CONFIG.SYS file that loads the disk cache device driver. Refer to your DOS documentation for more information on CONFIG.SYS; refer also to the documentation for your disk cache program to identify the disk cache device driver line.

- *Disable FASTOPEN.* If you use the DOS FASTOPEN command in either your CONFIG.SYS or AUTOEXEC.BAT files, disable it. FASTOPEN can cause problems during Stacker installation. To disable FASTOPEN, use a text editor such as the DOS EDIT program to change your CONFIG.SYS or AUTOEXEC.BAT file. Add REM to the beginning of the line that loads the FASTOPEN program. Refer to your DOS documentation for more information on FASTOPEN.

- *Make sure that you have enough disk space.* Stacker requires approximately 2.8M of space on your hard disk—before the disk is compressed. You cannot complete Stacker installation without adequate free space on your hard disk.

- *Delete the DoubleSpace program files.* Upgrading to DOS 6 automatically places DOS DoubleSpace program files on your hard disk. Because your DOS directory most likely is part of DOS's search path, you may inadvertently run the DoubleSpace program. DoubleSpace cannot determine whether your disks have been compressed by any disk compression scheme other than DoubleSpace. Installing DoubleSpace after installing Stacker, therefore, destroys your Stacker compressed drives and can result in severe data loss. Because both the Stacker

STOP

If you do not uninstall your copy-protected software before compressing your disk, that software is unusable after compression.

You also can disable device drivers in your CONFIG.SYS file by using DOS 6's capability to conditionally process lines in your CONFIG.SYS file. Press F8 to have DOS prompt you before loading each device driver, and then do not load the disk cache device drivers. Refer to your DOS documentation for more information on this feature.

NOTE:

After you install Stacker, you may again enable your disk cache device drivers and FASTOPEN command by removing the REM prefix from those lines in your CONFIG.SYS file.

> **NOTE:**
> Compressing all the files on your hard disks or partitions can require anywhere from a few minutes to a few hours, depending on how many disks you compress and how many files are on each disk. Begin the Stacker Setup only if you are certain you do not need your computer for several hours—at the end of a working day, for example, or on a Friday afternoon.

> **STOP**
> The Stacker Setup program restarts your computer twice. If you have data on a RAM disk or in TSR programs, save it *before* you begin the Stacker Setup.

> **NOTE:**
> If you use Windows, and a permanent swap file is located on any of your hard drives, Stacker Setup leaves enough uncompressed space on the appropriate hard drive to accommodate the swap file. Stacker moves the permanent swap file to the uncompressed portion of the drive and alters your Windows configuration to use the uncompressed drive's new drive letter when looking for the permanent swap file.

and DoubleSpace disk compression device drivers have the same name, DBLSPACE.BIN, you also may confuse the two files. If this occurs, you may temporarily lose access to your Stacker drives. To avoid these problems, delete the DOS DoubleSpace program files before you install Stacker. Use the DOS DEL command to delete all the files listed in Table 9.1. These files usually are located in the directory that contains your other DOS files. Make sure that you delete *only* the DoubleSpace files.

Table 9.1 DoubleSpace Program Files to Delete

Program File	Purpose
DBLSPACE.BIN	DoubleSpace device driver.
DBLSPACE.EXE	DoubleSpace program.
DBLSPACE.HLP	DoubleSpace Help file.
DBLSPACE.INF	Setup information for DoubleSpace.
DBLSPACE.SYS	Relocator for DBLSPACE.BIN.

After you complete all the steps in the preceding checklist, you are ready to install Stacker. As you install Stacker, remember to read all on-screen instructions for each step of the compression process. Avoid shortcuts, even if you are an experienced computer user. In areas involving the safety and integrity of your disk data, the adage "It is better to err on the side of caution" is particularly true.

Running Express Setup

This section describes how to start and use the Stacker Express Setup. Stacker Express Setup compresses all uncompressed disk drives in your system that are 5M or greater in overall size. If you have no hard drives, Stacker Express Setup compresses any removable media disks with capacities greater than 5M. If you previously installed DoubleSpace, Stacker Setup recognizes the DoubleSpace compressed drives and offers to convert them to Stacker format. To convert from DoubleSpace to Stacker, follow the instructions in the section "Converting to Stacker from Another Disk Compression Program," later in this chapter.

You can run the Stacker Express Setup from either DOS or Windows. If you run Stacker Express Setup from Windows, Stacker Setup adds a **S**tacker menu to the Windows File Manager. Stacker Setup also prepares Windows to create a program group for the Stacker Windows utilities. Use the instructions in the following section to install Stacker from the DOS command line. To install Stacker from Windows, begin the installation with the instructions in the section "Starting Express Setup from Windows," later in this chapter.

Starting Express Setup at the DOS Prompt

Stacker Express Setup compresses all your hard disks. To start Stacker Express Setup from the DOS prompt, follow these steps:

1. Go to the DOS prompt. If you use DESQview, GEM, or GEOworks, you must exit to DOS before starting Stacker. Exit also from any shell program that you may use, such as the DOS Shell, XTree, or Norton Desktop for DOS.
2. Insert the Stacker program disk 1 in whichever of your disk drives can accommodate it. You can install Stacker from either drive A or drive B.
3. Make the drive containing the Stacker program disk the current logged disk drive.
4. Type **SETUP** at the DOS prompt, and press Enter. Stacker displays a welcoming screen as the Setup program loads into memory and prepares your system.

    After Stacker Setup completes its preparations, it displays the Welcome to Setup dialog box. The dialog box displays a message advising you to back up your data before continuing and contains three command buttons: Continue, Help, and Exit.

5. To continue the installation, choose Continue. To access the Stacker Help system, choose the Help command button, or press F1. To halt the installation, choose the Exit command button. An Exit Verification dialog box asks you to cancel or verify the exit. Choose Cancel to return to Stacker Setup, or OK to return to DOS without completing the Stacker installation.

    If you continue with the installation, Stacker Setup displays the Personalize Stacker dialog box, which contains spaces to enter your name and your company's name.

6. Type your name in the Name text box, and then tab to the Company text box and enter your company name. (If Stacker Setup has run before, it already displays your personal information in this dialog box; you cannot change it.)
7. Choose Continue to continue the installation.

    After you update the Stacker files with your personal information, Stacker Setup displays the Express or Custom Setup dialog box (see fig. 9.1).

    If you were referred to these steps from the section "Starting Custom Setup at the DOS Prompt" or the section "Starting Double-Space Conversion from DOS," go now to step 2 in the appropriate section. The remaining instructions in this section cover Express Setup only.

    Express Setup installs the Stacker program files in a directory named STACKER on your drive C, compresses all hard drives, and installs the Stacker device driver with all appropriate settings. Custom Setup, on the other hand, enables you to

> **NOTE:** Many dialog boxes throughout Stacker Setup offer Continue, Help, and Exit commands. In each case, the commands operate as described in step 5 of this procedure. Any time during installation, you can access Help by pressing F1. Using the Stacker Help system is described in Chapter 11.

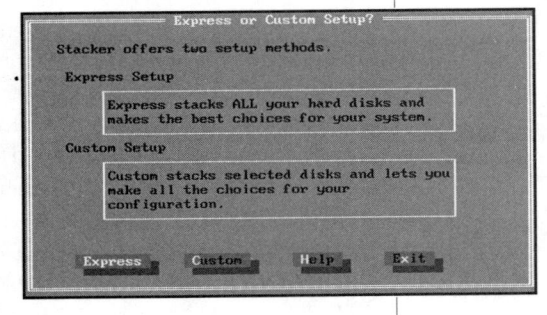

Fig. 9.1

The Stacker Express or Custom Setup dialog box.

specify which drives are to be compressed and to choose several different Stacker options. To perform a Custom installation, refer to the section "Running Custom Setup," later in this chapter.

8. Choose the **E**xpress command button. Stacker displays the Express Setup dialog box, as shown in figure 9.2.

This dialog box briefly describes the Express Setup process and displays the names of the drive and directory in which Setup installs the Stacker program files.

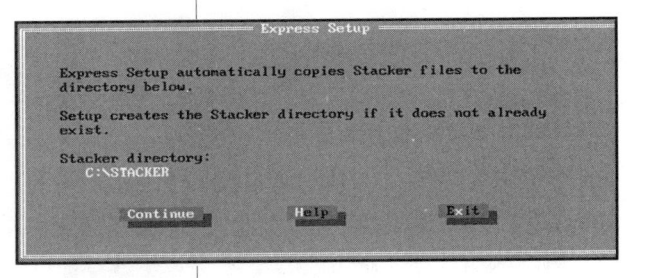

For Express Setup, the Stacker directory is always C:\STACKER.

9. Choose **C**ontinue to begin the Stacker Express Setup. Stacker begins copying files to your hard disk and displays a progress report.

Installing Stacker may take several hours, and Stacker cannot be interrupted after it begins the actual disk compression process. If you cannot do without your computer for several hours, E**x**it the Stacker Setup program and compress your disk some other time.

10. To finish installing Stacker, go to the section "Completing Stacker Express Setup," later in this chapter.

Fig. 9.2
The Express Setup dialog box.

Starting Express Setup from Windows

To begin the Stacker Express Setup from Windows, follow these steps:

1. Close any active Windows applications. Stacker must exit Windows to complete the Setup. Although you can save any open files later, closing all active Windows programs now makes your task easier.

2. Insert the Stacker program disk 1 in whichever of your floppy disk drives can accommodate it. You can install Stacker from either drive A or drive B.

3. From the Windows Program Manager, choose the **F**ile menu and then choose **R**un. Windows displays the Run dialog box.

4. In the **C**ommand Line text box of the Run dialog box, type the drive letter of the floppy disk drive that contains Stacker disk 1, followed by a colon, a backward slash, and the word **setup**, as shown in the following example. (This example assumes your Stacker disk is in drive B.)

    b:\setup

5. Choose OK to start the Stacker Setup program. Windows begins to load the Stacker Setup program from the floppy disk. The Stacker Setup program displays a greeting message as it loads.

After the Stacker Setup program finishes loading, it displays the Stacker 3.1 Setup dialog box. This dialog box displays a message reminding you to back up your data before continuing and contains three command buttons: **O**K, E**x**it, and **H**elp.

> **NOTE:** Many dialog boxes throughout Stacker Setup contain **O**K, E**x**it, and **H**elp command buttons. These command buttons always operate as described in step 6 of this procedure. Any time during installation, you can access Help by pressing F1. Using the Stacker Help system is described in Chapter 11.

6. To continue the Stacker Setup, choose the **OK** command button.

Choose **E**xit to halt the Stacker Setup installation. Stacker displays a dialog box asking you to verify the exit. Choose **N**o to continue Stacker Setup or **Y**es to return to Windows without completing the Stacker installation.

Choose **H**elp to access the Stacker Help system.

If you continue with the installation, Stacker Setup displays the Personalize Stacker dialog box, containing spaces to enter your name and your company name.

7. Type your name in the Name text box, and then tab to the Company text box and type your company name. (If Stacker Setup has run before, Stacker already displays your personal information; you cannot change it.)

8. Choose **OK** to continue the Stacker installation. Stacker updates the installation disk with your personal information and displays the dialog box shown in figure 9.3. This dialog box enables you to choose one of two methods for registering your software—by mail or by FAX.

You register by mail by completing and mailing the registration card supplied in your software package. To register by FAX, you must complete the registration form on-screen; Stacker Setup prints out your Warranty Registration in a form suitable for FAX transmission to Stac Electronics.

9. Choose Register by **M**ail to use the registration card supplied in your Stacker software package. Stacker displays a confirmation box in which you again choose Register by **M**ail to confirm your choice (or you can choose instead to Register by **F**AX if you change your mind). Stacker Setup proceeds to the dialog box shown in figure 9.5; skip to step 12 to continue the installation process if you are registering by mail.

To register by FAX, choose the Register by **F**AX button. Stacker Setup displays the dialog box shown in figure 9.4, with your personal information already entered.

Fig. 9.3, top

The Stacker Registration dialog box.

Fig. 9.4, bottom

The first page of the Stacker FAX Warranty Registration Form.

Installing Stacker   **181**

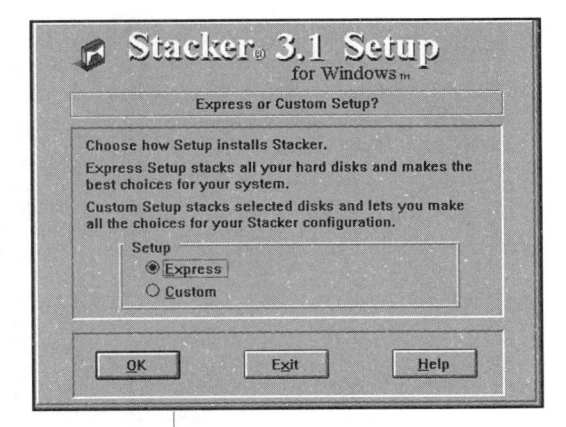

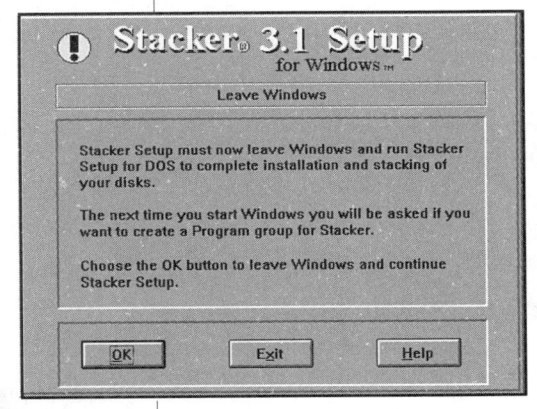

Fig. 9.5, top

The Stacker Express or Custom Setup dialog box.

Fig. 9.6, bottom

The Stacker Leave Windows confirmation dialog box.

10. Complete the first on-screen page of the FAX registration form, and choose **OK** to display the second page of the form; then complete that page.
11. Choose the **P**rint/FAX command button on the second page of the registration form. Windows displays a standard Print Setup dialog box. After you are satisfied with the printer settings, choose OK to print the form.

    After Stacker finishes printing the FAX registration form, Stacker Setup displays the Stacker Express or Custom Setup dialog box, as shown in figure 9.5.

    If you were referred to these steps from the section "Starting Custom Setup from Windows" or from the section "Starting DoubleSpace Conversion from Windows," go now to step 2 of the appropriate section. The remaining instructions in this section cover Express Setup only.

    Express Setup installs the Stacker program files in a directory named STACKER on your drive C, compresses all hard drives, and then installs the Stacker device driver with all appropriate settings. CustomSetup, on the other hand, enables you to compress specific drives and to choose from among several different Stacker options. For instructions on performing a Custom installation, refer to the section "Running Custom Setup," later in this chapter.

12. Select the **E**xpress radio button in the Setup area near the bottom of the dialog box. (Fig. 9.5 shows the **E**xpress button already selected.)
13. Choose **OK**. Stacker displays the Express Setup dialog box containing text that briefly describes the Express Setup process.
14. Choose **OK** again to confirm Express Setup. The Stacker Setup Leave Windows confirmation dialog box appears (see fig. 9.6). Stacker must leave Windows to continue the Express Setup.
15. Choose **OK** to continue the Stacker Express Setup. Stacker tells Windows to close all active applications and exit. If any Windows applications have unsaved data, an on-screen message asks if you want to save the data.

    After the exit from Windows is complete, a Stacker Express Setup confirmation dialog box appears (refer to fig. 9.2). The text in the screen briefly describes Express Setup and displays the drive and directory name into which the Stacker program files are to be installed. For Express Setup, the drive and directory location is always C:\STACKER.

16. Choose **C**ontinue in the Express Setup confirmation dialog box to begin the Stacker Express Setup. Stacker begins copying files to your hard disk. Stacker displays a progress report as it copies files.

    Installing Stacker may take several hours. Stacker cannot be interrupted after it begins the actual disk compression process. If you cannot do without your computer for several hours, E**x**it the Stacker Setup program and compress your disk some other time.

17. Go to the following section, "Completing Stacker Express Setup," to finish installing Stacker.

> **NOTE:**
> If you use Windows and do not have a mouse device driver loaded for your DOS applications, you cannot use your mouse in Stacker Setup after it exits from Windows. If you find you cannot use the mouse, use keyboard selection techniques (pressing highlighted keys or pressing Tab and Enter) to choose command buttons whenever Stacker Setup is in DOS.

Completing Stacker Express Setup

Whether you started the Stacker Express Setup from DOS or from Windows, after Stacker Setup begins copying files, the Express Setup process is the same. After Stacker Express Setup finishes copying all the files on disk 1, Stacker displays a screen message that prompts you to insert the second program disk and displays command buttons that enable you to **C**ontinue or E**x**it Setup.

To complete your Stacker Express Setup, follow these steps:

1. Replace Stacker disk 1 with Stacker disk 2, and choose **C**ontinue to finish copying the Stacker files to your hard disk. Choose E**x**it if you decide not to complete Stacker installation at this time.

    After Stacker Express Setup finishes copying all Stacker program files to your hard disk, Stacker displays the Start Stacking dialog box, as shown in figure 9.7. Stacker is ready to restart your computer and begin *stacking*—that is, compressing—your hard disks.

    The Start Stacking dialog box enables you to change your mind about compressing your disks. This is your last opportunity to do so. After Stacker actually begins compressing your disks, it cannot be interrupted. To halt the process now, choose E**x**it.

2. To continue, remove all disks from your floppy drives and choose **R**estart. Stacker now restarts your computer. Refer to the Stacker Reboot sidebar on the following page.

    After the Stacker Reboot is complete, Stacker Express Setup resumes operation.

Stacker Express Setup gathers information about your disk drives and then begins compressing each of your hard disk drives in turn. Stacker begins with the disk drive or partition with the highest drive letter and proceeds to the lowest. Stacker checks the integrity of your hard disk's File Allocation Table (FAT), tags all the files on your disk, and

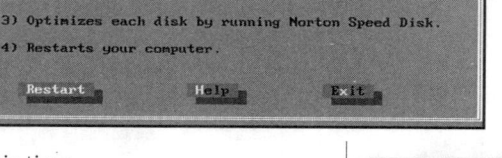

Fig. 9.7

The Stacker Express Setup Start Stacking dialog box.

> **NOTE:**
> After Stacker begins building drives, it can complete the Setup process unattended; you do not need to make additional choices or perform any other actions.

Installing Stacker 183

A Word about Stacker Reboot

If you use Stacker Express Setup or the DoubleSpace to Stacker conversion, Stacker Setup restarts your computer twice. The first time Stacker Setup restarts your computer, it does so to make sure that no software remains in memory that may interfere with Stacker Setup. If you use Stacker Custom Setup, this first restarting of your computer is optional. Stacker Setup restarts your computer a second time, after installation is complete, to make your new compressed volumes available. Stacker always restarts your computer after installation is complete, regardless of the installation method you chose. The first time Stacker restarts your computer is referred to as the *Stacker Reboot*. A few moments after Stacker restarts your computer, the message `Starting MS-DOS...` appears on-screen. DOS loads into your computer's memory, loads the Stacker DBLSPACE.BIN device driver, and begins processing CONFIG.SYS. If you use the DOS 6 feature to create multiple start-up configurations in your CONFIG.SYS, choose the same start-up configuration from the CONFIG.SYS menu that was in effect when you started Stacker Setup. (Refer to your DOS documentation for more information on multiple start-up configurations.) DOS then processes the rest of your CONFIG.SYS file and starts processing AUTOEXEC.BAT. If you pressed F8 to conditionally process lines in CONFIG.SYS, make sure that you process your AUTOEXEC.BAT file. (Refer to your DOS documentation for more information on conditional execution of CONFIG.SYS.) The following message should appear:

```
**** Stacker Reboot ****
```

Stacker Setup loads into memory and resumes operation where it left off. If your computer does not restart, or if you do not see the Stacker Reboot message, first make sure that drive A is empty. If a disk is in drive A, remove it, and press Ctrl+Alt+Del to restart your computer. Your computer should restart as described. In rare cases, your computer may not respond correctly to the method Stacker Setup uses to restart your computer. If your computer does not restart, and drive A is empty, turn your computer's power off and back on or press your computer's reset button if it has one. Your computer should now restart as described.

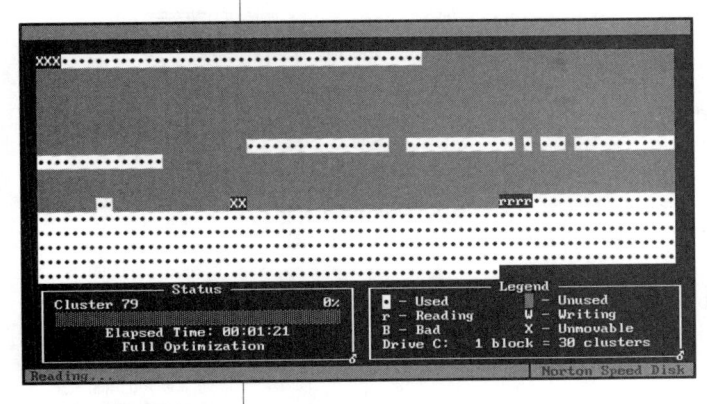

Fig. 9.8

Stacker runs Norton Speed Disk to optimize your new compressed drive.

then creates the Stacker compressed drive. Stacker then begins building the Stacker drive by compressing all the files on your disk and adding them to the Stacker compressed drive. As Stacker builds your compressed drive, it displays a Building Stacker Drive progress report.

After Stacker finishes building the Stacker drive, it loads a special version of the Norton Speed Disk program to optimize the newly created compressed drive. Norton Speed Disk displays a screen similar to the one shown in figure 9.8. The exact contents of the screen depend on your computer system.

After Norton Speed Disk finishes optimizing the new compressed drive, Stacker Setup checks all the compressed data on the Stacker drive and verifies the integrity of the drive. Stacker Setup displays a progress report screen while verifying the Stacker drive.

Stacker Express Setup repeats the cycle of creating a new Stacker drive, compressing files and adding them to the new Stacker drive, optimizing, and making final verifications for every hard disk or partition in your computer system. After Stacker Express Setup finishes compressing all the hard disks and partitions in your computer system, it displays the Stacking Results report shown in figure 9.9.

The Stacking Results report shows the results of compressing each of your drives. Your specific computer system determines the exact contents of the report. The report shows how much space was available on each drive before compression and how much space is available on each drive after compression. Usually, the free space after compression is much higher than the free space before compression, but the actual amount of free space after compression depends on how full your drives were before compression and how well the files compressed. In figure 9.9, for example, drive C was 73M in size before Stacker compression and had 26M free. After stacking, drive C is 143M in size and has 92M free.

The results report also lists the drives that are the host, or *working,* drives for the Stacker volumes. In figure 9.9, for example, drive G is the working drive for the Stacker drive E. If your system has more than four drives after Stacker is added, you can use the up- and down-arrow keys to scroll through the list of drives to review stacking results for drives not currently visible on-screen.

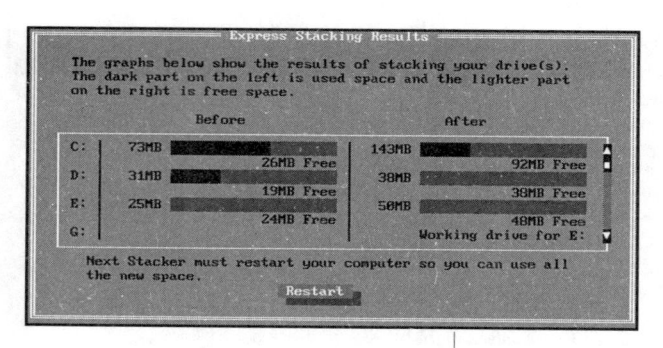

After you finish viewing the results report, Stacker must restart your computer to make your compressed drives available. To restart your computer, make sure that drive A is empty, and then choose the **R**estart button.

Stacker Express Setup is now complete. After Stacker restarts your computer this second time, you can use your compressed drives just as you used your drives before you installed Stacker. Now, however, you have much more available storage space.

If you start the Stacker setup from inside Windows, the next time you start Windows, you are asked if you want to create a program group for the Stacker Windows utility programs. Click the **O**K button for Stacker to create a Stacker program group. For information on creating the Stacker program group manually, see Chapter 10, "Configuring and Optimizing Stacker."

Fig. 9.9

The Express Stacking Results report.

NOTE:

If you needed to uninstall any copy-protected software before beginning the Stacker Express Setup, you can reinstall that software now.

NOTE:

After you finish installing Stacker, immediately perform the procedure described in the section "Making a DOS 6 Startup Disk Containing Stacker," later in this chapter. If you do not make a DOS 6 start-up disk that contains the Stacker DBLSPACE.BIN file, and you must start your computer from a floppy disk, you cannot access your Stacker compressed drives.

Running Custom Setup

This section describes how to start and use the Stacker Custom Setup. (For information on Express Setup, see the section "Running Express Setup," earlier in this chapter.) By using Custom Setup, you can choose the directory in which the Stacker program files are installed and which specific disk drives are compressed. Stacker Custom Setup also enables you to choose how much uncompressed free space to leave on a drive and to select the cluster size and expected compression ratio for the new compressed drive. If you previously installed DoubleSpace, Stacker Setup recognizes the DoubleSpace compressed drives and offers to convert them to Stacker format. To convert from DoubleSpace to Stacker, follow the instructions in the section "Converting to Stacker from Another Disk Compression Program," later in this chapter.

You can perform the Stacker Custom Setup from either DOS or Windows. If you run Stacker Custom Setup from Windows, Stacker Setup adds a **S**tacker menu to the Windows File Manager and prepares Windows to create a program group for the Stacker Windows utilities. To install Stacker from Windows, begin the installation with the instructions in the section "Starting Custom Setup from Windows," later in this chapter. To install Stacker from the DOS command line, proceed with the instructions in the following section.

Installing Stacker   **185**

Starting Custom Setup at the DOS Prompt

To start the Stacker Custom Setup from the DOS prompt, follow these steps:

1. Follow steps 1 through 7 in the procedure for starting Stacker Express Setup from DOS. (Refer to the section, "Starting Express Setup at the DOS Prompt," earlier in this chapter.)

2. Choose the **C**ustom command button in the Express or Custom Setup dialog box (refer to fig. 9.1). Stacker displays the Create a Directory for Stacker dialog box, as shown in figure 9.10.

   In this dialog box, Stacker indicates that, unless you specify otherwise, it will copy the Stacker program files to a directory named STACKER on drive C. You can change the target directory by entering a different drive and directory path in the Copy **S**tacker Files To text box, as instructed in the dialog box.

3. After you are satisfied with the drive and directory name for the Stacker program files, choose **C**ontinue. Stacker begins copying files to your hard disk. Stacker displays a progress report while it copies files.

   After Stacker Custom Setup finishes copying all files on disk 1, Stacker displays a dialog box prompting you to insert Stacker disk 2.

4. Replace Stacker disk 1 with Stacker disk 2, and choose Continue to finish copying the Stacker files to your hard disk.

   After Stacker Custom Setup finishes copying all the Stacker program files to your hard disk, Stacker displays the dialog box shown in figure 9.11. In this dialog box, you indicate whether the setup program is to add the Stacker directory to your DOS PATH statement in your AUTOEXEC.BAT file.

   If you do not add the Stacker directory to the PATH statement, you must use the Stacker commands or utilities from the Stacker directory or type the full Stacker directory name for each command. If you add the Stacker directory to the PATH statement, your Stacker commands and utilities are available to you at all times. Adding the Stacker directory to your PATH statement is recommended.

5. To add the Stacker directory to your PATH statement in AUTOEXEC.BAT, choose **A**dd to Path. To leave the Stacker directory out of your PATH statement, choose Do**n**'t Add. If your computer has EMS memory, Stacker Custom Setup displays the Expanded Memory dialog box, as shown in figure 9.12.

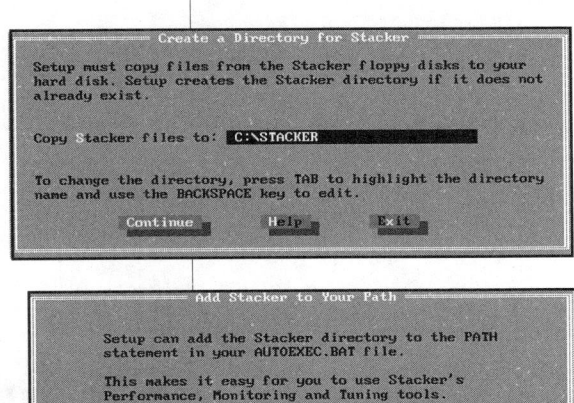

Fig. 9.10, top

The Create a Directory for Stacker dialog box.

Fig. 9.11, middle

Stacker Custom Setup's Add Stacker to Your Path dialog box.

Fig. 9.12, bottom

The Stacker Expanded Memory dialog box.

The Expanded Memory dialog box prompts you to indicate whether Stacker is to configure its device driver to use EMS memory to store the data Stacker compresses or decompresses.

Using EMS memory makes more of your computer's conventional memory available for other programs. Some programs—particularly early versions of Borland SE products—use EMS in a way that may interfere with Stacker. If you have any doubts about whether your programs use EMS safely, do not use EMS with Stacker. You also can enable or disable Stacker's use of EMS later, after you install Stacker. Using EMS is described in Chapter 10, "Configuring and Optimizing Stacker."

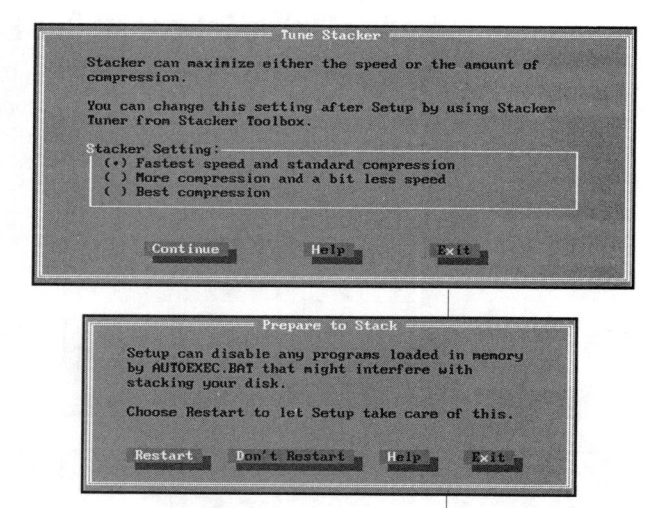

Fig. 9.13, top
The Tune Stacker dialog box.

Fig. 9.14, bottom
The Stacker Setup Prepare to Stack dialog box.

6. To enable Stacker to use EMS, choose **U**se EMS. If you do not want Stacker to use EMS, choose **D**on't Use EMS. Stacker displays the Tune Stacker dialog box, as shown in figure 9.13.
7. In the **S**tacker Setting area of the Tune Stacker dialog box, choose the radio button for the Stacker compression level you want: Fastest Speed and Standard Compression, More Compression and a Bit Less Speed, or Best Compression.
8. After you are satisfied with the compression level, choose **C**ontinue. Stacker displays the Prepare to Stack dialog box, as shown in figure 9.14. This dialog box prompts you to tell Stacker whether to restart your computer.

If you are certain that no programs are loaded in memory that may interfere with Stacker, you do not need to restart your computer. If any programs are loaded in memory that may write to the disk while Stacker is working (such as FAX receive software or electronic mail programs), restarting your computer temporarily disables these programs from loading. Having Stacker restart your computer is recommended.

9. Choose **D**on't Restart to proceed directly with the Stacker Custom Setup. If you choose **D**on't Restart, skip to step 11.
10. To restart your computer, remove all disks from your floppy drives and choose **R**estart. Stacker now restarts your computer. Refer to the Stacker Reboot sidebar on page 183.

After the Stacker Reboot is complete, Stacker Custom Setup resumes the Stacker installation.

11. Go to the section "Completing Stacker Custom Setup," later in this chapter, to finish installing Stacker.

NOTE:

The higher the compression level, the greater is the length of time Stacker requires to compress your data. Your choice of compression level represents a trade-off between speed and the amount of compression you want.

Installing Stacker 187

Starting Custom Setup from Windows

To start the Stacker Custom Setup from Windows, follow these steps:

1. Follow steps 1 through 11 in the procedure for starting Stacker Express Setup from Windows. (Refer to the section, "Starting Express Setup from Windows," earlier in this chapter.) After Stacker finishes printing the FAX registration form, Stacker Setup displays the Stacker Express or Custom Setup dialog box (refer to fig. 9.5).

2. Select the **C**ustom radio button near the bottom of the Express or Custom dialog box, and then choose **O**K. Stacker displays the Choose Stacker Directory dialog box, as shown in figure 9.15.

   In this dialog box, Stacker indicates that, unless you specify otherwise, it will copy the Stacker program files to a directory named STACKER on drive C. You can change the target directory by entering a different drive and directory path in the Copy Stacker Files To text box, as instructed in the dialog box.

3. Choose **O**K after you are satisfied with the drive and directory name for the Stacker program files. Stacker displays the Add Stacker Directory to Your Path dialog box. In this dialog box, you indicate whether the setup program is to add the Stacker directory to your DOS PATH statement in your AUTOEXEC.BAT file (see fig. 9.16).

   If you do not add the Stacker directory to the PATH statement, you must use the Stacker commands or utilities from the Stacker directory or type the full Stacker directory name for each command. If you add the Stacker directory to the PATH statement, your Stacker commands and utilities are available to you at all times. Adding the Stacker directory to your PATH statement is recommended.

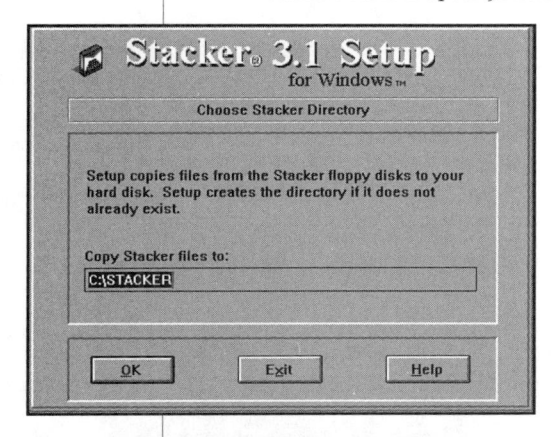

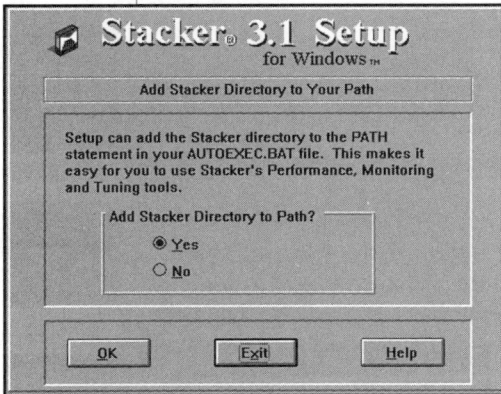

Fig. 9.15, top

The Choose Stacker Directory dialog box.

Fig. 9.16, bottom

The Stacker Custom Add Stacker Directory to Your Path dialog box.

4. Choose **Y**es to add the Stacker directory to the PATH in AUTOEXEC.BAT; choose **N**o to skip adding the Stacker directory to your PATH statement.

5. Choose **O**K to continue Stacker Custom Setup. Stacker displays the Tune Stacker dialog box, in which you choose the Stacker compression level (see fig. 9.17).

6. In the Stacker Setting area, choose the radio button for the compression level you want (**F**astest Speed and Standard Compression, **M**ore Compression and a Bit

Less Speed, or **B**est Compression), and then choose **OK**. Stacker displays the Leave Windows dialog box (refer to fig. 9.6).

Stacker must now leave Windows to continue the Custom Setup.

7. Choose **OK** in the Leave Windows dialog box to continue the Stacker Custom Setup. Stacker tells Windows to close all active applications and exit. If any Windows applications have unsaved data, an on-screen message asks if you want to save the data.

After Stacker Custom Setup exits from Windows, Stacker begins copying files to your hard disk. Stacker displays a progress chart while it copies files. After Stacker Custom Setup finishes copying the files on disk 1, it displays a dialog box prompting you to insert the second program disk.

8. Replace Stacker disk 1 with Stacker, and choose **C**ontinue to finish copying the Stacker files to your hard disk.

If you have EMS memory in your computer, Stacker Custom Setup displays the Expanded Memory dialog box after it finishes copying all the files to your disk (refer to fig. 9.12). This dialog box prompts you to indicate whether Stacker is to configure the Stacker device driver to use EMS memory to store the data that Stacker compresses or decompresses.

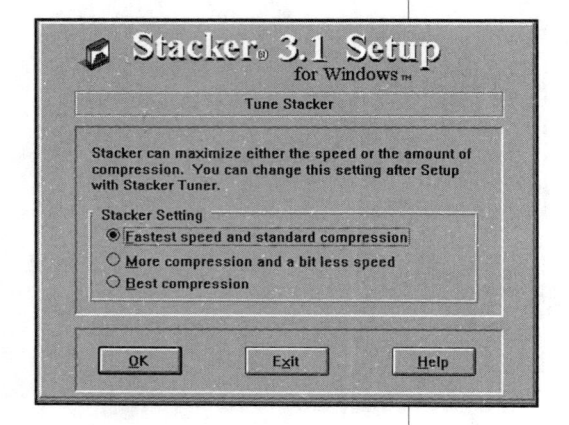

Using EMS memory makes more of your computer's conventional memory available for other programs. Some programs—particularly early versions of Borland SE products—make use of EMS in a way that may interfere with Stacker. If you have any doubts about whether your programs use EMS safely, don't use EMS with Stacker. You also can enable or disable Stacker's use of EMS later, after you install Stacker. Using EMS is described in Chapter 10, "Configuring and Optimizing Stacker."

9. To enable Stacker to use EMS, choose **U**se EMS. If you do not want Stacker to use EMS, choose **D**on't Use EMS. Stacker displays the Prepare to Stack dialog box (refer to fig. 9.14). This dialog box prompts you to indicate whether you want the Setup program to restart your computer.

If you are certain no programs are loaded in memory that may interfere with Stacker, you do not need to restart your computer. If any programs are loaded in memory that write to the disk while Stacker is working (such as FAX receive software or electronic mail programs), restarting your computer temporarily disables these programs from loading. Having Stacker restart your computer is recommended.

NOTE:
The higher the compression level, the greater is the length of time Stacker requires to compress your data. Your choice of compression level represents a trade-off between speed and the amount of compression you want.

Fig. 9.17

Stacker Custom Setup asks you to select the compression level.

> **NOTE:**
>
> If you use Windows and do not have a mouse device driver loaded for your DOS applications, you cannot use your mouse in Stacker Setup after it exits from Windows. If this occurs, use keyboard methods (pressing highlighted keys or Tab and Enter) to choose command buttons while Stacker Setup is in DOS.

10. To skip the Stacker restart and proceed immediately with the Stacker Custom Setup, choose **D**on't Restart, and then go to step 11.

    To restart your computer, remove all disks from your floppy drives and choose **R**estart. Stacker now restarts your computer. Refer to the Stacker Reboot sidebar on page 183.

11. Go to the following section, "Completing Stacker Custom Setup," for instructions on finishing your Stacker Custom installation.

Completing Stacker Custom Setup

From this point on, the Custom Setup process is the same, whether you started Stacker Custom Setup from DOS or from Windows. During this portion of the installation process, you decide which method Stacker uses to create the new Stacker Drive. At this point in the installation process, Stacker Custom Setup displays the Select a Disk to Stack dialog box, in which you choose the disk you want Stacker to compress (see fig. 9.18).

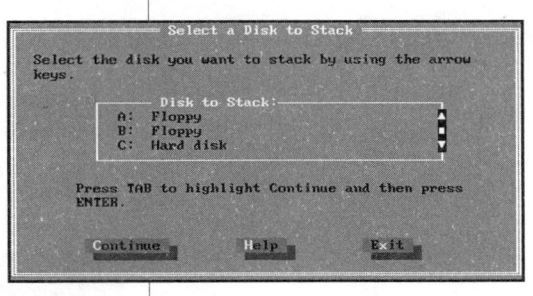

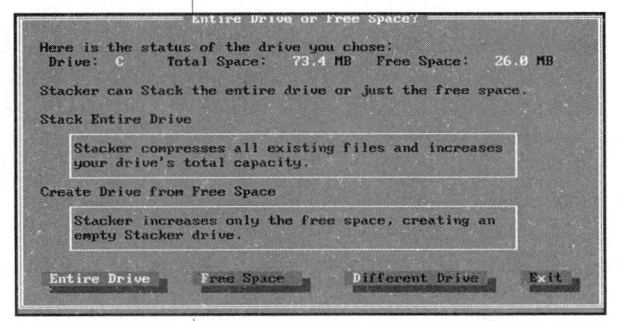

To complete your Stacker Custom Setup, follow these steps:

1. In the **D**isk to Stack list box, select the drive you want to compress.

2. Choose **C**ontinue. Stacker displays the Entire Drive or Free Space? dialog box, as shown in figure 9.19.

   If you change your mind about compressing this disk, choose **D**ifferent Drive. Stacker returns you to the Select a Disk to Stack dialog box (step 1).

3. In the Entire Drive or Free Space? dialog box, choose either the **E**ntire Drive or the **F**ree Space command button to begin stacking the selected disk drive.

   Choose **E**ntire Drive to compress the drive and all its current files, and then go to the following section, "Compressing an Entire Drive," to complete the creation of your Stacker drive.

   Choose **F**ree Space to leave the files on a disk uncompressed but create a compressed drive from the free space on that disk, and then go to the section "Compressing Free Space," later in this chapter, to complete the creation of your Stacker drive.

Fig. 9.18, top

The Select a Disk to Stack dialog box.

Fig. 9.19, bottom

Stacker's Entire Drive or Free Space? dialog box.

Compressing an Entire Drive

If you choose to compress the entire drive, Stacker compresses all the files on the selected drive and assigns drive letters so that the new Stacker volume replaces the existing uncompressed drive. To compress all the files on drive D, for example, and make D a compressed drive, you instruct Stacker to compress the entire drive. If you choose this method, Stacker immediately validates the drive you select and then displays the Stack Entire Drive dialog box, as shown in figure 9.20.

The Stack Entire Drive dialog box displays the letter of the drive you selected to compress, the drive's total physical space, and the current amount of free space on the drive. The dialog box also offers several choices for your next action: You can choose **S**tack to compress the drive you selected, **D**ifferent Drive to compress a drive other than the one already selected, or Ad**v**anced Options to choose among several options for the new compressed drive.

If you choose **D**ifferent Drive, Stacker returns you to the Select a Disk to Stack dialog box (refer to fig. 9.18). Follow all the instructions in the preceding section, "Completing Stacker Custom Setup," to select a new drive. If you choose Ad**v**anced Options, Stacker displays the Advanced Options (Entire Drive) dialog box, as shown in figure 9.21. In this dialog box, you can set the amount of free space that remains uncompressed, set the expected compression ratio, or choose the cluster size for the Stacker drive. You achieve the following results by setting these options in the dialog box:

- Increasing the Space to Leave **U**nstacked (uncompressed) reduces the amount of space on the Stacker drive and increases the amount of space on the uncompressed host drive. Stacker's default value for this option is for the smallest possible uncompressed drive; this setting produces the largest possible compressed volume. *(See also the Note on the following page.)*
- Changing the Expected Com**p**ression Ratio option affects Stacker's estimate of free space on the Stacker drive. Stacker assumes that all files compress at the expected compression ratio and bases its report of free space for a compressed volume on this expected compression ratio. If the expected compression ratio is 2:1 and the Stacker volume has 1M of uncompressed space, for example, Stacker reports 2M of free space on that compressed volume. Change the expected compression ratio only if you know that most of the files you intend to store on the Stacker drive will consistently compress with ratios higher or lower than 2:1.
- The C**l**uster Size option sets the size of the cluster Stacker uses for the new compressed drive. In general, the larger the physical drive you compress, the larger must be the cluster size. As a rule, never change the Stacker cluster size. Always leave the Stacker cluster size on Auto to enable Stacker to choose the cluster size.

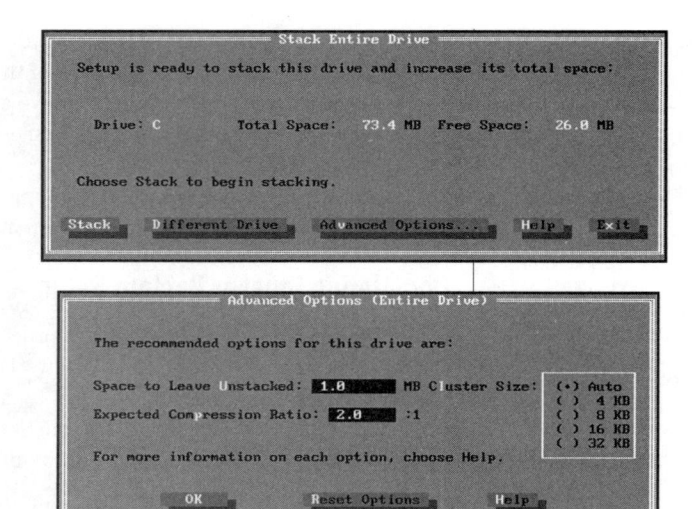

Fig. 9.20, top

The Stack Entire Drive dialog box.

Fig. 9.21, bottom

The Stacker Advanced Options (Entire Drive) dialog box.

Installing Stacker 191

> **NOTE:**
> The amount of uncompressed free space Stacker leaves on the uncompressed drive as a result of the setting for the Space to Leave **U**nstacked option is *in addition to* any files that must remain uncompressed. If compressing a drive containing a Windows permanent swap file that is 5M in size, for example, Stacker moves the swap file to the uncompressed drive and allocates 5M of space for it. If the uncompressed free space is set for 2M, the new uncompressed drive is actually about 7M in size, with 5M occupied by the Windows permanent swap file and 2M of empty uncompressed space.

To finish compressing the entire drive, follow these steps:

1. In the Stack Entire Drive dialog box, choose the **D**ifferent Drive command button to compress a drive other than the one you already selected; Stacker returns you to the Select a Disk to Stack dialog box, and you can follow the steps in the preceding section, "Completing Stacker Custom Setup," to select your new drive. To continue with the current drive, go to step 2.

2. To change other settings, choose the Ad**v**anced Options button. Stacker displays the Advanced Options dialog box (refer to fig. 9.21). If you do not want to set the advanced options, skip to step 4.

   To change the space to leave unstacked, type the amount of space (in megabytes) you want left uncompressed in the Space to Leave **U**nstacked text box.

   To change the expected compression ratio, enter the value you want to use in the Expected Com**p**ression Ratio text box. You can enter any number from 1.0 to 16.0; use only one decimal place.

   To change the cluster size, select the radio button for the desired cluster size in the C**l**uster Size list box. (Changing the cluster size is *not* recommended.)

   If you make a mistake or want to return to the original settings, choose the **R**eset Options command button. Stacker restores the original settings for the Ad**v**anced Options.

3. Choose **O**K after you are satisfied with your Advanced Options settings. Stacker returns to the Stack Entire Drive dialog box.

4. Choose **S**tack. Stacker immediately begins to compress the selected drive. Stacker checks the integrity of the selected hard disk's File Allocation Table (FAT), tags all the files on the disk, and creates the Stacker compressed drive. Stacker then begins building the Stacker drive by compressing all files on the disk and adding them to the Stacker compressed drive. Stacker displays a progress report as it builds your compressed drive.

After Stacker finishes building the Stacker drive, it loads a special version of the Norton Speed Disk program to optimize the newly created compressed drive. Norton Speed Disk displays a screen similar to that shown in figure 9.8. The exact contents of the screen depend on your specific computer. After Norton Speed Disk finishes optimizing the new compressed drive, Stacker Setup checks all the compressed data on the Stacker drive and verifies the integrity of the drive. Stacker displays a progress report during the verification process.

After Stacker Custom Setup finishes compressing the hard disk, it displays the Stacking Results report shown in figure 9.22. The Stacking Results report shows the results of compressing the drive. (The exact contents of the report depend on your computer system.) The report shows the disk's available space, before and after compression.

The free space after compression usually is much higher than the free space before compression. The actual amount of post-compression free space depends on how full your drive was before compression and how well the files on it compressed. The results report also lists the drive that is the host, or *working*, drive for the Stacker volume. In figure 9.22, for example, drive F is the working (host) drive for the Stacker drive C.

After you finish viewing the results report, you can choose the **S**tack Another command button to compress another disk. Stacker returns to the Select a Disk to Stack dialog box. Follow the instructions beginning with step 1 in the section "Completing the Stacker Custom Setup," earlier in this chapter, to stack another disk.

After you finish stacking your drives, Stacker must restart your computer to make the new Stacker drives accessible. To restart your computer, remove all disks from your floppy drives and choose the **R**estart command button at the bottom of the Stacking Results report. Stacker restarts your computer.

Your Stacker Custom Setup is complete. After Stacker restarts your computer, you can use your compressed drives just as you used your drives before you installed Stacker. Make sure that you follow the recommendations in the Notes on page 184 at the end of the section "Completing Stacker Express Setup," earlier in this chapter. In particular, make sure that you perform the procedure to make a Stacker bootable floppy disk, as described in the section "Making a DOS 6 Start-up Disk Containing Stacker," later in this chapter.

Fig. 9.22

The Custom Stacking Results report for an entire drive.

NOTE:

You can use the Stacker Toolbox to compress additional disks or drives at any time. If you are not sure you want to compress all your hard disk partitions now, compress just one or two, and use the Stacker Toolbox to compress the others later.

Compressing Free Space

Creating a free space drive leaves any existing files on your hard disk uncompressed and uses only the current free space on the disk to create the compressed volume. This option also is useful if you want to create a compressed volume on an empty disk or partition. If you choose to create a Stacker drive from free space, Stacker immediately validates the drive you selected and then displays the Create Drive from Free Space dialog box, as shown in figure 9.23.

The Create Drive from Free Space dialog box displays the letter of the drive you selected to compress, the drive's total physical space, and the current amount of free space on the drive. This dialog box enables you to choose how much of the uncom-pressed drive's available free space to use for the new Stacker drive. Stacker assumes that you want to use all the uncompressed free space on the drive; if you do not want to use all the drive's free space, you can change the Space to **U**se setting in this dialog box.

The Create Drive from Free Space dialog box also offers several command button choices for your next action. You can choose **S**tack to compress the drive you selected,

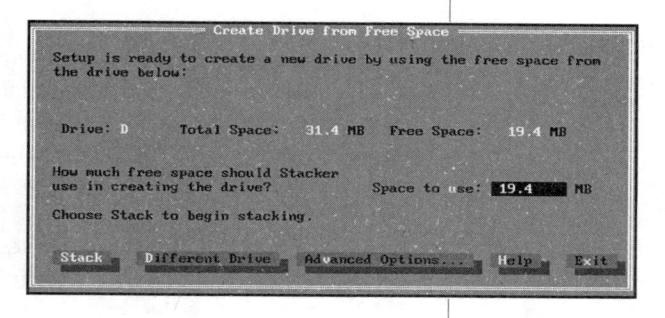

Fig. 9.23

The Create Drive from Free Space dialog box.

Different Drive to compress a drive other than the one already selected, or Ad**v**anced Options to choose other options for the new compressed drive.

If you choose **D**ifferent Drive, Stacker returns to the Select a Disk to Stack dialog box. You then can select a new drive and follow the instructions in the section "Completing Stacker Custom Setup," earlier in this chapter. If you choose Ad**v**anced Options, you can set the expected compression ratio or choose the cluster size for the Stacker drive. The Expected Com**p**ression Ratio and **C**luster Size settings are the same as in the Ad**v**anced Options settings described in the preceding section, "Compressing an Entire Drive." Refer to that section for information on these options.

To finish creating your free space drive, follow these steps:

1. In the Create Drive from Free Space dialog box, choose the **D**ifferent Drive command button to create a free space Stacker drive from free space on a drive other than the one already selected; Stacker returns you to the Select a Disk to Stack dialog box, and you can follow the instructions in the section "Completing Stacker Custom Setup," earlier in this chapter, to select your new drive. If you do not want to use a different drive, go to step 2.

2. To change the free space Stacker uses to create the new drive, type the amount of free space (in megabytes) Stacker is to use for the new compressed volume in the Space to **U**se text box. You can enter any number from 1M up to the maximum uncompressed free space available on the uncompressed drive. If you do not want to change the free space setting, go to step 3.

3. Choose Ad**v**anced Options to set the expected compression ratio or choose the cluster size for the Stacker drive. Stacker displays the Advanced Options (Free Space) dialog box, as shown in figure 9.24. If you do not want to set advanced options, skip to step 5.

   To change the expected compression ratio, type the value you want in the **E**xpected Compression Ratio text box. You may enter any number from 1.0 to 16.0; use only one decimal place.

   To change the cluster size, select the radio button for the desired cluster size in the C**l**uster Size list box.

   If you make a mistake or want to return to the original settings, choose the **R**eset Options command button. Stacker restores the original settings for the Ad**v**anced Options.

4. Choose **O**K after you are satisfied with your Ad**v**anced Options settings. Stacker returns to the Create Drive from Free Space dialog box.

5. Choose **S**tack. Stacker immediately begins to compress the selected drive.

Stacker checks the integrity of the selected hard disk's File Allocation Table (FAT) and then loads a special version of the Norton Speed Disk program to optimize the uncompressed drive. While Speed Disk is optimizing the uncompressed drive, it displays a screen

Reducing the free space used for the Stacker Free Space drive increases the amount of uncompressed space that remains available on the uncompressed drive. If you need more space on your uncompressed drive, decrease the space used for the Stacker Free Space drive.

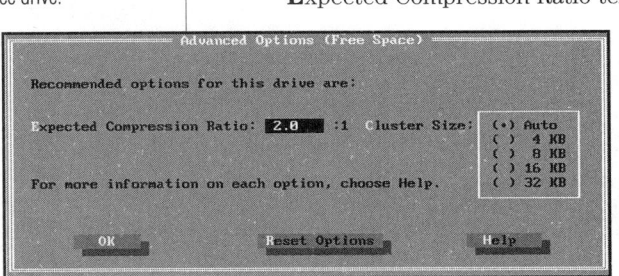

Fig. 9.24

The Stacker Advanced Options (Free Space) dialog box.

similar to that shown in figure 9.8. The exact contents of the screen depend on your specific computer.

Stacker then creates the free space compressed drive. Because Stacker creates the drive from free space on the uncompressed host drive, no files are added to the new Stacker drive. After Stacker creates the new compressed drive, it verifies the integrity of the drive. While verifying the Stacker drive, Stacker displays a progress chart. After Stacker Custom Setup finishes creating and verifying the free space drive, it displays the Stacking Results report shown in figure 9.25.

The Stacking Results report shows the results of creating the free space compressed drive. The exact contents of the report depend on your specific computer system. The report shows how much space was available on the drive both before and after compression. In figure 9.25, for example, Stacker used all the free space on drive D to create the new Stacker drive. Drive D had 31M free before creating the free space drive. Because all the free space was used for the Stacker drive, drive D has no free space left. The results report also lists the new Stacker drive that resulted from compressing free space. In figure 9.25, the new Stacker drive I has 62M of available space.

After you finish viewing the results report, you can choose to stack another disk by choosing the **S**tack Another command button. Stacker returns to the Select a Disk to Stack dialog box. Follow the instructions beginning with step 1 in the section "Completing the Stacker Custom Setup," earlier in this chapter.

After you finish stacking your drives, Stacker must restart your computer to make the new Stacker drives are accessible. To restart your computer, remove all disks from your floppy drives and choose the **R**estart command button at the bottom of the Stacking Results report. Stacker restarts your computer.

Your Stacker Custom Setup is now complete. After Stacker restarts your computer, you can use your compressed drives just as you used your drives before you installed Stacker. Make sure that you follow the recommendations in the Notes on page 184 at the end of the section "Completing Stacker Express Setup," earlier in this chapter. In particular, make sure that you perform the procedure to make a Stacker bootable floppy disk, as described in the following section, "Making a DOS 6 Start-up Disk Containing Stacker."

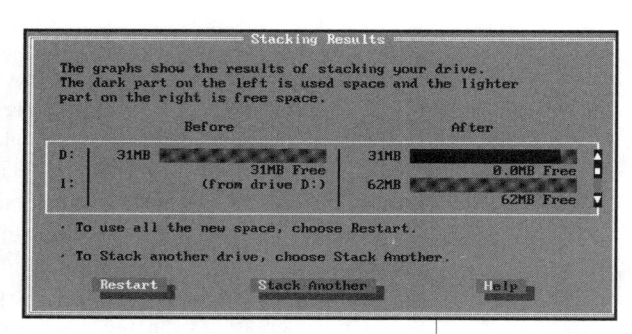

Fig. 9.25

The Custom Stacking Results report for a free space drive.

NOTE:

You can use the Stacker Toolbox to compress additional disks or drives at any time. If you are not sure you want to compress all your hard disk partitions now, compress just one or two, and use the Stacker Toolbox to compress the others later.

NOTE:

SYS is a DOS command that makes a floppy disk or other disk bootable. The SYS command copies the DOS hidden system start-up files, IO.SYS and MSDOS.SYS, to the floppy disk, along with the DOS command interpreter, COMMAND.COM. If the Stacker DBLSPACE.BIN file is present on your hard drive, the SYS command also copies this file to the floppy disk. (See step 3 on following page.)

Making a DOS 6 Start-up Disk Containing Stacker

After you install Stacker on your computer system, make at least one bootable floppy disk with the Stacker DBLSPACE.BIN device driver on it. If you ever need to start your computer from a floppy disk, you cannot access your Stacker drives unless your start-up floppy disk also contains the Stacker device driver. The bootable floppy disk you make must contain the DOS system files, the DOS COMMAND.COM command interpreter, and

Installing Stacker

the Stacker DBLSPACE.BIN file. Without these files, the disk cannot start your computer and provide access to your Stacker drives.

To make a DOS 6 start-up disk, you need one blank, formatted floppy disk compatible with your computer's drive A. If your drive A is a 3 1/2-inch drive, for example, you need a 720K or 1.44M floppy disk.

Follow these steps to make a DOS 6 start-up floppy disk containing the Stacker DBLSPACE.BIN device driver:

1. Install Stacker, if you have not already done so. Follow the appropriate instructions in this chapter for either the Stacker Express Setup or Custom Setup.

    As you install Stacker on your hard disk, the Stacker Setup program installs the Stacker DBLSPACE.BIN device driver on your hard disk.

2. Insert a blank, formatted floppy disk in drive A.
3. Type **SYS A:** at the DOS prompt, and press Enter. After a few moments, DOS displays the message `System Transferred`.
4. To test your start-up disk, first make sure that you do not have any unsaved data on a RAM disk or stored in any TSR programs, and then press Ctrl+Alt+Del to restart your computer.

If the system was correctly transferred to your floppy disk, your computer reboots from the floppy disk. After your computer finishes rebooting, use the DOS DIR command to make sure that you still can access your Stacker drives. If you can access your Stacker drives, your start-up disk is OK.

The DOS 6 start-up disk you make by following these steps contains only the files necessary to start your computer. You also may want to copy some of the DOS or Stacker utility programs to the start-up floppy. If your hard disks or compressed volumes become unavailable for any reason, you may need copies of your DOS, Stacker, or other utility programs for troubleshooting. Among the programs you may want to copy to the start-up floppy are FORMAT, ATTRIB, CHKDSK, and Stacker's CHECK program.

Some computers are set up so that they do not boot up from a floppy disk, but always go directly to the hard disk to read the DOS start-up files. If your computer does not boot from drive A, check your computer's BIOS setup program to see if it enables you to control which drives the computer checks for start-up disks. Refer to the documentation supplied with your computer, or consult with your vendor or company's computer support personnel for assistance in using your computer's BIOS setup program.

Converting to Stacker from Another Disk Compression Program

You currently may be using a disk compression program other than Stacker. To use Stacker, you first must convert your compressed data into a format Stacker can use. This section describes how to convert from another disk compression program to Stacker.

Converting from DoubleSpace to Stacker

If you currently use DoubleSpace, the Stacker Setup program recognizes your DoubleSpace compressed drives and converts them for you. The following sections describe how to use the Stacker Setup program to convert your DoubleSpace compressed drives to Stacker format.

Starting DoubleSpace Conversion from DOS

The Stacker Setup program converts all your DoubleSpace compressed hard disks. To start Stacker Setup from the DOS prompt, follow these steps:

1. Follow steps 1 through 7 in the procedure for starting Stacker Express Setup from DOS. (Refer to the section, "Starting Express Setup at the DOS Prompt," earlier in this chapter.)

196 The Disk Compression Book

After you complete step 7 in the section "Starting Express Setup at the DOS Prompt," Stacker Setup updates the files with your personal information and then displays the dialog box shown in figure 9.26, informing you that Stacker has detected DoubleSpace on your system.

2. Choose **C**ontinue to convert your DoubleSpace drives to Stacker. Stacker immediately begins copying files to your hard disk, displaying a progress chart of the copying process.
3. Go to the section "Completing The DoubleSpace Conversion," later in this chapter, to finish installing Stacker.

> **NOTE:**
> Follow the same preparation guidelines before converting from other disk compression software to Stacker that you follow if installing Stacker alone. Refer to the section "Preparing to Install Stacker," earlier in this chapter, for information on preparing for Stacker installation.

Starting DoubleSpace Conversion from Windows

The Stacker Setup program converts all your DoubleSpace compressed hard disks. To start the Stacker Setup from Windows, follow these steps:

1. Follow steps 1 through 11 in the procedure for starting Stacker Express Setup from Windows. (Refer to the section, "Starting Express Setup from Windows," earlier in this chapter.)

   After Stacker finishes printing the FAX registration form, Stacker Setup displays the Convert DoubleSpace Drives dialog box, as shown in figure 9.27. This dialog box lists the steps Stacker takes in converting mounted DoubleSpace hard drives to Stacker drives. DoubleSpace conversion installs the Stacker program files in a directory named STACKER on your drive C, converts all your hard drives, and installs the Stacker device driver with all the appropriate settings.

2. Choose **O**K to continue with the Stacker installation and conversion of your DoubleSpace drives to Stacker. Stacker Setup displays the Leave Windows confirmation dialog box (refer to fig. 9.6).

3. Choose **O**K to continue the Stacker Setup. Stacker tells Windows to shut down. As Windows closes each of your applications, an on-screen message prompts you to save any unsaved data.

   After Stacker Setup successfully exits from Windows, Setup displays the Setup for DoubleSpace Conversion dialog box (refer to fig. 9.26).

4. Choose **C**ontinue. Stacker begins copying files to your hard disk and displays a progress report as it copies the files.

The following section explains how to complete the DoubleSpace conversion.

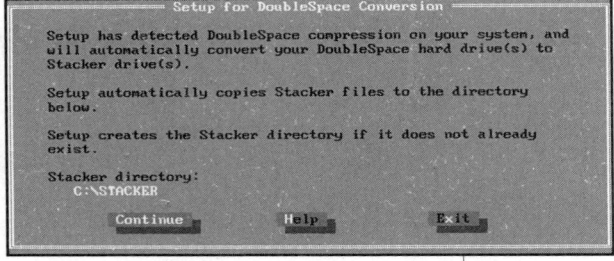

Fig. 9.26

The Stacker Setup for DoubleSpace Conversion dialog box.

> **NOTE:**
> If you use Windows and do not have a mouse device driver loaded for your DOS applications, you cannot use your mouse in Stacker Setup after it exits from Windows. In this situation, use keyboard selection techniques (pressing highlighted keys and Tab and Enter) to choose command buttons while Stacker Setup is in DOS.

Completing the DoubleSpace Conversion

After Stacker begins copying files, DoubleSpace conversion is the same whether you started the DoubleSpace to Stacker conversion from DOS or from Windows. At this point,

Installing Stacker **197**

Stacker is copying files to your hard disk and displaying a progress report screen. After Stacker finishes copying all files on disk 1, Stacker prompts you to insert disk 2.

To complete your DoubleSpace to Stacker conversion, follow these steps:

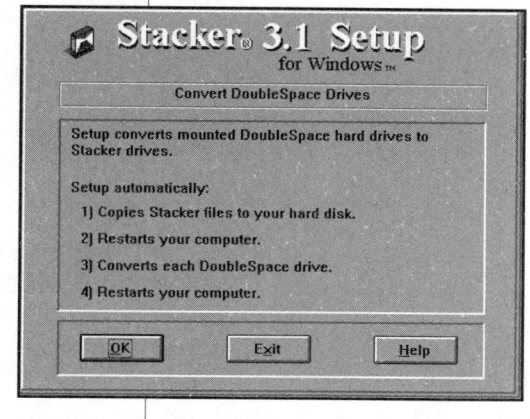

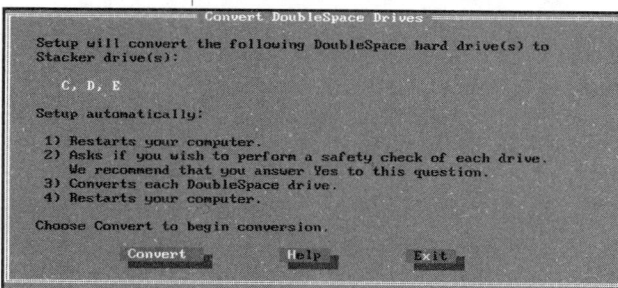

1. Replace Stacker disk 1 with Stacker disk 2, and choose Continue.

   After Stacker finishes copying all Stacker program files to your hard disk, Stacker displays the dialog box shown in figure 9.28.

   In this dialog box, Stacker lists all the drive letters for the DoubleSpace drives it has detected. Unless you change your mind and choose Exit, Stacker converts each DoubleSpace drive listed after you choose the Convert button. The text near the middle of the dialog box briefly describes what the Stacker Setup program does as it converts your DoubleSpace compressed drives to Stacker format.

   Stacker is ready to restart your computer and begin converting your DoubleSpace compressed drives to Stacker format.

2. To continue, remove all disks from your floppy drives, and choose Convert. Stacker restarts your computer. Refer to the Stacker Reboot sidebar on page 183.

   After the Stacker Reboot is complete, the DoubleSpace to Stacker conversion resumes operation. Stacker displays a dialog box informing you that Setup will run the DOS CHKDSK program.

3. Choose Continue. Stacker runs the DOS CHKDSK program to test both the DoubleSpace compressed drives and the uncompressed host drives to be certain no problems exist with any of the drives. CHKDSK tests the File Allocation Table and the file chains on the disk drives. Your screen clears, and the DOS CHKDSK program displays various messages as it checks each of your DoubleSpace compressed drives and their hosts.

   After running CHKDSK, Stacker checks each of your uncompressed drives to make sure that enough free space is available for the working room Stacker needs to make the conversion. If insufficient working room is available on the uncompressed host drive, Stacker displays the error message shown in figure 9.29. The specific drive in the error message depends on your computer.

   Choose Continue if this error message appears. Stacker restarts your computer. After your computer restarts, free up more disk space on your uncompressed

Fig. 9.27, top

The Stacker Convert DoubleSpace Drives dialog box.

Fig. 9.28, bottom

The Stacker Convert DoubleSpace Drives dialog box.

host drive, and begin the DoubleSpace to Stacker conversion process again.

You may be able to free up enough space by deleting unnecessary files from your uncompressed host drive. Otherwise, you must make your DoubleSpace compressed volume smaller. Follow the instructions in Chapter 6, "Using the DoubleSpace Utilities," for changing the size of a DoubleSpace compressed drive.

If each uncompressed host drive has adequate working room, Stacker displays a dialog box asking if you want to perform a safety check of the DoubleSpace drives.

4. Choose **Y**es in this dialog box to instruct Stacker to perform a safety check of the DoubleSpace compressed drives before it converts them. Choose **N**o to skip the safety check.

   As Stacker performs the safety check, it displays a progress report showing you the estimated time remaining in the safety check process. After Stacker completes the safety check, or if you skip the safety check, Stacker displays a dialog box announcing that Stacker is ready to begin the actual conversion from DoubleSpace format to Stacker format.

5. Choose **C**ontinue to begin the conversion of your DoubleSpace drives to Stacker drives. Stacker builds a Stacker volume for every mounted DoubleSpace drive on your system and converts each DoubleSpace drive into a Stacker drive.

   After Stacker converts all your DoubleSpace drives, it displays the dialog box shown in figure 9.30 (see next page). (The actual contents of this screen depend on your computer system.) Stacker is ready to restart your computer.

6. Make sure that drive A is empty, and then choose **C**ontinue. Stacker restarts your computer.

Your conversion from DoubleSpace to Stacker is complete. You can use your compressed drives just as you used your drives before you installed Stacker. All your compressed and uncompressed drives have the same drive letters as they had when you used DoubleSpace.

After your computer restarts, you may notice the following message:

    You have Stacker drive(s) which have been converted from DoubleSpace.
    Please run STAC, and select Restack on the converted drive(s)
    to take full advantage of Stacker's superior safety and compression.

Stacker is suggesting that you use the Stacker Toolbox to restack the compressed drives you just converted from DoubleSpace. Restacking the Stacker drives compresses your data to Stacker's maximum capability and completes the conversion of your drives to Stacker format. Perform the Restack operation as soon as possible. See Chapter 12, "Using the Stacker Utilities," for instructions on using the Stacker Toolbox and

Fig. 9.29

The Stacker error message reporting that insufficient working room exists on the uncompressed host drive.

Although this safety check of your DoubleSpace compressed drives takes time, performing it is highly recommended.

NOTE:

After Stacker actually begins converting your disks, it cannot be interrupted. If you cannot do without your computer for several hours, or if you change your mind about installing Stacker at this time, choose the E**x**it command button.

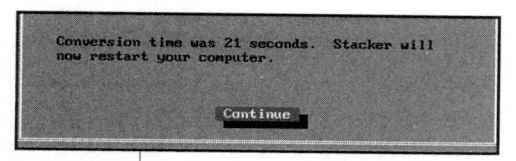

Fig. 9.30

The Stacker conversion completion report.

Optimizer to restack your drives. Make sure that you also follow all the recommendations in the Notes at the end of the section "Completing Stacker Express Setup," on page 183.

If any statements in your CONFIG.SYS file referred to DoubleSpace's DBLSPACE.SYS, Stacker Setup disables those lines. (DBLSPACE.SYS is the device driver DoubleSpace uses to relocate the DoubleSpace compression device driver in memory.) Stacker places REM (for *remark*) at the beginning of any line in CONFIG.SYS that refers to DBLSPACE.SYS. Stacker adds equivalent lines for the STACHIGH.SYS device driver (the device driver that Stacker uses to relocate its compression device driver in memory). The following line, for example, may have appeared in your CONFIG.SYS file:

```
DEVICEHIGH=C:\DOS\DBLSPACE.SYS /MOVE
```

Stacker disables that line and adds a line to your CONFIG.SYS file. In this example, the two lines read as follows:

```
REM DEVICEHIGH=C:\DOS\DBLSPACE.SYS /MOVE
DEVICEHIGH=C:\STACKER\STACHIGH.SYS
```

Converting from Other Disk Compression Programs

This section describes how to convert from another disk compression program to Stacker. Converting your data to Stacker compression format is a fairly demanding task and requires more than a little familiarity with DOS.

Follow the procedures in this section carefully, and observe all precautions and warnings. Do not attempt the conversion to Stacker if you are pressed for time. In this procedure, you perform actions that fundamentally affect your computer and the data stored on it. Patience and attention to procedural detail are important for you to successfully complete the conversion. Read through the following procedure before you begin the actual conversion, and make sure that you understand all the steps involved. If you have any doubts, consult a more experienced individual for advice and assistance (such as your company's computer support person).

If using an earlier version of DOS than DOS 6, install your DOS 6 upgrade before you attempt to convert your compressed data to Stacker. If you recently installed your DOS 6 upgrade, or you install it now, make sure that all your programs are working correctly before you add Stacker.

The manual conversion method described here essentially involves backing up all your disk data, reformatting your hard disk, installing Stacker, and then restoring your data to the hard disk from the backup. If your disk compression program provides a means of uncompressing your disk files and uninstalling itself, you may benefit from using that method instead of reformatting your disk drive. IIT's XtraDrive, for example, includes a utility to decompress all a disk's files and then remove the compressed volumes.

If you convert from DoubleSpace, permit Stacker to convert your DoubleSpace drives instead of doing it manually. Stacker's automatic conversion process is much easier.

NOTE: Using your disk compression's uninstall utility may not work on your system. If your compressed disk is nearly full, an uncompressed disk may not have sufficient room to store all your data.

To convert your disk compression software to Stacker, follow these steps:

1. Uninstall any copy-protected software you may have on your disk. Refer to the guidelines in the section "Preparing To Install Stacker," earlier in this chapter for more information about removing copy-protected software. After you convert your disk to Stacker, you can re-install any copy-protected programs.

2. Back up all the files on your compressed and uncompressed disks.

    Almost all disk compression schemes, including Stacker, use the same basic approach: The compressed data is stored in a file on an uncompressed host drive and accessed as a logical disk drive. Every compressed disk on your computer, therefore, has a matching uncompressed host drive.

    As you back up the files on the uncompressed host disk, do not back up the compressed volume files. The compressed volume file that contains all your compressed data usually has System, Hidden, and Read-Only file attributes. If your compressed drive is drive C, for example, and its host drive is drive D, you back up all files on drives C and D, except for the compressed volume file.

    Refer to your backup program's documentation for information on how to exclude certain files from a backup. Refer to your disk compression software's documentation for information on how to identify the compressed volume file.

3. Notice how much space is required on the uncompressed disk to hold all the files you back up from that disk. Notice also how much total space is required for the files you back up from each compressed disk. This information is useful when you create your Stacker compressed disks.

4. Keep track of which uncompressed disk is your boot disk. You must make sure that you restore files from this disk to the correct disk or disk partition.

5. Create a bootable floppy disk for DOS 6 if you do not already have one. Refer to your DOS documentation for instructions on creating a bootable floppy disk.

6. Make sure that you also have a floppy disk (or disks) that contain the following files:
    - The DOS FDISK utility.
    - The DOS FORMAT utility.
    - Any device drivers your system needs to operate, except for your old disk compression software. These device driver files must go on your bootable floppy disk.
    - CONFIG.SYS and AUTOEXEC.BAT files to start your computer and load any needed device drivers or other configuration information. These files must go on your bootable floppy disk.
    - Your backup and restore software.

7. Edit your CONFIG.SYS and AUTOEXEC.BAT files so that they no longer load the device drivers or TSR programs needed for your old disk compression software. Refer to your disk compression software's documentation for information on identifying the device drivers and TSR programs used with the old disk compression program.

STOP

If you do not uninstall your copy-protected software before performing the conversion to Stacker, you cannot use those programs after the conversion is completed.

NOTE:

Backing up the compressed volume files is not useful. Data in the compressed volume files is readable only if using the original disk compression software. You must back up the files from the compressed drive to transfer them to Stacker. If you do not back up the files from the compressed volume individually, you cannot transfer the files to Stacker, and you lose all your data. Refer to Chapter 1, "Understanding and Using Disk Compression," for more information about compressed volume files.

Installing Stacker 201

> ⚠️ Step 11 through the end of this procedure effectively wipes out *all* the data on your hard disks. *Make absolutely sure* that you have a complete, valid backup of all your files from all your hard disks, whether compressed or uncompressed; otherwise, you are certain to lose data.

> 📝 **NOTE:**
> The procedure in step 11 is optional. Perform this step only if you previously contemplated rearranging how your hard disk or disks are currently partitioned. Because you must reformat your hard disk and restore all your data anyway, this is a good time to repartition your disks.

8. Edit your CONFIG.SYS and AUTOEXEC.BAT files so that any disk caching programs are disabled.
9. Reboot your computer by using the bootable floppy disk you created for step 5. At this point, your compressed disks are unavailable. You are working directly with the actual physical disk drives and disk partitions in your computer. No drive letters are exchanged; your first hard disk or hard disk partition is drive C, the next is drive D, and so on.
10. Double-check to make sure that your floppy disks have all the utility programs and other software you need to complete the conversion (see the checklist in step 6).
11. If you want to change the way your hard disk or disks are physically partitioned, use the DOS FDISK utility to repartition your disk at this time. Refer to your DOS documentation for information about the FDISK utility. If you want only to convert from your old disk compression software to Stacker, you do not need to use FDISK.
12. Use the DOS FORMAT utility to format each of your disk's partitions. As you format your hard disk partitions, use the /U switch option. Using this option prevents the FORMAT utility from creating information necessary to unformat the disk. (This information is not useful to you.) The following example shows how to type the command for the FORMAT utility to format the second partition on a hard disk:

    FORMAT D: /U

    As you format the C partition of your hard disk, make sure that you use the /S switch to transfer the system files to the hard disk so that the C partition is bootable. If your hard disk has only one partition, that partition is drive C; otherwise, the first partition on your hard disk is drive C. Type the following command to format your drive C:

    FORMAT C:/ S /U

13. After you format your disk partitions, verify that drive C is bootable. Remove all floppy disks from your drives, and press Ctrl+Alt+Del to restart your computer. Your computer should start, load DOS, and leave you at the C prompt.
14. From the floppy disks you prepared in step 6, copy your CONFIG.SYS, AUTOEXEC.BAT, and any required device drivers to drive C.
15. Copy your backup software program from the floppy disks you prepared in step 6, or reinstall the backup software from its distribution disks. Refer to the documentation for your backup software for information on setting up the backup and restore programs.
16. Restore *only* your DOS 6 program files from the backup you made in step 2. Alternatively, you can run the DOS 6 Setup program again to reinstall the DOS 6 program files.
17. Restart your computer again. Remove any floppy disks from the drives, and press Ctrl+Alt+Del. Your computer should restart, load DOS, and leave you at the DOS prompt.

You are ready to compress your disks by using Stacker. Follow the instructions in this chapter for Stacker Express Setup to compress all your drives. Then continue with step 18.

18. Restore all remaining data from your backup to your hard disks. As you restore your data from the backup, configure your backup and restore program so that files from the backup do not replace files already on the hard disk.
19. To complete the restoration of your data, reinstall any copy-protected software you uninstalled earlier.

You have completed the conversion to Stacker disk compression. Your computer should now work as it did before, although you may need to make a few additional adjustments before you truly finish. Your system may have a few other differences as well.

As explained at the beginning of this chapter, Stacker has specific rules for how it assigns drive letters. Stacker's rules for assigning drive letters may be different from the rules that your previous disk compression software used. Some of your drive letters are likely to be different after you convert to Stacker. Your compressed volumes should all have the same drive letters they did before, but the drive letters for your uncompressed drives may be different.

Usually, having different drive letters for the uncompressed drives does not affect your computer's operation. You may need to adjust, however, to the new drive letters in your computer system. In a few situations, however, having different drive letters may make a difference. If your DOS PATH statement (in AUTOEXEC.BAT) refers to directories on your uncompressed drives, you may need to change the path statement to reflect the new drive letters. You also may need to reconfigure any software programs that refer to directories on an uncompressed drive.

In particular, Windows users may need to make some minor changes. As you may recall from the discussion in Chapter 1, "Understanding and Using Disk Compression," Windows permanent swap files do not work on a compressed drive; you must put the permanent swap file on an uncompressed drive. To get the most speed performance from Windows, many people place temporary swap files on an uncompressed drive. (Refer to your Windows documentation for more information about Windows swap files.) Because drive letters for your uncompressed drives are likely to change, Windows may report that it cannot open the swap file. If you have a permanent swap file, Windows may report that the swap file is corrupted. Refer to Chapter 13, "Troubleshooting Stacker," for information on correcting problems with the Windows swap file.

NOTE: If you need more than 2M of space on the uncompressed boot drive, use the instructions in this chapter for Stacker Custom Setup instead of Express Setup. Stacker Custom Setup enables you to specify how much uncompressed space to leave on the host drive.

STOP If your restore program replaces files that already exist on your hard disk, you will inadvertently replace your modified CONFIG.SYS and AUTOEXEC.BAT files with the old versions that still load your former disk compression device drivers. If these device drivers load into memory, your Stacker drives may become inaccessible or corrupted, and you must change CONFIG.SYS and AUTOEXEC.BAT again.

Summary

In this chapter, you learned about the changes Stacker makes to your computer system. You learned what files Stacker adds or changes on your boot disk, and how Stacker assigns drive letters and volume labels. You also learned what preparations to make before installing Stacker and were guided through step-by-step instructions for performing both Express and Custom setup for Stacker. The chapter concluded by explaining how to convert from DoubleSpace or another disk compression program to Stacker.

The next chapter gives you information on configuring and optimizing Stacker.

CHAPTER 10

Configuring and Optimizing Stacker

After you install Stacker, you may want to optimize it to make the best use of your computer's resources. If you change your computer's configuration after you install Stacker—adding or removing a disk drive or adding network software—you may need to make changes in how Stacker configures and assigns drive letters and uses memory. This chapter shows you how to configure Stacker to use the least amount of conventional memory and explains how Stacker redirects DOS disk commands to use Stacker's equivalent commands. The chapter then describes how to use the MS-DOS SMARTDRV disk cache to safely increase the speed of your Stacker compressed drives. (SMARTDRV comes with DOS 6.)

This chapter also describes when and how to adjust Stacker's compression levels and change the expected compression ratio for a Stacker compressed drive. The chapter then explains how to alter the way Stacker assigns drive letters and how to change the number of removable media drives that Stacker can accommodate. The chapter concludes by discussing how to set up a Stacker compressed RAM drive.

Understanding the Stacker Initialization File: STACKER.INI

As you install Stacker, it places a file called STACKER.INI in the root directory of your uncompressed boot drive. STACKER.INI contains information the Stacker DBLSPACE.BIN device driver uses to configure itself and assign disk drive letters. Almost all Stacker options are controlled through commands in the STACKER.INI file. STACKER.INI is a DOS text file, similar to many other files on your disk drive; unlike most other files on your disk, however, STACKER.INI has Hidden, System, and Read-Only file attributes. Because you normally do not need to be aware of this file, Stacker gives it the Hidden file attribute; the System and Read-Only file attributes prevent you from accidentally deleting the STACKER.INI file.

The following example shows a sample STACKER.INI file for a computer with three physical disk drive partitions. Each drive partition contains a compressed volume file created by compressing the entire drive. The uncompressed drive E partition also contains a compressed volume file created by compressing the free space on the drive.

```
/DIR=C:\STACKER\
/BD=G
/RP=2
/SW JF
A:
E:\STACVOL.DSK,SW
D:\STACVOL.DSK,SW
C:\STACVOL.DSK,SW
E:\STACVOL.000,NS
```

The STACKER.INI file provides the Stacker device driver with the information it needs to operate. Notice that STACKER.INI is generally structured so that all the commands preceded by a slash—referred to as *switches*—are located at the beginning of the file. The last four lines in the file refer to the Stacker compressed volume files that are to be mounted. These lines tell Stacker which compressed volumes to mount after your computer starts, where the compressed volumes are located, and how to handle drive letter assignments as the compressed volumes are mounted.

If you used earlier versions of Stacker, some of the switches in the STACKER.INI file may be familiar. Almost all the STACKER.INI command switches are the same as the command line switches used with the old Stacker device drivers. You control Stacker 3.1 in DOS 6 by using switches in the STACKER.INI file instead of using switches with the device driver in CONFIG.SYS. The remaining discussion in this section shows you how Stacker processes the STACKER.INI file; the following section describes the individual switches in more detail.

The first line in the preceding sample file—/DIR=C:\STACKER\—tells the Stacker device driver that the Stacker programs are located in the STACKER directory on drive C. If you use Stacker's redirection of DOS disk commands, described later in this chapter, the Stacker device driver uses this directory to locate the Stacker command files.

The second line—/BD=G—tells Stacker which drive letter to use as the *base drive*. (This is the first drive letter assigned by Stacker.) In this example, the base drive letter is G. You find this switch most often in systems that have been converted from DoubleSpace to Stacker.

The third line—/RP=2—tells Stacker to provide two replaceable drive letters for mounting additional Stacker compressed drives. Replaceable drive letters are typically used for removable disks.

The fourth line—/SW JF—tells Stacker to swap drive letters J and F so that the drive formerly accessible as drive J is now drive F, and the drive formerly accessible as drive F is now drive J.

The fifth line—A:—tells Stacker that drive A is used for Stacker compressed removable disks. If you access a disk in drive A that is compressed by Stacker, that disk is automatically mounted. Without such a line in STACKER.INI, you must manually mount at least one compressed removable disk in a disk drive to establish the link between the drive letter and the Stacker device driver that enables automatic compressed volume mounting in that drive.

The remaining lines in the file mount Stacker compressed volumes from the computer's hard drives. Each line specifies the uncompressed drive and the name of the compressed volume file to mount. The two letters at the end of each line specify how Stacker should handle drive letter assignments as it mounts the compressed drive.

The first of these lines in the sample file—`E:\STACVOL.DSK,SW`—mounts the STACVOL.DSK file stored on uncompressed drive E. The SW mounting option tells Stacker to swap drive letters. Stacker mounts the compressed volume file and assigns it the next available DOS drive letter. Normally, because this system has three hard disk partitions (C, D, and E), the next available drive letter is F. The /BD line, however, sets the base drive for Stacker as drive G. Stacker therefore assigns the drive letter G to the first mounted compressed volume.

Because the mounting method indicates that the drive letters are to be swapped, Stacker exchanges the drive letters of these two drives. The compressed volume is now accessible as drive E, and the uncompressed volume is accessible as drive G.

At this point, drive letters have the following assignments:

    A: Stacker automatic mounting.
    C: Uncompressed drive—not processed yet.
    D: Uncompressed drive—not processed yet.
    E: Stacker compressed volume.
    F: Not used by Stacker.
    G: Uncompressed host drive for E.

The next line to mount a compressed volume from a hard drive—`D:\STACVOL.DSK,SW`—mounts the STACVOL.DSK file stored on uncompressed drive D. Stacker mounts the compressed volume file and assigns it the next available DOS drive letter, H. As occurs with the first compressed volume mounted, drive letters are swapped so that the compressed volume is accessible as drive D and the uncompressed volume as drive H.

The next line—`C:\STACVOL.DSK,SW`—mounts a compressed volume from uncompressed drive C. Stacker assigns drive letter I to the newly mounted compressed volume and then swaps the drive letters so that the compressed drive is accessed as drive C and the uncompressed drive as drive I.

The last line of the sample STACKER.INI file—`E:\STACVOL.000,NS`—mounts the STACVOL.000 file stored on uncompressed drive E. This final Stacker compressed volume file is created by compressing the free space on drive E. The NS indicates that no swapping of drive letters is to take place. Stacker mounts this compressed volume file and assigns it the next available drive letter, J.

At this point, drive letters are assigned as shown in the following list:

    A: Stacker automatic mounting.
    C: Stacker compressed volume.
    D: Stacker compressed volume.
    E: Stacker compressed volume.

F: Not used by Stacker.
G: Uncompressed host drive for E.
H: Uncompressed host drive for D.
I: Uncompressed host drive for C.
J: Stacker compressed volume (free space drive).

After Stacker mounts all the compressed volume files, it swaps any additional drive letters indicated by the /SW switch. In the sample STACKER.INI file, the /SW switch indicates that drive letters F and J are to be exchanged. All the compressed drives now have contiguous drive letters; drives C through F all are Stacker compressed drives.

The final drive letter assignments are as shown in the following list:
A: Stacker automatic mounting.
C: Stacker compressed volume.
D: Stacker compressed volume.
E: Stacker compressed volume.
F: Stacker compressed volume (free space drive).
G: Uncompressed host drive for E.
H: Uncompressed host drive for D.
I: Uncompressed host drive for C.
J: Not used by Stacker.

Examining the STACKER.INI Commands

The example in the preceding section shows how Stacker processes the STACKER.INI file and provides a quick introduction to the most common switches and mounting options for compressed volume files. The example also helps illustrate how Stacker assigns drive letters. This section provides detailed information on each of the Stacker command switches and mounting options.

Command Switches

Table 10.1 summarizes the STACKER.INI command switches. Each switch is described in detail, with examples, following the table.

Table 10.1 The STACKER.INI Command Switches

Command Switch	Purpose/Function
;	Used at the beginning of a line to indicate that the line is a comment. Stacker does not process the line.
@	Reserves a replaceable drive letter for removable disks.
*	Reserves a Stacker drive letter.
d:	Represents any drive letter. Reserves the specified drive letter as a Stacker replaceable drive letter for use with removable disks.

Configuring and Optimizing Stacker

Command Switch	Purpose/Function
/-AUTO	Turns off all automatic mounting of removable disks.
/BD=	Sets the base drive letter that Stacker uses.
/C=	Sets the cluster size for Stacker volumes.
/DIR=	Specifies the directory for Stacker program files.
/EMS	Places Stacker buffers in expanded memory.
/M=	Sets the Stacker buffer size.
/P=	Sets the Stacker compression level.
/RP=	Sets the maximum number of replaceable drives for removable disks.
/SW	Specifies pairs of drive letters to be swapped.
/UM	Places Stacker buffers in upper memory.
/W–	Disables Stacker's search for the Windows permanent swap file.
/W=	Specifies a directory for the Windows SPART.PAR file.
/W+	Specifies a directory for the Windows permanent swap file.

; The semicolon (;) symbol is legitimate only as the first character on a line. Stacker does not process any line that begins with this symbol. Use this symbol to temporarily disable a command in the STACKER.INI file or to make comments documenting the file, as shown in the following example:

```
/DIR=C:\STACKER\
D:\STACVOL.DSK,SW
C:\STACVOL.DSK,SW
; this line is a comment: the following line to mount a free space volume
  is not processed
; D:\STACVOL.000,NS
```

@ The @ symbol instructs Stacker to allocate enough memory to accommodate a replaceable drive letter. The size of the Stacker device driver in memory increases by approximately 1.4K for every replaceable drive letter Stacker reserves. Replaceable drive letters are usually assigned to removable media disk drives. If you mount a Stacker compressed volume (on a removable disk or otherwise), the newly mounted volume uses a Stacker replaceable drive letter. After the Stacker device driver is loaded into memory and all the compressed volumes listed in STACKER.INI are mounted, you can mount only as many additional Stacker volumes as you have available replaceable drive letters to assign them.

Suppose, for example, that you have only one replaceable drive letter. If you mount a Stacker compressed volume in drive A and then try to mount another Stacker compressed volume in drive B, Stacker tells you that no more replaceable drive letters are available and that you must add the @ symbol to your STACKER.INI file. (See also the description of the /RP= switch for another method of reserving Stacker replaceable drive letters.)

* The asterisk (*) symbol reserves the next available DOS drive letter for Stacker's use. This drive letter becomes unavailable for use by DOS. Normally, you use this symbol with the /SW switch to reserve a drive letter that you intend to swap with another Stacker or DOS drive letter later. The following STACKER.INI file demonstrates the * symbol on a system with one hard disk:

```
/DIR=C:\STACKER\
*
C:\STACVOL.DSK,SW
```

As the computer first starts up, the next available DOS drive letter is D. Because the line with the * symbol is the first line in the sample STACKER.INI file that affects drive letter assignments, Stacker reserves drive letter D. The next available DOS drive letter is now E. The last line mounts the compressed volume on drive C. Because the swap mounting option is specified, Stacker mounts the compressed volume as drive C, and assigns the drive letter E to the uncompressed host drive for drive C.

d: In the *d:* command, the *d* stands for any drive letter. Placing this command in STACKER.INI causes Stacker to reserve the drive letter you specify for use as an automatically mounted replaceable drive letter. Use this command to ensure that Stacker automatically mounts compressed volumes in a specific removable media drive. (See also the description of the /RP= switch for another method of reserving Stacker replaceable drive letters.) The following STACKER.INI sample file instructs Stacker to automatically mount compressed removable disks in drives A and B:

```
/DIR=C:\STACKER\
A:
B:
C:\STACVOL.DSK,SW
```

/-AUTO This switch disables automatic mounting of compressed removable disks for your entire system. Use the /-AUTO switch if you do not use compressed removable disks or if you need more memory available. Using this switch reduces the size of the Stacker device driver by approximately 3K, whether the Stacker device driver is loaded in conventional or upper memory.

/BD=*d* This command switch tells Stacker to use the drive letter specified by *d* as the base drive. The Stacker base drive letter is the drive letter Stacker uses as the first drive letter it assigns. You may not specify a base drive letter lower than the highest drive letter allocated by DOS before any compressed volumes are mounted. You most often see the /BD= switch in systems converted from DoubleSpace. Use this switch to skip one or more drive letters. The drive letters that Stacker skips are still available to DOS. If your computer is connected to a network, you may need to specify the Stacker base drive letter to reserve certain drive letters for your network software.

The following example shows the STACKER.INI file of a system converted from DoubleSpace. Stacker Setup uses the /BD= switch to keep the compressed and uncompressed drive letters the same as those previously used by DoubleSpace.

```
/DIR=C:\STACKER\
/BD=H:
C:\STACVOL.DSK,SW
```

Because the Stacker base drive letter is set to H, the first drive letter Stacker assigns is H. Stacker therefore assigns drive letter H to the uncompressed host drive of the first compressed volume it mounts (specified by the last line in the example). Without the /BD= command switch, the uncompressed host drive in this example would be drive D.

/C=*n* This switch tells Stacker what cluster size to use. Stacker normally uses 8K clusters but may use 16K or 32K clusters for compressed volumes larger than 512M. If you plan to store only small files, you can set the cluster size to 4K. Usually, if this switch is needed, Stacker adds it to STACKER.INI while stacking your disk drives. In general, you never need to alter or add this switch yourself.

/DIR=*directory* In this switch, *directory* stands for a valid DOS directory path. This switch tells Stacker where to find its program files. Stacker adds this switch to STACKER.INI as you first install the program. You never need to change this switch unless you move your Stacker program files to a different disk or directory after you install Stacker.

/EMS This switch instructs Stacker to use expanded memory to store data in Stacker's internal disk cache. If expanded memory is available on your computer, Stacker uses as much as is available—up to a maximum of 64K. Add this switch to reduce the amount of conventional memory Stacker uses or to increase the size of the Stacker disk cache without using additional conventional memory. Placing the Stacker disk cache in EMS memory reduces the size of the Stacker device driver by about 20K, whether the device driver is loaded in conventional or upper memory. (See also the description of the /UM command switch.)

/M=*nn* This switch tells Stacker how much conventional memory to use for Stacker's internal disk cache. The *nn* stands for a two-digit number specifying the size of the disk cache in kilobytes. You can specify any number from 1 to 64. Increasing the size of Stacker's internal disk cache may increase the speed of your system's accesses to compressed drives. The /M= switch increases the Stacker device driver's size in memory by about 1K for every 1K increase in the disk cache size. The /M= switch has no effect if you use it with the /EMS switch.

/P=*n* This switch tells Stacker which compression level to use. Because compressing your data takes time, Stacker must make a trade-off between giving you the maximum speed and the maximum compression possible. You can adjust this trade-off by using the /P= switch. The *n* stands for any number from 0 to 9. The higher the number, the greater is the compression and the lower is the speed.

If you use the Stacker Tuner to tune Stacker's compression, Stacker changes this switch. If no /P= switch is found in STACKER.INI, Stacker uses a compression level equivalent to /P=1—the same as the Fastest Speed, Standard Compression option in the

STOP

Setting the Stacker cluster size too small or too large may degrade the performance of your Stacker drives and result in inefficient use of your compressed disk space. Let Stacker set the cluster size automatically.

STOP

Although most programs' current versions use EMS memory correctly, some programs do not, which prevents other programs from using EMS memory at all. This problem is more likely to occur if you use early versions of software products such as Borland's Paradox SE. Do not use the Stacker /EMS switch if you use such programs. If you have a program that interferes with EMS memory management, you may be able to upgrade to a current version for a relatively small cost. Contact the software publisher or your vendor for upgrade information.

Stacker Tuner. A setting of /P=9 is equivalent to the Best Compression option in the Stacker Tuner, and /P=5 is equivalent to More Compression, and a Bit Less Speed. Specifying /P=0 turns the compression tuning off completely and incidentally decreases the size of the Stacker device driver by approximately 4K.

/RP=*n* This switch sets the number of replaceable drive letters that Stacker reserves. The *n* represents any number from 0 to the maximum number of currently available DOS drive letters. Replaceable drive letters are normally used with removable disk drives. Use the /RP= switch if you need to allocate several replaceable drives. (Using /RP= is generally more convenient than placing several @ symbols in the STACKER.INI file.) The /RP= switch reserves only the space for replaceable drive letters in the Stacker device driver; it does not reserve actual drive letters. To reserve replaceable drives for specific drive letters, use the *d:* command instead. Stacker always reserves at least one replaceable drive letter, even if you specify 0 with the /RP= switch or if no /RP= switch or @ symbols are found in the STACKER.INI file. The size of the Stacker device driver in memory increases by approximately 1.4K for every replaceable drive letter that Stacker reserves.

/SW *dd* This switch enables you to specify additional pairs of drive letters for Stacker to swap. You may list more than one pair of drive letters on the same /SW line. Use a space to separate each pair of drive letters. Stacker first mounts all the compressed volume files listed in STACKER.INI and makes any necessary drive letter assignments or exchanges. Stacker then carries out the additional drive letter exchanges specified by the /SW switch. Use /SW to alter the order of your drive letters if you are not satisfied with how Stacker assigns drive letters. You can use /SW to swap any drive letter, even if that drive letter is not used directly by Stacker.

Suppose, for example, that you have a computer system with two disk drives and decide to create a third logical disk drive by compressing the free space on drive D. By itself, Stacker produces the following STACKER.INI file:

```
/DIR=C:\STACKER\
D:\STACVOL.DSK,SW
C:\STACVOL.DSK,SW
D:\STACVOL.000,NS
```

Stacker first mounts the STACVOL.DSK compressed volume from drive D and then swaps drive letters so that the compressed volume is drive D and the uncompressed volume is drive E—the next available drive letter. Stacker then mounts the STACVOL.DSK compressed volume from drive C and swaps drive letters so that the compressed volume is drive C and the uncompressed volume is drive F. The final line mounts as drive G the STACVOL.000 compressed volume, which is the compressed drive created from the free space on uncompressed drive D. After Stacker is done, the drive assignments are as follows:

- C: Stacker compressed volume.
- D: Stacker compressed volume.
- E: Uncompressed host drive for D.
- F: Uncompressed host drive for C.
- G: Stacker compressed volume (free space drive).

You may prefer that all the compressed volume drive letters be contiguous, with the uncompressed host drive letters as the last two drive letters. If so, add the /SW switch to the STACKER.INI file, as shown in the following example. Notice that the /SW switch swaps two different pairs of drive letters, and that drive letter G is swapped twice.

```
/DIR=C:\STACKER\
/SW EG FG
D:\STACVOL.DSK,SW
C:\STACVOL.DSK,SW
D:\STACVOL.000,NS
```

Stacker initially mounts the compressed volumes and assigns drive letters as before. After all the drives are mounted, Stacker performs any additional drive letter swapping specified by /SW. The /SW switch in the second line of this example causes Stacker to swap drive letters E and G and then drive letters F and G. The final drive assignments are as shown in the following list:

C: Stacker compressed volume.
D: Stacker compressed volume.
E: Stacker compressed volume (free space drive).
F: Uncompressed host drive for D.
G: Uncompressed host drive for C.

/UM This switch instructs Stacker to put its internal disk cache into the upper memory area if the upper memory area is available and has enough room. Use this switch if you need more available conventional memory but do not have enough upper memory available in which to load the entire Stacker device driver. Placing the Stacker internal disk cache in upper memory reduces the size of the Stacker device driver in conventional memory by approximately 20K.

If both the /UM and /EMS switches are in the STACKER.INI file, Stacker tries to use EMS memory first. If EMS memory is not available or has insufficient space for the Stacker cache, Stacker observes the /UM command and attempts to place its internal disk cache in upper memory.

/W– This switch tells Stacker to skip the search for the Windows permanent swap file. Without this switch, the Stacker device driver searches your uncompressed disks for a Windows permanent swap file whenever the driver loads into memory. If one is found, Stacker updates the Windows file SPART.PAR, which Windows uses to locate the permanent swap file. Stacker updates the SPART.PAR file because its reassignment of drive letters may have placed the Windows permanent swap file on a different drive than it was on previously. This file search increases slightly the time your computer requires for start-up. If Windows is not installed on your system or if you do not plan to relocate your permanent swap file, add the /W– switch to STACKER.INI to speed up your system's start-up.

/W=*directory* This switch also affects Stacker's search for a Windows permanent swap file. In this switch, *directory* represents the DOS directory—including the drive letter—that contains your Windows program files. Use this switch if Stacker reports that it cannot find the SPART.PAR file.

/W+*directory* This switch, like the other forms of the /W command, affects Stacker's search for a Windows swap file. In this switch, *directory* represents the DOS drive and directory that contains the Windows permanent swap file. Use this switch if Stacker reports that it cannot find the permanent swap file.

Drive Mounting Options

Along with configuration and control information it provides, the STACKER.INI file tells Stacker which compressed volume files to mount whenever you start your computer. Each line in STACKER.INI that specifies a compressed volume file for mounting also indicates how Stacker should assign drive letters. Stacker uses one of three different methods for handling drive letter assignments. Stacker places a special command switch—called a *mounting parameter*—at the end of each line in the STACKER.INI file that mounts a compressed volume. Table 10.2 summarizes the available mounting parameters. Each mounting parameter and its effect is described in detail following the table.

Table 10.2 Stacker Drive Mounting Parameters

Parameter	Effect
NS	*No S*wapping. The Stacker drive is mounted without swapping drive letters.
RP	*ReP*lace. The Stacker drive is mounted and replaces the uncompressed drive.
SW	*SW*ap. The Stacker drive is mounted, and Stacker swaps its drive letter with the uncompressed drive.

Each drive mounting parameter is placed at the end of the same line as the compressed volume file name and is separated from the file name by a comma. The following STACKER.INI line, for example, mounts the STACVOL.DSK compressed volume file on drive C and uses the SW mounting parameter:

```
C:\STACVOL.DSK,SW
```

SW The *SW*ap mounting parameter is the one most often used. If mounting a compressed volume that uses the SW parameter, Stacker exchanges the drive letter of the compressed volume with the drive letter of the uncompressed host drive that contains the compressed volume file. The Stacker compressed volume then becomes available through the drive letter of the original uncompressed drive, and the uncompressed drive is accessible through another drive letter. The STACKER.INI file shown in the following example is for a computer with a single hard disk and a single compressed volume:

```
/DIR=C:\STACKER\
C:\STACVOL.DSK,SW
```

While mounting the compressed volume, Stacker first assigns it the next available DOS drive letter, D. Stacker then immediately swaps this new drive letter for the drive letter of the original uncompressed drive—C in this example. The compressed drive, therefore, is drive C, and the uncompressed drive appears as a new drive letter, D.

NS The *No S*wapping parameter is the second most common mounting parameter. If mounting a compressed volume that uses this parameter, Stacker does not reassign any drive letters. The newly mounted compressed volume keeps the first drive letter assigned to it—the next available DOS drive letter. Most compressed drives created from free space are mounted by using the NS mounting parameter. As you create a free space compressed drive, Stacker adds a line to STACKER.INI to mount the new free space drive by using the NS mounting parameter.

The following example shows a compressed drive mounted by using the NS mounting parameter. This STACKER.INI file is for a computer with a single physical hard drive and two compressed volumes. The second compressed volume file is created from the free space on drive C.

```
/DIR=C:\STACKER\
C:\STACVOL.DSK,SW
C:\STACVOL.000,NS
```

In this example, Stacker mounts the first compressed volume file and swaps drive letters. After the first compressed volume is mounted, drive C refers to the Stacker drive, and drive D refers to the original uncompressed disk. As Stacker mounts the second compressed volume—STACVOL.000—Stacker assigns this volume the next available drive letter, which is E. Because the NS mounting parameter is used to mount this compressed volume file, Stacker does not reassign the compressed volume's drive letter or change the drive letter of the uncompressed host drive. The final drive assignments from this example are as shown in the following list:

   C: Stacker compressed volume.
   D: Uncompressed host drive for C and E.
   E: Stacker compressed volume (free space drive).

RP This is the *ReP*lace mounting parameter. If Stacker mounts a compressed volume by using the RP mounting parameter, the compressed volume replaces the uncompressed drive from which it is mounted. No new drive letters are created or assigned. The uncompressed host drive is inaccessible until the Stacker compressed drive is unmounted. Use this mounting parameter if you do not need to access the uncompressed portion of the drive or if you want to reduce the number of drive letters in your system.

```
/DIR=C:\STACKER\
D:\STACVOL.DSK,RP
C:\STACVOL.DSK,SW
```

The STACKER.INI file in the preceding example is configured for a computer with two hard drives, C and D. The first compressed drive mounted is from drive D. Because this drive has the RP mounting parameter, Stacker assigns drive letter D to the compressed volume as it is mounted. The uncompressed host drive—the original drive D—is now unavailable until the compressed volume is unmounted. The final assignment of drive letters in this example is shown in the following list:

   C: Stacker compressed volume.
   D: Stacker compressed volume.
   E: Uncompressed host drive for C.

Editing STACKER.INI

This section supplies the specific information you need to edit your STACKER.INI file.

Before making any changes in your STACKER.INI file, make sure that you have a bootable floppy disk containing the Stacker DBLSPACE.BIN device driver file. You may need to boot your computer from a floppy disk if you experience a problem after you change STACKER.INI. Refer to the section "Making a DOS 6 Start-Up Disk Containing Stacker," in Chapter 9, for information on creating a bootable floppy disk that contains the Stacker DBLSPACE.BIN files.

Make sure also that you save a copy of the DOS ATTRIB utility program on your bootable floppy disk. If you experience problems that require you to boot your computer from a floppy disk after changing STACKER.INI, you need the ATTRIB program to make the STACKER.INI file accessible.

You can use either of two methods to edit the STACKER.INI file. The most convenient method involves using a DOS batch file and a text editing program supplied with Stacker. The second method is more complex but involves only utility programs supplied with DOS. The following sections describe how to locate the STACKER.INI file and how to edit the file by using these two methods.

> **STOP** Be careful if you change your STACKER.INI file. The commands in STACKER.INI can fundamentally affect how the Stacker device driver operates and how your compressed volumes are mounted. Making hasty or incorrect changes in STACKER.INI may make one or more of your compressed volumes temporarily unavailable or may cause Stacker itself to operate incorrectly.

Locating STACKER.INI

Whether you use the Stacker tools or the DOS method to edit STACKER.INI, you must first locate the STACKER.INI file. STACKER.INI is located in the root directory of the uncompressed drive that is your system's boot drive *before* Stacker exchanges any drive letters. To identify your uncompressed boot drive, type the following command at the DOS prompt, and press Enter:

STACKER

Stacker displays a report listing all your disk drive letters, similar to that shown in the following example. The list shows which drive letters are swapped and also gives the name and location of each mounted compressed volume file if the drive letter is a Stacker drive letter. If a drive letter is used by Stacker but a compressed volume is not currently mounted on that drive, the report indicates the drive letter's status.

```
Stacker 3.10 for Windows and DOS   1990-93 Stac Electronics, Carlsbad, CA
Registered to:
        Matthew Harris
        Harris Programming Service

Stacker drive map:
   Drive A: was drive A: at boot time   [ Auto-mounting Stacker drive ]
   Drive B: was drive B: at boot time   [ Auto-mounting Stacker drive ]
   Drive C: was drive C: at boot time   [ F:\STACVOL.DSK = 57.1MB     ]
   Drive D: was drive D: at boot time   [ E:\STACVOL.DSK = 27.9MB     ]
   Drive E: was drive E: at boot time
   Drive F: was drive F: at boot time
No available replaceable drive(s).
```

If you start your computer from a hard disk, your boot drive is always drive C. In the preceding report, drive C is shown as stored in the STACVOL.DSK compressed volume file on drive F. Drive F is therefore the uncompressed boot drive for this system, and the STACKER.INI file is in the root directory of drive F. The uncompressed boot drive for systems with only one physical hard drive is usually drive D. If your drive C is not compressed, no information appears in the right-hand column of the report—as is the case in the lines for drives E and F in the example. STACKER.INI then is in the root directory of drive C. (Refer to Chapter 11, "Using Stacker," for more details about using the STACKER command to get information about your compressed drives.)

Editing STACKER.INI by Using the Stacker Utilities

Stacker installs into your Stacker program directory two tools for editing the STACKER.INI file. If you use Express Setup, or if you permit Custom Setup to change your AUTOEXEC.BAT file, Stacker adds the Stacker directory to your PATH statement and the Stacker tools are always available. If the Stacker program files on your hard disk become unavailable for any reason, you also can use the editing tools from your Stacker Program Disk 1.

The first editing tool is a simple, general-purpose text editor—ED.EXE. You can use ED.EXE to edit STACKER.INI or any other DOS text file. The ED.EXE program file is stored in the Stacker directory on your hard disk and in the root directory of disk 1 of your Stacker floppy disks. The second editing tool is a DOS batch file named STACINI.BAT. Unlike ED.EXE, you can use the STACINI.BAT file for only one purpose—to edit the STACKER.INI file.

STACINI.BAT performs three tasks. First, it removes the Hidden, System, and Read-Only file attributes from the STACKER.INI file so that the file can be edited. Then STACINI.BAT starts ED.EXE so that STACKER.INI is loaded into memory and displayed on-screen, ready for editing. After you exit from the text editor, STACINI.BAT restores the Hidden, System, and Read-Only file attributes to STACKER.INI.

If you intend to use the Stacker editing tools on your hard disk, and the Stacker directory is not part of your PATH statement, you must use the DOS CHDIR command to change to the Stacker directory before using the editing tools. To use the Stacker editing tools from the Stacker program disks, insert Stacker Program Disk 1 into whichever floppy disk drive can accommodate it, and make that drive the current disk drive. If the Stacker Program Disk is in drive A, for example, type **a:** at the DOS prompt, and press Enter.

To edit the STACKER.INI file by using STACINI.BAT, follow these steps:

1. Use the procedure described in the preceding section, "Locating STACKER.INI," to determine which drive letter is your uncompressed boot drive.

2. Type **STACINI *d:*** at the DOS prompt, and press Enter. (Substitute your uncompressed boot drive letter for ***d*** in this command.)

    STACINI.BAT displays a message describing its purpose and also displays the prompt Press any key to continue....

3. Press any key. STACINI.BAT uses the DOS ATTRIB command to remove the protective Hidden, System, and Read-Only attributes from STACKER.INI and

---

If you use the editing tools from the Stacker Program Disk 1, remember that the STACINI.BAT file is in the TOOLS directory on this disk. Use the following command to begin editing the STACKER.INI file (substitute your uncompressed drive letter for *d*):

TOOLS\STACINI *d:*

then starts ED.EXE to edit STACKER.INI. (If you decide not to edit STACKER.INI at this time, press Ctrl+C and then Y to cancel the batch file and return to the DOS command line.)

ED.EXE displays an on-screen printout similar to the one shown in figure 10.1. The exact contents of the STACKER.INI file displayed depend on your specific computer. Notice the status line at the bottom of the screen. This line identifies the ED text editor and displays the only two editing commands that ED recognizes, along with the name of the file being edited. The asterisk (*) at the left edge of the bottom line indicates that the file has been changed. The asterisk appears on the status line as soon as you make changes in the file you are editing.

Fig. 10.1
A STACKER.INI file as it appears on the ED text editor screen.

4. To change the STACKER.INI file, use the arrow keys to move the cursor to the line you want to edit, and type your changes. Use the Del or Backspace keys to erase characters; press Enter to start a new line.
5. After you finish making changes, press Ctrl+Z to save your changes and exit ED. If you change your mind about saving changes to the STACKER.INI file, press Esc. If you made any changes, ED asks whether you want to save the file before exiting. To exit without saving your changes, press N, and then press Enter.

Whether or not you save your changes, STACINI.BAT uses the DOS ATTRIB command to restore the protective Hidden, System, and Read-Only file attributes to the STACKER.INI file and then returns you to the DOS prompt.

6. To make the changes in STACKER.INI take effect, restart your computer by pressing Ctrl+Alt+Del.

NOTE:
Any changes you make in STACKER.INI do not take effect until you restart your computer. Stacker processes the STACKER.INI file only after the Stacker DBLSPACE.BIN device driver is loaded into memory.

Editing STACKER.INI by Using DOS Only

If the Stacker utility programs are not available or you prefer to use a text editor other than ED, you can edit the STACKER.INI file manually.

To edit the STACKER.INI file manually, follow these steps:

1. Use the procedure described in the section "Locating STACKER.INI," earlier in this chapter, to determine which drive letter is your uncompressed boot drive.
2. Make your uncompressed boot drive the current disk drive, and make the root directory the current directory.

3. Use the DOS DIR command to verify the presence of the STACKER.INI file by typing the following command at the DOS prompt and pressing Enter:

   DIR STACKER.INI /AH

   If the current drive and directory are correct, DOS displays a directory listing showing only the STACKER.INI file. If you are in the wrong directory or disk, DOS displays the message `No files found`. If you are in the correct directory and drive, go on to step 4; otherwise, repeat steps 1 and 2.

4. Type the following command at the DOS prompt, and press Enter:

   ATTRIB –S –H –R STACKER.INI

   This command removes the System, Hidden, and Read-Only file attributes from the STACKER.INI file. STACKER.INI now appears in regular directory displays and can be modified or deleted.

5. Copy STACKER.INI to a floppy disk. If you experience problems after modifying the STACKER.INI file, you can use this copy to restore STACKER.INI to its original condition.

6. Use a text editor—such as DOS EDIT—to edit the STACKER.INI file.

7. After you make your changes, save the file and exit from your text editor.

8. Restore the protective file attributes for STACKER.INI by typing the following command at the DOS prompt and pressing Enter:

   ATTRIB +S +H +R STACKER.INI

9. To make the changes in STACKER.INI take effect, restart your computer by pressing Ctrl+Alt+Del.

If your changes to STACKER.INI do not work as you anticipated, you may want to restore your original STACKER.INI file and try the editing process again. If you made a copy of your original STACKER.INI file, you can use the following procedure to restore the file:

1. Use the following ATTRIB command on the uncompressed boot disk to remove the file attributes of the STACKER.INI file:

   ATTRIB –S –H –R STACKER.INI

2. Delete the STACKER.INI file from your hard disk by typing **DEL STACKER.INI** at the DOS prompt and pressing Enter.

3. Copy the original STACKER.INI file from the floppy disk to your uncompressed boot disk.

4. Restore the correct file attributes by typing the following command and pressing Enter:

   ATTRIB +S +H +R STACKER.INI

5. Restart your computer to restore the original drive assignments and Stacker configuration.

After your computer restarts, the original drive assignments and configuration of your STACKER.INI file are restored.

Freeing Conventional Memory

This section describes how to make more of your computer's conventional memory available for your DOS programs by relocating the Stacker device driver in memory or by reducing its size in memory. Many DOS programs require substantial amounts of conventional memory. If enough conventional memory is not available for your application to run after you load it, the program may display insufficient memory error messages. DOS may even tell you that you do not have enough memory to load the program at all.

You may be able to load the Stacker device driver into your computer's upper memory area to make more conventional memory available for your other programs. Before you learn how to load the Stacker device driver into upper memory, however, you must understand the mechanism Stacker uses to control its placement in memory.

Using STACHIGH.SYS and DBLSPACE.BIN

You load device drivers into conventional memory by using the DEVICE command in your CONFIG.SYS file. Your CONFIG.SYS file, for example, may already contain a line similar to the following, which loads a mouse device driver:

    DEVICE=MOUSE.SYS

Similarly, you load device drivers into upper memory by using the DEVICEHIGH command in your CONFIG.SYS file; DEVICEHIGH tells DOS to use the memory manager to load the device driver into upper memory. (Refer to your DOS documentation for more information about the DEVICE and DEVICEHIGH commands.)

As described in Chapter 9, "Installing Stacker," Stacker places the DBLSPACE.BIN file in the root directory of your boot disk as you install Stacker. The DLBSPACE.BIN file is the device driver for your Stacker compressed disk drives. DOS loads DBLSPACE.BIN into memory before processing your CONFIG.SYS file. DOS, therefore, must always load DBLSPACE.BIN in conventional memory as your computer first starts—DOS has no way of knowing where you want the device driver to ultimately reside.

The commands in your CONFIG.SYS file cannot directly apply to DBLSPACE.BIN, because the device driver is already loaded into memory as DOS processes CONFIG.SYS. Instead of directly controlling where DBLSPACE.BIN loads into memory, the makers of Stacker provided a way to indirectly control the location of the Stacker device driver. Instead of using statements in your CONFIG.SYS file that refer to DBLSPACE.BIN, you use statements referring to a different file, called STACHIGH.SYS. The STACHIGH.SYS file is a device driver that enables you to move DBLSPACE.BIN from one part of your computer's memory to another. Stacker gets all its configuration information from the STACKER.INI file, so no switches are available for STACHIGH.SYS.

If you use DEVICEHIGH in your CONFIG.SYS file to load STACHIGH.SYS, DOS moves the DBLSPACE.BIN device driver to upper memory. Otherwise, the STACHIGH.SYS device driver just adds the DOS disk command redirection described in the section "Redirecting DOS Disk Commands to Stacker," later in this chapter.

> **NOTE:** The subject of memory management is fairly complex. This book cannot adequately cover all the issues involved in using your computer's memory most efficiently. To learn more about DOS memory management, consult *Using MS-DOS 6*, also published by Que.

> **STOP** If you load disk drive device drivers that make logical disk drives available to DOS—such as a RAM disk or network software—adding STACHIGH.SYS to your CONFIG.SYS file may affect how DOS and Stacker assign drive letters to these other drives. So that STACHIGH.SYS does not affect these drive letters, make sure that the STACHIGH.SYS statement in CONFIG.SYS comes *after* all other statements that load disk drive device drivers. You may even want to make STACHIGH.SYS the last line in your CONFIG.SYS file.

Using STACHIGH.SYS To Relocate the Stacker Device Driver

To load any device driver into upper memory, you must use an expanded memory manager program. DOS cannot control the upper memory area without the additional services provided by an expanded memory manager. You can use the expanded memory manager supplied with DOS—EMM386—or third-party memory managers such as QEMM or 386MAX. This book describes only the memory managers supplied with DOS. If you use another memory manager, refer to its documentation for details on that program. The commands you use in your CONFIG.SYS file to control the Stacker device driver's location in memory are the same, however, whether you use DOS memory management software or another memory manager.

To use the DOS EMM386 memory manager, your computer must have an 80386 or higher CPU and you also must load the DOS HIMEM.SYS extended memory manager. To load the Stacker device driver into upper memory, you need to edit your CONFIG.SYS file. To edit CONFIG.SYS, use any text editor program, such as DOS EDIT or the ED program supplied with Stacker. (Refer to your DOS documentation for information about using EDIT.)

Follow these steps to add the instructions to your CONFIG.SYS that load Stacker into upper memory:

1. Open the CONFIG.SYS file for editing with any suitable text editor.
2. If not already present, add the following line to the beginning of your CONFIG.SYS file:

    DEVICE=C:\DOS\HIMEM.SYS

    This line installs the HIMEM.SYS extended memory manager the next time you restart your computer.

    After the HIMEM.SYS line, you must add the line for the DOS EMS memory manager, EMM386. The EMM386 line must come after the HIMEM.SYS line because EMM386 uses services provided by HIMEM.SYS.

    To make upper memory available for device drivers, you must use one of two switches with EMM386. The first switch—/RAM—enables the upper memory area and also enables expanded memory for use by other programs. The second switch—/NOEMS—enables only the upper memory area.

3. To make upper memory available for DOS and device drivers and provide expanded memory for other programs, add the following line to CONFIG.SYS:

    DEVICE=C:\DOS\EMM386.EXE /RAM

    If no other programs use expanded memory, and you want upper memory available only for device drivers, add the following line to CONFIG.SYS instead:

    DEVICE=C:\DOS\EMM386.EXE /NOEMS

4. Add the following line after the HIMEM.SYS and EMM386 statements in CONFIG.SYS:

    DOS=UMB

If you use the new DOS 6 feature to create start-up menus by using CONFIG.SYS, make sure that you put the statements for STACHIGH.SYS in the common area of your configuration menu. Refer to your DOS documentation for more information on creating CONFIG.SYS start-up menus.

Before editing your CONFIG.SYS file, copy the original file to a floppy disk so that you can restore your original CONFIG.SYS if you make a mistake or have other problems.

DEVICE statements for HIMEM.SYS and EMM386 may already appear in your CONFIG.SYS file. The EMM386 line in particular may include several other switches, especially if you used the DOS MEMMAKER command. Do not alter these other switches; doing so may make your computer inoperable or may cause a memory conflict.

This statement enables DOS's access to the upper memory area. No device drivers can load into upper memory without this statement.

Alternatively, you may add the following line:

DOS=UMB,HIGH

This statement enables DOS's access to the upper memory area and also loads parts of DOS into upper memory.

So far, you have added only the required memory management device drivers that enable DOS to use the upper memory area. Next you must add the statement that loads the Stacker device driver into upper memory.

5. If not already present, add the following line at the end of your CONFIG.SYS file:

    DEVICEHIGH=C:\DOS\STACHIGH.SYS

    The DEVICEHIGH statement causes DOS to relocate the Stacker device driver into upper memory.

6. Save your revised CONFIG.SYS file, and exit your text editor.
7. Press Ctrl+Alt+Del to restart your computer and make the changes in CONFIG.SYS take effect.

DOS is now configured to use STACHIGH.SYS to relocate the Stacker DBLSPACE.BIN device driver into your computer's upper memory.

> If a DEVICE statement for STACHIGH.SYS already is in your CONFIG.SYS file, you can use the DOS MEMMAKER command to change the statements in CONFIG.SYS to load the device driver high. Refer to your DOS documentation for information on using DOS MEMMAKER.

Verifying that Stacker Is Using Upper Memory

If upper memory has insufficient room to load a device driver, DOS loads the device driver into conventional memory without displaying an error message. To determine which device drivers load into upper memory, you must use the DOS MEM command to display a report describing how your computer's memory is used by DOS and other programs. (Refer to your DOS documentation for full information about MEM.)

To determine whether the Stacker device driver is loaded into upper memory, type the following command at the DOS prompt, and press Enter:

MEM /C /P

The /C switch for the MEM command instructs it to classify memory usage by the program using the memory. The /P switch tells the MEM command to pause after every screenful of information displayed.

Upper Memory Conflicts

If you already use upper memory, and you load the Stacker device driver into upper memory, you may begin to receive disk drive read error messages from DOS similar to the following example:

    Error reading drive C:

Read errors may result from conflicts between Stacker and other software that uses the upper memory area. If the upper memory area becomes too crowded, device drivers may interfere with one another's data areas. Another cause of read errors may be a conflict between Stacker and a feature called *shadow RAM*. Computers using shadow RAM copy the BIOS software from their ROM chips into RAM. This "shadow" copy of the BIOS ROM enables your computer to operate faster, because RAM typically operates faster than ROM. If you experience disk read errors after loading the Stacker device driver into upper memory, remove the DEVICEHIGH command for Stacker from your CONFIG.SYS. If you think the errors result from a conflict with your computer's shadow RAM, you can try turning off the shadow RAM instead of removing Stacker from upper memory. Refer to your computer's hardware documentation to determine whether your computer uses shadow RAM and how to disable it.

Configuring and Optimizing Stacker

After you issue the MEM command with the specified switches, a display similar to the following appears:

```
Modules using memory below 1 MB:

  Name          Total         =   Conventional   +   Upper Memory
  --------      ----------------  ----------------   ----------------

  MSDOS         16845  (16K)      16845  (16K)           0    (0K)
  HIMEM          1168   (1K)       1168   (1K)           0    (0K)
  EMM386         3120   (3K)       3120   (3K)           0    (0K)
  COMMAND        2976   (3K)       2976   (3K)           0    (0K)
  STACHIGH      52160  (51K)          0   (0K)       52160   (51K)
  Free         737744 (720K)     631072 (616K)      106672  (104K)


Memory Summary:
  Type of Memory           Total          =        Used         +         Free
  ----------------         ----------------        ----------------       ----------------

  Conventional             655360   (640K)         24288   (24K)          631072   (616K)
  Upper                    158832   (155K)         52160   (51K)          106672   (104K)
  Adapter RAM/ROM          131072   (128K)        131072  (128K)               0     (0K)
  Extended (XMS)          3249040  (3173K)        222096  (217K)         3026944  (2956K)
                          ----------------        ----------------       ----------------
  Total memory            4194304  (4096K)        429616  (420K)         3764688  (3676K)
  Total under 1 MB         814192   (795K)         76448   (75K)          737744   (720K)

  Largest executable program size                 630976  (616K)
  Largest free upper memory block                 106672  (104K)

MS-DOS is resident in the high memory area.
```

The first section of the MEM report, under the heading Modules using memory below 1MB, indicates where the device driver is loaded in memory. The first column shows the name of the device driver or program, and the remaining columns show the total memory used and how much conventional and upper memory is consumed. Notice in the STACHIGH entry (first section, fifth entry) that 0K of conventional memory and 51K of upper memory are used. This indicates that the Stacker device driver—STACHIGH.SYS—is loaded into upper memory.

The specific contents of your report varies depending on the configuration of your computer. If the report shows that STACHIGH uses conventional memory and that 0K of upper memory is used, the device driver is not loaded into upper memory. If the Stacker device driver is not loaded into upper memory, carefully review the configuration steps in the preceding section. Make sure especially that you included either the /RAM or /NOEMS switch with EMM386 and that you also included the DOS=UMB statement. If you performed the procedures correctly but are loading many device drivers into upper memory, you simply may not have enough upper memory available to accommodate the Stacker device driver.

Using Stacker with EMS Memory

If your computer has EMS memory, you can use that memory to reduce the amount of conventional or upper memory consumed by the Stacker device driver. Stacker maintains an internal disk cache in which it stores the data read from your disk drive. If you use EMS memory with Stacker, Stacker places its internal disk cache into EMS memory, which reduces the size of the Stacker device driver by about 20K, whether the device driver is loaded in conventional or upper memory.

To place Stacker's disk cache in EMS memory, your system must have EMS memory enabled. If you do not already have EMS memory enabled on your computer, follow the steps in the section "Using STACHIGH.SYS To Relocate the Stacker Device Driver," earlier in this chapter, to add the HIMEM.SYS and EMM386.EXE memory managers, which enables your computer system to use EMS memory.

After you make sure that EMS is enabled for your computer, you must add the /EMS switch to your STACKER.INI file, on a line by itself, so that STACKER.INI appears as shown in the following example:

```
/DIR=C:\STACKER\
/EMS
C:\STACVOL.DSK,SW
```

For the change to take effect, you must restart your computer. (See the section "Understanding the Stacker Initialization File: STACKER.INI," earlier in this chapter, for full information on the /EMS switch and on editing STACKER.INI.)

Disabling Automatic Removable Disk Mounting

If you need to squeeze every bit of memory possible out of your computer system, and you do not often use compressed removable disks, you can disable automatic mounting of removable disks. Disabling automatic drive mounting reduces the size of the Stacker device driver by about 3K, whether loaded in conventional memory or upper memory.

Add the /-AUTO switch, on a line by itself, to your STACKER.INI file to disable automatic mounting of removable disks, so that STACKER.INI appears as shown in the following example:

```
/DIR=C:\STACKER\
/-AUTO
C:\STACVOL.DSK,SW
```

For any changes in STACKER.INI to take effect, you must restart your computer. (See the section "Understanding the Stacker Initialization File: STACKER.INI," earlier in this chapter, for full information on the /-AUTO switch and on editing STACKER.INI.)

Redirecting DOS Disk Commands to Stacker

Stacker includes several utilities that provide services equivalent to certain DOS commands but are specially adapted for use with Stacker compressed drives. Stacker provides the SDIR command, for example, which is equivalent to the DOS DIR command but also displays such information as the specific compression ratios for individual files on Stacker compressed drives. (SDIR is described in Chapter 11, "Using Stacker.")

If you have used DoubleSpace in DOS 6, you already know that DOS 6 disk commands (such as DIR and CHKDSK) recognize DoubleSpace compressed disks and provide special services pertaining to DoubleSpace compressed drives. The DOS DIR command, for example, now has an additional command line switch to display the compression ratios of files on a DoubleSpace compressed disk. Stacker 3.1 provides a similar capability in DOS 6. Stacker 3.1 can intercept DOS disk commands and utilities and instead invoke the appropriate Stacker utility programs. If you use the DOS DIR command on a Stacker compressed drive, for example, the Stacker SDIR command is invoked instead.

Because DOS 6 commands do not recognize Stacker compressed drives, Stacker adds this capability to DOS through a device driver. You can load this DOS disk command redirection device driver in one of two ways. The first method is to use the STACHIGH.SYS device driver. The DOS command redirection is built into STACHIGH.SYS and is enabled whenever STACHIGH.SYS loads into either conventional or upper memory. The second way to load the DOS disk command redirection device driver into memory is by using the REDIRECT.COM utility program. REDIRECT.COM installs another file—REDIRECT.BIN—into memory as the DOS disk command redirection device driver. Stacker copies the REDIRECT.COM and REDIRECT.BIN files into your Stacker directory on installation.

Use REDIRECT.COM if you do not want to use STACHIGH.SYS but still want to load DOS disk command redirection, or to make DOS disk command redirection an optional feature for your system. To load the redirection device driver, type the following command at the DOS prompt, and press Enter:

REDIRECT

Stacker displays a message on-screen informing you that command redirection is loaded. To load REDIRECT every time your computer starts, add a line containing the REDIRECT command to your AUTOEXEC.BAT file.

Improving Stacker Performance by Using SMARTDRV.EXE

Stacker is compatible with almost all disk cache programs. (Disk caching is described in Chapter 1.) This section discusses using the SMARTDRV.EXE version 4.1 disk cache program supplied with DOS 6. Although other suitable disk cache programs are available (such as NCache in the Norton utilities), providing specifics for all disk cache programs available is beyond the scope of this book. You can, however, apply the general guidelines for using SMARTDRV.EXE to any other disk caching program you may use with Stacker.

Stacker can recognize most disk cache programs. Stacker assumes responsibility for keeping your data safe by recognizing the disk cache instead of relying on the disk cache to recognize Stacker.

The easiest approach usually is to install DOS command redirection by loading the STACHIGH.SYS device driver in your CONFIG.SYS file. Refer to the section "Freeing Conventional Memory," earlier in this chapter, for information on adding STACHIGH.SYS to your CONFIG.SYS file.

NOTE:
Stacker adds the STACHIGH.SYS device driver to your CONFIG.SYS file as you install Stacker, so the DOS disk command redirection is automatically enabled.

SMARTDRV is a TSR program that loads through your AUTOEXEC.BAT file. Locating SMARTDRV near the beginning of AUTOEXEC.BAT is a good idea so that the benefits of the cache are available as early as possible. You load SMARTDRV by adding the following line to AUTOEXEC.BAT (assuming that your DOS files are in the DOS subdirectory on drive C):

C:\DOS\SMARTDRV

SMARTDRV 4.1 automatically caches all your disk drives, using write-delay caching for all your hard disks. SMARTDRV does not normally use write-delay caching for removable media drives, because the program cannot tell when the disk may be removed from the drive. Using a disk cache on a logical disk drive, however, is not effective. Disk caching works only if you cache the physical disk drive or a physical disk partition. Stacker, therefore, prevents SMARTDRV from caching your mounted compressed volumes but not your physical hard disks.

You can obtain information about how SMARTDRV is operating by entering the following command at the DOS prompt:

SMARTDRV /S

This command instructs SMARTDRV to display a status report. The following status report shows the type of information that appears on-screen:

```
Microsoft SMARTDrive Disk Cache version 4.1
Copyright 1991,1993 Microsoft Corp.


Room for     128 elements of    8,192 bytes each
There have been      724 cache hits
     and     543 cache misses
Cache size:  1,048,576 bytes
Cache size while running Windows:    524,288 bytes


              Disk Caching Status
   drive   read cache   write cache    buffering
   ---------------------------------------------
     A:       yes          no             no
     B:       yes          no             no
     F:       yes          yes            no
     G:       yes          yes            no
     H:       yes          yes            no

For help, type "Smartdrv /?".
```

This sample report is for a computer with three physical disk partitions, each of which hosts a compressed volume file. The compressed volumes are drives C, D, and E. Their respective host disks are H, G, and F. Notice that only the floppy drives A and B and the three physical disk drives—currently referred to as F, G, and H—are cached. Stacker prohibits SMARTDRV from caching the compressed volumes. (For a complete explanation of the SMARTDRV report, refer to your DOS documentation.)

> **NOTE:**
> This section discusses only aspects of SMARTDRV relevant to using Stacker. For more information on SMARTDRV, refer to your DOS documentation, or read *Using MS-DOS 6*, also published by Que.

Configuring and Optimizing Stacker 225

To use a disk cache other than SMARTDRV, configure your disk cache so that caching for your compressed volumes is disabled. Refer to the documentation for your cache program to determine the correct method of disabling the cache for particular drives.

One SMARTDRV 4.1 feature requires careful consideration: its write-delay caching. Although the write-delay cache—along with the regular read cache—does increase the speed of your disk operations, it poses an inherent danger. Because the write-delay cache holds information in memory before writing the data to the disk, some data may be lost if your computer experiences a power failure or a problem that requires you to restart the computer by turning it off instead of using Ctrl+Alt+Del. (SMARTDRV does write all its write-delay cache data to the disk if you use Ctrl+Alt+Del to restart your computer.)

Although the risk of data loss from a write-delay cache may be small, it does exist, and the consequences can be serious. If data loss occurs, and the lost data is part of your compressed volume's structural information, your compressed volume may become corrupted. A corrupted compressed volume file may result in the loss of all files on the compressed volume. Because of this increased risk of severe data loss, you should turn off the write-delay cache for any disk drives that contain compressed volume files. On an 80386 or higher computer running at 33MHz or greater, you may not even notice any speed difference after the write cache is turned off.

Notice that, in the sample SMARTDRV status report, the write cache is active for all hard disk drives. SMARTDRV 4.1 uses write caching for all your hard disk drives and partitions unless you specify otherwise.

To turn off the SMARTDRV write cache for one or more disk drives, follow these steps:

1. Type **STACKER** at the DOS prompt, and press Enter. Stacker displays a report similar to that shown in the following example, listing all your disk drives, and— if a drive is compressed—the name and location of its compressed volume file.

```
Stacker 3.10 for Windows and DOS  1990-93 Stac Electronics,
Carlsbad, CA
Registered to:
        Matthew Harris
        Harris Programming Service

Stacker drive map:
   Drive A: was drive A: at boot time
   Drive B: was drive B: at boot time
   Drive C: was drive C: at boot time  [ H:\STACVOL.DSK = 57.1MB  ]
   Drive D: was drive D: at boot time  [ G:\STACVOL.DSK = 27.9MB  ]
   Drive E: was drive E: at boot time  [ F:\STACVOL.DSK = 20.9MB  ]
   Drive F: was drive F: at boot time
   Drive G: was drive G: at boot time
   Drive H: was drive H: at boot time
Total of 1 available replaceable drive(s).
```

NOTE:
If you are concerned about problems with the SMARTDRV write-delay cache, you may want to know that Microsoft now has available SMARTDRV version 4.2. SMARTDRV 4.2 does not automatically use write-delay caching; instead, write-delay caching for all drives is off unless you explicitly turn it on. You can obtain SMARTDRV 4.2 through the Microsoft Software Library on CompuServe Information Services, or contact Microsoft Customer Service directly. The DOS 6 Upgrade continues to include SMARTDRV version 4.1.

In this sample report, drive C is compressed, and its compressed volume file— listed to the right of the line—is on drive H. You therefore want to disable write caching for drive H.

2. Use a text editor such as DOS EDIT or the ED program supplied with Stacker to edit your AUTOEXEC.BAT file. If your AUTOEXEC.BAT does not already contain a line to load SMARTDRV, add the following line to the file (assuming that SMARTDRV is in your DOS directory on drive C):

   C:\DOS\SMARTDRV

3. Add to the SMARTDRV line the drive letters for which you want to disable write caching. To disable write caching for drive H, for example, leave a space at the end of the preceding line and then type **H** after the space so that the complete line in AUTOEXEC.BAT appears as in the following example:

    `C:\DOS\SMARTDRV H`

   If your computer's drives C, D, and E are compressed, for example, hosted by drives H, G, and F, respectively, this line in AUTOEXEC.BAT must appear as follows, after all changes, to disable write caching for all drives:

    `C:\DOS\SMARTDRV H G F`

4. Save the changes to your AUTOEXEC.BAT file, and exit your text editor.
5. Use Ctrl+Alt+Del to restart your computer. After your computer restarts, SMARTDRV is reconfigured so that write caching for the selected drives is disabled.
6. To check your work, type **SMARTDRV /S** at the DOS prompt and press Enter to display the SMARTDRV status report. SMARTDRV displays a status report similar to the one shown following step 1, except that all drives should list "no" in the write cache column of the report.

If the write cache is still on for any of drives, carefully work your way through these steps again. Make sure especially that you use the correct drive letters in the SMARTDRV line of AUTOEXEC.BAT.

> **NOTE:** Remember that you must control disk caching for your compressed drives through their host drives. If you accidentally specify the drive letter for a Stacker compressed drive, rather than for the physical drive, SMARTDRV displays the following error message on-screen:
>
>   Warning: Unable to
>   use a disk cache
>   on the specified
>   drive

Tuning Stacker Compression Levels

Stacker makes a trade-off between giving you maximum compression and maximum speed. The trade-off is necessary because compressing data takes time. Generally, the more thoroughly Stacker compresses your data, the longer the process takes and the more likely you are to notice a slowdown in your computer's operations. Stacker enables you to adjust the level of compression applied to your data to accommodate your computer's operating capabilities and your own preferences regarding compression time and speed. Unless you specify otherwise, Stacker uses a compression level that provides the fastest speed and a standard level of compression.

To change Stacker's compression level, you can either use the Stacker Tuner utility program or you can alter the STACKER.INI file.

Setting Compression Levels by Using the Stacker Tuner Utility

You can use the Stacker Tuner utility from either DOS or Windows. The following sections describe these two ways to use the Stacker Tuner.

Using the DOS Stacker Tuner

To use the DOS Stacker Tuner utility, follow these steps:

1. Type **TUNER** at the DOS prompt, and press Enter. The Stacker Tuner utility starts and displays the dialog box shown in figure 10.2. Three choices appear in the **S**peed/Space Balance area at the center of the dialog box. These options represent the three compression levels you can choose.

2. To select a compression level, choose the radio button for the compression level you want, as shown in the **S**peed/Space Balance area of the dialog box.

3. Choose the **C**ontinue command button after you select the compression level. Stacker displays a message indicating that the STACKER.INI file has been updated and that the new compression level has been set. (If you decide not to change the compression level, choose the E**x**it command button instead. The Stacker Tuner exits to DOS without changing the compression levels.)

4. To clear the notification message from your screen and return to DOS, choose **O**K or press Enter.

The new compression level is now set and active. If Stacker tuning was completely turned off prior to changing compression levels, however, you must restart your computer for the new compression level to take effect. Refer to the description of the /P= command switch in the section "Understanding the Stacker Initialization File: STACKER.INI," earlier in this chapter, for information on turning off the compression tuning.

Fig. 10.2

The Tune Stacker dialog box.

NOTE:

If you install Stacker from Windows, the Stacker program group is set up for you. If you install Windows after you install Stacker, or if you install Stacker from DOS, you must manually run the SGROUP utility program. Using the SGROUP utility program is described in the section "Creating the Stacker Program Group in Windows," later in this chapter.

Using the Windows Stacker Tuner

To use the Windows Stacker Tuner utility, follow these steps:

1. To start the Windows Stacker Tuner, double-click the Stacker Tuner program icon in the Program Manager's Stacker program group. (The Stacker Tuner icon is depicted in fig. 10.10, later in this chapter.) The Stacker Tuner program displays the dialog box shown in figure 10.3.

2. To select a compression level, choose the radio button for the compression level you want, as shown in the Software Speed/Compression Setting area of the dialog box.

3. To change compression levels, choose **O**K after you select a compression level. The Stacker Tuner changes the compression level and closes the dialog box. No additional messages appear.

If you decide not to change the compression level, choose the E**x**it command button. The Stacker Tuner closes without changing the compression levels.

The new compression level is now set and active. As in using the DOS Stacker Tuner, if Stacker tuning was completely turned off prior to changing compression levels, you must restart your computer for the new compression level to take effect. The section "Understanding the Stacker Initialization File: STACKER.INI," earlier in this chapter, provides information on the /P= command and on turning off the compression tuning.

Setting Compression Levels by Using STACKER.INI

You also can set the Stacker compression levels by directly editing the STACKER.INI file to add or change the /P= switch. If no /P= switch appears in the STACKER.INI file, Stacker uses a compression level of 1, which is the equivalent of the Fastest Speed and Standard Compression option in the Stacker Tuner. A /P=9 switch is the equivalent of the Best Compression option in the Stacker Tuner, and /P=5 is the equivalent of the More Compression and a Bit Less Speed.

You can set the /P= switch for any number between 0 and 9, which enables you to adjust the compression level for Stacker more precisely than is possible by using the Stacker Tuner. For information on setting the /P= switch, see the section "Understanding the Stacker Initialization File: STACKER.INI," earlier in this chapter.

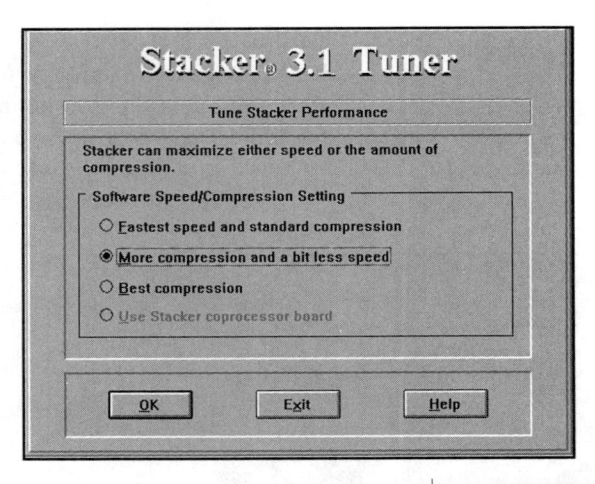

Fig. 10.3

The Windows Stacker Tuner dialog box.

Changing the Expected Compression Ratio

The reported free space on your compressed disk drive is based on a calculation that uses the expected compression ratio. This expected compression ratio is usually 2:1. If 10M is physically available on the disk, for example, and the expected compression ratio is 2:1, the free space reported is 20M.

If files on your compressed disk consistently compress with a higher or lower ratio than 2:1, the amount of free space reported on your disk may be inaccurate. If you store many files that compress well, and your overall compression ratio is greater than 2:1, for example, the free space reported by using the standard expected compression ratio is less than the amount of data you can actually store on the compressed disk. This may lead you to believe you have less storage available than you really do.

If, on the other hand, you store many files that do not compress well, and your overall compression ratio is less than 2:1, the free space reported by using the standard expected compression ratio is greater than the amount of data you can actually store on the disk. This situation is more annoying, because it may lead you to believe you have more storage available than you actually do.

You may want to change the expected compression ratio so that the free space reported for your compressed disk more accurately reflects the amount of additional storage actually available. Raising the expected compression ratio causes Stacker to report a larger amount of space available on the compressed disk. Lowering the estimated compression ratio causes Stacker to report less space as available on the compressed disk. Usually, you change the expected compression ratio to match the actual overall compression ratio, because this approach provides the best free space reports. You can, however, specify any ratio to use for the expected compression. You can change the estimated compression ratio by using either the Stacker Toolbox or the Windows Stackometer utility. These techniques are explained in the following sections.

Changing the Expected Compression Ratio by Using the Stacker Toolbox

To change your expected compression ratio by using the Stacker Toolbox, follow these steps:

1. Start the Stacker Toolbox by typing **STAC** at the DOS prompt and pressing Enter. The Stacker Toolbox loads into memory and displays the menu screen shown in figure 10.4.
2. Choose **E**xpected Compression. Stacker displays the screen shown in figure 10.5, listing your Stacker compressed drives.
3. Choose the drive for which you want to change the expected compression ratio. Stacker displays a message indicating that it must run the SDEFRAG utility to optimize (defragment) the compressed drive before changing the expected compression ratio. By running the SDEFRAG utility with full optimization, Stacker makes sure that all data on your compressed drive is compressed as much as possible. Fully optimizing your compressed disk also enables Stacker to gather the information it needs to make sure that the expected compression ratio you enter later is a reasonable value.
4. Press any key on your keyboard. Stacker optimizes the compressed drive you selected. Depending on how full your compressed drive is and how badly fragmented its files, this process may take from a few minutes to an hour or more. During this time, Stacker displays various status messages as it defragments and optimizes your compressed drive.

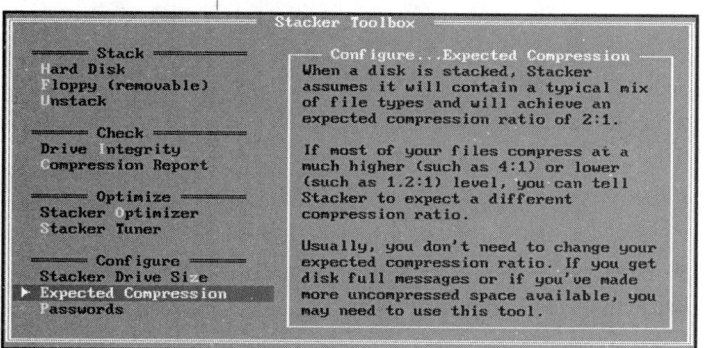

After SDEFRAG optimizes your compressed drive, a report appears on-screen showing the size of the Stacker drive and the current expected compression ratio on which the size calculation is based. The report also shows the actual compression ratio of the Stacker drive and the new size of the Stacker drive if you accept the expected compression ratio Stacker suggests.

Finally, the report shows the range of values Stacker accepts for the expected compression ratio. Stacker limits the range to make sure that the expected compression ratio does not deviate too far from the actual compression ratio. If, for example, your actual compression ratio is 1.8:1, you cannot change to an

Fig. 10.4

The Stacker Toolbox main menu display.

expected compression ratio of 3.0:1. The higher compression ratio would clearly produce unrealistically high free space estimates. Similarly, Stacker does not accept an expected compression ratio that results in unrealistically low free space estimates.

At the bottom of the expected compression ratio report is a text box in which you can enter a new expected compression ratio. Stacker's suggested compression ratio is already entered in the text box.

5. Press Enter to use the expected compression ratio that Stacker suggests.

   To enter your own expected compression ratio, use the Backspace key to erase Stacker's suggested ratio, and then type the expected compression ratio you want to use and press Enter.

   Stacker displays the screen shown in figure 10.6, listing the Stacker drive size, the new expected compression ratio, and the amount of uncompressed space on the working host drive. At the bottom of this screen, Stacker also displays a menu of three choices: **P**erform Changes on Stacker Drive, **M**odify Settings, and **E**xit without Changes.

6. Choose the menu option for the action you want to perform.

   Choose **P**erform Changes on Stacker Drive to change the expected compression ratio. Stacker immediately makes the specified change to the Stacker volume and displays a progress chart while it makes the change. Stacker then displays a message telling you that it must restart your computer. Press Enter, and your computer restarts.

   Choose **M**odify Settings to return to the previous screen and select a different expected compression ratio.

   Choose **E**xit without Changes if you decide not to change the expected compression ratio. Stacker returns to the Stacker Toolbox main menu.

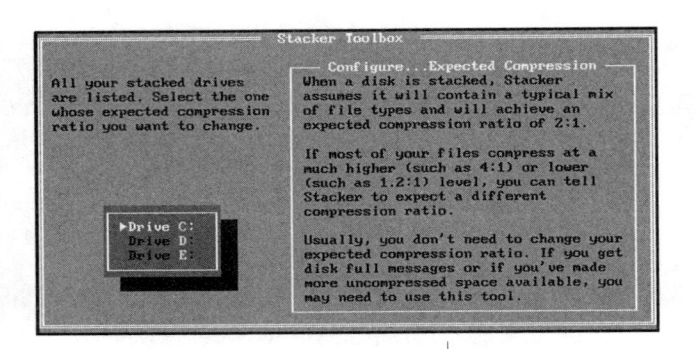

Fig. 10.5

The Stacker Toolbox main menu screen's list of compressed drives.

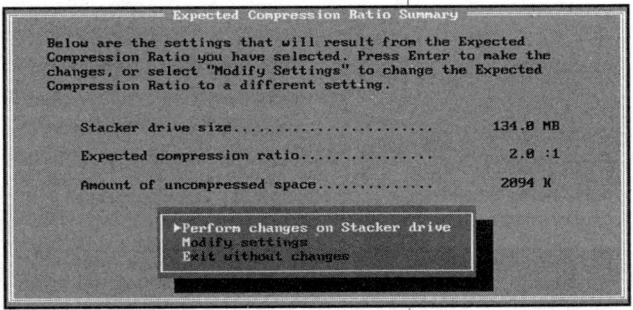

Fig. 10.6

The Expected Compression Ratio Summary screen.

Changing the Expected Compression Ratio by Using the Windows Stackometer

You use the Stacker Stackometer utility program to change the expected compression ratio from Windows. Follow these steps to use the Stackometer:

Configuring and Optimizing Stacker   **231**

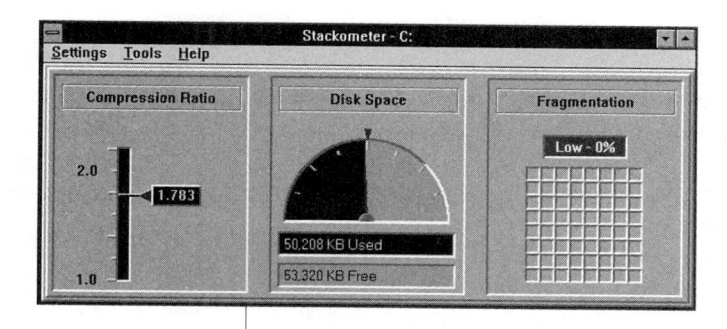

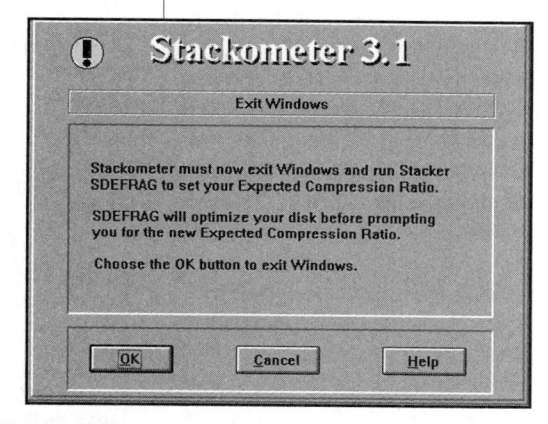

Fig. 10.7, top

The Stackometer opening window and main menu bar.

Fig. 10.8, bottom

The Stackometer Exit Windows dialog box.

1. Double-click the Stackometer program icon in the Program Manager's Stacker program group. (The Stackometer icon is depicted in fig. 10.10, later in this chapter. If you do not have a Stacker program group, refer to the section "Creating the Stacker Program Group," also later in this chapter.)

    After the Stackometer program starts, the window and main menu bar shown in figure 10.7 appears on-screen.

2. Choose **T**ools; Stackometer displays the **T**ools menu.

3. Choose **S**et Expected Compression; Stackometer displays the dialog box shown in figure 10.8, informing you that Stacker must leave Windows to change the expected compression ratio.

4. Choose **O**K to leave Windows. Stacker tells Windows to shut down, and Windows closes any running applications. If any applications have unsaved data, the application asks whether you want to save the data.

    If you decide not to change the expected compression ratio at this time, click **C**ancel. Stacker returns to the Stackometer window and main menu.

5. After exiting Windows, Stacker displays a message telling you that SDEFRAG must optimize the Stacker drive.

    From this point on, the steps for using the Stackometer to change the expected compression ratio are identical to those for using the Stacker Toolbox.

6. Go to step 4 in the section, "Changing the Expected Compression Ratio by Using the Stacker Toolbox," and follow the remaining steps in that section to finish changing the expected compression ratio.

Changing Stacker Drive Letter Assignments

As explained in Chapter 9, "Installing Stacker," Stacker assigns drive letters by using the next available DOS drive letter as it mounts each compressed volume. Usually, you need not be concerned about the drive letter assignments Stacker makes. In a few circumstances, however, you may need to alter how Stacker assigns drive letters.

If you connect your computer to a network after you install Stacker, you may find that a conflict exists between drive letters used by Stacker and the most convenient drive letters for your network drives. If you have two hard disks or partitions, for example, and you compress both of these, Stacker usually assigns the drive letters E and F as the host drives for the compressed volumes. If you want to configure your network software to use drive F as a network drive, however, that drive letter is currently unavailable, because Stacker is using it. You eliminate drive letter conflict problems by changing how Stacker assigns drive letters.

Another situation in which you may want to change how Stacker assigns drive letters occurs if you create one or more Stacker drives from the free space on your uncompressed drives. Because Stacker assigns the next available DOS drive letter to these drives as they are mounted, the free space drives usually are assigned drive letters that come after the letters assigned to the uncompressed host drives. Many users prefer all their compressed drives to have contiguous drive letters and that all uncompressed drives be at the end of the series of drive letters.

To change Stacker's drive letter assignments, you must manually alter the STACKER.INI file in the root directory of your uncompressed boot disk. Using the /SW command switch is one way to change drive letter assignments. This switch enables you to specify one or more pairs of drive letters to exchange. Stacker swaps the drive letters in each pair. Adding the following /SW command to STACKER.INI, for example, makes Stacker exchange the drive letters for drives G and K:

/SW GK

After the swap is complete, the drive formerly accessed through drive letter K is accessible through drive letter G—and vice versa. The /SW command switch is described in the section "Examining the STACKER.INI Commands," earlier in this chapter. The section "Editing STACKER.INI" describes how to edit STACKER.INI.

Another way to alter Stacker drive letter assignments is by adding the /BD= command switch to your STACKER.INI file. The /BD= switch tells Stacker which drive letter to use as the base drive letter (the first letter Stacker assigns on your system). You can use the /BD= switch to skip over one or more drive letters. Drive letters skipped by Stacker are still available to DOS. The following example shows the entire STACKER.INI file for a system with one hard disk partition; the /BD= switch in the example causes Stacker to assign drive letter H as the first drive letter. The skipped drive letters (D, E, F, and G) remain available to DOS for network drives, RAM drives, and so on.

```
/DIR=C:\STACKER\
/BD=H
C:\STACVOL.DSK,SW
```

The /BD= switch is described in more detail in the section "Command Switches," earlier in this chapter. The section "Editing STACKER.INI" describes how to edit STACKER.INI.

You also can change Stacker drive letter assignments for both compressed and uncompressed drives by changing the order in which Stacker mounts the compressed volumes. Stacker mounts compressed volumes in the same order they appear in STACKER.INI and assigns the next available DOS drive letter to each volume as it is

In many cases, you can resolve conflicts over drive letter assignments to network drives, external disk drives, and RAM drives by altering the order of the device drivers in your CONFIG.SYS file—especially if you use the STACHIGH.SYS device driver. If other device drivers that create logical disk drives come before STACHIGH.SYS in your CONFIG.SYS file, these drivers receive their drive letters directly from DOS before STACHIGH.SYS changes any drive letters.

mounted. Changing the order in which compressed volumes are mounted, therefore, changes the drive letter assigned to each drive. The following example shows the STACKER.INI file for a system with two hard disk partitions:

```
/DIR=C:\STACKER\
D:\STACVOL.DSK,SW
C:\STACVOL.DSK,SW
```

On this system, after Stacker mounts all the drives and makes the drive letter changes specified by the mounting parameters, the drive letter assignments are as shown in the following list:

    C: Stacker compressed volume
    D: Stacker compressed volume
    E: Uncompressed host for drive D
    F: Uncompressed host for drive C

You may find this result confusing or undesirable, however, because the uncompressed host drive for drive C has a higher drive letter than the uncompressed host drive for drive D. If you simply switch the order of the last two lines of this sample file (so that the line that mounts C:\STACVOL comes before the line that mounts D:\STACVOL), your final drive letter assignments are as shown in the following list:

    C: Stacker compressed volume
    D: Stacker compressed volume
    E: Uncompressed host for drive C
    F: Uncompressed host for drive D

Refer to the sections "Editing STACKER.INI" and "Drive Mounting Options," earlier in this chapter, for information on editing the STACKER.INI file and on mounting parameters.

Adjusting the Number of Removable Media Drives

Stacker can mount only a specified maximum number of removable media drives at one time. If your system has more physical removable media drives than Stacker can mount, you may need to unmount one compressed volume before you can mount another. This situation may arise if you add a floppy disk or a Bernoulli, Floptical, or Syquest removable media drive to your computer.

To change the number of removable media drives Stacker can accommodate, you must increase the number of replaceable drive letters that Stacker can support. To do so requires changing your STACKER.INI file. You can increase the number of replaceable drive letters by adding the @ symbol, the /RP= switch, or one or more specific drive letters to your STACKER.INI file. (Editing the STACKER.INI file is described in the section "Editing STACKER.INI," earlier in this chapter.)

Stacker always reserves at least one replaceable drive letter. Stacker reserves one additional replaceable drive letter for each @ symbol you add to your STACKER.INI file. Adding the /RP= switch, however, usually is more convenient. For more information, see the section "Command Switches," earlier in this chapter.

> **NOTE:**
> Increasing the number of replaceable drive letters that Stacker reserves increases the size of the Stacker device driver in memory. The size of the driver increases by about 1K for each replaceable drive letter added.

To reserve a specific drive letter as a replaceable drive letter and also enable automatic drive mounting for that drive letter, the drive letter must appear in your STACKER.INI file, as shown in the following example:

```
/DIR=C:\STACKER\
A:
B:
C:\STACVOL.DSK,SW
```

In this example, automatic mounting is enabled for drive A first, and the first replaceable drive letter reserved by Stacker is used. The next line instructs Stacker to reserve another replaceable drive letter and enable automatic drive mounting for drive B. After Stacker reserves the replaceable drive letter for drive B, no additional replaceable drive letters are available.

Creating a Stacker RAM Disk

A *RAM disk* is an area of your computer's memory set aside by a device driver and configured to be used like a disk drive. Like the Stacker device driver, the RAM disk device driver makes a logical disk drive available to DOS. Because the RAM disk's data is stored in your computer's memory, access to a RAM disk is extremely fast. RAM disks often are used to hold temporary files or files that must be read frequently. Many users, for example, set the DOS TEMP environment variable to use a RAM disk, thus speeding up the operation of programs that use the TEMP environment variable to specify the location of their temporary files.

RAM disks have limitations and drawbacks, however. Apart from the fact that a RAM disk's data is lost whenever you turn your computer off (unless you copy the data to one of your hard disks), a RAM disk takes up computer memory. A RAM disk usually must be about 1M to 2M in size to be useful. On many computers, this represents 25, 50, or 100 percent of total available memory. You can somewhat compensate for a RAM disk's heavy memory use by compressing the RAM disk. A RAM disk 500K in size, for example, will yield about 1M of storage after it is compressed.

You can use any of three methods to apply Stacker disk compression to a RAM disk. The first two methods involve placing the appropriate Stacker commands in your AUTOEXEC.BAT or CONFIG.SYS file and making corresponding changes in your STACKER.INI file. These two methods are often preferred because they are fast and, after established, automatic.

The third method involves copying the compressed volume file for the RAM disk onto one of your uncompressed drives and then copying it back to the RAM disk whenever your computer starts. After the compressed volume file is copied to the RAM disk, you use Stacker to mount the drive. This method is useful if you want to save and restore all the files on the RAM disk without copying individual files. The method does, however, use space on your uncompressed disk drive, is more difficult to set up, and slows your system's start-up process more than do the first two methods.

Using a RAM disk with some programs, such as Windows, may be counterproductive. The RAM disk may leave other programs "starved" for memory and force them to access the disk more often, slowing them down. You may get better results by using a disk cache program such as SMARTDRV to speed up disk operations for many of your programs.

Compressing the RAM Disk by Using CONFIG.SYS

This method is perhaps the easiest way to create a Stacker compressed RAM disk. It is effective, however, only on RAM disks created by device drivers in your CONFIG.SYS file, such as the DOS RAMDRIVE.SYS. To use this method, you first must set up your RAM disk device driver software. Then you add commands to CONFIG.SYS to compress the RAM disk and to STACKER.INI to mount the compressed RAM disk. If you intend to use the DOS RAMDRIVE.SYS device driver—as do the examples in this section—refer to your DOS documentation for instructions.

After you set up your RAM disk, you add a line to CONFIG.SYS to load the Stacker SCREATE.SYS program, which compresses the RAM drive. Technically, SCREATE.SYS is not a device driver, even though it loads into memory through your CONFIG.SYS file. SCREATE.SYS creates one or more compressed volumes and then unloads itself from memory. Because SCREATE.SYS does not remain in memory, trying to load SCREATE.SYS into upper memory is pointless.

You specify which disk drives SCREATE.SYS compresses by placing the drive letters on the same line in CONFIG.SYS as the SCREATE.SYS device driver. The SCREATE.SYS line must come after the device driver that creates the RAM disk. The following example shows the RAMDRIVE.SYS device driver used to create a RAM disk, followed by the SCREATE.SYS line that compresses the RAM disk. The final line in the example loads the STACHIGH device driver into upper memory.

```
DEVICE=C:\DOS\RAMDRIVE.SYS 1026 /E
DEVICE=C:\STACKER\SCREATE.SYS F:
DEVICEHIGH=C:\STACKER\STACHIGH.SYS
```

The system in which these lines are used has three physical disk partitions: C, D, and E. As the RAM disk is created, DOS assigns it the next available drive letter, F. SCREATE.SYS, therefore, must compress drive F. Notice that the drive letter F is placed as a command line switch after the SCREATE.SYS device driver.

Your system is now configured to create and compress a RAM disk, but Stacker does not yet mount the compressed volume. You first must change your STACKER.INI file by adding a line containing the RAM disk drive letter so that Stacker mounts the RAM disk compressed volume. Refer to the section "Editing STACKER.INI," earlier in this chapter, for instructions on editing your STACKER.INI file.

The following sample shows how the STACKER.INI file appears after adding the drive letter line:

```
/DIR=C:\STACKER\
F:
E:\STACVOL.DSK,SW
D:\STACVOL.DSK,SW
C:\STACVOL.DSK,SW
```

> **NOTE:** Whether you use the RAMDRIVE.SYS provided with DOS or another RAM disk, make sure that the RAM disk device driver loads *before* any references to STACHIGH.SYS are read in CONFIG.SYS. Stacker assigns drive letters differently depending on whether the RAM disk device driver—or other disk device drivers—load before or after STACHIGH.SYS. If your computer has, for example, two physical drives (C and D), and the RAM disk device driver loads before STACHIGH.SYS, the RAM disk is assigned drive letter E. If the RAM disk device driver loads after STACHIGH.SYS, the RAM disk is assigned the next available DOS drive letter after all the Stacker drives are assigned drive letters.

After these changes are made to CONFIG.SYS and STACKER.INI, your computer is ready to create, compress, and mount the RAM disk. The new lines in CONFIG.SYS create and compress the RAM disk, and the new line in the STACKER.INI file mounts the compressed RAM drive. In the example, the next time the computer is started, RAMDRIVE.SYS creates the RAM disk, DOS assigns drive letter F to it, and SCREATE.SYS compresses it. Next, the F: line in STACKER.INI causes Stacker to mount the compressed volume on drive F.

Compressing the RAM Disk by Using AUTOEXEC.BAT

You must use this method if your RAM disk device driver loads as a TSR program from your AUTOEXEC.BAT file. The method of adding SCREATE.SYS to your CONFIG.SYS file does not work with a TSR RAM disk device driver, because the RAM disk does not exist at the time the SCREATE.SYS command is processed in CONFIG.SYS. If you want more control over the mounting parameters Stacker uses to mount the RAM disk compressed volume, you also can use this method, even if your RAM disk device driver loads from CONFIG.SYS. Mounting a compressed volume from AUTOEXEC.BAT uses the Stacker mounting commands, giving you control over how the drive is mounted. You do not get this kind of control if you mount the drive from STACKER.INI.

To compress and mount a RAM disk by using commands in your AUTOEXEC.BAT file, follow these steps:

1. Create a RAM disk (if you do not already have one) by adding an appropriate line to your CONFIG.SYS or AUTOEXEC.BAT file. Refer to your RAM disk software documentation for information on setting up the RAM disk.
2. Restart your computer, and notice which drive letter DOS assigns to the RAM disk.
3. If your RAM disk software loads from your AUTOEXEC.BAT file, add the following line to your AUTOEXEC.BAT file:
   CREATE d:
   Substitute the drive letter of your RAM disk for *d*. The new line must come immediately after the line in AUTOEXEC.BAT that creates the RAM disk. This line compresses the specified disk drive.
   Do *not* perform this step if your RAM disk device driver loads from CONFIG.SYS. Instead, compress your RAM disk by using SCREATE.SYS, as described in the preceding section, "Compressing the RAM Disk by Using CONFIG.SYS."
4. To mount the compressed volume, add the following line to your AUTOEXEC.BAT file, immediately after the CREATE line (if you added one in the preceding step):
   STACKER d:
   Replace *d* in this line with the drive letter of your RAM disk. This command tells Stacker to mount the compressed volume file STACVOL.DSK on drive *d*. You also

NOTE:
Whenever Stacker mounts a drive for a replaceable drive letter, as shown in the example in the preceding section, Stacker mounts the compressed volume as if the RP (replace) mounting parameter were specified. The original uncompressed drive for the RAM disk is therefore inaccessible until the compressed volume is unmounted. Usually, this situation is not a problem. If you want to use a mounting parameter other than RP to mount your compressed RAM disk, use the mounting method described in "Compressing the RAM Disk by Using AUTOEXEC.BAT."

NOTE:
A RAM disk device driver loaded from AUTOEXEC.BAT receives a different drive letter than a RAM disk device driver loaded from CONFIG.SYS. A RAM disk device driver loaded from AUTOEXEC.BAT receives its drive letter from DOS after Stacker has already mounted the hard disk compressed volumes and assigned drive letters to their host drives. In a system with physical drives C and D, for example, the RAM drive receives drive letter E if loading from CONFIG.SYS and drive letter G if loading from AUTOEXEC.BAT.

Configuring and Optimizing Stacker   **237**

can use any of the variations of the STACKER mounting command described in the section "Mounting and Unmounting Compressed Drives," in Chapter 11, "Using Stacker."

The next time you start your computer, Stacker compresses the RAM disk and then mounts the compressed drive.

Compressing the RAM Disk by Copying the Compressed Volume

Use this method if you want to preserve all the data on your compressed RAM disk without copying individual files and can make one or two megabytes of space available on one of your uncompressed drives. In this technique, you copy a compressed volume file from your hard disk to the RAM disk and then mount the drive.

Before beginning this procedure, set up your RAM disk software to create a RAM disk, and then restart your computer. Notice which drive letter is assigned to your RAM disk. Now follow these steps to compress the RAM disk and copy its compressed volume file:

1. Compress the RAM disk by typing **CREATE *d*:** at the DOS prompt. Substitute for *d* the drive letter of your RAM disk. This command instructs Stacker to compress the existing disk drive. After Stacker finishes compressing the RAM disk, a screen appears displaying a message to that effect.
2. Choose **OK** to return to DOS. You are ready to copy the compressed volume file to the uncompressed portion of one of your hard disks.
3. Make the RAM disk the current disk drive.
4. Type the following command at the DOS prompt, and press Enter:
    ATTRIB –S –H –R STACVOL.DSK
    This command removes the protective file attributes from the compressed volume file so that you can copy it.
5. Copy the compressed volume file to an uncompressed hard disk. As you copy the compressed volume file, you also must give it a different name so that it does not interfere with any other compressed volume files on the uncompressed hard disk. To copy the compressed volume file to an uncompressed hard disk with drive letter D, for example, type the following command at the DOS prompt:
    COPY STACVOL.DSK D:\RAMVOL.CVF
    Remember to use your uncompressed drive letter in the command if it is not D. You also can use a different file name for the copy of the compressed volume file. DOS copies the compressed volume file to the uncompressed drive you specify.
6. To protect the compressed volume file you copied from the RAM disk from accidental deletion, type the following command at the DOS prompt, and press Enter:
    ATTRIB +R D:\RAMVOL.CVF

NOTE:
The Stacker CREATE command only creates compressed volumes on an existing disk drive; it does not create the RAM disk. You must use a RAM disk device driver, such as the RAMDRIVE.SYS supplied with DOS, to create a RAM disk.

The compressed volume file from the RAM disk requires about as much uncompressed hard disk space as the size of the RAM disk in memory. If, for example, you created a RAM disk that uses 2M of memory, the compressed volume file for that RAM disk requires about 2M of uncompressed disk space. If your uncompressed hard disk does not have enough room for the compressed volume file from the RAM disk, you may be able to resize one of your compressed volumes to free enough space on its uncompressed host drive. See Chapter 12, "Using the Stacker Utilities," for information on changing the size of Stacker compressed drives.

ATTRIB sets the Read-Only attribute for the RAMVOL.CVF file. (Remember to use your uncompressed drive letter in this command if it is not D, and use your own file name if you chose a different one.)

The necessary preparation for setting up your compressed RAM disk is complete. Now you must make changes to your AUTOEXEC.BAT file.

7. Use a text editor to add the following two lines to your AUTOEXEC.BAT file:

    COPY D:\RAMVOL.CVF F:\STACVOL.DSK
    STACKER F:

    Remember to substitute the drive letter of your RAM disk for F and to substitute the drive letter of your uncompressed drive for D if your drives use different drive letters. Remember also to use your own file name if you chose a name other than RAMVOL.CVF for your copy of the RAM disk's compressed volume file.

The next time you start your computer, the AUTOEXEC.BAT commands copy the compressed volume file onto the RAM disk and then mounts the Stacker compressed volume. Your computer's start-up is delayed by only as much time as is required to copy and mount the compressed volume file. As soon as the compressed volume mounts, control returns to DOS, and any other commands in your AUTOEXEC.BAT file are carried out.

> To preserve all of the data on the compressed RAM disk before you turn off or restart your computer, first unmount the RAM disk compressed volume and then remove the Read-Only attribute from your previous hard disk copy of the RAM disk's compressed volume file. Finally, repeat steps 4 through 6 to again copy the RAM disk's compressed volume file to your uncompressed hard disk. Unmounting compressed volumes is described in Chapter 11, "Using Stacker."

Creating the Stacker Program Group in Windows

If you install Stacker from Windows, Stacker instructs Windows to create a program group and program icons for the Stacker Windows utilities. If you install Windows after you install Stacker, or if you install Stacker from DOS, you must run a Stacker utility program called SGROUP to create the Stacker program group and program items.

SGROUP is a Windows program. To run the SGROUP program and create the Windows Stacker program group, follow these steps:

1. From the **F**ile menu in the Windows Program Manager, choose **R**un . Windows displays the Run dialog box.
2. Type the following in the **C**ommand Line text box of the Run dialog box:

    C:\STACKER\SGROUP.EXE

    If your Stacker program files are in a different directory or on a drive other than C, substitute the appropriate directory and drive.
3. To run the SGROUP program, press Enter or click OK. The SGROUP program displays the dialog box shown in figure 10.9.
4. To create the Stacker program group, press Enter or click OK. Stacker creates the program group shown in figure 10.10.

    If you change your mind about creating the program group at this time, press Esc or click Cancel. Stacker returns to the Windows Program Manager without creating the program group.

Summary

In this chapter, you learned how Stacker uses the STACKER.INI file to configure itself. You also learned how to change Stacker drive letter assignments by changing the STACKER.INI file. You then learned how to make more conventional memory available by loading the Stacker device driver into upper memory, loading the Stacker disk cache into EMS memory, and disabling automatic drive mounting.

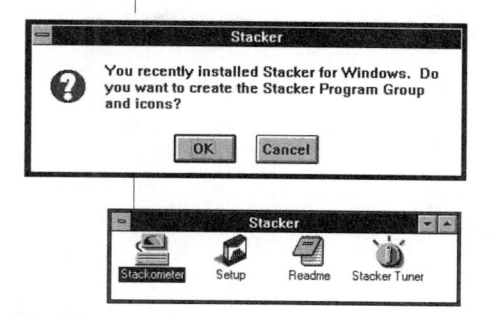

The chapter then described how Stacker redirects certain DOS commands to use Stacker equivalents and how this redirection is loaded into memory and controlled. You also learned how to correctly set up disk cache programs with Stacker—in particular, how to configure SMARTDRV for the greatest safety with Stacker. This chapter also explained how to change Stacker compression levels and when and how to change the expected compression ratio. The chapter then discussed when and how to adjust the maximum number of removable media drives that Stacker can mount at one time.

Finally, you learned three ways to compress a RAM disk by using Stacker. You learned how to compress a RAM disk by using commands in your CONFIG.SYS or AUTOEXEC.BAT file. You also learned how to preserve the RAM disk's compressed volume file and restore it after your computer restarts.

The next chapter describes how to use Stacker in day-to-day operations.

Fig. 10.9, top

The dialog box for creating the Stacker program group.

Fig. 10.10, bottom

The Stacker program group.

CHAPTER 11

Using Stacker

This chapter provides the information you need to use Stacker successfully on a day-to-day basis. The information in the chapter assumes you have already installed and configured Stacker. (Installing Stacker is the topic of Chapter 9, and configuring Stacker is discussed in Chapter 10.) This chapter begins with a general discussion of file management on your Stacker compressed drives and then describes the DOS commands that work differently with your compressed drives. The chapter also explains how to get information about your Stacker compressed drives and discusses how to mount and unmount compressed volumes.

This chapter gives special attention to using Stacker with removable media drives. You learn how to compress removable media drives, how to mount and unmount the drives, and how to solve the most common problems you may encounter with removable media. The chapter then describes how to use Stacker's password security feature and how to set and enter passwords. You learn the correct methods for backing up your compressed and uncompressed drives and which files not to back up. The chapter also discusses various issues involved in using third-party disk-maintenance utility programs and concludes by describing how to use Stacker's Help system.

Performing File Management on Compressed Drives

Because Stacker disk compression is transparent—that is, not noticeable to the user—you manage your files the same as you did before you installed Stacker. The DOS commands for creating directories, copying files, and displaying directory listings work the same with your Stacker compressed disks as with uncompressed disks. Whenever DOS reads information from a disk, Stacker determines whether the disk is compressed. If the disk is compressed, Stacker uncompresses the information before making it available to DOS. Similarly, whenever DOS writes information to a disk, Stacker determines whether the disk is compressed and compresses the information if necessary.

If you save a file on an uncompressed disk, Stacker does not compress the data, and the file is stored in standard DOS format. With Stacker, you never need to be concerned about translating your data if you copy a file from a compressed disk to an uncompressed disk or vice versa. Stacker handles all the work behind the scenes, reading or writing the disk's information, with or without compression, as appropriate for that disk. The main difference you notice after adding Stacker to your computer system is that your computer system has more disk drive letters. These additional drive letters represent either the host drives—or *working drives*—for your compressed volumes or the compressed volumes themselves.

Keeping track of these additional drive letters may seem tricky at first. Usually you need not concern yourself with the host drives for your compressed volumes. Because Stacker exchanges drive letters, your compressed volumes replace your original uncompressed hard drives. You normally use your compressed volumes as if they are the only disk drives in your computer.

You need to be concerned with the host drives for your compressed volumes only if you perform maintenance on your disk drives or alter your Stacker configuration. The following section shows you how Stacker enables you to obtain information about your compressed volumes and their host drives.

Using the DIR and SDIR Commands on Stacker Drives

Among the first DOS commands any computer user learns is the DIR (directory) command. Stacker provides an equivalent command—SDIR—that displays the same information as the DOS DIR command. If the Stacker DOS disk command redirection is installed, you can use either the DOS DIR or the Stacker SDIR commands to list files and obtain information about their compression ratios. Stacker automatically adds the DOS disk command redirection to your system when you install it. (The Stacker DOS disk command redirection is described in Chapter 10, "Configuring and Optimizing Stacker.") If you disable the Stacker DOS disk command redirection (by removing the STACHIGH.SYS device driver from your CONFIG.SYS file), you can use only the Stacker SDIR command to obtain compression ratio information. The regular DOS DIR command still displays file listings for a compressed volume but cannot display information about the compression ratios. If you used earlier versions of Stacker, you may feel more comfortable using the SDIR command. If you have used DoubleSpace or have never used disk compression at all, you may prefer the regular DOS DIR command.

Both the Stacker SDIR command and the DIR command in DOS 6 provide a command line switch—the /C switch—for compressed drives. The /C switch causes DIR or SDIR to display the actual compression ratio for each file in the directory listing. Occasionally viewing the actual compression ratios for files on your compressed volumes can be useful.

To view all the files in the Stacker directory that end with COM, for example, and to show their actual compression ratios, enter the following command at the DOS prompt:

DIR C:\STACKER*.COM /C

The preceding command works only if the DOS command redirection is installed; otherwise, use the following equivalent command:

SDIR C:\STACKER*.COM /C

Whether you use the DOS DIR command redirected to the Stacker SDIR command or use the SDIR command directly, these commands produce a listing similar to the following:

```
SDIR - 3.10, Copyright 1990-93 Stac Electronics, Carlsbad, CA

Volume in drive C is STACVOL_DSK

Directory of   C:\STACKER
AUTORCVR COM      1043  05-25-93   3:10a   5.3:1
CREATE   COM      1042  05-25-93   3:10a   8.0:1
DBLSPACE COM     21948  05-25-93   3:10a   1.6:1
DCONVERT COM      1043  05-25-93   3:10a   8.0:1
DIR      COM      7744  05-25-93   3:10a   1.3:1
REDIRECT COM     12901  05-25-93   3:10a   2.1:1
REMOVDRV COM      1046  05-25-93   3:10a   5.3:1
SDEFRAG  COM      1045  05-25-93   3:10a   8.0:1
SETUP1   COM      1040  05-25-93   3:10a   8.0:1
STAC     COM      1036  05-25-93   3:10a   8.0:1
STACKER  COM     48453  06-03-93   3:27p   1.3:1
UNSTACK  COM      1045  05-25-93   3:10a   8.0:1
       12 file(s)        99386 bytes

Overall compression ratio of files listed = 2.1:1
             54673408 bytes free
```

The /C switch adds the following information to a standard directory listing: The actual compression ratio of each individual file appears to the right of the file listing, in a column after the file size, date, and time. The CREATE.COM file shown in this listing, for example, has a compression ratio of 8.0:1. The average compression ratio for all listed files appears on a new line, between the lines that show the number of files listed and the number of bytes free. In this example, all the COM files compressed at an average ratio of 2.1:1.

The /C switch shows the compression ratio for the files in the directory listing based on the cluster size the compressed volume uses (usually 8K). The /CH switch shows the compression ratio for files as based on the actual cluster size of the uncompressed disk. To display the same listing as the previous example, therefore, but using the actual cluster size of the uncompressed disk, type the following command at the DOS prompt:

DIR C:\STACKER*.COM /CH

The preceding command works only if the DOS command redirection is installed; otherwise, use the following equivalent command:

SDIR C:\STACKER*.COM /CH

Both commands produce a directory listing similar to that of the following example:

```
SDIR - 3.10, Copyright 1990-93 Stac Electronics, Carlsbad, CA
Volume in drive C is STACVOL_DSK
Directory of   C:\STACKER
AUTORCVR COM       1043    05-25-93   3:10a   1.3:1
CREATE   COM       1042    05-25-93   3:10a   2.0:1
DBLSPACE COM      21948    05-25-93   3:10a   1.5:1
DCONVERT COM       1043    05-25-93   3:10a   2.0:1
DIR      COM       7744    05-25-93   3:10a   1.3:1
REDIRECT COM      12901    05-25-93   3:10a   1.9:1
REMOVDRV COM       1046    05-25-93   3:10a   1.3:1
SDEFRAG  COM       1045    05-25-93   3:10a   2.0:1
SETUP1   COM       1040    05-25-93   3:10a   2.0:1
STAC     COM       1036    05-25-93   3:10a   2.0:1
STACKER  COM      48453    06-03-93   3:27p   1.3:1
UNSTACK  COM       1045    05-25-93   3:10a   2.0:1
     12 file(s)       99386 bytes
Overall compression ratio of files listed = 1.4:1
           54673408 bytes free
```

Notice that some of the reported compression ratios are different—the compression ratio for CREATE.COM, for example, is now shown as 2.0:1. The average compression ratio also is lower than the compression ratio reported if you use the /C switch. The calculation of the compression ratio in this listing is now based on how many clusters the compressed data occupies on the physical disk instead of how many clusters the uncompressed data would occupy. Computing the compression ratio by using the actual cluster size of the uncompressed disk produces different results than does using the cluster size of the compressed volume. If the actual cluster size on your disk is smaller than 8K, you may see slightly lower reported compression ratios. If the actual cluster size on your uncompressed disk is greater than 8K, you may see slightly higher reported compression ratios.

For most purposes, use the information provided by the /C switch instead of that obtained from using the /CH switch.

Using the CHKDSK and CHECK Commands on Stacker Drives

CHKDSK is the basic disk troubleshooting and repair program supplied with DOS. CHKDSK tests the logical integrity of a disk drive. Stacker provides a similar command—CHECK—that checks the internal integrity of your Stacker drive. You use the DOS CHKDSK command to check the compressed drive's integrity at the DOS level of organization, and you use the Stacker CHECK command to test the integrity of your compressed drive at Stacker's level of organization. The Stacker CHECK program also runs every time you use the DOS CHKDSK command on a compressed drive if the Stacker DOS disk command redirection is installed. (See Chapter 10, "Configuring and Optimizing Stacker," for more information on the Stacker DOS disk command redirection.)

Most users are familiar with the standard report displayed by using the DOS CHKDSK command on an uncompressed disk. (Chapter 13, "Troubleshooting Stacker," contains detailed information on using CHKDSK to locate and correct errors on your disks.) If the Stacker DOS disk command redirection is installed, CHKDSK performs the same logical integrity checks on your compressed drives as it does on your uncompressed drives, but with a difference: After CHKDSK performs the standard DOS integrity checks on the compressed volume and displays the usual report, the Stacker command redirection invokes the Stacker CHECK command, which performs additional integrity checks on the compressed volume.

After you use the CHKDSK command on a compressed disk, a report similar to the following example appears on-screen:

```
Volume STACVOL_DSK created 06-03-1993 9:20p

106594304 bytes total disk space
   139264 bytes in 3 hidden files
   229376 bytes in 28 directories
 51552256 bytes in 1011 user files
 54673408 bytes available on disk

     8192 bytes in each allocation unit
    14520 total allocation units on disk
     8182 available allocation units on disk

   655360 total bytes memory
   580400 bytes free

CHECK - 3.10, Copyright 1990-93 Stac Electronics, Carlsbad, CA

Volume in drive C is STACVOL_DSK

No errors found

Stacker Drive Compression Ratio = 1.8:1
Projected Bytes Free            = 54,673,408
```

Stacker produces the last few lines of this report after it checks the compressed drive's integrity. The actual report varies in content depending on your specific compressed drive. Chapter 13, "Troubleshooting Stacker," contains more information about the Stacker CHECK command.

Getting Information about Your Compressed Drives

As you work with your compressed drives, you want to obtain information about them. Along with the amount of free space remaining on a compressed drive (which you can determine by using the DOS DIR command), you may want to know the overall compression ratio for a disk, which drive hosts a particular compressed volume, how much free space remains on the host drive, or other information about your compressed and uncompressed drives. Stacker enables you to obtain information about your compressed and uncompressed drives directly at the DOS prompt, from menu commands in the Stacker Toolbox utility, or, if you use Windows, from the Stacker menu in the Windows File Manager.

Obtaining Information at the DOS Prompt

The simplest way to get information about your compressed and uncompressed drives is to obtain it directly at the DOS prompt. You can use either the STACKER command or the REPORT utility from the DOS prompt to instruct Stacker to display information about your drives. The STACKER command reports on Stacker drive letter assignments and tells you the name of each compressed volume file and the drive letter used for that compressed volume's host drive. To use the STACKER command to obtain a map of drive letters and the compressed volume file information, type **STACKER** at the DOS prompt and then press Enter.

The STACKER command produces a display similar to that of the following example:

```
Stacker 3.10 for Windows and DOS  1990-93 Stac Electronics, Carlsbad, CA

Registered to:
        Matthew Harris
        Harris Programming Service

Stacker drive map:
   Drive A: was drive A: at boot time  [ Auto-mounting Stacker drive ]
   Drive B: was drive B: at boot time
   Drive C: was drive C: at boot time  [ H:\STACVOL.DSK = 57.1M ]
   Drive D: was drive D: at boot time  [ G:\STACVOL.DSK = 27.9M ]
   Drive E: was drive E: at boot time  [ I:\STACVOL.DSK = 20.9M ]
   Drive F: was drive I: at boot time  [ I:\STACVOL.000 = 2.9M  ]
   Drive G: was drive G: at boot time
   Drive H: was drive H: at boot time
   Drive I: was drive F: at boot time
   Drive J: was drive J: at boot time  [ * — Not mounted ]
No available replaceable drive(s).
```

The computer system that generated this report has three physical disk partitions and one drive created from the free space on the third partition. The STACKER.INI file for this system contains a /SW statement to swap the drive letters F and I. The STACKER.INI file also contains a line to set up drive A to automatically mount compressed volumes. (See the section "Understanding the Stacker Initialization File: STACKER.INI," at the beginning of Chapter 10, for a discussion of the STACKER.INI command switches and for information on swapping drive letters and setting up drives for automatic mounting.)

At the beginning of the report generated by the STACKER command, Stacker displays a copyright notice and the personal information you entered when you installed Stacker. Stacker then displays a map of all the drive letters in your computer. Each drive letter is followed by the letter originally assigned to it by DOS during your computer's start-up. (In this report, for example, drive F originally was drive I.)

At the end of each line, inside square brackets, Stacker lists the name of the compressed volume file and the current drive and path that point to that compressed volume file. If the drive letter in the drive map is not a Stacker drive letter, or if the drive is not compressed, the right-hand column shows no file name or any other information. In this sample report, for example, drive C is a compressed volume stored in the file named STACVOL.DSK in the root directory of drive H; drive H has no information to the right of it, because it is an uncompressed drive.

You can use any of the standard DOS output redirection commands to send the STACKER information report to a printer or to a disk file. The following command, for example, uses the redirection command > to send the information report to your printer:

STACKER > PRN

Refer to your DOS documentation for more information about the DOS redirection commands.

> **NOTE:**
> If you attempt to access a drive that uses a drive letter Stacker has reserved but is not currently using, the DOS `Drive not ready` error message appears on-screen instead of the DOS `Invalid drive` error message you may expect. The drive letter exists for DOS because Stacker reserved it. Because Stacker has not assigned it to a compressed or uncompressed drive, however, DOS considers that drive "not ready."

> You also can start the Stacker Report utility directly from DOS by entering the following command at the DOS prompt:
> **REPORT** *d:*
> Substitute the letter of the drive that you want information about for the *d* in the example above. If, for example, you want information about your C drive, enter the following command:
> **REPORT C:**
> If you start the Report utility this way, the report program loads directly into memory and displays a progress chart as it gathers information about the indicated drive.

Notice the line for drive A in the sample report. The information at the right indicates that, whenever DOS accesses drive A, Stacker checks to see if a compressed volume is on the disk. If a compressed volume exists, Stacker mounts the compressed volume before DOS completes the requested disk access. Notice also the line for drive J in the report. This line indicates that Stacker has reserved the drive letter but is not currently using the drive. This drive may be used later to mount another compressed volume—in drive B, for example. A drive letter is reserved by adding a line that contains only the asterisk (*) symbol to the STACKER.INI file. See Chapter 10, "Configuring and Optimizing Stacker," for more information on the STACKER.INI file and its commands.

The STACKER report also shows how many replaceable drive letters are still available. This line at the bottom of the report does not list the total number of replaceable drive letters Stacker has reserved; it reports only how many replaceable drive letters of the total number allocated remain available. In the sample report, no replaceable drive letters remain available.

Obtaining Information by Using the Stacker Toolbox

You can display more detailed information about your compressed drives by using the Stacker Toolbox. The Stacker Toolbox enables you to access the Stacker report utility. By using the Stacker report utility you can learn the size of your compressed drive, the compression ratios of various files, the overall compression ratio, and other information.

To use the Stacker Toolbox to obtain information about your compressed drives, follow these steps:

1. To start the Stacker Toolbox, type **STAC** at the DOS prompt and press Enter. The Stacker Toolbox displays the main menu screen shown in figure 11.1. The available menu choices appear on the left side of the screen.

2. Choose **C**ompression Report from the main menu. The left side of the Stacker Toolbox screen changes to display a list of all your compressed drives, as shown in figure 11.2.

3. Select the drive about which you want information. Stacker immediately starts gathering information about the selected drive, displaying a progress chart while it does so.

    After Stacker finishes gathering information, it displays the report and menus shown in figure 11.3.

    Disk **U**sage is a Stacker Show **F**iles report form that reports on the different types of files on your compressed drive, sorted by how much disk space the files consume. Stacker determines the file types based on the files' extensions.

4. Select how you want the files in the Show **F**iles report arranged by moving the highlight bar in the Sort By menu box to a different option (if you do not want the files sorted by Disk **U**sage). Stacker changes the report display as you highlight each different choice.

    Choose **E**xtension to display the Show **F**iles report based on file extensions. Choose File **C**ount to display the Show **F**iles report based on the number of files of each extension present on the disk. Choose Comp **R**atio (Compression Ratio) to display the Show **F**iles report based on the compression ratio of the different file extension groups.

5. After you select the basis for sorting the files in your report, you can choose to view the list in Ascending or Descending order by selecting one of these options in the Sort Order box.

    To choose Ascending order, press the plus sign (**+**) key on your keyboard. To choose Descending order, press the minus sign (**–**) key on your keyboard. The report display changes to reflect the new sort order, and the highlight in the Sort Order box changes to indicate the current sort order.

6. Select other options in the Actions menu across the top of the screen by highlighting the different report actions. The report display changes as the highlight moves from action to action.

    Show **S**ummary reports on how the Stacker compressed volume file uses the space on your physical disk drive, as shown in figure 11.4. A bar chart at the top of the Summary report compares the expected and actual compression ratios. The lower portion of the Summary report reveals additional statistics about your compressed volume.

    Change **D**rive chooses a different disk drive for the Show **F**iles and Show **S**ummary reports. After you select the Change **D**rive action, Stacker displays a list of all compressed drives in your system, similar to that shown in figure 11.5.

7. Select the drive for which you want report information by highlighting that drive, and then move the highlight in the Actions menu to view either a Show **F**iles or a Show **S**ummary report for that drive.

8. After you finish viewing the reports on your compressed drives, press Esc or F10 to exit from Stacker's Report screen. Stacker displays an exit confirmation dialog box. Choose **Y**es to exit the Stacker Report screen; press Esc or choose **N**o if you decide to remain in the Report screen.

If you started Report from the Stacker Toolbox, leaving Report returns you to the Stacker Toolbox main menu. If you started Stacker Report from DOS by using the REPORT command, you return to the DOS prompt after you leave Stacker Report.

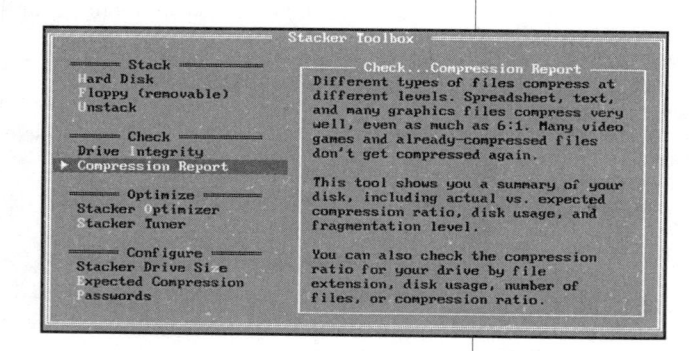

Obtaining Information from Windows

The methods described in the preceding section for obtaining information about your Stacker compressed drives work only if you start from the DOS command line. If you use Windows, you may want to obtain information about your compressed drive from inside Windows without exiting to DOS. Stacker provides two different ways to get information about compressed drives from within Windows.

Fig. 11.1

The Stacker Toolbox.

Using Stacker   **249**

Fig. 11.2
The Stacker Toolbox list of compressed drives.

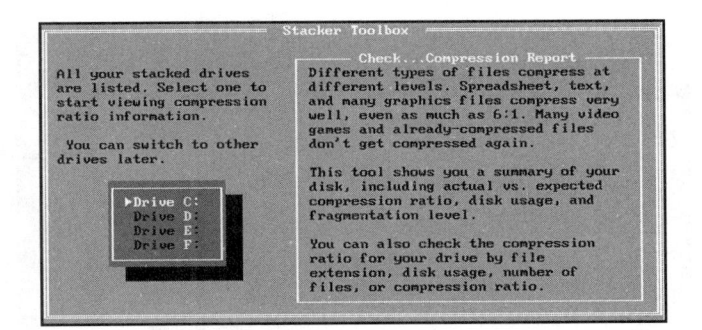

Stacker adds a new menu, called Stacker, to the main menu bar of the Windows File Manager. By using the **S**tacker menu, you can view information about your Stacker compressed drives and also obtain information about specific files and their compression ratios. Another Stacker tool for displaying information about your compressed drives is the Stackometer utility. The Stackometer utility displays information about your compressed drive's level of fragmentation, overall actual compression ratio, and used and free space. The Stackometer utility is located in the Stacker program group.

Using the File Manager's Stacker Menu

To obtain information about your compressed drives by using the **S**tacker menu in the Windows File Manager, follow these steps:

1. Access the Windows File Manager if it is not already running. (Refer to your Windows documentation for information on starting and using Windows and the Windows File Manager.)
2. Open a file list window for the drive for which you want information. Refer to your Windows documentation for specific information on opening a file list window.
3. Open the Stacker menu in the File Manager. Figure 11.6 shows the open Stacker menu.

Fig. 11.3
The Stacker Show **F**iles report, based on Disk **U**sage.

4. Choose **F**ile Info in the **S**tacker menu to view information about specific selected files. Stacker displays a dialog box similar to that shown in figure 11.7. To view summary information for the entire disk drive, skip to step 6.

If the current file list box is not a Stacker compressed drive, Stacker instead displays a dialog box containing the error message `Not a Stacker drive`. If this error dialog box appears, press Enter or click the **O**K command button to clear the dialog box, and then try another drive.

If you have not selected any files, Stacker instead displays a dialog box containing the error message `You must select a file(s) to view file information`. If this error dialog box appears, just press Enter or click the **O**K command button to clear the dialog box. Select one or more files on the file list, and then try again.

The Stacker File Info dialog box indicates the current drive in the title bar of the dialog box and, in the lower-right corner of the dialog box, displays the overall compression ratio for the selected files and their total *uncompressed* size in bytes. In figure 11.7, for example, the Stacker File Info dialog box displays files from the file list on drive C. The overall compression ratio for the files is 1.8:1, and their total size in uncompressed bytes is 2,779,531.

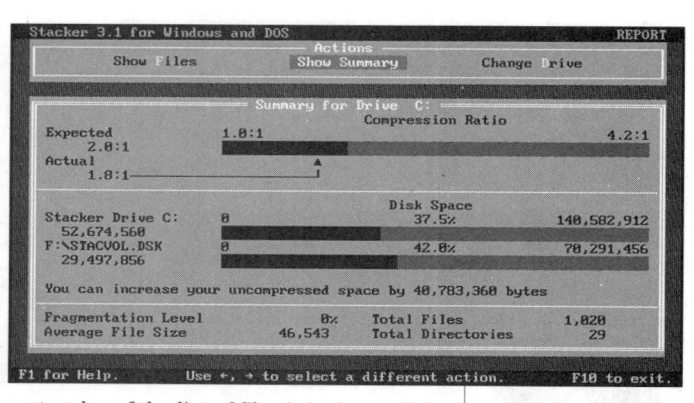

The Stacker File Info dialog box lists all the selected files and shows their **N**ame, **T**ype (extension), **S**ize, and Comp (Compression) **R**atio. The sort order of the list of files is in Ascending or Descending order based on name, file extension, size, or compression ratio.

By default, the file list in the Stacker File Info dialog box is sorted by file name in ascending order. To change the basis for sorting the file list, choose one of the command buttons across the top of the dialog box. Stacker immediately changes the list display to reflect the new sort criterion.

To sort the file list by name, choose the **N**ame command button at the top of the column of file names in the list. To sort the file list by file extension, choose the **T**ype command button at the top of the column of file extensions in the list. To sort the file list by size, choose the **S**ize command button at the top of the column of file sizes in the list. To sort the list by compression ratio, choose the Comp **R**atio command button at the top of the column of compression ratios in the list.

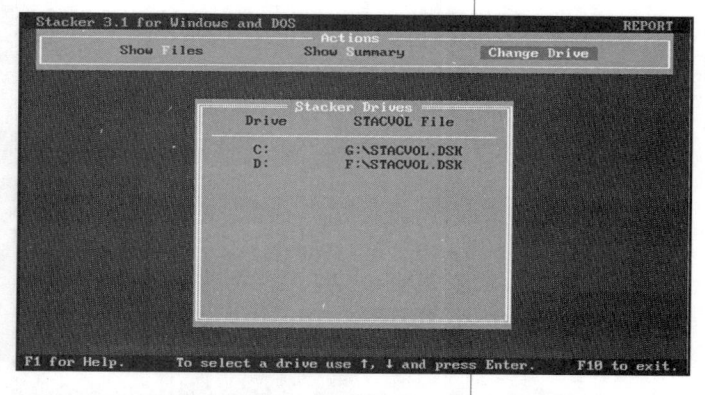

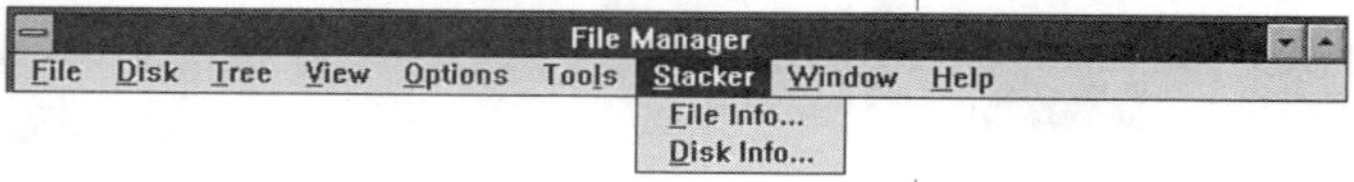

Fig. 11.4

The Stacker Show **S**ummary report.

Fig. 11.5, top

The Stacker Change **D**rive report's list of compressed drives.

Fig. 11.6, bottom

The **S**tacker menu in the Windows File Manager.

To change the sort order, click the Ascending or Descending radio buttons in the lower left of the File Info dialog box. Stacker immediately redisplays the list according to the new sort order.

5. After you finish viewing the file information in the Stacker File Info dialog box, choose the **O**K command button to close the dialog box and return to the Windows File Manager.

6. Choose **D**isk Info from the **S**tacker menu in the Windows File Manager to view information about how the space on your compressed drive is used instead of viewing information about specific files. Stacker displays the Drive Info dialog box, as shown in figure 11.8.

Using Stacker   251

Fig. 11.7

The Stacker File Info dialog box.

NOTE: Stacker adds the **S**tacker menu to the File Manager and the Stacker program group in the Program Manager *only* if you install Stacker from inside Windows. If you install Windows after you install Stacker, or if you install Stacker from DOS, you must use the SGROUP utility to add the **S**tacker menu to the File Manager and the Stacker program group to the Program Manager. See Chapter 10 for more information on the SGROUP utility.

The title bar of the Stacker Drive Info dialog box shows the compressed drive, the compressed volume file name, and its location. The Stacker Drive Info dialog box itself displays a graphic representation of the used and free space on your compressed drive, the total free space and expected compression ratio for the drive, and the total used space and actual compression ratio of the files.

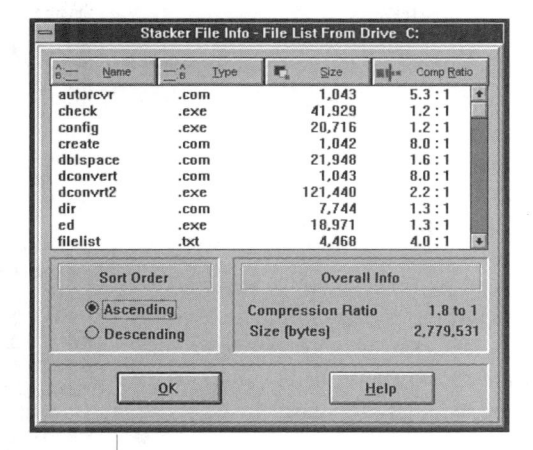

If the current file list box is not a Stacker compressed drive, Stacker instead displays a dialog box containing the error message Not a Stacker drive. Press Enter or click the **O**K command button to clear the dialog box, and then try another drive.

7. After you finish viewing the drive information, press Enter or choose the **O**K command button to close the Stacker Drive Info dialog box and return to the Windows File Manager.

Using the Stackometer Information Display

The Stackometer program provides access to a variety of Stacker utilities from inside Windows. The various Stackometer utilities are described throughout Part III of this book, whenever they are appropriate for the tasks at hand. The main display of the Stackometer program provides some basic information about your compressed drives. You can use the Stackometer to view the overall compression ratio of a disk drive, the amount of used and free disk space, and the fragmentation level of the compressed drive.

To use the Stackometer to view information about a compressed drive, follow these steps:

1. To start the Stackometer, double-click the Stackometer program icon in the Stacker program group of the Windows Program Manager. The Stackometer program icon is shown in figure 11.9.

   After the Stackometer program starts, the window and main menu shown in figure 11.10 appear. The *title bar* of the Stackometer window identifies the drive for which Stackometer is showing statistics. In figure 11.10, the Stackometer shows statistics for compressed drive D.

   The *bar scale* at the extreme left of the main window shows the actual overall compression ratio of the compressed drive. The bottom of the compression ratio bar scale is a compression ratio of 1.0 :1—that is, no compression. The top of the compression ratio bar scale is the expected compression ratio for the compressed drive. The compression ratio chart is updated as the overall compression ratio of your compressed drive changes.

   The *disk space meter* in the center of the Stackometer main window shows the amount of used and free space on the compressed drive. The dark colored area is the amount of used space, and the light colored area is the amount of free space available. In figure 11.10, a little more than half the space on the compressed drive is in use. Notice also the small triangle near the halfway mark of the meter in this figure. Your Stackometer disk space meter has a similar triangle. This triangle marks the physical capacity of the working drive for your Stacker compressed volume file. The triangle indicates how much space you would have without Stacker, relative to the entire amount of compressed space available. In figure 11.10, the triangle is at the halfway mark of the disk space meter, meaning that Stacker has doubled the storage for the drive.

The *fragmentation display* at the right of the Stackometer main window shows a graphic representation of the compressed disk's clusters and the level of file fragmentation on the compressed volume. This display helps you determine when to use the Stacker SDEFRAG optimization utility described in Chapter 12, "Using the Stacker Utilities." Defragment your compressed volume whenever the fragmentation level is medium to high.

NOTE: If you use Stackometer to display information about an uncompressed drive, only the disk space meter and compression chart appear in the Stackometer main window. The compression chart always shows a compression ratio of 1.0:1, and the disk space meter appears in black (for used space) and white (for unused space) instead of in color (shades of blue).

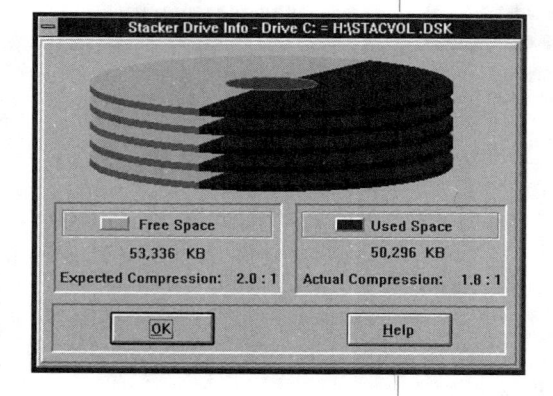

2. To view information for another drive, open the Stackometer **S**ettings menu and choose **S**elect Drive. Stackometer displays the Select Drive dialog box, as shown in figure 11.11. The Select Drive dialog box displays a list of all your disk drives.

3. Select from the **D**rives list the drive you want to view, and choose the **O**K button. Stackometer returns to the Stacker main window and updates its title bar and displays to reflect the current information for the new drive.

Click the **C**ancel command button or press Esc if you decide not to change the disk drive for the Stackometer display.

You can have more than one Stackometer running at a time. You can start several Stackometers and set each to display a different disk drive. If you minimize the Stackometer, the Stackometer minimized icon is a miniature version of the free space meter; this miniature free space meter continuously updates to reflect the actual free space available on the drive.

Fig. 11.8
The Stacker Drive Info dialog box.

Fig. 11.9
The Stackometer program icon.

Mounting and Unmounting Compressed Drives

Except for compressed removable media disks, you usually need not be concerned about mounting or unmounting your compressed disks. Your compressed hard disks are automatically mounted as your computer starts. Chapter 10 describes how Stacker uses the STACKER.INI file to mount compressed disks and exchange drive letters as your

Using Stacker **253**

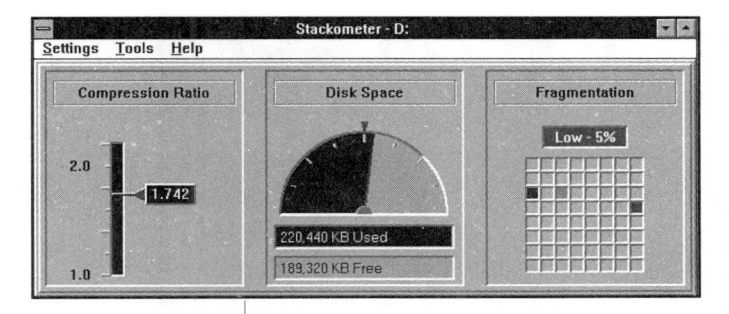

Fig. 11.10

The Stackometer window and main menu.

STOP

Do not run Stacker or use any Stacker commands from a DOS prompt opened while running Windows, DESQview, GEM, or GEOworks.

computer starts. You may, however, want to unmount a compressed hard disk for safety if you perform disk diagnostic or repair procedures. (See Chapter 13, "Troubleshooting Stacker.") The section "Using Disk Utilities with Stacker," later in this chapter, discusses considerations you must observe when using various disk optimization and repair utilities. Keep in mind that you cannot use many of the Stacker utilities while you are running Windows, DESQview, GEM, or GEOworks. You can mount or unmount compressed drives with Stacker *only* while you are at the DOS prompt.

You use only the STACKER command to mount or unmount your drives. You can add various command line switches to the STACKER command to specify which compressed volume to mount and how to mount it. You also can use command line switches to unmount your compressed volumes. The following sections describe how to use the STACKER command to mount and to unmount compressed drives.

Mounting a Compressed Drive

The simplest way to mount a drive is to use the following STACKER command syntax at the DOS prompt:

STACKER *d*:

This command tells Stacker to mount the STACVOL.DSK compressed volume file on the drive specified by *d*. Stacker mounts the compressed volume, assigns it the next available drive letter, and then exchanges the drive letter between the uncompressed drive and the compressed drive—just as if the volume were mounted from the STACKER.INI file with the SW mounting parameter. The following command, for example, mounts the STACVOL.DSK compressed volume file on drive F:

STACKER F:

If the drive letter you use to mount the compressed volume is listed in the STACKER.INI file, Stacker mounts the compressed drive and assigns it the same drive letter as the original uncompressed drive. The original uncompressed drive is inaccessible until you unmount the compressed volume. Suppose, for example, that you have a Floptical or Bernoulli drive that is drive E, and your STACKER.INI file contains a line with the drive letter E. If you use the following command, Stacker mounts the compressed volume as drive E (the uncompressed volume is unavailable until you unmount drive E):

STACKER E:

If you use the * symbol in your STACKER.INI file to reserve additional drive letters, you can use the following form of the STACKER command:

STACKER *d1*:=*d2*:\STACVOL.*nnn*

In the preceding example, *d1* represents a Stacker drive letter you want assigned to the compressed volume after the volume is mounted; *d2* represents the drive letter for the uncompressed drive that contains the compressed volume file you want to mount; *nnn* represents the three-letter file extension of the compressed volume file. If you created the compressed volume file by compressing an entire drive, the compressed volume file is named STACVOL.DSK. If you created the compressed volume file from free space on the drive, the first compressed volume file is named STACVOL.000, the second free space compressed volume file is named STACVOL.001, and so on.

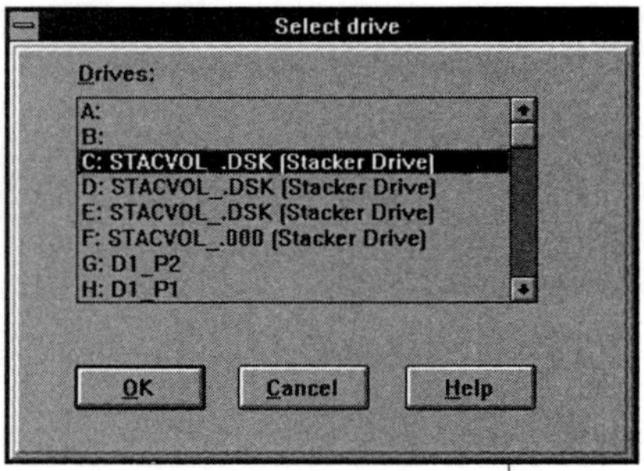

Fig. 11.11

The Stackometer Select Drive dialog box.

To mount the first free space compressed volume file on drive F as drive J, for example, use the following command:

STACKER J:=F:\STACVOL.000

Stacker mounts the STACVOL.000 compressed volume file as drive J.

For Stacker to mount the drive and assign it the drive letter J, drive letter J must be reserved for use by Stacker and not currently be in use for another compressed or uncompressed drive. If you try to mount a compressed volume file and assign it a drive letter that has not been reserved by Stacker, Stacker displays an error message telling you that the drive letter is not a Stacker drive letter. The drive letter you use, therefore, must be a drive letter for a removable disk drive, a drive letter formerly used by another compressed volume, or an additional drive letter you reserved for Stacker.

To reserve additional drive letters for Stacker, add the * symbol to your STACKER.INI file. The section "Examining the STACKER.INI Commands," in Chapter 10, "Configuring and Optimizing Stacker," shows how to use the * symbol to reserve drive letters. You can always reuse a drive letter for a Stacker volume you have unmounted or a drive letter for a removable media drive that does not already have a compressed removable disk mounted.

The third form of the STACKER command for mounting compressed volumes is issued as follows:

STACKER @*d*:\STACVOL.*nnn*

In this example, *d* stands for the drive letter that contains the compressed volume file you want to mount. The *nnn* stands for the three-letter extension of the compressed volume file, as described earlier in this section. This form of the STACKER command mounts the specified compressed volume file from the specified disk drive and replaces the uncompressed volume with the mounted compressed volume. The compressed volume is now accessible through the drive letter you specified, and the original uncompressed volume is unavailable until the compressed volume is unmounted.

The following command, for example, mounts the STACVOL.DSK file on drive E:

STACKER @E:\STACVOL.DSK

This command instructs Stacker to mount the compressed volume and assign it drive letter E. The original uncompressed volume is unavailable until the compressed volume is unmounted. This last form of the STACKER command usually is issued for removable media drives.

You may run into one special problem while trying to mount a compressed volume, whether from a hard disk or from a removable disk. If you mount several compressed volumes (usually removable media), Stacker may run out of replaceable drive letters. If you try to mount another drive after Stacker runs out of replaceable drive letters, the following error message appears on-screen:

```
ERROR:  No replaceable drives available.
        You must add '@' to your Stacker configuration and reboot,
        OR you should unmount a replaceable Stacker drive
```

To correct the problem, add a line containing the @ symbol to your STACKER.INI file, or increase the number of replaceable drive letters reserved by adding the /RP= command to your STACKER.INI file. (Chapter 10, "Configuring and Optimizing Stacker," describes the STACKER.INI file and the @ and /RP= commands.) After you have made the change, you must restart your computer for the change to take effect.

Unmounting a Compressed Drive

After you know how to mount a compressed volume, you also may want to know how to unmount a compressed volume. Unmounting a compressed volume is easy and straightforward. Only one form of the STACKER command is used to unmount drives.

To unmount a Stacker compressed volume, use the following syntax in the STACKER command you type at the DOS prompt:

STACKER –*d*:

In the preceding syntax example, *d* represents the letter of the drive you want to unmount. You unmount compressed volume files by referring to the drive letter currently assigned to the mounted compressed volume. To unmount the compressed volume in drive B, for example, use the following command:

STACKER –B:

Stacker unmounts the compressed volume drive B.

As you can see, unmounting a compressed volume is very simple. A few situations that can arise while you unmount compressed volumes do, however, deserve additional attention.

If you unmount a drive while it is the current logged drive, and the original compressed volume was mounted with swapped drive letters, you receive a message from DOS that the current drive is no longer valid—which is true. DOS prompts you for a new drive letter. Type any valid disk drive letter and press Enter. DOS does not always recover from this error, so you may need to restart your computer.

Occasionally, you may accidentally use the STACKER unmounting command on a drive that is not compressed. If you use compressed removable media, for example, you may forget whether you have already unmounted a disk before removing it from the drive and end up using the unmount command twice. The second time you issue the unmount command, no compressed volume is present to unmount. If you try to unmount a drive that is not a compressed volume, Stacker displays the following error message. (The

NOTE: If you unmount a compressed volume that had its drive letters swapped, Stacker does *not* swap the drive letters back to their original positions. If your drive D is a compressed drive hosted by drive E, for example, and you unmount drive D, you still must access the uncompressed drive through drive E. If you attempt to access drive D while it is unmounted, you receive an `invalid drive` error message from DOS. You can, however, use the swapped drive letter to mount a compressed volume—either to remount the first compressed volume or to mount a different compressed volume. Stacker *does* restore the drive letters for removable disks and other compressed volumes where the mounted compressed volume replaced the original uncompressed drive.

precise drive letter in the error message depends on the specific disk drives in your system and the drive you tried to unmount.)

```
ERROR:  Drive G: is not a Stacker drive letter
```

Another potentially serious situation involves your compressed drive C. Drive C is usually your start-up drive. DOS must have continuous access to certain files on your start-up disk. If you unmount your drive C, however, DOS cannot locate the files it needs on that drive. If you do accidentally unmount drive C, regardless of whether it is the current disk drive, you receive one or more of several different error messages from DOS. In such situations, you almost always must restart your computer.

If you need to work on your computer with the compressed volume on your drive C unmounted, you must start your computer from a floppy disk.

> Do not unmount your drive C. If you unmount drive C, you almost always must restart your computer.

Using Stacker with Removable Media

This section describes how to use Stacker with removable media. You mount and unmount compressed removable media drives the same way you mount and unmount compressed volumes on your hard disks. (Mounting and unmounting compressed volumes is described in the preceding section of this chapter.)

Mounting Removable Disks Automatically

Stacker automatic removable drive mounting is built into the Stacker device driver. Stacker automatic mounting requires you to mount a compressed removable drive only once. After you mount the first compressed volume in a removable media drive, Stacker establishes a connection to that removable media drive. You may insert additional compressed or uncompressed removable disks in the drive, and Stacker mounts or unmounts the compressed volumes as necessary.

You may use the STACKER.INI file to pre-establish Stacker's connection to a particular drive letter for automatic mounting of compressed volumes in that drive. To do so, add a line containing only the drive letter to your STACKER.INI file. (The STACKER.INI file is discussed in the section "Understanding the Stacker Initialization File: STACKER.INI," in Chapter 10, "Configuring and Optimizing Stacker.")

The following STACKER.INI file example pre-establishes automatic volume mounting for drives A and B:

```
/DIR=C:\STACKER\
A:
B:
C:\STACVOL.DSK,SW
```

Adding the drive letter line to STACKER.INI also reserves a replaceable drive letter for that drive so that you do not run out of replaceable drive letters as long as you mount compressed volumes in that drive.

> Stacker does not mount compressed removable drives that also are password-protected. You must mount password-protected compressed volumes manually on removable disks. Refer to the section "Using Passwords," later in this chapter, for more information on setting and entering passwords.

> **NOTE:**
> If you manually unmount a compressed volume in a removable media drive, Stacker severs the automatic mounting connection with that drive. The following command for example, unmounts the compressed volume in drive B so that Stacker stops automatically mounting compressed disks in drive B:
> **STACKER –B:**
> Stacker severs the automatic mounting connection even if you have pre-established the automatic mounting in the STACKER.INI file. To mount another compressed removable disk in the drive, you must manually mount the compressed volume. After you mount a second compressed volume manually, the Stacker automatic drive mounting takes over again. The following command, for example, mounts the compressed volume on the disk in drive B and re-establishes automatic mounting for drive B:
> **STACKER B:**

> **NOTE:**
> The STACKER.EXE program is not the same as the STACKER.COM program, which provides the utilities for a computer that already has Stacker installed. Do not confuse the two.

If Stacker mounts a compressed volume in a removable media drive, the compressed volume is mounted so that it replaces the original drive. If you change disks and insert an uncompressed disk, Stacker unmounts the compressed volume and the original drive letter again accesses the physical, uncompressed drive. If a removable disk with a compressed volume is inserted in the drive again, Stacker mounts the compressed volume.

To mount a compressed volume on a removable disk and also make the uncompressed portion of the disk accessible, you must mount the compressed volume manually by using the second mounting syntax, described in the section "Mounting a Compressed Drive," earlier in this chapter.

Compressing Removable Media

Compressing removable media disks is slightly different from compressing your hard disks. Usually, after you compress all your hard drives, you do not compress any others unless you get a new computer or add more hard drives to your system. You are more likely to compress removable media disks—such as floppy disks—on a day-to-day basis. This section describes how to compress your removable media disks successfully.

Whenever you compress a removable media disk, Stacker creates a compressed volume file named STACVOL.DSK in the uncompressed root directory of the removable disk and assigns the file the Hidden, System, and Read-Only file attributes—just as on a hard disk. After it creates the compressed volume file, Stacker adds an informational file to the uncompressed root directory of the removable disk. This file, called README.STC, is a DOS text file that contains a message informing you that the disk is compressed by Stacker. README.STC also includes brief instructions on how to mount the disk. The README.STC file appears as follows:

```
This is a Stacker compressed disk.
Type "STACKER d:", where "d" is the drive letter of this disk.
```

As you compress a removable media drive, Stacker places another file in the uncompressed root directory of the removable disk. This is the STACKER.EXE program file. The STACKER.EXE program is the Stacker Anywhere program—a special version of Stacker that enables you to use Stacker compressed removable media with computers that do not have Stacker installed. Using Stacker Anywhere is described in the section, "Using Stacker Compressed Removable Media in Other Computers," later in this chapter.

You may compress removable media drives either from the DOS command line or by using the Stacker Toolbox.

Compressing Removable Media Disks from the DOS Prompt

You can compress a removable disk drive directly from the DOS prompt by using the Stacker CREATE command. (You also use this command to compress hard drives and RAM drives.) The full syntax for the CREATE command and its command line switches is described in Chapter 12, "Using the Stacker Utilities." The following discussion describes only those aspects of the CREATE command you use most often to compress removable media drives.

To compress a removable media drive, use the following command syntax:

CREATE *d*:

In this form, the CREATE command tells Stacker to compress a drive specified by the drive letter you substitute for *d* and to use the entire disk for the compressed volume file. The following example tells Stacker to compress the floppy disk in drive A and to compress all the space on the disk:

CREATE A:

Usually, you want to make the largest possible compressed volume file. Except for the README.STC and STACKER.EXE files, you generally have no reason to store any files on the uncompressed part of a removable disk.

To compress a removable media disk from the DOS command line, type the Stacker CREATE command at the DOS prompt, using the syntax just described, and press Enter. Stacker compresses the removable disk in the drive you specified. Stacker makes the compressed volume file as large as possible and then places the README.STC and the Stacker Anywhere files in the uncompressed root directory of the removable disk.

After you press Enter, Stacker begins to compress the removable disk. While Stacker is compressing the disk, it displays various messages as it creates and then verifies the compressed volume. After Stacker CREATE finishes compressing the removable disk, it displays a dialog box indicating the successful creation of the compressed volume file. To return to the DOS prompt, press Enter or choose the **OK** command button displayed in the dialog box. To compress more than one removable disk in the same drive, put the next disk you want to compress in that drive, and issue the CREATE command again; you do not need to unmount the drive.

> **NOTE:** Stacker CREATE only compresses the disk; it does not mount the resulting compressed volume. If Stacker automatic mounting is active for the drive in which you compressed the removable disk, Stacker mounts the drive if you try to access it. Otherwise, you must mount the new compressed drive on the removable disk manually.

Compressing Removable Media Disks by Using the Stacker Toolbox

You also can compress removable disks through the menu system in the Stacker Toolbox. To compress a removable disk by using the Stacker Toolbox, follow these steps.

1. To start the Stacker Toolbox program, type **STAC** at the DOS prompt and press Enter. The Stacker Toolbox program starts and displays its main menu (refer to fig. 11.1).
2. To compress a removable disk, choose **F**loppy from the Stack portion of the menu. Stacker displays the drive list shown in figure 11.12, which lists all your removable media drives.
3. If you have not yet done so, put the removable disk you want to compress in the drive in which you want to compress it.
4. Select from the drive list the drive that contains the disk you want to compress. If you change your mind about compressing a disk, press Esc.

    Stacker begins to compress the disk in your selected drive. Various messages appear on-screen as Stacker creates and then verifies the compressed volume.

    After Stacker finishes compressing the disk, it displays a dialog box indicating the successful creation of the new compressed volume.
5. Press Enter or choose **O**K to continue. Stacker returns to the main Toolbox menu.

> **STOP**
>
> The usual precautions regarding using removable disks in general also apply to using compressed removable disks. Never remove a disk while data is being written to it or while the disk is still in use by an application. Doing so may result in loss of data. Remove or change disks *only* if the disk drive activity light is off and you are sure the disk is not being used by an application.

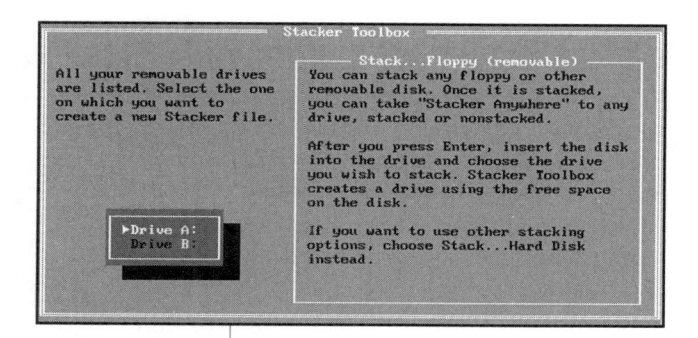

6. To exit from the Stacker Toolbox and return to DOS, press Esc or F10. Stacker asks you to confirm that you want to return to DOS. Select **Y**es to return to DOS or **N**o to return to the Toolbox.

Using Removable Media

This section describes several issues involved in using removable media on a day-to-day basis: changing disks, using write-protected disks, and transporting disks to another computer.

Fig. 11.12

The Stacker list of removable media drives.

Changing Disks

Before you can access the files on a compressed removable disk, you (or Stacker) must mount that disk. After the compressed volume on a removable disk is mounted, however, you may eventually want to insert a different disk in the drive to access a different group of files.

If you replace a mounted compressed removable disk with an uncompressed disk, Stacker recognizes that the new removable disk is not compressed and unmounts the previous drive. If you later insert another compressed removable drive, Stacker recognizes that a compressed volume is again on the disk and automatically mounts it for you—if enough replaceable drive letters still remain. If you replace a mounted compressed removable disk with another compressed removable disk, Stacker keeps the removable drive mounted. The new removable disk is available immediately without needing to be mounted.

Using Write-Protected Removable Media

You can use write-protected removable disks with Stacker. In accordance with the protected status of the disk, you cannot change or add to any of the data on the disk. Stacker can mount the compressed volume, however, and enable you to access files on the write-protected removable disk.

After you mount a compressed volume on a write-protected removable disk, Stacker displays an additional message informing you that the volume is write-protected. The Stacker information display—described at the beginning of this chapter—shows you that the compressed volume is write-protected. If you try to write data to a mounted, write-protected removable disk, you receive the standard DOS error message that a write-protect error is present on the disk.

Using Stacker Compressed Removable Media in Other Computers

You can use your Stacker compressed removable disks on any other computer on which Stacker is installed. If you use the Stacker Anywhere program, your Stacker compressed removable disks also can be read by computers that do not use Stacker.

If you need to make files from a compressed removable disk available on a computer on which Stacker is not installed, follow these steps:

1. Insert the disk containing the Stacker compressed volume into any disk drive that accommodates it on the computer without Stacker.
2. Make the disk with the Stacker compressed volume your current disk drive.
3. Use the DOS DIR command to verify that the STACKER.EXE file is on the Stacker compressed disk, along with the README.STC file. (If the STACKER.EXE program file is not present, you cannot use the Stacker compressed removable disk on a computer without Stacker.)
4. Use the STACKER.EXE (Stacker Anywhere) program to make the compressed volume on the disk available by typing **STACKER** at the DOS prompt and then pressing Enter.

   The Stacker Anywhere program loads into memory and mounts the compressed volume file. Stacker Anywhere prints out a copyright notice, information on how to contact Stac Electronics to order the full Stacker software, and the advisement that Stacker Anywhere may be used only to make the data on the compressed disk readable. Stacker Anywhere indicates that it has mounted the drive and then returns to the DOS prompt. The files on the compressed volume are now available. Stacker Anywhere provides only the capability to read and write to the compressed volume on the Stacker compressed removable disk. Stacker Anywhere does not provide any other features of the full Stacker package. Stacker Anywhere remains in memory as long as the compressed removable disk is mounted. You can tell if Stacker Anywhere is loaded into memory because Stacker Anywhere adds a line to the DOS prompt reminding you to type **exit** to unmount the drive.
5. To unmount the compressed volume after you finish with it, type **exit** at the DOS prompt and press Enter. Stacker Anywhere unmounts the compressed drive and unloads itself from memory.

Using Passwords

Stacker enables you to protect the data on your compressed volumes with two levels of security, whether the volumes are on your hard disk or on a removable disk. The first level of security is a password that enables the user to both read and write data to the compressed volume. This type of password is called a *read/write password*, because it enables the user to perform both activities. The second level of security is a password that enables the user to read data from the compressed volume, but does not enable the user to change any data on the volume. This type of password is called a *read-only password*, because it enables only that activity.

If a compressed volume is *password-protected*, Stacker asks you (or any other user) to enter the password whenever Stacker mounts the compressed volume file. To enter the password, you type the password when prompted by Stacker and press Enter. Stacker does not display any characters on-screen as you enter the password, so no one looking over your shoulder can easily determine what you type.

NOTE: Make sure that you remember the password you select. If you forget the password, the data on the password-protected compressed volume becomes permanently inaccessible. Even Stac Electronics, the publishers of the Stacker program, cannot determine a password you have forgotten.

Using Stacker 261

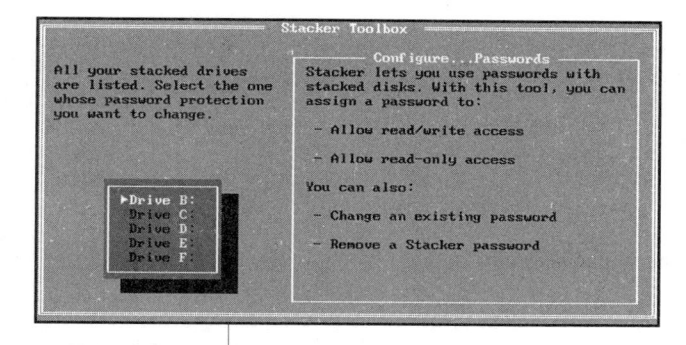

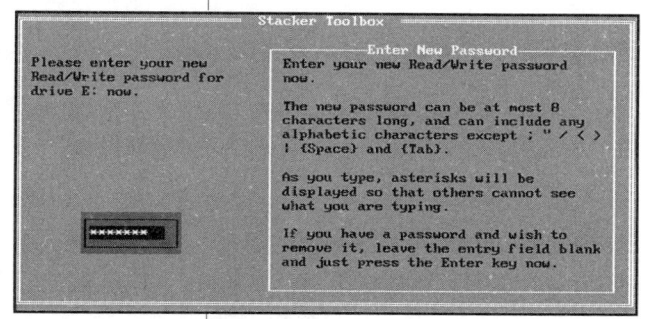

Fig. 11.13, top

The Stacker Toolbox list of compressed drives.

Fig. 11.14, bottom

The Stacker Toolbox password entry screen.

In choosing a password, do not pick words that other people can guess easily. Your spouse's name, your birthday, the name of your favorite sports team, and so on all are bad choices for a password.

If a user cannot enter either a valid read/write or read-only password, Stacker does not mount the compressed volume, whether during your computer's start-up or by a manual mounting command. Stacker permits one attempt at entering the password and then refuses to mount the compressed volume. You can always use the STACKER command to try mounting the drive and entering the password again. If you fail to use a valid password, however, Stacker continues to refuse to mount the compressed volume, no matter how many times you try.

To use the Stacker Toolbox to set or change passwords, follow these steps:

1. To start the Stacker Toolbox, type **STAC** at the DOS prompt and press Enter. The Stacker Toolbox starts and displays the main menu screen (refer to fig. 11.1).

2. Choose **P**asswords from the Configure section of the Toolbox main menu. The Stacker Toolbox displays the screen shown in figure 11.13, which lists all your compressed drives.

3. Select the appropriate drive. If this is the first time a password is set for this compressed volume, Stacker displays the screen shown in figure 11.14. If this screen appears, skip to step 6.

   If a read/write password is already set for this compressed volume, Stacker instead displays the screen shown in figure 11.15. Continue with step 4 to create a read-only password or to change an existing read/write password.

4. Choose the type of password you want to change or create.

   After you choose the password type, Stacker displays a screen similar to the one already shown in figure 11.14. The exact contents of the screen depend on the type of password you are setting: Read/**W**rite or **R**ead-Only.

5. If changing an existing password, type the old password and press Enter. Stacker displays another screen similar to this, ready for you to type the new password.

6. Type the new password you want to use. Stacker displays asterisks as you type so that no one looking over your shoulder can easily determine what you are typing.

7. After you type your password, press Enter. Stacker immediately displays another screen almost identical to the one in which you just entered the new password. Stacker asks you to enter the new password a second time, not only to confirm your choice of a password but also to make sure that you did not make a typing mistake.

8. Type your password again, and press Enter. If you typed the password the same both times, Stacker displays a message confirming the change in the password and returns to the Stacker Toolbox main menu. If you did not type the password the same both times, Stacker asks you to re-enter the password. Go back to step 6.

If you decide not to change a password, you can press Esc or F10 to cancel the process and return to the Stacker Toolbox main menu. To create a read-only password, you must first create a read/write password and then follow the preceding steps again. The second time these steps are performed, the password type menu shown in figure 11.15 appears; choose **R**ead-Only in step 4, and proceed as described for a read/write password.

> **NOTE:** If entering the first password for this compressed volume, you are actually creating the read/write password for that volume. Stacker requires you to create a read/write password before you can create a read-only password.

To remove a password from a compressed volume, follow the preceding steps as if you intended to change the read/write password. Instead of entering a new password, however, just press Enter, and then press Enter again to confirm the blank password the second time Stacker asks for it.

If you use both a read-only password and a read/write password, you must remove the read-only password before you can remove the read/write password. Stacker enforces this rule because a password that provides read-only security without a password for read/write security makes no sense.

Backing Up Your Compressed Drives

You back up your compressed volumes the same way you backed up your uncompressed drives before installing Stacker. The main difference is that, if using Stacker, you have more drives to back up. As your compressed volumes become full, you also must use more disks or tapes to perform your backup, because you effectively double your disk storage by installing Stacker. Whenever you perform a backup, make sure that you back up both your compressed volumes and your uncompressed drives. Back up all files on your compressed volumes, and back up all files on your uncompressed volumes, except the compressed volume file itself. (Refer to the documentation for your backup program for information on excluding files from a backup.)

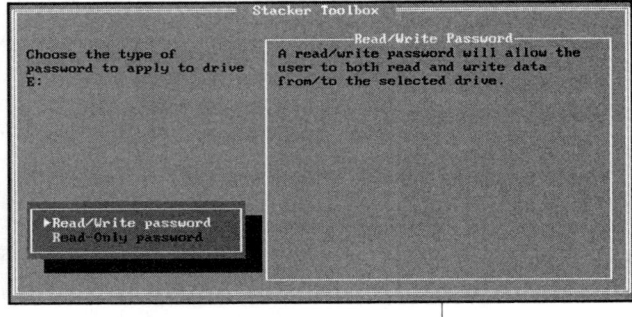

Fig. 11.15

The Stacker Toolbox password type selection screen.

Although backing up an entire compressed volume file is possible, doing so is pointless. If you back up individual files from your compressed volumes and then back up the compressed volume file itself, you duplicate your effort and use many more disks or tapes than necessary. Especially avoid the temptation to back up only your compressed volume file instead of all the individual files from the compressed volume. If you back up only the compressed volume file without backing up the individual files on the compressed volume, you cannot restore single files. You can restore only the entire compressed volume file, which results in the loss of any files you changed or added to your compressed volume since your last backup.

For information on a comprehensive and cost-effective backup technique that enables you to restore any file for a period of up to three months past, refer to Appendix C, "The 'Grandfather' Backup Technique."

Using Disk Utilities with Stacker

Most hard disk utilities are compatible with your compressed volumes as long as these utilities also are compatible with your version of DOS and your specific hardware. In general, always use the most current version of your disk utilities available. If you are unsure about the compatibility of a particular disk utility, consult the utility's manufacturer or your vendor for information on the product's compatibility with DOS 6 and Stacker.

Among the most frequently used disk utilities are those categorized as *disk optimizers*, or *defragmentation programs*. Many software publishers offer disk optimization programs; DOS 6 even supplies its own version of a disk optimization utility, called DEFRAG. Disk optimization programs improve your hard disk's performance by *defragmenting* the files on the disk. As discussed in Chapter 1, "Understanding and Using Disk Compression," DOS divides your disk into small chunks called *clusters* (also referred to as *allocation units*). DOS stores files on your disk by dividing the information in the file into several different clusters; the actual number of clusters used by a file depends on the size of the file and the size of the clusters.

DOS uses whatever unused clusters it finds as it writes new information to the disk. Files that change frequently usually are stored in clusters that are scattered all across the surface of your hard disk. If the clusters used by a file are scattered widely across the surface of the disk, the disk's read/write heads must move farther and more often to retrieve all the information in the file. A disk that contains many files consisting of clusters that are physically separated is said to be *fragmented*. Disk optimization, or defragmenting, programs rearrange the file clusters on your disk so that all clusters in use by a particular file are contiguous. Making the clusters for a file contiguous can speed up disk access, because the disk's read/write heads need not move around as much to retrieve the entire file.

Using an optimization program on your compressed volume does not necessarily speed up your compressed volume. Your compressed volume file is already grouped in contiguous clusters on the physical hard disk. Defragmenting your compressed volume normally is useful only if you must change the size of your compressed volume. Chapter 12, "Using the Stacker Utilities," describes how to change the size of a compressed volume. Using an optimization program on your uncompressed drives, however, can speed up access to the files on the uncompressed drive if the uncompressed drive is fragmented. But be careful if you do use optimization programs on your uncompressed drives. Most defragmentation programs do not move files marked with the System, Hidden, or Read-Only attributes. Your compressed volume file, therefore, is usually not affected by running defragmentation programs on your uncompressed hard disk.

Do not run a defragmentation program on your uncompressed disk if you have altered the Hidden, System, or Read-Only attributes on your compressed volume file. You can lose data from the compressed volume if you defragment the uncompressed host drive while the compressed volume file is unprotected. As you run your defragmentation program on the uncompressed disk, the defragmentation program moves clusters using the cluster size of the host drive as the basis for the cluster size to move. If the host drive's cluster size is different than Stacker's cluster size—as is usually the case—some Stacker clusters can become corrupted if moved by the defragmentation program.

Using the Stacker Help System

Stacker provides a fairly comprehensive Help system. You can obtain help from Stacker either for the Stacker DOS commands or for activities you perform by using the Stacker Toolbox. If you use the Stacker DOS commands frequently, you may need a short refresher on the command line switches and their effects. For a brief description of all the Stacker DOS commands and their command line switches, add the /? command line switch to those commands. The following command, for example, displays a short Help screen for the STACKER command itself:

STACKER /?

Stacker displays a list of all its command line switches and their options, along with a brief description of the action or effect associated with each switch.

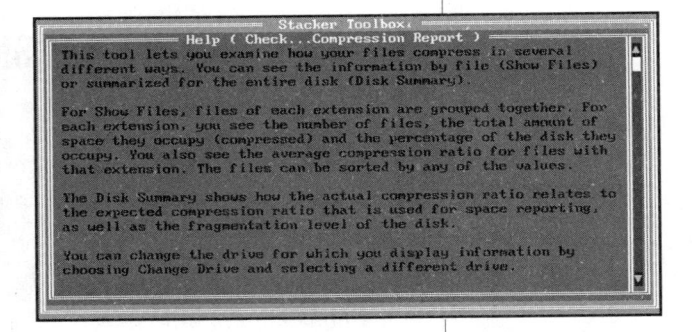

Fig. 11.16

The Help screen for the Stacker Toolbox Check Compression Report choice.

You are most likely to need help while performing tasks by using the Stacker Toolbox or the Stackometer utility in Windows. This section describes only how to use the Stacker Toolbox Help system. The Help system for the Stackometer utility is the same as any other Windows Help system.

Stacker provides you with *context-sensitive help*—that is, help that relates to the immediate task on which you are working (the context). To access context-sensitive help, press the F1 key at any time while in the Stacker Toolbox. Stacker displays a Help screen related to your current activity. Stacker uses the currently selected menu choice, currently open dialog box, or other cues to determine your operating context and display the appropriate Help screen. You also may access context-sensitive help by choosing the **H**elp button that appears on many Stacker Toolbox screens. The same Help screen appears whether you use the **H**elp command button or press F1.

After you press the F1 key or choose the **H**elp command button, Stacker Toolbox displays a screen of text explaining the task on which you are working. Figure 11.16 shows the Help text for the **C**ompression Report choice in the Check area of the Stacker Toolbox menu.

If the Help text is more than one page long, use the PgUp and PgDn keys to move forward and backward through the Help text. After you finish reading the Help text, press the Esc key. Stacker returns to whatever was on-screen at the time you pressed the F1 key.

Summary

In this chapter, you learned about issues affecting the day-to-day use of your compressed drives. You learned about managing your files on your Stacker compressed drives and about how Stacker redirects DOS disk commands to use the Stacker equivalent commands so that you do not need to learn any new commands. You learned how to get information about your compressed drives, whether from the DOS prompt or from the Stacker utility menus in DOS or Windows. You also learned how to mount and unmount a compressed drive and how the Stacker automatic removable drive mounting works.

This chapter then explained how to compress your removable media drives and described the special concerns associated with using compressed removable media. The chapter also provided brief descriptions of how to back up your compressed drives and how to use disk utilities with Stacker safely. Finally, the chapter explained how to use the Stacker Help system.

The following chapter explains how to use the Stacker utilities to perform some less common tasks with Stacker.

CHAPTER 12

Using the Stacker Utilities

> **NOTE:**
> This chapter focuses on creating compressed drives on hard disks. To compress a removable disk, refer to Chapter 11, "Using Stacker."

> ⚠️ Some programs—such as early versions of Lotus 1-2-3 and most contemporary DOS-based music programs—use copy-protection schemes that rely on finding certain data in certain areas of the disk. Compressing a disk moves the data for which the copy-protec-tion scheme searches. You must uninstall any software that uses this type of copy protection before compressing a disk; otherwise, the copy-protection scheme no longer recognizes your software as a legitimate copy, and you cannot use it. After you compress the drive, you can reinstall the copy-protected program.

This chapter discusses tasks you do not need to perform on a daily basis, although you eventually will want or need to perform them. Some procedures—such as creating a new compressed volume—you need to perform only once for each of your compressed drives. This chapter describes how to use the Stacker Toolbox, Stackometer, and command line utilities to create additional compressed drives, change the size of a compressed drive, and check the integrity of your compressed drives. You also learn how and when to defragment a compressed drive, how to delete a compressed drive, and how to remove Stacker compression.

Creating Additional Compressed Drives

This section explains how to compress disk drives by using the Stacker Toolbox or the Stacker CREATE utility. Stacker enables you to create two different types of compressed drives by compressing an entire disk (and all files on it) or by using only free space from the uncompressed disk.

If you add another disk drive to your computer, or decide to repartition your existing hard disks, you may need to perform the procedures in this section to create or re-create compressed drives. After you create a compressed drive, you normally do not need these procedures again. If, after you create a compressed drive, you decide that it is too large or too small, you can change the size of the compressed drive as described in the section "Changing the Size of a Compressed Drive," later in this chapter.

Compressing Drives by Using the Stacker Toolbox

To compress drives by using the Stacker Toolbox, follow these steps:

1. Type **STAC** at the DOS prompt and press Enter to start the Stacker Toolbox, if it is not already running. The Stacker Toolbox starts and displays the main menu, as shown in figure 12.1. The menu choices are arranged vertically along the left side of the screen.

2. Choose **H**ard Disk in the Stack section of the main menu. Stacker displays the Prepare to Stack dialog box, as shown in figure 12.2.

   If TSR programs that write to the disk (such as FAX receive or electronic mail) currently are loaded in memory, you should restart your computer so that Stacker can temporarily disable them. If you are certain no programs that can interfere with Stacker are loaded in memory, you do not need to restart your computer. Having Stacker restart your computer is, however, recommended.

3. To restart your computer, first make sure that floppy drive A is empty, and then choose **R**estart. Choose **D**on't Restart to proceed immediately to step 4.

   If you choose **R**estart, Stacker restarts your computer. (If your computer does not restart, or if you have a start-up menu in your CONFIG.SYS file, refer to the Stacker Reboot sidebar on page 186, in Chapter 9, "Installing Stacker.") After a few moments, you see the on-screen message `**** Stacker Reboot ****`. Stacker loads into memory and resumes operation.

   Whether or not you choose to have Stacker restart your computer, Stacker displays the Select a Disk to Stack dialog box, as shown in figure 12.3.

   The list of drives in the Select a Disk to Stack dialog box can include disks you already have compressed. If you select a disk that is already compressed, you can compress only the free space on the uncompressed host drive for the compressed volume you select.

4. Select the drive you want to compress from the Disk to Stack list in the Select a Disk to Stack dialog box (refer to fig. 12.3), and choose **C**ontinue.

   If you select a hard disk that is not already compressed, Stacker displays the Entire Drive or Free Space? dialog box, as shown in figure 12.4 (see next page). If you select a hard disk that is already compressed, Stacker instead displays the Create Drive from Free Space dialog box. If this dialog box appears, skip to step 1 in the section "Creating a Free Space Drive," later in this chapter, for instructions.

   The Entire Drive or Free Space? dialog box lists the drive you selected, the current total space on the drive, and the currently available free space on the drive.

5. Choose **E**ntire Drive to compress a drive and all files currently on it. If you choose **E**ntire Drive, refer to the instructions in the following section, "Compressing an Entire Drive," to finish creating your Stacker drive.

   Choose **F**ree Space to create a compressed drive from the free space on a disk without compressing existing files on that disk or to create more than one

STOP

If you use the Stacker Toolbox to compress a drive, Stacker restarts your computer near the end of the process and, optionally, near the beginning of the process. If you have a RAM disk, preserve any data on it that you want to keep *before* you begin this procedure. Similarly, any TSR programs you use may have open files or unsaved data in memory. Make sure that all files used by TSR programs are closed and all data saved before you use the Stacker Toolbox to compress a drive.

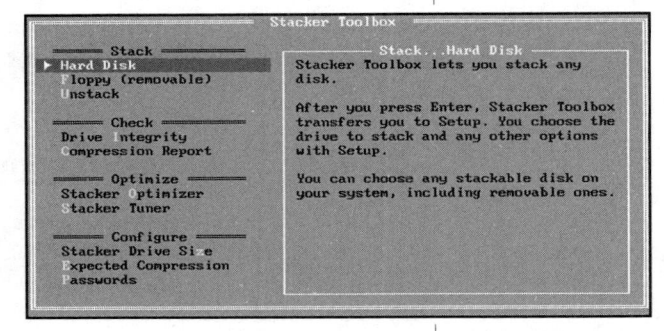

Fig. 12.1

The Stacker Toolbox main menu.

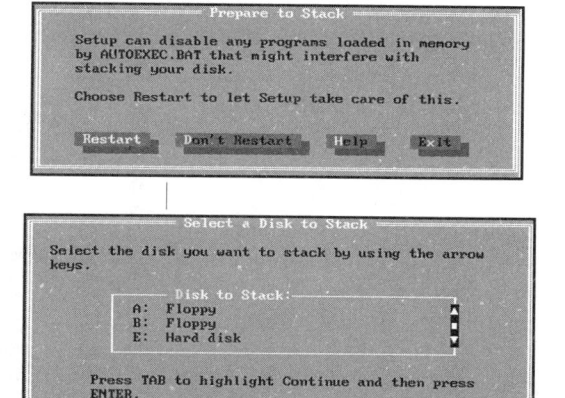

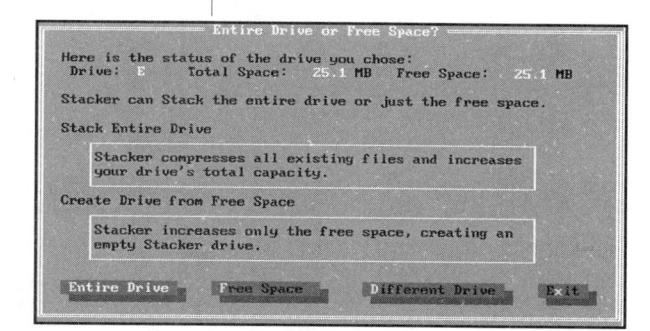

Using the Stacker Utilities   **269**

compressed volume on the same host drive. If you choose Free Space, refer to the instructions in the section "Creating a Free Space Drive," later in this chapter, to finish creating your Stacker drive.

If you change your mind about compressing the disk, choose **D**ifferent Drive. Stacker returns you to the Select a Disk to Stack dialog box (refer to fig. 12.3). If you change your mind about compressing any disks, choose E**x**it.

Compressing an Entire Drive

If you use the Stacker Toolbox to compress an entire drive, Stacker creates the new compressed volume and then it compresses any existing files and moves them to the new compressed volume. Stacker then exchanges drive letters between the newly compressed volume and the original uncompressed drive so that the new compressed drive now uses the drive letter of the original uncompressed drive. The original uncompressed drive becomes accessible through a new drive letter.

After you choose to compress an entire drive, Stacker immediately validates the drive you selected and displays the Stack Entire Drive dialog box, as shown in figure 12.5. The Stack Entire Drive dialog box lists the letter of the drive you selected to compress, the drive's total physical space, and the current amount of free space on the drive. In this dialog box, you can choose to compress the selected drive, choose a different drive, or choose advanced options for the newly compressed drive. If you change your mind, you can cancel the compression operation by choosing E**x**it.

As you create the new compressed drive, you can control how much free space remains uncompressed on the host drive, the expected compression ratio for the compressed drive, and the cluster size for the Stacker drive. You control these elements by choosing the Ad**v**anced Options button in the Stack Entire Drive dialog box.

Change the amount of space that remains unstacked (uncompressed) only if you need more uncompressed space on the original drive than the minimum amount that Stacker sets aside or if you want a smaller compressed volume. Increasing the amount of space left unstacked decreases the size of the new compressed volume.

Change the expected compression ratio only if you know that the files you intend to store on the new Stacker drive will consistently compress with compression ratios greater or less than 2.1:1. Changing the expected compression ratio affects the estimate of free

Fig. 12.2, top

The Prepare to Stack dialog box, in which Stacker asks whether you want to restart your computer.

Fig. 12.3, middle

The Select a Disk to Stack dialog box.

Fig. 12.4, bottom

Stacker asks whether to com-press the entire drive or create a new drive from free space.

space on the Stacker drive. Stacker assumes that all files compress at the expected compression ratio and bases its report of free space on the expected compression ratio. If the expected compression ratio is 3.1:1, for example, and 1M of unused physical space is on the Stacker volume, Stacker reports 3M of compressed space available on that volume.

Usually, you should not change the Stacker drive's cluster size; leave the cluster size option set to Auto, enabling Stacker to choose the cluster size. In general, the larger the physical drive you compress, the larger the cluster size needs to be. If you are certain that you will store only very small files on the new Stacker drive, a 4K cluster may improve the efficiency of the Stacker drive. Forcing the cluster size to be too large or too small, however, may cause Stacker to operate more slowly and use the physical disk space inefficiently.

To finish compressing the entire drive, follow these steps:

1. Choose the Ad**v**anced Options button in the Stack Entire Drive dialog box to set the amount of free space left unstacked, set the expected compression ratio, or set the cluster size for the new Stacker drive. Stacker displays the Advanced Options (Entire Drive) dialog box, as shown in figure 12.6 (see next page). If you do not want to set any advanced options, skip to step 6.
2. To change the space to leave unstacked, select the Space to Leave **U**nstacked text box, and type the amount of space you want to leave uncompressed in megabytes (M) and tenths of a megabyte. (To leave 3,500,000 bytes uncompressed, for example, type **3.5**.) If you do not want to change this value, skip to step 3.
3. To change the expected compression ratio, select the Expected Com**p**ression Ratio text box, and type the new expected compression ratio for the compressed drive. You can type in any number from 1.0 to 16.0; use only one decimal place. To leave the expected compression as displayed, skip to step 4.
4. To change the cluster size, select the appropriate radio button in the C**l**uster Size section of the Advanced Options dialog box; otherwise, skip to step 5. (Normally, you should leave this setting on Auto.)

   If you make a mistake or want to restore the original settings for any of these options, choose **R**eset Options. Stacker restores the original suggested settings for the Advanced Options.
5. Choose **O**K. Stacker returns to the Stack Entire Drive dialog box.
6. Choose **S**tack to compress the selected drive. Stacker immediately begins to compress the selected drive.

Stacker checks the integrity of the selected hard disk's File Allocation Table (FAT), tags all files on the disk, and then creates the Stacker compressed drive. Stacker then begins building the drive by compressing all the files on the disk and adding them to the Stacker compressed drive. After Stacker finishes building the new drive, it loads the Stacker SDEFRAG program to optimize the newly created compressed drive. After SDEFRAG finishes optimizing the new compressed drive, Stacker checks all the data on the compressed drive and again verifies the integrity of the drive.

> **NOTE:**
> To compress a drive other than the one already selected, choose the **D**ifferent Drive command button of the Stack Entire Drive dialog box. Stacker displays the Select a Drive dialog box. Follow the instructions beginning with step 4 in the preceding section, "Compressing Drives by Using the Stacker Toolbox."

> **NOTE:**
> The amount of free space Stacker leaves unstacked is *in addition to* any files that must remain uncompressed. If you compress a drive containing a Windows permanent swap file that is 5M in size, for example, Stacker moves the swap file to the uncompressed host drive, allocating 5M of space for it. If the space to leave unstacked is set for 2M, the new uncompressed drive is actually about 7M—5M occupied by the Windows swap file and 2M empty space.

After Stacker finishes compressing the hard disk, it displays the Stacking Results report, as shown in figure 12.7. The Stacking Results report shows the available space on the drive before and after compression. Usually, the amount of free space after compression is much greater than the free space before compression, but the amount of free space after compression depends on how full the drive was before compressing it and how well the files on it compressed. The results report also lists the host, or *working,* drive for the Stacker volume. In figure 12.7, for example, drive I is the working drive for the Stacker drive E.

After you finish viewing the results report, you can choose the **S**tack Another command button at the bottom of the report to compress another disk drive. If you choose **S**tack Another, Stacker returns to the Select a Drive dialog box. Follow the instructions beginning with step 4 in the section "Compressing Drives by Using the Stacker Toolbox," earlier in this chapter.

Stacker adds a line to the STACKER.INI file for each compressed volume you create on a hard disk. Stacker must restart your computer so that the new compressed volumes are mounted. To restart your computer, make sure that floppy drive A is empty, and then choose the **R**estart button at the bottom of the Stacking Results report.

> **NOTE:**
> If you uninstalled any copy-protected software before creating the compressed drive(s), you can reinstall that software now.

Creating a Free Space Drive

If you choose to create a new compressed drive from the free space on an uncompressed drive, or if you choose to create a new compressed volume on a host drive that already contains a compressed volume, Stacker displays the Create Drive from Free Space dialog box, as shown in figure 12.8. This dialog box lists the letter of the drive you selected to compress, the uncompressed drive's total space, and the current amount of free space on the uncompressed drive.

For this type of drive, Stacker creates the new compressed drive without compressing any existing files or exchanging any drive letters. Instead, Stacker uses free space on the host drive to create a new compressed drive that is empty. Stacker gives the new compressed drive the next available DOS drive letter, but does not exchange the drive letter with the host drive. In effect, Stacker adds the new compressed drive to your system as a new disk drive.

Stacker assumes you want to make the new compressed drive as large as possible. Stacker therefore uses all the available uncompressed space on the specified drive to create the new compressed drive, leaving only the minimum working space uncompressed. If you need more uncompressed space on that drive, you can change the amount of

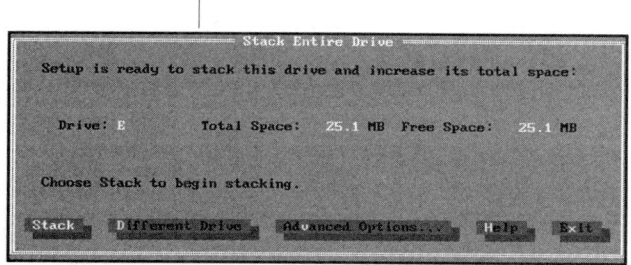

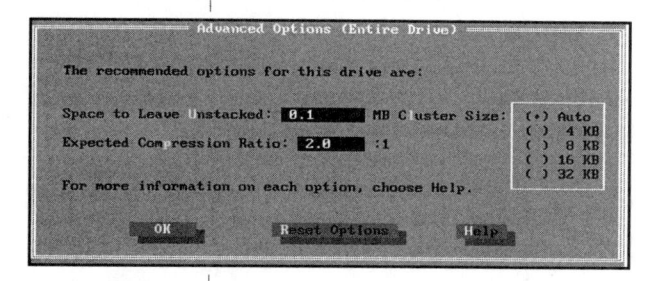

Fig. 12.5, top

The Stack Entire Drive dialog box.

Fig. 12.6, bottom

The Stacker Advanced Options dialog box for compressing an entire drive.

uncompressed space Stacker uses to create the new compressed drive. As you create the compressed drive, you also can control the expected compression ratio and cluster size of the new compressed drive through the Ad**v**anced Options settings. These settings have the same effects as described in the preceding section, "Compressing an Entire Drive."

To finish creating your free space drive, follow these steps:

1. To change the amount of uncompressed space Stacker uses for the new compressed drive, select the Space to **U**se text box, and type the amount of free space you want to use for the new Stacker drive in megabytes (M) and tenths of a megabyte. You can enter any number from 1M up to the total free space available on the uncompressed drive. If you do not want to change the amount of uncompressed space, skip to step 2.
2. Choose Ad**v**anced Options if you want to change the expected compression ratio or choose the cluster size for the new Stacker drive. Stacker displays the Advanced Options (Free Space) dialog box, as shown in figure 12.9. If you do not want to set any advanced options, skip to step 6.
3. To change the expected compression ratio, select the **E**xpected Com**p**ression Ratio text box, and type the expected compression ratio for the new compressed drive. You can type any number from 1.0 to 16.0; use only one decimal place. To leave the expected compression ratio as displayed, skip to step 4.
4. To change the cluster size, select the appropriate radio button in the C**l**uster Size section of the Advanced Options dialog box; otherwise, skip to step 5. Normally, you should leave this setting on Auto.

   If you make a mistake or you want to return to the original settings for any of these options, choose **R**eset Options. Stacker restores the original suggested settings for the Advanced Options.
5. Choose **O**K. Stacker returns to the Create Drive from Free Space dialog box.
6. Choose **S**tack to create the free space drive. Stacker immediately begins to create the new compressed drive.

> **NOTE:**
> To compress a drive other than the one already selected, choose the **D**ifferent Drive command button in the Create Drive from Free Space dialog box. Stacker displays the Select a Drive dialog box. Follow the instructions beginning with step 4 in the section "Compressing Drives by Using the Stacker Toolbox," earlier in this chapter.

> Reducing the free space used by the Stacker drive increases the amount of uncompressed space that remains available on the uncompressed drive and decreases the size of the new compressed drive.

Stacker checks the integrity of the selected hard disk's File Allocation Table (FAT) and then loads the Stacker SDEFRAG utility to optimize the uncompressed drive. Stacker then creates the free space compressed drive. Because the new Stacker drive is created from free space on the uncompressed host drive, no files are added to the new Stacker drive. After Stacker finishes creating and verifying the free space drive, it displays the Stacking Results report, as shown in figure 12.10.

This report lists the space available on the uncompressed drive before and after compression, as well as the space available on the newly compressed drive. In figure 12.10, for example, drive E had 5M free space, and all this free space was used to create the new Stacker drive. Because all the free space was used for the Stacker drive, drive E now has

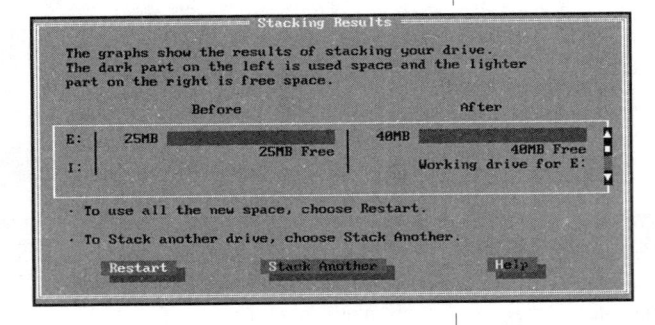

Fig. 12.7

The Stacking Results report for an entire drive.

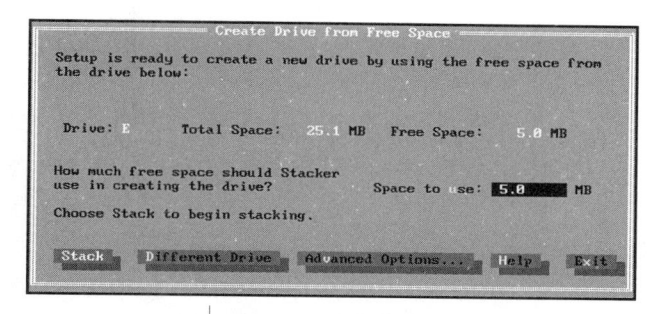

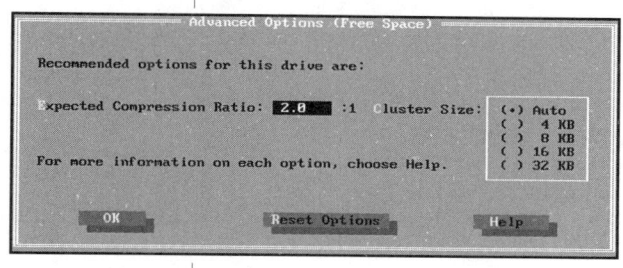

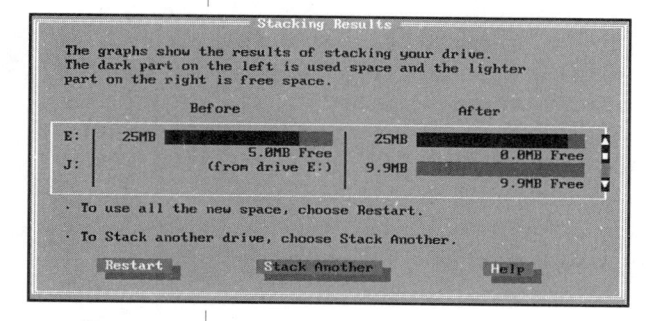

Using the Stacker Utilities   **273**

no free space left. Because the expected compression ratio was 2:1, new drive J has a little less than 10M space available. The new compressed drive is not exactly 10M in size, because approximately 100K remains uncompressed for Stacker's minimum working space.

After you finish viewing the results report, you can choose the **S**tack Another command button at the bottom of the report. Stacker returns to the Select a Drive dialog box. Follow the instructions beginning with step 4 in the section "Compressing Drives by Using the Stacker Toolbox," earlier in this chapter.

Stacker adds a line to the STACKER.INI file for each compressed volume you create on a hard disk. Stacker must restart your computer so that the newly compressed volumes are mounted. To restart your computer, make sure that floppy drive A is empty, and then choose the **R**estart button at the bottom of the Stacking Results report.

Use the STACKER command described in Chapter 11, "Using Stacker," to view information about your newly compressed drive and your system's drive letters.

Fig. 12.8, top
The Create Drive from Free Space dialog box.

Fig. 12.9, middle
The Stacker Advanced Options dialog box for creating a free space drive.

Fig. 12.10, bottom
The Stacking Results report for a free space drive.

Compressing Drives by Using the CREATE Utility

You also can use the Stacker CREATE command and its switches to create a new compressed drive. If you create a compressed drive by using the CREATE command, Stacker creates a new compressed volume file using all the available free disk space on the drive you compress. The CREATE command is most useful for compressing removable media disks or to create Stacker volumes on hard disks or empty partitions. The CREATE command does not compress existing files and add them to the compressed volume. CREATE does not add new hard drive compressed volumes to the STACKER.INI file, as happens if you use the Stacker Toolbox to create compressed volumes.

Use the following syntax when typing the Stacker CREATE command:

CREATE *d:***\STACVOL.***nnn* **/S=***nnn.n* **/R=***n.n*

The \STACVOL file name and the /S= and /R= switches, however, are all optional. You can use the switches in any combination. The *d* represents the letter for the drive on which you want to create the compressed volume. The following command, for example, compresses drive E:

CREATE E:

Stacker uses all available free space on drive E and creates a Stacker compressed volume file named STACVOL.DSK.

The /S= switch enables you to specify the size of the new compressed volume in megabytes. Because the CREATE command normally uses all available free space on the drive you compress, you use the /S= switch to reserve some uncompressed space on the drive. If, for example, your uncompressed drive E has 10M of free space but you need to keep 2M of uncompressed space available while compressing the rest, you use the following command to make Stacker create a compressed volume file using only 8M free space on drive E:

CREATE E: /S=8

The /R= switch enables you to specify the expected compression ratio for the new drive. The following command, for example, compresses all the free space on drive E and gives the new compressed volume an expected compression ratio of 2.2:1.

CREATE E: /R=2.2

Use the /R= switch only if you know that the data you intend to store on the compressed volume will consistently compress at greater or less than the standard expected 2:1 compression ratio.

The first compressed volume file Stacker creates on any disk receives the name STACVOL.DSK. Compressed volume files created on the same uncompressed disk must, obviously, have different file names. Stacker gives the second compressed volume file on a single uncompressed disk the name STACVOL.000. The third compressed volume file created on the same uncompressed disk is given the name STACVOL.001, and so on.

As you create compressed volumes by using the Stacker Toolbox, Stacker automatically chooses the correct STACVOL file name for you, whether the compressed volume file is the first, second, fifth, or tenth compressed volume created on that same hard disk. The Stacker CREATE command, however, is not as sophisticated. Only when you use CREATE to make the first compressed volume on an uncompressed disk does CREATE automatically choose the correct file name. Unless you specify the STACVOL file name, CREATE always tries to create a compressed volume file with the name STACVOL.DSK. If a STACVOL.DSK file already exists on the disk you compress, CREATE displays an error message and refuses to create another compressed volume.

To solve this problem, use the \STACVOL file name option for the CREATE command. If you manually provide the file name, CREATE is able to create multiple compressed volumes on the same hard drive. The following command, for example, creates a new compressed volume on drive E and gives the new compressed volume file the name STACVOL.001:

CREATE E:\STACVOL.001

Changing the Size of a Compressed Drive

Eventually, you may want to change the size of your compressed volumes. If a compressed volume begins to get full and you still have free space on the uncompressed host drive, you may want to increase the size of a compressed volume so that you can store more data on it. On the other hand, you may need more room on the uncompressed host drive and, therefore, may want to make a compressed volume smaller. If, for example, you decide to create or enlarge a Windows permanent swap file—which must be stored on an uncompressed drive—you may need to make more space available on the uncompressed drive by reducing the size of a compressed volume.

In general, you can usually reduce the size of a compressed volume file by about half as much free space as is on the compressed volume—depending on the expected compression ratio. If, for example, a compressed volume has 20M free space and an expected compression ratio of 2:1, you can usually reduce the size of the compressed volume file by about 10M.

To change the size of a compressed volume by using the Stacker Toolbox, follow these steps:

1. Type **STAC** at the DOS prompt and then press Enter to start the Stacker Toolbox. The Stacker Toolbox starts and displays its main menu screen (refer to fig. 12.1). The main menu choices are arranged vertically along the left side of the screen.
2. To change a compressed volume's size, choose Stacker Drive Size in the Configure section of the main menu. Stacker displays a list of your compressed drives (see fig. 12.11).
3. Choose the compressed drive the size of which you want to change. Stacker displays the Stacker Drive Size dialog box, as shown in figure 12.12.
4. Choose Increase Stacker Drive Size to make your compressed volume larger. Increasing the Stacker drive size increases the size of the compressed volume and reduces the space on the uncompressed host drive. If no free space remains on the uncompressed host drive, you cannot increase the size of the Stacker drive. If you choose this option, skip to the last paragraph of step 5.

    Choose More Uncompressed Space Available to make your uncompressed volume larger. Increasing the available space on the uncompressed drive reduces the size of the Stacker compressed volume file, decreasing the available space on the compressed drive. If the compressed drive is full, you cannot make more uncompressed space available.

    If you choose More Uncompressed Space Available, Stacker displays a message saying that it must run the SDEFRAG program to optimize the Stacker drive. The SDEFRAG program defragments the compressed drive so that it can be made larger or smaller.

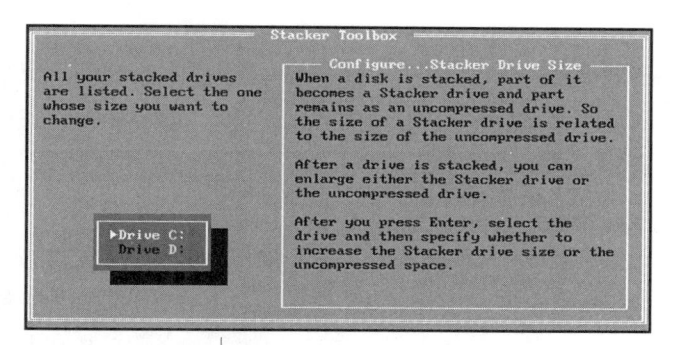

Fig. 12.11

Stacker displays a list of compressed drives.

STOP

If you use the Stacker Toolbox to change the size of a compressed drive, Stacker restarts your computer near the end of the process. If you have a RAM disk, preserve any data on it that you want to keep *before* you begin this procedure. Similarly, any TSR programs you use may have open files or unsaved data in memory. Make sure that all files used by TSR programs are closed and all data saved.

NOTE:

Remember that if you increase the size of a compressed volume, you use free space on its uncompressed host drive. If you make more space available on an uncompressed host drive, you make the compressed volume smaller.

5. Press any key to continue. Stacker SDEFRAG optimizes your compressed volume, displaying various messages as it operates. Depending on how full your compressed drive is and how badly fragmented its files, this step may take a few minutes to an hour or more.

Stacker displays a screen showing the range of acceptable values for the size of either the compressed volume or the uncompressed space, plus a text box for you to enter the new size for the Stacker drive or the new amount of free space for the uncompressed drive, depending on the option you selected.

6. To use the size that Stacker suggests, press Enter. To use a different size, type in the text box the value you want, and press Enter.

Stacker displays a screen showing the new Stacker drive size, the expected compression ratio, and the new amount of uncompressed space on the working host drive. At the bottom of this screen, Stacker also displays a menu of three choices: **P**erform Changes on Stacker Drive, **M**odify Settings, and **E**xit without Changes.

7. Choose **P**erform Changes on Stacker Drive to actually change the size of the compressed drive. Stacker immediately begins making the specified changes to the Stacker volume. Stacker displays a progress chart as it makes the changes and then displays a message that it must restart your computer. Press Enter to restart your computer.

Choose **M**odify Settings to return to the previous screen and select a different size value.

Choose **E**xit without Changes if you decide not to change the size of the compressed volume or uncompressed space at this time. Stacker immediately returns you to the Stacker Toolbox main menu.

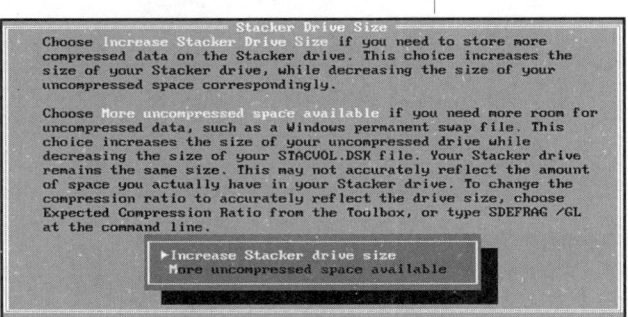

Fig. 12.12

The Stacker Drive Size dialog box enables you to choose whether to make the compressed volume larger or more uncompressed space available.

Removing a Compressed Drive

You may at some point decide that you no longer need a compressed volume. Perhaps you created a compressed volume from free space on a drive and now no longer need it. The best way to remove a compressed drive in Stacker is to *unstack* the drive. Unstacking a compressed drive moves all the files on the compressed volume to the uncompressed volume. Each file and directory from the compressed volume is uncompressed and moved to the uncompressed host drive.

After all the files have been uncompressed and moved to the uncompressed drive, Stacker removes the compressed volume file from the uncompressed disk. Stacker also adds a semicolon (;) to the beginning of each line in STACKER.INI for the compressed

STOP

If you use the Stacker Toolbox to unstack a compressed drive, Stacker restarts your computer near the end of the process. If you have a RAM disk, preserve any data on it that you want to keep *before* you begin this procedure. Similarly, any TSR programs you use may have open files or unsaved data in memory. Make sure that all files used by TSR programs are closed and all data saved.

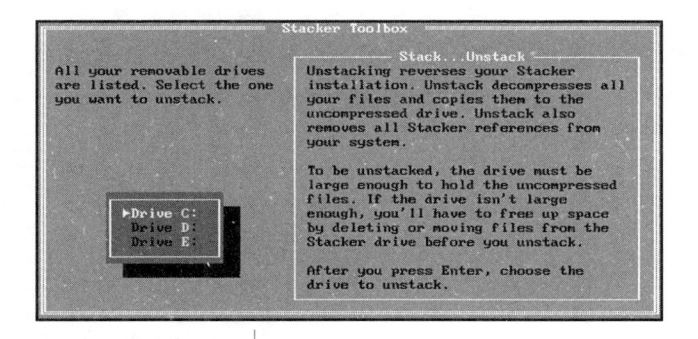

Fig. 12.13

The Stacker Toolbox's list of compressed drives.

You also can unstack a compressed drive by using the UNSTACK command. Type **UNSTACK d:** at the DOS prompt, and press Enter. Substitute the drive letter of the compressed drive you want to unstack for the *d*. After UNSTACK loads into memory, begin with step 4 of these instructions.

volume file you just unstacked. As explained in Chapter 10, a semicolon symbol at the beginning of a line in STACKER.INI indicates that the line is not to be processed.

To use the Stacker Toolbox to unstack a compressed volume, follow these steps:

1. Type **STAC** at the DOS prompt and press Enter to start the Stacker Toolbox. The Stacker Toolbox starts and displays its main menu (refer to fig. 12.1). The main menu choices are arranged vertically along the left side of the screen.

2. To unstack a compressed volume, choose **U**nstack in the Stack section of the menu. Stacker displays a list of compressed drives (see fig. 12.13).

3. Choose the compressed drive you want to unstack. Stacker searches for the compressed volume file, verifies the FAT, checks the directory tree, and then checks the file fragmentation of the compressed volume.

   If the compressed volume is not completely optimized, Stacker displays a message that it must run the SDEFRAG utility to optimize the disk and asks whether you want to continue or exit.

   If your compressed volume is already fully optimized, Stacker displays the screen shown in figure 12.14. If this screen appears, skip to step 5.

4. Choose **C**ontinue to run SDEFRAG to optimize the compressed volume you want to unstack and remove. If you decide not to unstack your compressed drive at this time, choose **E**xit.

   If you choose Continue, Stacker runs SDEFRAG to optimize the compressed volume. SDEFRAG displays various messages as it defragments the compressed volume. After SDEFRAG finishes optimizing, Stacker displays the screen shown in figure 12.14.

   Stacker displays an error message if the uncompressed drive is not large enough to hold all the data from the compressed volume. To unstack the drive, you must delete some files from the compressed volume. Remember to back up the files if you want to keep them, before you delete them. The last line in the error message states how many kilobytes of data you must remove from the compressed volume before you can unstack it. Press Enter to clear the error message and return to the Stacker Toolbox main menu.

5. To continue unstacking the drive, choose Unstack; if you decide not to unstack the drive, choose Exit.

   If you choose Unstack, Stacker again asks for confirmation that you want to unstack and remove the compressed volume.

6. To unstack and remove the drive, choose Yes. Stacker unstacks the drive, displaying a progress chart as it does so. If you decide not to unstack and remove the compressed drive at this time, choose No.

If the drive you unstack is the last compressed drive in your computer system, Stacker asks whether you want to remove Stacker from your system completely.

7. Choose Yes to have Stacker make alterations to your system so that the Stacker device driver no longer loads into memory as your computer starts up. Choose No to leave your system set up so that the Stacker device driver still loads into memory. Stacker displays the screen shown in figure 12.15.

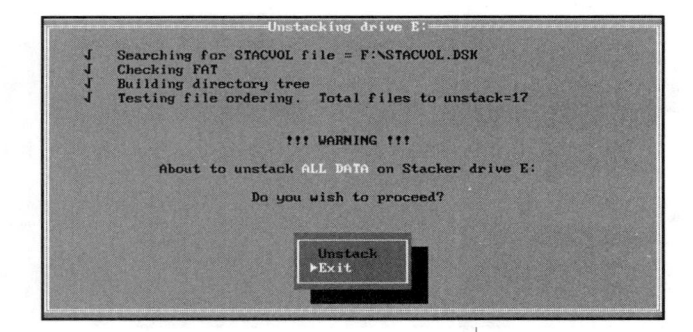

8. Press Enter. Your computer restarts.

As an alternative to unstacking and removing a compressed drive by using the Stacker Toolbox, you can remove a compressed drive by using the Stacker REMOVDRV command. To use REMOVDRV, type the following command at the DOS prompt:

REMOVDRV d:

Substitute the drive letter of the compressed drive you want to remove for *d*. Unlike what occurs when unstacking a compressed drive, however, REMOVDRV removes the specified compressed drive and *all files on it*. If you want to keep any files on the compressed drive, you must back them up before using REMOVDRV.

After you finish unstacking and removing a compressed drive, you may want to perform some additional housekeeping. After Stacker finishes unstacking a compressed drive, it deletes the compressed volume file (REMOVDRV also deletes the compressed volume file). Another file, however, is left behind. As discussed in Chapter 9, "Installing Stacker," Stacker uses a file named STACKER.LOG (located in the root directory of the host drive) to keep track of error information about your compressed volumes. You may want to keep the STACKER.LOG file, or you may want to delete it.

The STACKER.LOG file has a Read-Only file attribute; you must remove the file attribute before you can delete the file. Use the following command to remove the Read-Only file attribute from the STACKER.LOG file:

ATTRIB –R STACKER.LOG

You can now delete the STACKER.LOG file.

If you unstacked the last compressed drive on your system and you answered Yes to have Stacker removed from your system, Stacker deletes the DBLSPACE.BIN file in the root directory of your boot disk and changes the statements in your CONFIG.SYS and AUTOEXEC.BAT files that refer to Stacker commands into comments; these lines are not actually deleted. Stacker also leaves behind the STACKER.INI file. You may want to delete these unneeded lines from your CONFIG.SYS and AUTOEXEC.BAT files. If you want to delete the STACKER.INI file as well, you need to remember that this file is located in the root drive of your boot disk and has Hidden, System, and Read-Only file attributes. You must remove these file attributes before you can delete the STACKER.INI file.

Fig. 12.14

Stacker asks for confirmation before unstacking and removing a compressed volume.

NOTE:

If you unstack a drive of which the uncompressed host drive contains a Windows permanent swap file, you may receive an error message the next time you start Windows, telling you the permanent swap file is corrupted. Follow the procedures in Chapter 13, "Troubleshooting Stacker," for information on dealing with this problem.

To remove the STACKER.INI file attributes, use the following command:
ATTRIB –R –S –H STACKER.INI

The ATTRIB command removes the file attributes from the STACKER.INI file. You can now delete the STACKER.INI file.

Defragmenting a Compressed Drive

Occasionally, you must use the Stacker defragmentation utility, SDEFRAG, to defragment your compressed drives. (Refer to Chapter 11 for an explanation of file fragmentation.)

Use SDEFRAG to speed up access to your compressed drive, to apply the highest level of compression to all the data on the compressed volume—regardless of the Stacker Tuner setting—and to ensure that the greatest possible amount of free space is available on the compressed drive. Like regular defragmentation programs for uncompressed disks, SDEFRAG arranges disk clusters so that all the clusters for all the files are contiguous. SDEFRAG is particularly useful if you intend to change the size of a compressed volume. Using SDEFRAG to move all the file fragments so that they are contiguous enables you to make the compressed volume as small as possible.

As you use the Stacker Toolbox to carry out various tasks (such as changing the size of a compressed volume or changing the expected compression ratio), the Stacker Toolbox automatically runs SDEFRAG whenever necessary. In fact, several Stacker Toolbox tasks are actually carried out by SDEFRAG.

The best and easiest way to use SDEFRAG is from the Stacker Toolbox or from the menus in the Stackometer Windows utility. Whether you start the defragmentation and optimization process through Stackometer or Stacker Toolbox, SDEFRAG offers you the following three methods of optimization:

- **Q**uick Optimize makes all the clusters for each file contiguous. Although all the clusters in each file are contiguous after a quick optimize, the free space on the compressed volume may still be in several different pieces. This optimization method is fastest and speeds up access to files on the compressed volume moderately.
- **F**ull Optimize makes all the clusters for each file contiguous and gathers all the files at the beginning of the compressed volume. All the free space on the compressed volume is in one contiguous area at the end of the compressed volume. This optimization method takes longer than **Q**uick Optimize, but increases the speed of access to your compressed volume file more than does **Q**uick Optimize.
- **R**estack (or Full Optimize and **R**estack in the Stackometer) performs a full optimization and recompresses every file on the disk at the maximum compression level, regardless of the Stacker Tuner settings. Restacking a drive ensures that all files on the disk are contiguous and as small as possible. Restacking a drive also ensures you the greatest possible amount of free space available on the compressed volume. You should **R**estack any compressed volumes you convert from DoubleSpace as soon as possible.

NOTE:
If you recently converted your compressed drives to Stacker from DoubleSpace, perform a full restack optimization on each compressed drive as soon as possible. Perform the restack optimization to fully complete the conversion from DoubleSpace and to ensure that your data is as safe and fully compressed as is possible with Stacker.

If you use the DOS DEFRAG utility on a compressed drive while Stacker DOS disk command redirection is installed, Stacker SDEFRAG runs instead of DOS DEFRAG on Stacker drives. Refer to your DOS documentation for more information about DEFRAG. You also can start the Stacker SDEFRAG utility directly from the DOS prompt by typing **SDEFRAG d:** and pressing Enter. Substitute the drive letter of the drive you want to optimize for *d*. For a list of the command switches you can use with SDEFRAG, type **SDEFRAG /?** at the DOS prompt, and press Enter.

Defragment a Drive by Using the Stacker Toolbox

To defragment a compressed volume by using the Stacker Toolbox, follow these steps:

1. Type **STAC** at the DOS prompt and press Enter to start the Stacker Toolbox. The Stacker Toolbox starts and displays the main menu (refer to fig. 12.1). The main menu choices are arranged vertically along the left side of the screen.
2. To optimize and defragment a compressed drive, choose Stacker **O**ptimizer in the Optimize section of the main menu. Stacker displays a list of compressed drives.
3. Select the compressed drive you want to optimize. Stacker displays the screen shown in figure 12.16, asking you to choose the optimization method to use.
4. Select the optimization method you want: **Q**uick Optimize, **F**ull Optimize, or **R**estack. (These options are described in the preceding section.)

    If you choose **Q**uick Optimize or **F**ull Optimize, Stacker runs the SDEFRAG program, which checks the integrity of your compressed volume's FAT and clusters and then analyzes the compressed volume. After SDEFRAG completes the analysis, it displays a report listing the current drive, the current fragmentation level as a percentage, and a recommendation as to whether you should continue with the optimization or exit.

    If you choose **R**estack, SDEFRAG does not show this report; instead, SDEFRAG continues immediately with the optimization of the compressed volume, displaying a map of the disk's clusters as it defragments them. Skip to step 6.

5. To continue with the optimization, choose **C**ontinue. SDEFRAG begins optimizing your compressed volume and displays a map of the clusters on your disk as it performs the actual defragmentation process.

    If you decide not to optimize your disk at this time, choose **E**xit. Stacker returns to the Toolbox main menu.

    After Stacker finishes optimizing your compressed drive, it displays an on-screen message indicating that it is finished.

6. Press Enter to continue. If you chose **Q**uick Optimize or **F**ull Optimize, Stacker returns you to the Toolbox main menu. If you chose **R**estack, Stacker displays a report indicating how much additional free space was obtained on the drive by compressing the files to the maximum of which Stacker is capable. After you finish viewing the report, press any key to continue.

You have completed optimizing and defragmenting your compressed volume.

> **NOTE:**
> Defragmenting a compressed volume may take from several minutes to several hours, depending on how many files are on the drive and how badly they are fragmented. Stacker does not give an estimate of how long defragmentation may take. You may want to use SDEFRAG at the end of a work day or on a Friday evening so that you are not inconvenienced by a long defragmentation. To interrupt SDEFRAG to use your computer for some other task, press Esc or F10.

> **NOTE:**
> If you use **R**estack on a compressed volume you just converted from DoubleSpace, Stacker restarts your computer.

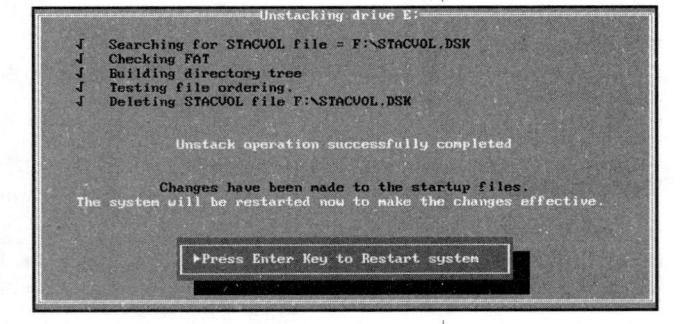

Fig. 12.15

Stacker is finished unstacking and removing the compressed volume.

Using the Stacker Utilities **281**

> **NOTE:**
> If you installed Stacker from Windows, the Stacker program group has been set up for you. If you installed Windows after you installed Stacker, or if you installed Stacker from DOS, you must manually run the SGROUP utility program described in Chapter 10, "Configuring and Optimizing Stacker."

> **NOTE:**
> If you choose Full Optimize and **R**estack for a compressed volume you just converted from DoubleSpace, Stacker restarts your computer.

Defragment a Drive by Using the Stackometer

To defragment or optimize a compressed volume by using the Stackometer, follow these steps:

1. To start the Windows Stackometer, double-click the Stackometer program icon in the Stacker program group.
2. Change the Stackometer current drive to the drive you want to optimize. Refer to the section "Using the Stackometer Information Display," in Chapter 11, for instructions on changing the Stackometer current drive.
3. Access the Stackometer **T**ools menu, as shown in figure 12.17.
4. Select the optimization method you want to use for the current drive: **Q**uick Optimize, **F**ull Optimize, or Full Optimize and **R**estack. The effect of each of these options is described in the section "Defragmenting a Compressed Drive," earlier in this chapter.

   Stackometer displays the Exit Windows dialog box. Stacker must leave Windows to run the SDEFRAG program and optimize the compressed volume.
5. Choose **O**K to leave Windows and perform the optimization. Stacker tells Windows to shut down. Windows, in turn, shuts down any running programs; if any have unsaved data, you are asked whether you want to save the data before exiting. After Windows exits, the SDEFRAG program begins to run.

   Choose **C**ancel if you decide not to optimize the compressed disk now. Stacker returns to the Stackometer main display.

   From this point on, optimizing your disk by using the Stackometer is the same as if using the Stacker Toolbox. Go to step 5 in the preceding section, "Defragment a Drive by Using the Stacker Toolbox," to finish optimizing the compressed drive. After SDEFRAG finishes, Stacker restarts Windows for you.

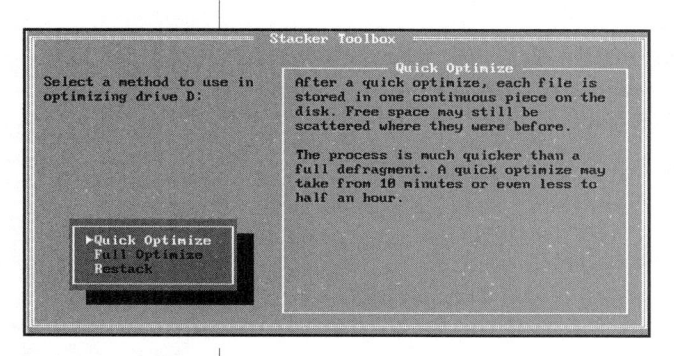

Fig. 12.16

Stacker asks you to choose the optimization method.

Checking the Integrity of a Compressed Drive

Periodically checking the logical integrity of your disk drives is a good idea, whether the drives are compressed or not. Checking the logical integrity of a drive ensures that all clusters on the drive are correctly allocated and accounted for and that all file chains on the disk are intact and correctly linked. Just as you use the DOS CHKDSK command to check the integrity of an uncompressed disk, you use the Stacker CHECK utility to test the integrity of your Stacker drives.

In some operations (such as changing the size of a compressed drive), using the CHKDSK and CHECK utilities before you perform the operation is an important step. Doing so ensures that no problems exist on the compressed drive—or uncovers any that do exist. If problems do exist on the compressed drive, you must correct them as soon as possible; otherwise, you risk losing data.

Using the DOS CHKDSK and the Stacker CHECK utilities to solve specific problems is discussed in Chapter 13, "Troubleshooting Stacker." This section describes how to operate the CHKDSK and CHECK utility and how to use the CHECK utility so that it attempts to correct any problems it finds.

Stacker's CHECK utility is designed to identify and repair problems in compressed volumes. You must use the DOS CHKDSK utility, however, to repair problems at the DOS level of organization on your compressed volumes. The DOS CHKDSK utility is designed to identify two different types of problems: *lost clusters* and *cross-linked files*. Repairing lost clusters is explained in the following section, which also provides instructions for starting the DOS CHKDSK and Stacker CHECK utilities. Repairing cross-linked files is described in Chapter 13.

Using Stacker CHECK from the DOS Prompt

The Stacker CHECK utility has several command line switches. Each command line switch is described in this section, although this discussion emphasizes those command line switches used for correcting problems with your compressed volumes.

Use the following syntax to instruct Stacker CHECK to examine a compressed volume and correct any errors it finds:

CHECK *d*: /F

The /F switch is optional; it causes CHECK to fix and report any errors it finds on the compressed volume. Without the /F switch, CHECK reports any errors it finds, but does not repair the errors. In the syntax example in the preceding example, *d* represents the drive letter of the compressed volume you want to check. If you do not specify the drive letter, CHECK examines the current disk drive.

If Stacker finds any errors on the compressed volume it checks, it displays a report that appears similar to the following example. The report lists the number of lost clusters, cross-linked files, or other problems that CHECK found.

```
CHECK - 3.10, Copyright 1990-93 Stac Electronics, Carlsbad, CA

Volume in drive I is STACVOL_000

Invalid cluster in file detected (Run CHKDSK I:)

Errors detected in file I:\FRAGCHKN\X1.

Error Summary:

        1 Files with errors
CHECK has found lost sectors which may be reclaimed.

Run CHECK /F I: to repair errors
```

Whenever you use DOS CHKDSK while the Stacker DOS disk command redirection is loaded in memory, the Stacker CHECK utility runs automatically as soon as CHKDSK is done.

Fig. 12.17

The Stackometer **T**ools menu.

Keep in mind that Stacker CHECK may detect problems on a compressed drive that are not detected by DOS CHKDSK. You always want to use *both* DOS CHKDSK and the Stacker CHECK utilities on your compressed drives. Just because DOS CHKDSK and Stacker CHECK uncover no problems on the compressed volume, however, do not assume that no problems exist on the uncompressed host drive. Use DOS CHKDSK on the uncompressed host drive to check its integrity, too.

```
CHECK has detected errors which should be repaired with CHKDSK or a disk
repair utility.

Stacker Drive Compression Ratio = 4.7:1
Projected Bytes Free            = 3,391,488
```

In this report, CHECK found errors in the DOS level of organization and tells you that the errors should be corrected by using the DOS CHKDSK utility.

To have CHECK repair any problems it finds as it checks your compressed volume, include the /F switch. To check the integrity of compressed volume D and to have CHECK fix any lost clusters it finds, for example, use the following command:

CHECK D: /F

If you use the /F switch, Stacker CHECK displays the same report as it does without the /F switch, but asks whether you want to repair the problems it finds. Figure 12.18 shows a Stacker CHECK report for drive I after the /F switch is specified and errors found.

To have CHECK repair errors, you must type the entire word **yes** in response to the question Repair drive?. CHECK interprets anything else, even just the letter **y**, as **no**. If you type **yes**, CHECK attempts to repair the compressed volume. Some errors cannot be corrected, however, without deleting the files involved. Depending on the specific type of error, CHECK may ask whether you want CHECK to delete damaged files. If you do not have recent backup copies of the damaged files, answer **no** to this question.

If you have backups or otherwise want CHECK to delete damaged files, type **yes** in response to the question. If you answer **no**, CHECK does not delete the damaged files. Instead, CHECK displays on-screen a recommendation that you copy the damaged files to another disk and then use the CHECK utility with the /F switch on the same drive. The second time you run CHECK with the /F switch, answer **yes** to have CHECK delete the damaged files.

Finally, CHECK asks whether you want to perform a surface scan of the compressed volume you are checking. Usually, you should answer **yes** to this question. As CHECK performs the surface scan of the compressed volume, it checks the entire physical surface of the physical disk containing the compressed volume file. The surface scan ensures that no physical defects exist on the disk and that you can read and write data throughout the entire compressed volume, including both used and unused areas.

Another CHECK switch—/WP—also is important in detecting and repairing damaged compressed volumes. The /WP switch causes CHECK to seek out all mounted, write-protected Stacker drives and attempt to repair them

As Stacker mounts compressed volumes during your computer's start-up, it automatically performs basic checks on each compressed volume it mounts. In some circumstances—such as if your computer is rebooted while SDEFRAG is running—Stacker may determine that possible damage has occurred to a compressed volume. To prevent further damage to the compressed volume, Stacker marks the compressed volume with a write-protect attribute as it mounts the volume. If a Stacker compressed volume has a write-protect attribute, you can access all the data on the drive, but you cannot change existing data or write new data to the compressed drive. The Stacker write-protect causes DOS

> **NOTE:**
> Some errors that CHECK can detect must be repaired by using DOS CHKDSK or repaired manually by you. If your CHECK report includes the following line, you also should run the CHKDSK utility on the compressed drive to fix additional errors:
>
> ```
> CHECK has
> detected errors
> which should be
> repaired with
> CHKDSK or a
> disk repair
> utility.
> ```

to treat the write-protected Stacker drive similar to how it treats a write-protected removable disk.

The following example shows how to use the /WP switch with the CHECK command so that CHECK seeks out and attempts to repair all mounted, write-protected Stacker drives:

CHECK /WP

This command causes Stacker to check each mounted Stacker volume. If the volume is write-protected, Stacker attempts to repair it. This command is automatically added to the beginning of your AUTOEXEC.BAT file when you install Stacker so that CHECK tests and repairs any write-protected drives whenever you start or restart your computer.

The following additional CHECK command switches do not directly relate to the identifying or repairing of problems in your compressed volumes but affect such factors as the amount of detail shown in the CHECK reports, whether individual file names are listed when your compressed volume is checked, and so on:

/B This command switch causes CHECK to run in "batch mode." Use this switch if you write a DOS batch file that uses the CHECK utility. If this switch is used, CHECK does not pause to ask questions as long as no errors are found.

/D This command switch increases the amount of detail that the CHECK utility displays in its reports.

/V This command switch simply tells CHECK to list each file as it is checked.

> **NOTE:**
> CHECK asks whether you want to perform a surface scan only if you use the /F switch. If you use the /F switch, CHECK always asks if you want to perform a surface scan, whether or not CHECK detects any errors in the logical structure of the compressed volume.

```
C:\>CHECK I: /F
CHECK - 3.10, (c) Copyright 1990-93 Stac Electronics, Carlsbad, CA
Volume in drive I is STACVOL_000
Invalid cluster in file detected (Run CHKDSK I:)
Errors detected in file I:\FRAGCHKN\X1.
Error Summary:
            1 Files with errors
CHECK has found lost sectors which may be reclaimed.
Repair drive I? ["yes"/no]:
```

Fig. 12.18

If the /F switch is added, CHECK asks to repair the errors it finds.

Using Stacker CHECK from the Stacker Toolbox

You also can check the integrity of your compressed drives from the Stacker Toolbox. If you use the Stacker Toolbox, you do not get to choose which command switches to use with the CHECK command; the Stacker Toolbox always starts the CHECK utility with the /F switch.

To use the Stacker Toolbox to check the integrity of your compressed drives, follow these steps:

1. Start the Stacker Toolbox by typing **STAC** at the DOS prompt and pressing Enter. The Stacker Toolbox starts and displays its main menu (refer to fig. 12.1). The main menu choices are arranged vertically along the left side of the screen.
2. To check a compressed disk, choose Drive **I**ntegrity in the Check section of the main menu. Stacker displays a list of your compressed drives.
3. Choose the compressed drive you want to check. Stacker immediately starts the CHECK utility.

CHECK runs and behaves as described in the preceding section, "Using Stacker CHECK from the DOS Prompt." Refer to that discussion for information on correcting any errors that CHECK may detect.

After CHECK finishes checking and repairing the compressed volume you selected, it displays the following message:

```
<press any key to continue.>
```

4. Press any key. Stacker returns to the Stacker Toolbox main menu.

You have completed checking your compressed volume.

Summary

In this chapter, you learned why and how to use the Stacker utilities to perform a variety of tasks. You learned how to add compressed drives to your system and how to change the size of a compressed drive. The chapter also explained how to defragment and restack a compressed drive. Most important, this chapter showed you how to use the Stacker CHECK utility to test the integrity of your Stacker compressed drives.

The following chapter deals with how to solve specific problems you can encounter

CHAPTER 13

Troubleshooting Stacker

In this chapter, you learn the causes of and solutions for many problems Stacker users encounter. The chapter begins with a discussion of measures you can take to prevent common errors and then explores some of the most common problems you may encounter—as well as some that are more rare.

Preventing Problems

In life, the best way to solve a problem is to prevent it. The same rule is true of Stacker. You can take several precautionary steps to circumvent most common problems. A few of these steps can even prevent severe data loss or corruption of your compressed volume files.

Memory Manager and Upper Memory Conflicts

Conflict with device drivers and programs in upper memory can cause a variety of problems, from relatively harmless disk read errors to corrupted data files—and even a corrupted compressed volume file. By giving up memory needed only for loading, or by taking over more memory for data, device drivers and TSR programs often change their size. Thus DOS cannot always tell whether a program or device driver can fit into upper memory. Occasionally, programs in upper memory inadvertently use memory locations that overlap. If overlap occurs, each program can corrupt the other's data or program instructions.

Corrupted memory data results in corrupted data on your disk files. If the corrupted memory data is part of the disk's File Allocation Table, serious data loss can result. If overlap results in corrupted program instructions, your computer can stop operating or may operate erratically, requiring you to restart it. Restarting your computer while programs run often results in lost clusters on your disk. Memory manager programs usually provide command line switches that enable you to expressly include or exclude areas of upper memory. If you include an area of memory already in use by a hardware device, any program or data the memory manager places in that memory area also is likely to become corrupted.

To prevent programs from conflicting with one another or from being corrupted by incorrect inclusions with your memory manager, follow these guidelines:

- *Update your memory manager configuration whenever your system changes.* Whenever you install a new device driver or a new piece of hardware, run your memory manager's configuration program again. By rerunning its configuration program—such as DOS MEMMAKER or QEMM's Optimize—you ensure that your memory manager is adjusted to the system revisions. If you add a new video board to your computer, for example, and you use as your memory managers HIMEM.SYS and EMM386 (supplied with DOS), you want to run the DOS MEMMAKER utility again. Consult the documentation supplied with your memory management software for information about its configuration program and how to use it.
- *Use conservative settings.* The more aggressively you configure your memory manager to use all the nooks and crannies of upper memory, the more likely you are to inadvertently create a situation where programs using upper memory interfere with each other or with your computer's hardware. If you use the DOS MEMMAKER utility, for example, do not use its aggressive scanning at first. (Refer to your DOS documentation for more information about MEMMAKER.) If you use EMM386 and suspect problems caused by memory conflicts, do not use the HIGHSCAN switch. (Refer to your DOS documentation for more information on EMM386.)
- *Add only one device driver or program to upper memory at a time.* Load a single device driver into upper memory and then use your system for a while to make sure that everything operates correctly. If you do not experience any difficulties, add the next device driver or program to upper memory, and so on.

For more details on configuring your specific memory manager, refer to your DOS documentation and the documentation provided with your memory management program.

STACKS Statement in CONFIG.SYS

DOS provides a command to use in your CONFIG.SYS file to tell DOS how much memory to allocate for stacks. (A *stack* is an area of memory DOS or another program uses as a temporary working area.) The STACKS= command in CONFIG.SYS tells DOS how many stacks to create and the number of bytes to allot each stack. DOS and other programs need stacks for use as temporary working areas and require them all the time, continuously. DOS, for example, requires stack space to process every key you press at the keyboard.

If DOS or a device driver attached to DOS needs a stack to perform a requested service, DOS usually exchanges the current stack for a new stack, leaving the contents of the original stack unaffected. After DOS or the device driver has completed the requested service, DOS restores the original stack that was in use at the time the service request was performed. Whatever program was running before the service request now continues with its original stack, as if it had never been interrupted. Because specific services are often performed by different layers of software (refer to Chapter 1), several different parts of DOS and/or a device driver may need space on a stack at the same time.

The STACKS command statement in the CONFIG.SYS file usually is similar to that shown in the following line, although specific numbers may differ:

```
STACKS=9,256
```

Because the number and size of the stacks you allocate affects how much memory DOS uses, some computers are configured to include the following statement in the CONFIG.SYS file:

```
STACKS=0,0
```

This statement tells DOS not to reserve any memory for stacks. With the number and size of the stacks set to zero, DOS does not exchange stacks whenever a new working space is needed. Instead, DOS permits the service that needs the working space to use the current stack.

If all the service requests in your computer use the same working stack, however, the stack may grow too large and the information in the stack may overwrite or corrupt other information in memory. If the information that is overwritten or corrupted is the disk's File Allocation Table or is other data waiting to be written to the disk, a damaged file or a corrupted compressed volume can result. To avoid this problem, examine your CONFIG.SYS file. If the file includes a STACKS=0,0 command, remove it. You can either replace STACKS=0,0 with the standard STACKS=9,256 or simply delete it, leaving no STACKS= command at all in the file. Refer to your DOS documentation for more information on CONFIG.SYS and the STACKS command.

Write-Delay Disk Cache

A disk cache program with a write-delay cache may cause some of the greatest problems with Stacker. Many difficulties users experience with corrupted data or corrupted compressed volume files are traceable to a write-delay cache program. You can learn more about disk cache programs in Chapter 1, "Understanding and Using Disk Compression," and Chapter 10, "Configuring and Optimizing Stacker." As described in these chapters, a write-delay cache involves holding some disk data in memory before physically writing it to the disk to speed up your computer's disk operations. Stacker is compatible with a number of disk cache programs, many of which use a write-delay cache.

Some specific problems may occur if you use write-delay cache programs: If your computer experiences a power failure, if you turn the computer off, or if the computer is restarted by using its Reset switch, for example, any data in the cache that has not been written to the disk is lost. The result may be lost clusters, lost or damaged files, or a corrupted compressed volume file.

Among the first things novice users learn is that turning the computer off while the cursor is at the DOS prompt is safe. This statement usually is true—but *not* if a write-delay cache is in use. Unwritten data still can be in the cache, even if the DOS prompt is visible. Although most write-delay caches write the data to disk after a certain period of inactivity—usually a few seconds—a vulnerable period still exists after the DOS prompt is visible but before data is written to the disk. You may think turning off the computer is safe when, in fact, turning off the computer results in data loss.

To avoid problems caused by cache programs that use a write-delay cache, you can adopt one of the following three approaches:

- *Disable the write-delay cache.* This approach is the most highly recommended. Disable write-delay caching for the host drives of your compressed volumes, because your compressed volumes are more likely to be severely affected by a write-delay cache problem. If you use SMARTDRV, follow the instructions in Chapter 10, "Configuring and Optimizing Stacker," for disabling write delay caching. Read caching remains active even if write caching is disabled, so you still obtain a speed benefit by using the cache program.
- *Clear the cache buffers before turning the computer off.* Most cache programs that use write-delay caches provide a command line switch that forces the cache program to write to disk any data currently held in memory. The SMARTDRV disk cache provided with DOS 6, for example, uses the following command and switch to clear the write-delay cache:

    SMARTDRV /C

    After you clear the cache, you can safely turn off the computer. Refer to the documentation for your specific cache program to learn how to clear the write-delay cache.
- *Wait before turning off your computer.* Make sure that you wait at the DOS prompt a couple minutes before turning off your computer. Waiting gives the cache program time to write data to the disk. Most write-delay cache programs clear the write cache after a period of inactivity.

Other Precautions

In general, never use software that rearranges data in a compressed volume unless the software is compatible with Stacker. This prohibition includes almost all disk repair and optimization utilities such as Norton Disk Doctor and Central Point PC Tools. Check with your vendor or the publisher of your utility software to determine whether your utilities are compatible with Stacker.

In particular, never use the SETVER program to enable a disk or any other system utility that reports that you are using an incorrect DOS version. Refer to your DOS documentation for more information on the SETVER program. Passive disk utilities, such as surface scan utilities, are safe to use, however, because they read data from the disk and do not change or move data.

Solving Drive Letter Problems

You occasionally experience difficulty with some drive letters Stacker assigns. Drive letter difficulties are most likely to occur immediately after you install Stacker or after you add additional disk drives to your computer system.

For the cache-clearing technique to be successful, you must always clear the write-delay cache yourself or clear it through a DOS batch file. If you forget and turn your computer off before the write-delay cache writes to the disk, you can lose data.

If you load Windows, the DOS Shell, or another shell program from your AUTOEXEC.BAT file, add the SMARTDRV /C command to AUTOEXEC.BAT. The command appears after the line that starts Windows or the shell program. If the last line in your AUTOEXEC.BAT starts Windows, for example, add the SMARTDRV /C command to the next line, as in the following example:

```
WIN
SMARTDRV /C
```

With this line in your AUTOEXEC.BAT file, the SMARTDRV write-delay cache automatically clears after you exit Windows or your shell program. You now can turn your computer off right away.

Local Drive Letter Problems

If you use a RAM disk or a disk drive that requires a device driver loaded in CONFIG.SYS, you may notice that your drives are assigned unusual drive letters. If so, check your CONFIG.SYS file for a line that refers to STACHIGH.SYS. If you find such a line, make sure that it follows those of any other device drivers that make disk drives available to DOS. STACHIGH.SYS and using RAM disks with Stacker are described in Chapter 10, "Configuring and Optimizing Stacker."

If the STACHIGH.SYS line in CONFIG.SYS already comes after those of all other device drivers that make disk drives available to DOS, you may want to change the STACKER.INI file to alter how Stacker assigns drive letters. Editing STACKER.INI also is described in Chapter 10.

Network Drive Letter Problems

To resolve problems with network drive letters, you can try the following solutions:

- *Change the network drive letter.* If possible, change the drive letter you use for your network drive.
- *Change how Stacker assigns drive letters.* If changing your network drive letter is inconvenient, you can edit the STACKER.INI file to change the drive letters Stacker uses. Editing STACKER.INI is described in Chapter 10, "Configuring and Optimizing Stacker." You may be able to make the usual network drive letter, F, available by using the /BD= command in STACKER.INI. This command shifts upward the drive letters Stacker uses. Shifting the drive letters upward makes the lower drive letters available to DOS. You also can use the /SW command in STACKER.INI to exchange drive letters on your system. Use this command to exchange a network drive letter with another drive letter, resulting in a more convenient configuration.

Solving Windows Swap File Problems

If you use Windows, you already know that a swap file enables Windows to work much faster. (Programs use a *swap file* on a hard disk to store data from the computer's memory. Programs access data in the swap file as if the swap file is actually part of the computer's memory.) Windows enables you to set up two different types of swap files, but you can use only one type at a time. You can configure Windows to use either a temporary swap file or a permanent swap file.

The *temporary swap file* uses regular DOS file services. You can put a temporary swap file on any disk, whether compressed or not. Windows performs better if you put your temporary swap file on an uncompressed disk, because data in a temporary swap file does not compress well and the compression time can slow down Windows. Although temporary Windows swap files pose no problems for your Stacker compressed drives, the Windows *permanent swap file* does not function correctly if you install it on a compressed drive. The permanent swap file does not use DOS disk services to manage the

STOP

Edit the STACKER.INI file very carefully. If you make a mistake while altering STACKER.INI, you can make your compressed volumes inaccessible.

swap file. For maximum speed, Windows instead uses BIOS services to access the permanent swap file or directly accesses the disk hardware itself. Because Windows bypasses DOS to access its permanent swap file, Windows also bypasses the Stacker device driver to access the permanent swap file. The Windows permanent swap file is therefore incompatible with a compressed drive, and so you must place this file on an uncompressed drive.

You need not worry about problems with the Windows permanent swap file when you install Stacker. If Windows is already installed on your computer before you add Stacker, and you use a permanent swap file, Stacker automatically moves the permanent swap file to an uncompressed drive. Stacker also changes the Windows configuration information so that Windows uses the new uncompressed drive letter to search for the permanent swap file. If you install Windows after you install Stacker, however, or you later change your swap file configuration, you may inadvertently install the permanent swap file on a compressed volume. If so, the next time you start Windows, a message appears indicating that the permanent swap file is corrupted.

Every time Stacker loads into memory, it checks your Windows configuration files and updates them if you have made changes in your drive letter assignments. If you made radical changes in the assignment of your drive letters, however, Stacker cannot locate all the Windows files and may display error messages saying so. The /W command in the STACKER.INI file controls whether or not Stacker searches for the Windows configuration files as it loads into memory and also controls which directories Stacker searches. If you make changes in your system, and the /W command is in your STACKER.INI file, Stacker may not update the Windows configuration files. You receive Windows error messages saying that the permanent swap file is corrupted or cannot be found. The /W command and its effects are described in Chapter 10, "Configuring and Optimizing Stacker."

If Windows cannot find the temporary or permanent swap file, the Stacker drive letter assignments for your uncompressed host drives have probably changed. This change usually occurs after you edit the STACKER.INI file to change Stacker's drive letter assignments or after adding another disk drive to your computer. To correct this problem, follow these steps:

1. After Windows displays the message that it cannot open the swap file, press any key to continue. Windows finishes loading.
2. After Windows loads, immediately exit from Windows.
3. Use the STACKER command described in Chapter 11, "Using Stacker," to determine which drive letters represent uncompressed drives. Notice which uncompressed drive has enough room for your temporary or permanent swap file.
4. Restart Windows. You may see the message that Windows cannot open the swap file again. Press any key to continue; Windows should finish loading.
5. After Windows is loaded, use the Control Panel to change the swap file location to match the drive letter you determined in Step 3. Refer to your Windows documentation for information on using the Windows Control Panel and setting Virtual Memory options.

NOTE:

If you use Windows with a permanent or temporary swap file, you may receive an error message from either Stacker or Windows after you swap additional drive letters or add the /BD= command to STACKER.INI. Stacker may report that it cannot locate the Windows permanent swap file or the file Windows uses to store the location of the permanent swap file. Windows may report that it cannot open the swap file or that the permanent swap file is corrupted. These messages simply mean that the disk drive on which Windows was configured to use a swap file now has a different drive letter. Ignore the Stacker error messages. If necessary, follow the procedures in this section. Then use the Windows control panel to change the virtual memory settings to re-establish the swap file, assigning it the correct drive letter. Refer to your Windows documentation for information on using the Windows control panel. How to obtain information about the Stacker drive letters is described in Chapter 11, "Using Stacker."

If Windows reports that your permanent swap file is corrupted, you probably inadvertently configured Windows to put a permanent swap file on a compressed volume. To correct the problem, follow these steps:

1. After Windows displays the message that the permanent swap file is corrupted and asks whether you want to delete the permanent swap file, press **Y** to answer **Y**es. Windows should finish loading into memory.
2. After Windows finishes loading, exit immediately from Windows.
3. Use the STACKER command described in Chapter 11, "Using Stacker," to determine which drive letters represent uncompressed drives. Notice which uncompressed drive has enough room for your temporary or permanent swap file.
4. Restart Windows. The message that the permanent swap file is corrupted may appear again. Press **Y** to answer **Y**es to delete the permanent swap file. Windows should finish loading into memory.
5. After Windows is loaded, use the Windows Control Panel to change the permanent swap file location.
6. After Windows asks if you want the corrupted permanent swap file set to zero length, press **Y** to answer **Y**es.

    If your corrupted permanent swap file results from a change in Stacker drive letters, Windows may report that it has found a permanent swap file not created by your Windows installation.
7. After Windows asks if this permanent swap file should be deleted, answer **Y**es.
8. Set the permanent swap file location to the uncompressed drive letter you determined in Step 3. Refer to your Windows documentation for information on using the Windows Control Panel and setting Virtual Memory options.

Examining Lost Clusters

A *lost cluster*, or *lost allocation unit*, is any disk cluster marked as being in use but not actually part of a file chain legitimately connected to an entry in your disk's file directory. Lost clusters usually do not cause problems. They do, however, occupy disk space because the cluster is marked as being in use and is not available to accept new data. Using the DOS CHKDSK and Stacker CHECK utilities is the only way to detect lost clusters.

What Causes Lost Clusters?

Lost clusters result from several causes. Usually, lost clusters result from power failures or from restarting your computer before all information in a file is written to disk. Lost clusters also result from incorrect use of disk optimization utilities on compressed volumes and from the use of incompatible versions of optimization or repair utilities on compressed volumes. If you use a disk repair utility that is not compatible with Stacker or DOS 6, for example, many lost clusters can result. If you use a disk cache program that has a write-delay cache, you can create lost clusters by turning off your computer before the write cache has physically written to disk.

To avoid lost cluster problems, make sure that any disk optimization utilities you use are compatible with Stacker and DOS 6. Especially avoid restarting your computer or turning your computer off while Windows or another program is running. Refer also to the "Write-Delay Disk Cache" section, earlier in this chapter, for more information on difficulties with disk cache programs and write-delay caches.

Repairing Lost Clusters

To detect and repair lost clusters on your compressed volumes, use both the DOS CHKDSK and the Stacker CHECK utilities. Use DOS CHKDSK to repair lost clusters on both Stacker compressed and uncompressed drives. To repair lost clusters on a compressed or uncompressed volume by using the DOS CHKDSK utility, issue the following command:

   CHKDSK /F *d*:

Substitute the drive letter of the drive you want to check and repair for the *d* in this command. If DOS CHKDSK finds any lost clusters, it gathers the clusters into legitimate file chains and places each file chain in the root directory of the disk drive you check. The files that DOS CHKDSK creates from the lost clusters all have file names ending with an extension of CHK. For more information about the DOS CHKDSK command and the CHK files it produces, refer to your DOS documentation. For information on using the Stacker CHECK command, refer to Chapter 12, "Using the Stacker Utilities."

Examining Cross-Linked Files

Cross-linked files occur if two file chains include the same cluster or clusters. File chains should never share clusters. Because subdirectories on your disk are actually special files that point to other files, two subdirectories can be cross-linked, and a subdirectory can be cross-linked with a file. Cross-linked files can cause additional problems. Because the files that are cross linked have one or more clusters in common, updating one cross-linked file can cause data in a cluster belonging to the second file to be overwritten.

You must repair cross-linked files as quickly as possible. You can use either the DOS CHKDSK command or the Stacker CHECK command to detect these files. Although both programs detect cross-linked files, only CHKDSK reports cross-linked files as such. The Stacker CHECK program merely reports that a problem exists with the files and recommends running CHKDSK.

What Causes Cross-Linked Files?

Cross-linked files are not as common as lost clusters. Both, however, can be caused by power failures and incorrect restarting of your computer. Cross-linked files also can result from conflicts among programs in upper memory or from overly aggressive use of upper memory. Having a STACKS=0,0 statement in your CONFIG.SYS file, using the HIGHSCAN switch with EMM386, or using a disk cache program with a write-delay cache all may cause

> **NOTE:**
> Even if you do not expect to recover the data in any of your cross-linked files, you must perform one of the repair methods described in the following section to remove the cross-linked files from your disk.

programs in memory to corrupt each other's data, creating cross-linked files. Refer to the section "Preventing Problems," earlier in this chapter, for information on dealing with upper memory conflicts, problems with the STACKS command in CONFIG.SYS, and write-delay disk caches.

Repairing Cross-Linked Files

To detect cross-linked files on an uncompressed volume, you must use the DOS CHKDSK utility. To detect cross-linked files on a compressed volume, you can use either the DOS CHKDSK or the Stacker CHECK utility. If many cross-linked files exist or other problems are present in a compressed volume, Stacker reports the situation after the drive is mounted. Neither CHKDSK nor the Stacker CHECK utility, however, can repair cross-linked files. You must repair them manually.

Notice that cross-linked files almost always involve some lost data from one or both of the files that are cross-linked. Because one or more clusters are shared between the two files, one or both of the files inevitably have invalid data in one or in several clusters. You often can retrieve one of the two cross-linked files; successfully retrieving both cross-linked files, however, is rare. Often, you cannot retrieve either file, and your only recourse is to restore the files from backup. Refer to Appendix C, "The 'Grandfather' Backup Technique," for information on a backup method that enables you to restore any file up to three months past.

To repair cross-linked files and to attempt to retrieve the affected files, follow these steps:

1. Run CHKDSK for either a compressed or uncompressed drive. Refer to your DOS documentation for more information on CHKDSK.

2. Record the names of any files or directories reported as cross-linked. You do not need to note the specific cluster numbers.

3. If the cross-links are for files only—that is, they do not include a subdirectory name—copy each cross-linked file to a separate directory, preferably on a separate disk. (Skip to step 4 if a subdirectory name appears as part of the cross-link.) Assume, for example, that two cross-linked files, FILE1.DOC and FILE2.DOC, are located in the root directory of drive C. You can copy both FILE1.DOC and FILE2.DOC to a floppy disk in drive A or to a directory other than the root directory on drive C.

4. If any cross-linked files include subdirectory names—such as two subdirectories linked together or a subdirectory cross-linked with a file—you must copy all the files in each affected subdirectory to another subdirectory or disk. If DIR1 and DIR2, for example, are cross-linked subdirectories, you can copy all the files and subdirectories in DIR1 to drive A or to any subdirectory other than DIR2. You then can copy all the files and subdirectories in DIR2 to drive B or to any subdirectory other than DIR1.

5. After copying the cross-linked files, delete the originals. If the cross-linked files include any subdirectories, use the DOS DELTREE command to delete the directory and all its files. Deleting the files or removing the subdirectory marks all clusters in both chains as unused, eliminating the cross-link.

NOTE: The compressed volume file can become cross-linked to files on the uncompressed host drive. The only way to detect this condition is to use the DOS CHKDSK utility on the uncompressed host drive. If the compressed volume file becomes cross-linked with one or more files on the uncompressed host drive, you can try to recover the files from the uncompressed host drive as described in this section. You then must remove and re-create your compressed volume.

NOTE: Make sure that you *copy* the files to another directory; do not use the DOS RENAME or MOVE commands or the Windows File Manager to simply move the files into another directory. Copying the files forces DOS to allocate an entirely new file chain for each copy of each file. Moving a file simply relocates the directory entry for the file without affecting the clusters in the file chain.

6. Check each file you copied to determine whether the files are damaged or have lost data, and delete any damaged files.
7. If the files are OK, move them back to their original directory. If you deleted a directory, re-create the directory and copy the files into it.
8. Use the DOS CHKDSK utility again to make sure that all the cross-linked files are eliminated and that no lost clusters are present.

This procedure can be time-consuming. If you have a current backup and you do not need to retrieve the cross-linked files or directories, use the following alternative:

1. Follow steps 1 and 2 from the preceding procedure.
2. Delete all cross-linked files. If a subdirectory is cross-linked, use the DOS DELTREE command to delete the subdirectory and its contents.
3. Restore the affected files and directories from your backup. Refer to the documentation for your backup program for information on restoring selected files or subdirectories. If you deleted a directory, make sure that you restore all its subdirectories and files.

By following either of these procedures, you can repair any cross-linked files and directories.

> **STOP**
> If you repair cross-links that involve a subdirectory, make sure that you copy not only all the files in the affected subdirectory, but also all the subdirectories farther down the directory tree—and all their files, too. If you do not copy all the files and subdirectories, you can lose even more data than just that in the immediately affected files.

Recovering a Deleted Compressed Volume File

From time to time, all computer users accidentally delete something they really want to keep. The proliferation of delete-protection utilities clearly testifies to this problem. (DOS, in fact, even includes its own UNDELETE program.) Accidentally deleting a compressed volume file from the DOS prompt, however, is difficult; Stacker protects compressed volume files by assigning them the System, Hidden, and Read-Only file attributes. The Windows File Manager and some shell and menu programs, on the other hand, do enable you to delete Hidden, System, and Read-Only files—although they usually ask for confirmation before deleting. You also may use the Stacker REMOVDRV command to delete a compressed volume file and then realize you deleted the wrong compressed volume. However such an accidental deletion occurs, you still may be able to recover the compressed volume file.

> **STOP**
> Make sure *before* you delete them that you have current backups for the files or subdirectories you delete.

You must attempt to recover the compressed volume file as soon as you realize you deleted it. The sooner you attempt recovery, the more likely is your success. If new data is written to the uncompressed drive that hosted the compressed volume file, the possibility exists that disk clusters that were part of the compressed volume file are now being used by other files. If so, you cannot recover the compressed volume file at all. Instead, you must re-create the compressed volume file and restore your files from backup.

Follow these steps to recover a deleted compressed volume file:

1. Make the current disk drive the uncompressed drive that hosted the compressed volume you want to recover.

    The uncompressed host drive usually now reflects its original drive letter, which is the same as the drive letter of the deleted compressed drive. If you accidentally deleted compressed volume D, for example, its uncompressed host drive is probably drive D now.

2. Make sure that you are in the root directory of the uncompressed drive. If necessary, use the DOS change directory (CD or CHDIR) command.
3. Type **UNDELETE** at the DOS prompt, and press Enter.

    The UNDELETE utility displays text on-screen similar to that shown in figure 13.1. The number and names of the files UNDELETE finds depends on the specific files and recent deletions on your computer's hard disk.
4. After UNDELETE asks if you want to delete a file, press N to answer No for all files except those with an extension of DSK or a three-digit extension and for which UNDELETE shows the first name as ?TACVOL.
5. Where UNDELETE asks for the first letter of the file name, type **s** (either uppercase or lowercase).

    UNDELETE undeletes the compressed volume file. Because the compressed volume file usually is large, the undeleting process can take several seconds, depending on your computer's speed. After UNDELETE finishes undeleting the compressed volume file, it returns to the DOS prompt.
6. Use the STACKER command (as described in Chapter 11, "Using Stacker") to mount the compressed volume file you just recovered.
7. If the compressed volume mounts, check its integrity by using Stacker's CHECK utility. Refer to Chapter 12, "Using the Stacker Utilities," for information on using CHECK.

The deleted compressed volume file is recovered.

```
D:\>UNDELETE

UNDELETE - A delete protection facility
Copyright (C) 1987-1993 Central Point Software, Inc.
All rights reserved.

Directory: D:\
File Specifications: *.*

    Delete Sentry control file not found.

    Deletion-tracking file not found.

    MS-DOS directory contains    2 deleted files.
    Of those,    2 files may be recovered.

Using the MS-DOS directory method.

    ?TACVOL  DSK    340992  7-07-93 10:49p  ....  Undelete (Y/N)?Y
    Please type the first character for ?TACVOL .DSK: S
File successfully undeleted.

    ?TACVOL  000    340992  7-07-93 10:49p  ...A  Undelete (Y/N)?
```

Fig. 13.1

The DOS UNDELETE display as it recovers Stacker compressed volume files.

Correcting Write-Protected Drive Error Messages

If the structure of your compressed volume file is faulty, Stacker reports after mounting the compressed drive that the Stacker drive is write-protected or damaged. These problems usually are caused by a power failure or by restarting your system while the SDEFRAG disk optimization program is running. Because Stacker places the CHECK /WP command in the AUTOEXEC.BAT file, the CHECK command usually attempts to repair these damaged Stacker drives as soon as you restart your computer. Refer to Chapter 12, "Using the Stacker Utilities," for more information on the CHECK program.

After the CHECK program finishes repairing the damaged compressed volumes, use the DOS CHKDSK command on each compressed and uncompressed drive to make sure that no additional problems exist. After you repair or eliminate all drive errors, restart your computer. Stacker now mounts your compressed drives without error messages.

Correcting Chronic Disk Read Errors

If you receive frequent error messages as DOS or your applications read data from your disk drives, try to identify the cause immediately. Frequent Error reading drive... messages indicate potentially serious problems in your computer's hardware or in your software. Chronic read errors from *all* your disk drives, both compressed and uncompressed, are probably caused by a problem in your computer's hardware. You should seek assistance from your vendor or a qualified hardware technician to determine the specific cause of the problem.

If the read errors occur *only* on your compressed drives, a memory conflict of some kind is the probable cause of the errors. If you use EMM386 with the HIGHSCAN switch, try removing the HIGHSCAN switch to see if the read errors cease. If you have loaded the Stacker device driver into upper memory, relocate the Stacker device driver to the conventional memory area; the read errors should cease.

Summary

This chapter serves as a troubleshooting guide for Stacker users. It began by acquainting you with measures you can take to head off many common problems associated with using Stacker. The chapter then described ways to solve problems involving Stacker drive letter assignments and Windows swap files. The chapter next described typical causes of lost clusters and cross-linked files and offered techniques for repairing them.

You also learned how to recover an accidentally deleted compressed volume file and how to deal with the `Write-protected drive` error message—the most common start-up error message. The chapter concluded with a discussion of the causes and possible remedies for chronic disk read errors.

PART IV
Appendixes

- A. Glossary
- B. Using the Microsoft Stacker to DoubleSpace Conversion Disk
- C. The "Grandfather" Backup Technique

APPENDIX A
Glossary

Allocation Unit. See *Cluster*.

AUTOEXEC.BAT. A special file containing DOS commands. On start-up, your computer first seeks out the CONFIG.SYS file and configures itself according to commands in that file. It then searches for the AUTOEXEC.BAT file. The AUTOEXEC.BAT file instructs your computer to carry out certain commands or to start certain programs. See also *CONFIG.SYS*.

Bernoulli Drive. A type of removable disk drive that uses large, removable disk cartridges. The disk inside the cartridge is similar in construction to a floppy disk. Bernoulli disk cartridge capacities range from 10M to 150M or more. Both Stacker and DoubleSpace are compatible with Bernoulli drives.

BIOS. An acronym for *Basic Input/Output System*, the software part of your computer that most directly controls its hardware. BIOS software performs various services for DOS—such as writing characters on-screen or reading or writing data to disk.

Boot. Term used to refer to starting a computer, originating from the idea that, after you turn on your computer, it must "lift itself by its own bootstraps."

Boot Disk. A floppy disk or hard disk specially prepared to store the BIOS and other DOS files needed to operate your computer. You cannot start your computer without a boot disk. To make compressed disks accessible, the disk compression device driver also must be on the boot disk. You may prepare a boot disk as you format it or by using the DOS SYS command.

Button. See *Command Button*, *Radio Button*.

CD-ROM. A type of removable media disk drive. CD-ROM stands for *Compact Disk-Read Only Memory*. CD-ROM drives store data as light and dark patterns and read the data back by using a laser beam. CD-ROM drives enable you only to read information from a disk; you cannot write new information to the disk. CD-ROM drives cannot be compressed by either DoubleSpace or Stacker but are otherwise compatible.

Check Box. A type of control in a dialog box. You use a check box to select options offered by a program if those options are not exclusive. A check box usually appears on-screen as a hollow square or a pair of square brackets. If the check box contains a check mark or "X," the choice is selected. If the check box is empty, the choice is not selected.

Clean Boot. Booting your computer without loading any device drivers or TSR programs not absolutely necessary to the operation of your computer. See also *Boot*, *Boot Disk*.

Click. To quickly press and release a button on your mouse. Most programs that use a mouse to select on-screen items—such as menu choices—have you position the mouse pointer over the item and then click the left mouse button to select that item. See also *Double-click*.

Cluster. The smallest unit of disk space DOS can access at one time. Refer to Chapter 1, "Understanding and Using Disk Compression," for more information about clusters.

Command Button. A type of control in a dialog box. You use a command button to carry out an action associated with that button. You select a command button by moving the mouse pointer over the button and clicking.

Command Line. Another name for the DOS prompt. The DOS prompt is sometimes referred to as the command line because it is the line at which you type commands. See also *Command Line Switch*.

Command Line Switch. Many DOS and other commands have various options you may select. You select these options by adding switches to the end of the command, on the same line.

Compressed Volume File. The general term given to the file that stores your compressed data. Whether you use Stacker or DoubleSpace, both programs work by using a large disk file to store your compressed data and then presenting that disk file to DOS as a logical disk drive.

Compression Ratio. The measurement of how much data compresses. A compression ratio of 1 to 1—written as 1:1—indicates that data did not compress at all. A compression ratio of 2:1 indicates that your data compressed to a size half as large as the original data. Both DoubleSpace and Stacker have maximum compression ratios of 16:1.

CONFIG.SYS. A special file your computer seeks out every time it starts, as soon as DOS is loaded into memory. DOS uses the information in the CONFIG.SYS file to load device drivers and configure itself and then searches for the AUTOEXEC.BAT file. See also *AUTOEXEC.BAT*.

Conventional Memory. The first 640K of your computer's memory, which is the portion used most often by DOS and your applications. If your programs run out of memory, you probably need to free more conventional memory. Both DoubleSpace and Stacker enable you to load their device drivers into areas of memory other than conventional memory.

CPU. An abbreviation for *Central Processing Unit*, the computer chip that is the main "brain" of your computer.

CVF. Abbreviation for *Compressed Volume File*. See *Compressed Volume File*.

DBLSPACE.BIN. The device driver file that DOS 6 is designed to preload. Whenever DOS 6 loads into memory on start-up, it searches the root directory of the start-up disk for a file named DBLSPACE.BIN. If DOS finds this file, it loads the file into memory as a device driver. Both DoubleSpace and Stacker 3.1 have device drivers named DBLSPACE.BIN. The DBLSPACE.BIN file usually has Hidden, System, and Read-Only file attributes.

DBLSPACE.INI. The file that contains the initialization information for DoubleSpace. After the DoubleSpace DBLSPACE.BIN device driver loads into memory, it searches for the DBLSPACE.INI file. DoubleSpace uses information in this file to determine which compressed volume files to mount and where those files are located. The DBLSPACE.INI file also controls how DoubleSpace exchanges drive letters as it mounts the compressed volumes.

DBLSPACE.*xxx*. The name used for the DoubleSpace compressed volume files stored on the uncompressed host drive. DoubleSpace gives System, Hidden, and Read-Only file attributes to each DBLSPACE.*xxx* file. The first DoubleSpace compressed volume file created on a disk is always DBLSPACE.000. Each successive DoubleSpace compressed volume file created on the same physical disk or partition is assigned a file extension one number higher. The second compressed volume file, for example, is DBLSPACE.001.

Defragment. To arrange all a file's data so that it lies in contiguous clusters on the disk. See also *Disk Optimizer*.

Device Driver. A piece of software especially written to attach itself to DOS and extend DOS's capabilities to control various types of hardware. Both DoubleSpace and Stacker use a device driver to present DOS with logical disk drives created from space on your physical disks.

Dialog Box. A tool of application programs to enable you to choose options and enter data. Dialog boxes are named from the idea that the program is conducting a dialog with the user. Dialog boxes usually contain command buttons, check boxes, radio buttons, and text boxes. You make choices and enter data in a dialog box by using the keyboard or, usually, a mouse.

Disk Drive. Any device that DOS treats as a disk drive. A disk drive may be a physical disk drive or a logical disk drive. See also *Drive Letter*.

Disk Optimizer. A program designed to rearrange data in files so that the data is stored in contiguous disk clusters. Disk optimizers also are referred to as defragmentation programs. DOS, DoubleSpace, and Stacker all provide their own disk optimization and defragmentation programs. See also *Fragmentation*.

Disk Partition. A part of a hard disk that is set up so that DOS treats it as a completely separate disk drive. This technique is not as common now as in the past.

Double-click. To quickly press and release a button on your mouse twice in a row. In most programs that use a mouse, you double-click with the left mouse button to initiate some action. See also *Click*.

Drive Letter. DOS identifies different disk drives by assigning each drive a letter of the alphabet. The first disk drive in your computer (usually a floppy disk) is drive A, the second is drive B, the third is drive C, and so on. The exception is that your first hard disk is always assigned drive letter C, even if you have only one floppy drive.

EMS. See *Expanded Memory*.

Expanded Memory. A special type of memory beyond the first 1M of your computer's memory. Expanded memory was used to expand memory beyond 1M in earlier computers that were physically incapable of addressing more than 1M of memory. The standard for using and controlling expanded memory is the EMS standard. Expanded memory is often referred to as *EMS memory*.

Extended Memory. Memory in your computer beyond 1M. Only computers that use the 80286 or later CPU chips can access extended memory. To prevent conflicts, almost all programs that use extended memory do so through a special software controller called an *extended memory manager*. The standard for using and controlling extended memory is the XMS standard. Extended memory is sometimes referred to as XMS memory.

Fixed Disk. See *Hard Disk*.

Floptical Drive. A type of removable media disk drive designed to read and write Floptical disks. *Floptical disks* are similar to normal floppy disks in construction and record information in magnetic patterns, but read the information back by using a laser beam.

Fragmentation. The information in a file on your disk is usually stored in several different clusters. Because DOS uses clusters on a first-come, first-served basis, files that frequently change often end up stored in clusters that are physically scattered across the surface of the disk. Because the disk's read/write heads must move farther and more often to read or write data on a disk, access to files may become slower if the files are badly fragmented. See also *Disk Optimizer*.

Hard Disk. A hard disk is a rigid platter, usually made of aluminum and coated with a magnetic material. The term *fixed disk* is often used instead of *hard disk*. Hard disks are not removable from your computer, hence the term *fixed*.

Host Drive. Compressed drives are stored as files on your physical disk drives. The physical disk drive that contains one or more compressed volume files is referred to as the host drive for those compressed volume files. See also *compressed volume file*.

Lempel-Ziv. The generic data compression algorithm used by both DoubleSpace and Stacker. Its name is derived from the last names of the two Israeli mathematicians who devised the compression algorithm.

Logical Disk Drive. A storage device that appears to DOS as a disk drive, although no actual disk drive may be involved at all. Your Stacker and DoubleSpace compressed volumes are logical disk drives.

LZS. The variation of the Lempel-Ziv compression algorithm used by Stacker and patented by Stac Electronics, the publishers of Stacker.

Memory-Resident Program. See *Terminate Stay Resident (TSR) Program*.

Mount. The process of establishing a connection between DOS and a compressed drive. Your compressed drives are not accessible through DOS until they are mounted.

Option Switch. See *Command Line Switch*.

Partition. See *Disk Partition*.

Physical Disk Drive. A disk drive that is physically present in your computer.

Radio Button. A type of control in a dialog box. You use a radio button to select options that are mutually exclusive. A radio button usually appears on-screen as a circle or a pair of parentheses. If the radio button's circle (or parentheses) is filled in by a solid dot, that option is selected. If the radio button is empty, the option is not selected.

RAM Disk. An area of computer memory that is set aside and then accessed by DOS as if it were a disk drive. RAM disks are created by device drivers or TSR programs.

RAM Drive. See *RAM Disk*.

Removable Media. Any disk you can remove from its drive and replace with a different disk—such as a floppy disk. Removable media drives include floppy disk drives, Bernoulli drives, Floptical drives, Syquest drives, and CD-ROM drives.

Stack. To add Stacker disk compression to a disk drive.

STACKER.INI. The file that contains the initialization information for Stacker. After the Stacker DBLSPACE.BIN device driver loads into memory, it seeks out the file named STACKER.INI. Stacker uses information in this file to determine which compressed volume files to mount and where those files are located. The STACKER.INI file also controls how Stacker assigns drive letters as it mounts the compressed volumes.

STACVOL.*xxx*. The name used for Stacker compressed volume files stored on the uncompressed host drive. Stacker gives System, Hidden, and Read-Only file attributes to each STACVOL.*xxx* file. The first Stacker compressed volume file created on a disk is always named STACVOL.DSK. Each successive Stacker compressed volume file created on the same physical disk or partition receives a file extension that is a three digit number. The second compressed volume file is named STACVOL.000, for example, while the third Stacker compressed volume is named STACVOL.001.

Syquest Drive. A type of removable media disk drive. Syquest drives are very similar to regular hard disk drives except that the part of the drive that encloses the actual disks is removable—like a pull-out car stereo.

Terminate Stay Resident (TSR) Program. A special type of program that loads into memory, attaches itself to DOS, and then terminates. The parts of the program that attach to DOS remain in memory and are invoked by DOS as necessary. All or part of the program remains in memory even if the program is not running.

Text Box. A type of dialog box control. You enter words or numbers into a text box. This information is then passed on to the application.

TSR. See *Terminate Stay Resident Program*.

UMB. Upper Memory Block. DOS divides the upper memory area into blocks. See also *Upper Memory Area*.

Uncompressed Drive. See *Host Drive*.

Uncompressed Volume. See *Host Drive*.

Unmount. The process of breaking the connection between DOS and a compressed drive.

Upper Memory Area. The 384K of memory between 640K and 1M. This area is generally reserved for the memory addresses of your computer's hardware devices. To use the upper memory area, an expanded memory manager must be installed in your computer.

Volume. Another name for a disk or disk drive. The term *volume* does not imply that the drive is either a physical drive or a logical drive.

Working Drive. See *Host Drive*.

XMS. See *Extended Memory*.

APPENDIX B

Using the Microsoft Stacker to DoubleSpace Conversion Disk

Converting compressed volumes from Stacker to DoubleSpace usually requires several hours. (In systems with large drives, conversion may even take an entire day or two.) The exact time required depends on the speed of your computer and its disk drives, how badly fragmented the disks are, and how full they are. Start the conversion from Stacker to DoubleSpace only if you do not need your computer for several hours. Start the conversion on a Friday afternoon or at the end of a working day, when you do not need your computer.

This appendix explains how to use the Stacker to DoubleSpace conversion disk, which is available from Microsoft. The appendix begins by outlining the preparations you must make before converting your disks from Stacker to DoubleSpace and continues through the actual conversion process. This appendix also describes how your system is changed by the conversion and offers several post-conversion "housekeeping" tips. The final section of the appendix describes how to use the new DoubleSpace command-line switch and the new **T**ools menu choice to convert your Stacker compressed floppy disks to DoubleSpace format.

Preparing To Convert

Converting from Stacker to DoubleSpace represents a major change in your computer system's configuration. Certain preparations are therefore necessary to ensure the safety of your data and the success of the conversion process.

Preparing to convert from Stacker to DoubleSpace is similar to preparing to install DoubleSpace on a computer that does not currently have disk compression. To prepare to convert from Stacker to DoubleSpace, first follow the preparation guidelines in Chapter 3, "Installing DoubleSpace," and then perform these additional steps:

- *Make a working copy of the Stacker to DoubleSpace conversion disk.* Use the DOS DISKCOPY command to copy your Stacker to DoubleSpace conversion disk. Use the working copy to perform the actual conversion. Refer to your DOS documentation for information on using the DOS DISKCOPY command.
- *Make sure that the drives you convert have enough working room.* To convert your compressed drives from Stacker to DoubleSpace, the uncompressed host drive must have a minimum amount of working room available. To convert a compressed boot disk, you must have at least 1.7M free space on the uncompressed host drive. Other disks require at least 1M free space on the uncompressed host drive. To determine which drives are the host drives for your Stacker volumes, type the following command at the DOS prompt, and press Enter:

    STACKER

    Stacker displays a report showing how drive letters were exchanged when your computer started and listing the drive letter and file name for the Stacker compressed volume. The following example shows a line from a Stacker drive report:

    ```
    Drive I: was drive K: at boot time    [ K:\STACVOL.DSK = 16.0MB  ]
    ```

    In this example, drive I is compressed by Stacker, and drive K is the uncompressed host drive for the Stacker compressed volume file. You must therefore ensure that drive K has at least 1M free space before starting the Stacker to DoubleSpace conversion. If the uncompressed host drive does not have enough working space, you may need to delete files from the uncompressed host or change the size of the Stacker drive.
- *Use the DOS CHKDSK command.* The DOS CHKDSK command checks the integrity of your disk drive. Although the Stacker to DoubleSpace conversion runs this command for you, using this command ahead of time and resolving any problems that CHKDSK may reveal at that point is a good idea. Refer to your DOS documentation for instructions on using the DOS CHKDSK command. CHKDSK also is discussed in Chapter 7, "Troubleshooting DoubleSpace."
- *Use the Stacker CHECK or SCHECK command.* The Stacker CHECK and SCHECK commands check the integrity of your compressed drives. If you use Stacker 2.0, use SCHECK; in Stacker 3.x, use CHECK. Although the Stacker to DoubleSpace conversion also runs these commands for you, using the appropriate command ahead of time and resolving any problems that are revealed at that point is a good idea. Although this book does not explicitly cover any version of Stacker prior to 3.1, Stacker CHECK is discussed in Chapter 13, "Troubleshooting Stacker."
- *Disable disk cache programs.* If you have any disk cache programs that load as device drivers in your CONFIG.SYS file or as TSR programs in your AUTOEXEC.BAT file—such as DOS SMARTDRV—you should disable them. To disable the device drivers in your CONFIG.SYS file, use a text editor (such as DOS EDIT) to change your CONFIG.SYS file. Add REM (for *remark*) to the beginning of the line in your CONFIG.SYS file that loads the disk cache device driver. Refer

> **NOTE:**
> If you used Stacker version 1.1 to compress your disks, if your Stacker compressed drive is larger than 512M, or if your Stacker compressed drives use a cluster size other than 8K, you cannot use the Stacker to DoubleSpace conversion program. You must convert to DoubleSpace by using the manual backup and restore technique described in Chapter 3, "Installing DoubleSpace." If your Stacker drive is larger than 512M, you must divide it into two smaller drives; DoubleSpace can support compressed drives only up to 512M.

to your DOS documentation for more information on CONFIG.SYS; refer also to the documentation for your disk cache program. To disable TSR programs in your AUTOEXEC.BAT file, use a text editor to change your AUTOEXEC.BAT file. Add REM (for *remark*) to the beginning of the line in your AUTOEXEC.BAT file that loads the disk cache TSR.

- *Restart your system with a "clean" configuration.* The Stacker to DoubleSpace conversion program requires an extremely large amount of your computer's conventional memory and environment space. Many users report that their Stacker to DoubleSpace conversion process is interrupted by running out of memory.

After you complete the preparation steps, you are ready to convert your Stacker compressed drives to DoubleSpace. Remember to read and follow all the on-screen instructions for each step of the conversion process. Do not try to take shortcuts, even if you are an experienced user. In areas regarding the safety and integrity of your disk data, do not take chances.

> **NOTE:** Whether you create an entirely new CONFIG.SYS file or use the F8 conditional processing, remember to load the Stacker device drivers. If you do not load these device drivers, the conversion program cannot access the Stacker drives to convert them.

Making Memory Available for the Stacker to DoubleSpace Conversion

To make as much of your computer's memory available as possible, you should restart your computer by using a special CONFIG.SYS file. This special CONFIG.SYS file should not load any more device drivers than are absolutely necessary to operate your system. You do not need device drivers for your mouse or display screen (such as MOUSE.SYS and ANSI.SYS), for example, to run the Stacker to DoubleSpace conversion. Instead of creating an entirely new CONFIG.SYS, you may want to press F8 to use the DOS 6 conditional processing of your CONFIG.SYS file to load only the device drivers necessary to operate your system. If you do decide to create a special CONFIG.SYS file, however, you can use the following example as a model. The correct Stacker device driver lines for your computer are, of course, different. Use the same Stacker device driver lines that are in your current CONFIG.SYS file. The example assumes that your DOS files are on drive C in a directory named DOS. If your COMMAND.COM file is in a different drive or directory, substitute the appropriate drive and directory.

```
DEVICE=C:\DOS\HIMEM.SYS
DEVICE=C:\DOS\EMM386.EXE /NOEMS
DOS=HIGH
DOS=UMB
FILES=40
BUFFERS=40
STACKS=9,256
SHELL=C:\DOS\COMMAND.COM C:\DOS\ /E:512  /P
DEVICEHIGH=C:\STACKER\STACKER.COM /P=1 I:\STACVOL.DSK
    I:\STACVOL.000 A:
DEVICEHIGH=C:\STACKER\SSWAP.COM I:\STACVOL.DSK
```

Notice the SHELL command in the preceding example, and notice the /E switch near the end of the line. This command allocates more environment space for DOS. If you receive an error from the conversion program telling you that your computer does not have enough environment space, increase the number used after the /E switch. Refer to your DOS documentation for more information on the SHELL command and the COMMAND.COM /E switch.

Making the Stacker to DoubleSpace Conversion

This section takes you through the conversion process step by step. If you have not read the previous section on preparing to convert from Stacker to DoubleSpace, go back and read it before proceeding with the conversion. Some follow-up and housekeeping activities you may want to perform are presented after the instructions for performing the conversion.

Performing the Conversion

The Stacker to DoubleSpace conversion process converts all your mounted Stacker drives to DoubleSpace format, including any removable media drives. To start the conversion process, follow these steps:

1. Make sure that you are at the DOS prompt. If you use Windows, DESQview, GEM, or GEOworks, you must exit to DOS before starting the Stacker to DoubleSpace conversion. You also should exit from any shell program you may use, such as the DOS Shell, XTree, or Norton Desktop for DOS.

2. Insert the working copy of your conversion disk into a floppy disk drive that can accommodate it, and make that drive the current disk drive.
3. Type **CONVERT** at the DOS prompt, and press Enter. The conversion program displays a message briefly describing what the program does. At the end of this display, the conversion program asks if you want to read the CONVERT.TXT file. (This file contains last-minute information and special instructions for using the conversion disk. You should at least skim through it.)
4. Press Y to read the CONVERT.TXT file now; the conversion program displays the CONVERT.TXT file. Press any key to display a new page from the CONVERT.TXT file each time —More— appears at the bottom of the screen. After you reach the end of CONVERT.TXT, you are asked if you want to read this file again. Press Y to read the CONVERT.TXT file again.

    To skip the CONVERT.TXT file and continue immediately with the conversion process, press N; the conversion program copies the updated DoubleSpace files to your hard disk.

    If you change your mind about performing the conversion now, press C to cancel the conversion. You return to the DOS prompt.

    After the conversion program finishes copying files, it displays a screen informing you that it will run the Stacker SCHECK or CHECK programs and DOS CHKDSK to test the integrity of your disk drives, compressed and uncompressed. If you have not yet run SCHECK, CHECK, and CHKDSK, have a pencil and paper handy to write down any error messages that appear as you run these programs. If you followed the preparation guidelines in the previous section, however, you have already identified and corrected any errors on your hard disks and Stacker compressed volumes.
5. Press any key to continue the conversion process. Depending on your version of Stacker, either Stacker CHECK or SCHECK runs. These programs ask whether you want to run a surface scan on your disks. A surface scan checks the surface of your disk for physical defects in areas not already marked by DOS as defective.
6. For maximum safety, press Y and then press Enter to have the CHECK or SCHECK program make the surface scan. If you are certain that your disk's surface is in good condition, press N and then press Enter to skip the surface scan.

    Regardless of whether you chose to perform the surface scan, the Stacker CHECK or SCHECK now executes. As this program runs, it displays various status messages. The CHECK or SCHECK program runs for every Stacker compressed drive that is currently mounted, including any removable media drives. Make sure that you write down any errors CHECK or SCHECK report.

    The Stacker to DoubleSpace conversion program now executes the DOS CHKDSK utility for every Stacker volume that is currently mounted and for their corresponding uncompressed host drives. Make sure that you write down any errors CHKDSK reports.

    After the compressed and uncompressed drives have been checked for errors, the conversion program displays a message asking whether any errors were detected.

STOP

After DoubleSpace converts your Stacker compressed volumes to DoubleSpace format, it restarts your computer. Make sure that you save any data on a RAM disk *before* beginning this procedure.

NOTE:

The Stacker to DoubleSpace conversion program installs an updated copy of the DBLSPACE.EXE and DBLSPACE.HLP files to the first directory in your PATH statement that contains a copy of the DBLSPACE program. Normally, only one copy of the DBLSPACE program should be on your hard disk, located in your DOS directory. If you have multiple copies of the DBLSPACE program, you must use the DOS COPY command to manually update any additional copies of DoubleSpace by copying the DBLSPACE.EXE and DBLSPACE.HLP files from the conversion disk.

Using the Microsoft Stacker to DoubleSpace Conversion Disk   311

7. If errors are reported, press Y; otherwise, skip to step 8. The conversion program displays a message stating that you must correct any errors before you convert your drives and then stops. Begin the conversion process again from step 1 after you correct all errors.

   Although this book does not explicitly cover any version of Stacker prior to 3.1, Chapter 13, "Troubleshooting Stacker," contains information on correcting problems detected by CHECK and DOS CHKDSK.

8. If no errors are reported, press N to continue the conversion process. Your screen clears, and the Stacker to DoubleSpace conversion program asks for confirmation to start the conversion process.

9. Press Y to convert your Stacker drives to DoubleSpace. The conversion program clears your screen; the DoubleSpace Setup program now loads into memory.

   Press N if you decide not to start the Stacker to DoubleSpace conversion; you return to the DOS command line.

   After a few moments, the DoubleSpace program displays the DoubleSpace Setup opening screen. This screen is intended for users who are installing DoubleSpace for the first time. These messages do not directly pertain to the Stacker to DoubleSpace conversion process.

10. Press Enter to continue the Stacker to DoubleSpace conversion. DoubleSpace Setup displays the screen shown in figure B.1.

    Notice that the message in figure B.1 warns you to run Stacker CHECK or SCHECK. Because the conversion program ran these utilities for you earlier, you do not need to run them again. Be certain, however, that you corrected any errors previously identified by Stacker CHECK/SCHECK and DOS CHKDSK.

11. Press Enter to continue with the Stacker to DoubleSpace conversion. DoubleSpace displays the screen shown in figure B.2, asking for final confirmation before starting the actual conversion of your Stacker compressed drives to DoubleSpace.

12. Make sure that drive A is empty. During the conversion process, DoubleSpace restarts your computer. If drive A is not empty, your computer does not restart correctly.

13. Press C to continue the Stacker to DoubleSpace conversion. DoubleSpace Setup now searches all your physical disk drives for mounted Stacker volumes. DoubleSpace converts any mounted Stacker volumes it finds, including removable media disks.

    After searching for Stacker drives, DoubleSpace Setup begins checking each of your Stacker compressed volume files. It displays a screen showing its progress as it checks each Stacker compressed volume file. DoubleSpace checks the compressed volume file for every Stacker drive currently mounted on your computer. DoubleSpace then performs several other checks of your system. If a floppy disk is in drive A, it displays the error message shown in figure B.3.

NOTE: After you begin the conversion process, you cannot interrupt it. The conversion process can take several hours or possibly an entire day or two, depending on your computer's speed and the amount of data to be converted. If you cannot do without your computer for that length of time, press F3 to quit the conversion process and then perform it at a more convenient time.

Remove the disk from drive A, and choose **R**etry; DoubleSpace checks your system again. If you decide not to convert from Stacker to DoubleSpace, choose **C**ancel instead. If you choose **C**ancel now, DoubleSpace restarts your computer anyway, but it does not convert any Stacker drives.

DoubleSpace Setup displays a message telling you that it will restart your computer. The message is displayed on-screen for a few seconds, and then your computer restarts. As your computer restarts, the message `Starting MS-DOS...` appears. After a few more moments, you see the message `DoubleSpace is continuing....`

DoubleSpace Setup now resumes operation. DoubleSpace examines your system, creates the new DoubleSpace compressed volumes, and then begins converting your Stacker drives to DoubleSpace format. As the conversion proceeds, DoubleSpace Setup displays a progress chart for each Stacker drive that it converts.

As each Stacker drive is converted, DoubleSpace resizes and then mounts each new DoubleSpace compressed volume. After the conversion of the currently mounted Stacker compressed drives is complete, DoubleSpace displays the screen shown in figure B.4.

Fig. B.1
The DoubleSpace Setup screen for Stacker users.

NOTE:
After DoubleSpace displays its progress screen, it can complete the conversion process unattended. DoubleSpace does not need you to make additional choices or perform any other actions until the conversion is complete.

14. After you read the message shown in figure B.4, press Enter or choose **O**K. DoubleSpace restarts your computer again so that the DoubleSpace device driver is loaded into memory and your new DoubleSpace compressed volumes are accessible.

    DoubleSpace does not check drive A before restarting your computer this time. Make sure that drive A is empty so that your computer restarts correctly.

15. If you made a special CONFIG.SYS file for starting your computer—as recommended in the guidelines for preparing to run the Stacker to DoubleSpace conversion program—you may now restore your original CONFIG.SYS file. After restoring this file, edit it and remove any references to the Stacker device drivers.

    If you pressed F8 to conditionally process your CONFIG.SYS file, DoubleSpace has already disabled the Stacker device drivers in your CONFIG.SYS file. DoubleSpace has also disabled the Stacker CHECK program that was formerly invoked from your AUTOEXEC.BAT file.

16. After you restore and edit your CONFIG.SYS file, restart your computer manually by pressing Ctrl+Alt+Del. Your computer starts up with the same configuration you had before converting to DoubleSpace.

    If you uninstalled any copy-protected software before beginning the Stacker to DoubleSpace conversion, reinstall that software now.

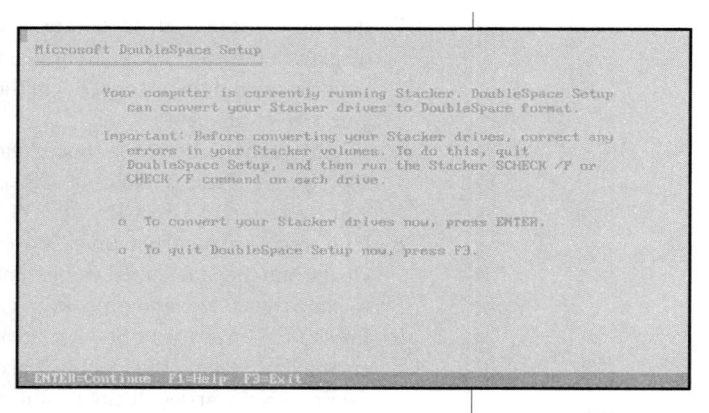

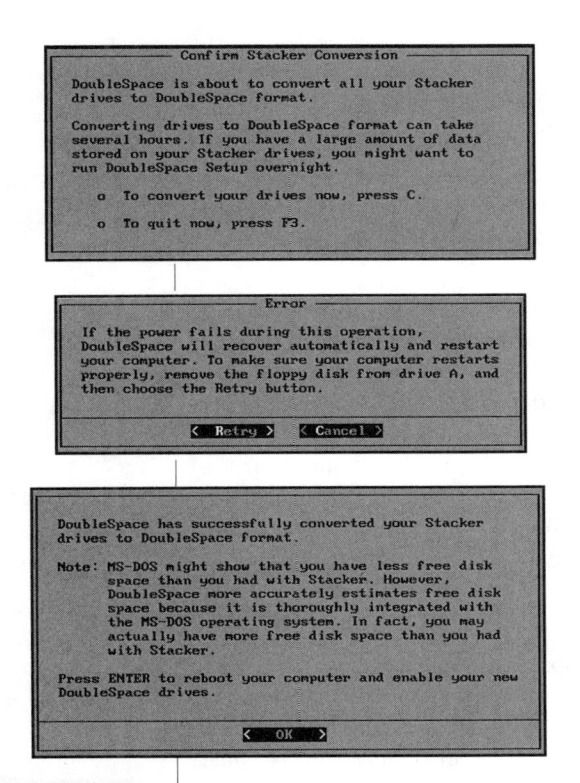

Fig. B.2, top

The DoubleSpace Setup final confirmation for converting your compressed drives from Stacker to DoubleSpace.

Fig. B.3, middle

The DoubleSpace disk in drive A error message.

Fig. B.4, bottom

DoubleSpace has completed the Stacker to DoubleSpace conversion.

The conversion of your Stacker compressed drives to DoubleSpace format is now complete. You may now want to perform a few follow-up and "housekeeping" activities, described in the following section.

After the Conversion

After the Stacker to DoubleSpace conversion is complete, a few of your system's details are slightly different than they were before the conversion. One minor difference you may notice is in the estimated compression ratio for your new DoubleSpace compressed drives. As DoubleSpace creates the compressed volumes that replace each of your Stacker drives, it sets the estimated compression ratio for the new volume to be the same as the actual compression ratio of the files on the compressed drive. If all the files on a converted compressed volume actually compressed at 1.8:1, for example, the new DoubleSpace drive has an estimated compression ratio of 1.8:1. Another minor difference is that DoubleSpace alters the volume labels of the Stacker drives it converts. Each DoubleSpace drive is given the volume label COMPRESSED, regardless of the previous volume label.

At the end of the Stacker to DoubleSpace conversion, DoubleSpace disables the Stacker device driver lines in your CONFIG.SYS file by adding REM (for *remark*) at the beginning of each line that loads a Stacker device driver. DoubleSpace also disables the lines in the AUTOEXEC.BAT file that ran the Stacker CHECK or SCHECK program by adding REM at the beginning of that line.

At this point, you may want to perform a few tasks to completely tidy up your system. You may want to edit your CONFIG.SYS and AUTOEXEC.BAT files to remove the old Stacker program lines entirely. Removing these lines is not essential; as long as these lines start with REM, they are not processed by DOS. If you remove the unneeded lines, however, you help keep your CONFIG.SYS and AUTOEXEC.BAT files simpler and easier to understand or troubleshoot in the future.

Another task you may want to perform involves removing the STACKER.LOG files on your uncompressed host drives. Stacker uses these files to help track information about your Stacker drives, but they are not needed or used by DoubleSpace. A STACKER.LOG file is located on each uncompressed drive that hosted a Stacker compressed volume. To remove the STACKER.LOG files, you must first remove the file's Read-Only attribute. Use the following command to remove the Read-Only file attribute:

ATTRIB –R STACKER.LOG

After you remove the Read-Only attribute, you can use the DOS DEL command to delete the file. Refer to your DOS documentation for more information on the ATTRIB and DEL commands.

Converting Stacker Compressed Removable Media to DoubleSpace

You may have removable disks, such as floppy or Bernoulli disks, that you compressed with Stacker and now want to convert to DoubleSpace. You can convert your removable disks directly from the DOS command line, by using the new command-line switch, or through the new Convert **S**tacker menu choice on the DoubleSpace **T**ools menu. DoubleSpace requires .9M (about 900K) of free uncompressed disk space on the removable disk to convert it to DoubleSpace. Some of your Stacker compressed removable disks may not have enough working room for DoubleSpace to convert the disk. In that case, follow the manual conversion procedure described at the end of this section.

Converting from the DOS Prompt

As with other DoubleSpace utility functions, DoubleSpace has command-line switches for converting Stacker removable disks to DoubleSpace format. If you use the command-line switches, DoubleSpace converts a Stacker drive without going into the DoubleSpace menus; DoubleSpace does, however, display some of the report screens you see while using the menus. Think of using the command-line switches as shortcuts for converting your removable disks.

The DoubleSpace command-line switches for converting a removable media drive use the following syntax:

DBLSPACE /CONVSTAC=*d1*:*volname* /NEWDRIVE=*d2* /CVF=*nnn*

The /NEWDRIVE and /CVF switches are optional. In this example, *d1* represents the drive containing the Stacker volume you want to convert, and *volname* represents the name of the Stacker compressed volume file to convert. (Normally, the Stacker compressed volume file is named STACVOL.DSK.) The following command, for example, converts the Stacker compressed volume file on drive A to DoubleSpace format:

DBLSPACE /CONVSTAC=A:\STACVOL.DSK

The /NEWDRIVE switch tells DoubleSpace which drive letter to use for the host drive as it mounts the converted compressed disk after converting it from Stacker. In the preceding syntax example, *d2* represents the drive letter for the host drive. You do not need to use this switch very often. The following command, for example, converts a Stacker compressed volume in drive A and mounts it with the host drive letter as G:

DBLSPACE /CONVSTAC=A:\STACVOL.DSK /NEWDRIVE=G:

The /CVF switch tells DoubleSpace to assign the converted compressed volume file a name other than DBLSPACE.000. In the same syntax example, *nnn* represents a three-digit whole number DoubleSpace uses as the file extension for the new compressed

Using the Microsoft Stacker to DoubleSpace Conversion Disk

volume file. To convert the Stacker compressed volume in drive A and have the DoubleSpace compressed volume file named DBLSPACE.001—instead of DBLSPACE.000—you use the following command:

DBLSPACE /CONVSTAC=A:\STACVOL.DSK /CVF=001

Whenever you convert a Stacker compressed removable disk to DoubleSpace by using the DoubleSpace command-line switches, DoubleSpace behaves just as if you converted the Stacker compressed volume through the DoubleSpace menus. DoubleSpace displays the same message screens if converting from the command line as you see if you convert from the DoubleSpace menus. After the conversion is complete and DoubleSpace mounts the new compressed volume, however, DoubleSpace returns to the DOS prompt instead of remaining in the DoubleSpace menus.

NOTE: After you convert a Stacker compressed removable drive to DoubleSpace, you cannot convert it back to Stacker.

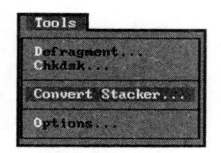

Converting by Using the DoubleSpace Menus

You also can convert removable disks by using the menu system in the updated DoubleSpace utility provided on your conversion disk. To convert a Stacker removable disk to DoubleSpace by using the DoubleSpace menus, follow these steps:

1. To start the DoubleSpace utility, type **DBLSPACE** at the DOS prompt and press Enter. The DoubleSpace program starts and displays its main menu and compressed drive list.
2. If you have not already done so, put the removable disk you want to convert into your disk drive.
3. From the **T**ools menu, choose Convert **S**tacker (see fig. B.5). DoubleSpace scans your computer system for Stacker drives that can be converted and then displays the Convert Stacker dialog box, as shown in figure B.6.
4. Select from the list of drives in the Convert Stacker dialog box the drive containing the removable disk you want to convert, and press Enter or choose **O**K. DoubleSpace immediately begins to convert the Stacker volume to DoubleSpace format.

If you change your mind about converting a disk, press Esc or choose **C**ancel.

As DoubleSpace performs the conversion, various status messages appear; DoubleSpace displays a progress report as it converts the disk.

If the removable disk contains insufficient uncompressed free space to convert the Stacker volume, DoubleSpace displays an error dialog box. If this error message appears, press Enter. DoubleSpace returns to the main menu and list of compressed drives. See the following section, "Converting If Insufficient Working Room Is Available," for information on converting the Stacker volume manually.

After DoubleSpace finishes converting the removable disk, it mounts the new DoubleSpace compressed drive and returns to the main menu and list of compressed drives. The removable disk you converted is now mounted and displayed in the list of compressed drives.

Fig. B.5
The updated DoubleSpace Tools menu.

NOTE: If the drive containing the removable disk you want to convert is not listed, first make sure that a disk is actually in the drive. If a disk is in the drive, make sure that it is in fact a Stacker compressed disk.

Converting If Insufficient Working Room Is Available

If you cannot convert your Stacker compressed removable disks because insufficient uncompressed free space is available, you may need to use the manual conversion method described in this section.

To use this method, first make sure that you have enough uncompressed hard disk space to accommodate the compressed volume file from the Stacker compressed removable disk. To determine how large the Stacker compressed volume file is, follow these steps:

1. Use the DOS DIR command to view the contents of the uncompressed root directory of the removable disk.
2. Notice the size of the STACVOL.DSK file. (It has Hidden, System, and Read-Only file attributes.)
3. Use any of the methods described in Chapter 5, "Using DoubleSpace," to determine which drive letters are your uncompressed host drives and whether any of the host drives have enough space to hold STACVOL.DSK.

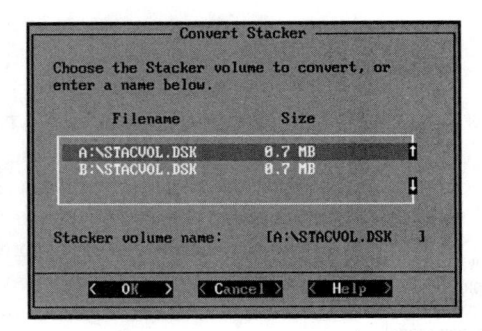

Fig. B.6

The DoubleSpace Convert Stacker dialog box.

If you do not have enough uncompressed disk space to hold the STACVOL.DSK file, you cannot use this method. You must make more free space available on one of your uncompressed host drives.

To actually make the conversion, you need a blank, formatted removable disk of the same size and physical capacity as the Stacker compressed disk that you are trying to convert. If converting a Stacker compressed disk on a 3 1/2-inch, 1.44M floppy disk, for example, you need a blank, formatted 3 1/2-inch, 1.44M floppy disk.

To begin the conversion process, follow these steps:

1. Use the DOS COPY command to copy the STACVOL.DSK file to one of your uncompressed disk drives. Use the method described earlier in this section to identify which of your uncompressed drives is suitable for this task.
2. Start DoubleSpace, and use the menus to convert the STACVOL.DSK file to a DoubleSpace compressed volume. Follow the steps in the preceding section for instructions on converting a Stacker compressed removable disk.

    DoubleSpace can still convert the Stacker compressed volume file, even though it is on your hard disk.

    DoubleSpace converts the Stacker volume and mounts the new DoubleSpace compressed volume. After the conversion is complete, DoubleSpace displays its main menu and list of compressed drives. You should notice a new compressed drive in the list. This drive is the Stacker volume you just converted.
3. Use any of the methods described in Chapter 5, "Using DoubleSpace," to determine the name of the new DoubleSpace compressed volume file. In most cases, the new compressed volume file is named DBLSPACE.001.
4. Unmount the new compressed volume file.
5. Make the uncompressed host drive to which you copied the original STACVOL.DSK file the current logged drive.
6. Type the following DOS ATTRIB command at the DOS prompt, and then press Enter:

    ATTRIB –S –H –R DBLSPACE.001

This command removes the Hidden, System, and Read-Only file attributes from the DoubleSpace compressed volume file that was created as you converted the Stacker compressed volume. (Substitute the name of the compressed volume file you obtained in step 3 for the file name in the preceding example.)

7. Remove the original Stacker removable disk from the drive.

To complete the transfer of the converted compressed volume file to a removable disk, follow these steps:

1. Insert a blank, formatted disk of the same size and capacity as the removable disk that contained the original Stacker volume into the disk drive.
2. Use the DOS MOVE command to move the DoubleSpace compressed volume file to the root directory of the blank, formatted disk. If the new DoubleSpace compressed volume file is named DBLSPACE.001, for example, and you move it to a removable disk in drive A, use the following command:

    MOVE DBLSPACE.001 A:

    Refer to your DOS documentation for more information about the DOS MOVE command.
3. Use the DOS RENAME command to rename the DoubleSpace compressed volume file so that it is called DBLSPACE.000.
4. To protect the DoubleSpace compressed volume, you must use the DOS ATTRIB command to restore its protective Hidden, System, and Read-Only file attributes. If your compressed volume file is on the disk in drive A, for example, use the following command:

    ATTRIB +H +S +R A:\\DBLSPACE.000

    ATTRIB adds the file attributes to the file; you can no longer view the DBLSPACE.000 file in your regular directory listings.
5. Copy the READTHIS.TXT file from one of your other DoubleSpace compressed removable disks, or put a similar file on the new disk so that other users know the disk is compressed by DoubleSpace.
6. Test the new compressed volume. If the volume mounts correctly, you can be reasonably certain that the conversion is successful.

    For added certainty, you may want to run either the DOS CHKDSK program or the DoubleSpace CHKDSK utility on the new compressed drive. Refer to Chapter 6, "Using the DoubleSpace Utilities," for information on using DoubleSpace CHKDSK.

Your manual conversion of the Stacker compressed volume is now complete.

> **NOTE:**
> If you do not rename the DoubleSpace compressed volume file to DBLSPACE.000, you cannot mount the volume on the removable disk.

APPENDIX C

The "Grandfather" Backup Technique

The "Grandfather" backup technique is named from the idea that the backup spans several "generations" of data. The Grandfather backup is a cost-effective, comprehensive, and secure method for backing up your hard disks. This technique uses a rotational system over a period of twelve weeks. After you go through the twelve-week cycle at least once, you can restore any lost file up to three months after the file's last backup.

To use the Grandfather backup system, you need ten sets of *backup media* (the disks or tape cartridges you use to store backup files). Base your estimate of the number of tapes or disks you need in each set on the total storage capacity of your compressed volume, plus the remaining space on the uncompressed volume. If you have a drive with a physical capacity of 40M, for example, and you compress that drive using DoubleSpace, you end up with a compressed drive approximately 76M in size and an uncompressed drive about 2M in size. You therefore need enough tapes or disks per set to back up approximately 78M of data (76M plus 2M).

After you gather together your ten sets of backup media, label the first four sets as follows: **Monday**, **Tuesday**, **Wednesday**, and **Thursday**. You use these backup sets for daily backups on Monday through Thursday.

Label the next three sets of backup media as follows: **Friday 1**, **Friday 2**, and **Friday 3**. You use one of these backup sets on each Friday for the first three weeks of each month in the twelve-week cycle.

Finally, label the remaining three sets of backup media as follows: **Month 1**, **Month 2**, and **Month 3**. You use one of these backup sets at the end of each of the three months in the twelve-week cycle.

Start the twelve-week backup cycle on a Friday, at the end of the work day. Use the backup media set labeled "Friday 1." Perform a *full backup*—that is, back up all the files on every compressed and uncompressed disk (except the compressed volume files themselves).

At the beginning of the next week, use the backup media set labeled "Monday." Perform an *incremental backup*—that is, back up only files that were added or modified since the last backup. Remember to back up files from your uncompressed drives as well as the individual files from your compressed drives. Remember also that you do not need to back up the compressed volume themselves.

Perform incremental backups on each remaining day of the week, using the appropriately labeled backup media sets. The process should take little time and require few disks or tapes if performed every day. On Friday, use the backup media set labeled "Friday 2" to perform another full backup. Repeat the daily Monday through Thursday incremental backups each day during the following week.

At the end of the second week, on the third Friday, use the backup media set labeled "Friday 3" to perform another full backup. Repeat once more the weekly cycle of incremental backups on Monday through Thursday. On the fourth Friday—which completes the first four weeks of the twelve-week cycle—perform a full backup using the backup media set labeled "Month 1."

During the next four weeks, repeat the monthly cycle just described: Each Monday through Thursday, perform an incremental backup using the appropriate backup set. On each Friday, perform a full backup using a different backup set so that, over a three-week period, you rotate through the Friday backup sets from "Friday 1" through "Friday 3" again.

On the eighth week—the week after you use the "Friday 3" backup set the second time—perform the usual Friday backup, but use the backup media set labeled "Month 2." During the next three weeks, repeat the monthly cycle of incremental backups on Mondays through Thursdays and full backups on Fridays.

On the twelfth week—the week after you use the "Friday 3" backup set a third time—perform the usual Friday backup, but use the backup media set labeled "Month 3." This gives you a set of backup files that enables you to reconstruct your entire disk or any single file to match its status on any day during the past three months.

Start the cycle over again: Continue performing incremental daily backups and full backups on each Friday and at the end of each month. At the end of the first month, use the "Month 1" backup media set again; use "Month 2" again at the end of the second month; and so on. As long as you continue this cycle, you can use your backup sets to reconstruct your entire disk or any single file to match its status on any day during the past three months. Thus by using this technique, you can never lose more than a single day's work.

If you ever need to reconstruct an entire disk, use the most recent Friday or Month backup set, and then restore your daily backups in order until you reach the most recent day you backed up. To restore a single file, start with the most recent day, and work backward through the backup sets until you locate the version of the file that you want.

Index

Symbols

* command switch, STACKER.INI, 206-208
; command switch, STACKER.INI, 206-207
@ command switch, STACKER.INI, 206-208
386MAX memory-management program, 30, 40-41, 72-73, 219-220
80286 CPUs, DPMI (DOS Protected-Mode Interface) program, 151

A

Access (Microsoft), 15
add-in programs, SPACEMANager, 149-153
   FortuneTeller free space estimator, 152
   SelectCompress, 150-151, 162-163
   SuperExchange, 151-152, 163-168
   SuperMount, 151, 166-168
ADDX utility command, switches, 163-164
algorithms
   Lempel-Ziv compression, 18-20, 304
applications, *see* programs
ARC file name extension, 151
Archive attribute, 13
attributes, file, 13, 23
AutoCAD, 16
AUTOEXEC.BAT file, 36, 301
   compressing RAM disks, 89, 236-237
   DoubleSpace installation changes, 52
   SPACEMANager installation, 153-155
   Stacker installation changes, 172-173
AutoSKETCH, 16
AVI files, 17

B

backing up
   compressed disks, 110, 262-263
   hard disks, 27-28
      "grandfather" technique, 319-320
backup media, 319
bar scale, Stackometer, 251
BAT file name extension, 150
Bernoulli drives, 10, 301
   compatibility with DoubleSpace and Stacker, 38-39
   mounting, 28
BIN file name extension, 150
binary files, 150
BIOS, files, compression ratio, 18
BIOS (*B*asic *I*nput/*O*utput *S*ystem), 11, 301
bitmap graphics files (BMP or PCX), 15
boot disks, 301
   files added by DoubleSpace, 51-52
   root directory, adding Stacker files, 172
booting computers, 301
   clean, 302
buffers, memory, 40

C

cache programs, write-delay, troubleshooting with Stacker, 289-290
CADD (Computer Aided Drafting and Design) files, compression ratio, 16
CD-ROM drives, 10, 301
Central Processing Units (CPUs), 302
   disk compression/decompression, 22-23
      hardware, 21-22
      software, 21
CHECK (Stacker), 281-282, 295
   from DOS prompt, 282-284
   from Toolbox, 284-285
check boxes, 302
CHKDSK (DOS), 96-97, 107, 119, 141-143, 148, 244-245, 295-296
CHKDSK (DoubleSpace)
   running from DOS prompt, 131-132
   running with menus, 132
clicking with mouse, 302
client/server networks, 14
clusters, lost, 12, 263, 282, 302
   causes, 293-294
   problems with DoubleSpace, 141-142
   repairing, 294
co-processor cards, 21-22
COM file name extension, 150
command buttons, 302
command line, *see* DOS prompt
commands, *see* DOS commands; DoubleSpace commands; Stacker commands
compressed disks, 23-27
   availability, 26
   backing up, 27-28, 110, 262-263
   by DOS versions prior to DOS 6, 27
   creating from free space, 271-273
   defragmenting, 129
      from DOS prompt, 129-130
      with DoubleSpace menus, 130
   with SDEFRAG, 279
   with Stackometer, 281
   with Toolbox, 280
DoubleSpace, 38
   changing sizes from DoubleSpace menus, 126-127
   creating additional disks, 115-125
   creating from free space, 120-125
   file management, 93-97
   formatting from DOS prompt, 133
   formatting with menus, 133-134
   from DOS prompt, 126
   information at DOS prompt, 97-99
   information from menus, 99-100
   information from Windows File Manager, 100-101
   mounting/unmounting at DOS prompt, 102-104
   mounting/unmounting with menus, 104-105
logical integrity, 131-132, 281-282
mounting, 253-255
removing, 127, 276-279
   at DOS prompt, 127-128
   with DoubleSpace menus, 128-129
Stacker, 38
   file management, 241-245
   information at DOS prompt, 246-247
   information from Toolbox, 247-248
   information from Windows, 248-252
   passwords, 260-262
   software compatibility with, 290
   troubleshooting with CHECK, 282-285
   utilities compatible, 263
unmounting, 255-256
with DOS versions prior to DOS 6, 27

compressed removable media disks,
28, 31-32
    changing disks, 259
    disabling mounting, 222
    DoubleSpace, 106-108
    mounting with SuperMount, 152
    on other computers, 109-110,
        259-260
    Stacker, 257-259
    SuperExchange, 163-164
    write-protected, 259
compressed volume files (CVFs),
23-26, 151, 302
    compression ratio, 17
    copying, compressing RAM disks,
        237-238
    deleting, 30
    DoubleSpace, 52-54
    FortuneTeller free space
        estimator, 152
    mounting with SuperExchange,
        165-166
    RAM disks, 90-92
    recovering deleted, 146-147,
        296-297
    sizes, problems, 144-146
    Stacker, 173-175
    troubleshooting, 147-148
    uncompressed, 23-26
compression ratios, 14-18, 228-229,
302
    changing
        with Stacker Toolbox, 229-230
        with Stacker Windows
            Stackometer, 230-231
    DIR or SDIR command, 242-244
    Fortune Teller free space
        estimator, 152
CONFIG.SYS file, 36, 302
    commands
        DEVICE, 72
        DEVICEHIGH, 72
        STACKS=, 136
    compressing RAM disks, 235
    installation changes
        DoubleSpace, 52
        Stacker, 172-173

local drive letters, 139
    STACKS= statement, 288-289
context-sensitive help, DoubleSpace,
    111-112
conventional memory, 30-31, 302
    freeing with Stacker, 218-222
converting
    from Stacker to DoubleSpace, 66,
        309-313
        post-conversion steps, 313-314
        pre-conversion steps, 307-309
        removable media disks, 314-317
    to DoubleSpace from other disk
        compression programs, 66-70
    to Stacker
        from DoubleSpace, 195-202
        from other disk compression
            programs, 199-202
copying compressed volumes to
    compress RAM disks, 237-238
CorelDRAW, 15
CPUs (Central Processing Units), 302
    compression/decompression, 22-23
    hardware, 21-22
    software, 21
cross-linked files, 142, 282, 294
    causes, 294-295
    repairing, 143-144, 295-296
Custom Setup (DoubleSpace), 37,
    59-66
Custom Setup (Stacker), 37, 184
    installation-final steps, 189-194
    starting
        from DOS prompt, 185-186
        from Windows, 187-189
CVFs, *see* compressed volume files

D

data compression, *see* disk
    compression
database files, compression ratio, 15
DBLFLOP utility command, switches,
    164-165

DBLSPACE.BIN file, 51-52, 303
   adding to boot disk root directory, 172
   device driver, 195, 203
   loading into upper memory, 218-221
DBLSPACE.INI file, 51-52, 82-85, 303
   commands, 85-86
   editing, 85-86
DBLSPACE.SYS file
   relocating DoubleSpace device drivers, 72
      into upper memory, 73-74
   /MOVE switch, 73
DBLSPACE.xxx, 303
decompressing data, *see* disk compression
DEFRAG (DOS), 58, 119, 144-146
defragmenting
   compressed disks, 129
      from DOS prompt, 129-130
      with DoubleSpace menus, 130
      with SDEFRAG, 279
      with Stackometer, 281-284
      with Toolbox, 280
   files, 303
      compatibility with DoubleSpace, 110-111
      programs compatible with Stacker, 263
deleting, *see* removing
DESQview, Stacker utilities, 253
device drivers, 11, 303
   DBLSPACE.BIN, 52, 195, 203
      loading into upper memory, 218-221
   DoubleSpace, relocating in memory, 71-92
   lost, 29-30
   memory-management programs conflicts, 135-136
   preloading, 36
   RAMDRIVE.SYS, 235-236
   STACHIGH.SYS, 173
diagnostic tools, DoubleSpace/Stacker, 42-44

dialog boxes, 303
   Add Stacker Directory to Your Path, 187
   Add SuperExchange to a Diskette, 164
   Advanced Options (Entire Drive), 190-191
   Change Size, 127
   Chkdsk, 132
   Choose Stacker Directory, 187
   Compress a Formatted Diskette, 165
   Compressed Drive Information, 99
   Convert DoubleSpace Drives, 196
   Create Drive from Free Space, 192-194
   Defragment, 130
   Delete a Compressed Drive, 128
   Delete Confirmation, 128
   DOS SelectCompress options, 163
   DoubleSpace Info, 100
   DoubleSpace Options, 87
   Enable SuperMount, 167
   Entire Drive or Free Space?, 189
   Exit Verification, 178
   Expanded Memory, 188
   Express Setup, 179-181
   Format a Compressed Drive, 134
   Leave Windows, 188
   Mount a Compressed Drive, 104
   Prepare to Stack, 186
   Run, 179
   SelectCompress Options, 162
   Stack Entire Drive, 190-192
   Stacker File Info, 249
   text boxes, 305
   Tune Stacker, 186
   Unmount Confirmation, 105
dictionaries, tokens, 19-20
directories, entries, 13
disk cache programs, 28-29, 176
   DoubleSpace
      improving with SMARTDRV, 76-79
      write-delay problems, 137-138

Index

disk compression, 9, 14, 22-23
   algorithms, Lempel-Ziv, 18-20
   device drivers, lost, 29-30
   DoubleSpace
      existing drives, 60-63
      file management, 93-97
      from DOS prompt, 116-117
      from menus, 117-120
      new drives, 63-66
   floppy disks from Windows, 165
   hardware, 21-22
   levels with SPACEMANager, 150-151, 162-163
   networks, 14
   program files, 23-26
   programs
      converting from others to Stacker, 199-202
      selection criteria, 47
   RAM, 89-92
   ratio, 14-18, 228-229
      changing with Stacker Toolbox, 229-230
      changing with Stacker Windows Stackometer, 230-231
      DoubleSpace, 79-81
   software, 20-21
   upgrade problems, 32
   with Stacker, 9, 189-194
      CREATE command, 273-274
      levels, 226-228
      Toolbox, 267-273
   with SuperExchange, 164-165
disk drives, 10, 13, 303-304
   backing up, "grandfather" technique, 319-320
   compatibility with DoubleSpace and Stacker, 38-39
   compressing, *see* disk compression
   letter assignments, 13, 24, 214
      DoubleSpace, 53-54, 81-87
      Stacker, 231-233
      troubleshooting problems, 139, 290-291
   logical, 13, 24, 304
   mounting, 304
      at DOS prompt, 102-104
      compressed, 101-102
      parameters, STACKER.INI file, 212-213
      with DoubleSpace menus, 104-105
   physical, 13, 24, 305
   read errors, troubleshooting, 298
   unmounting, 305
      at DOS prompt, 102-104
      compressed, 101-102
   volume labels, 54
   write-protected, correcting error messages, 297
   see also compressed disks; disks; floppy disks; removable media disk drives
disk operating system, *see* DOS
disks
   boot, 301
      adding DoubleSpace files, 51-52
      adding Stacker files, 172
   clusters, 12, 302
      errors, 148
   fixed, 304
   fragmenting, 304
   optimizing, 303
      compatibility with DoubleSpace, 110-111
      compatibility with Stacker, 263
   partitioning, 13-14, 303
   RAM, 305
      creating with DoubleSpace, 88-91
      drive names, 139
      Stacker, 239
   repair programs, 44
   sectors, 12
   space meter, Stackometer, 251
   storage systems, 10-14
   see also compressed disks; floppy disks; removable media disk drives
DLBSPACE.BIN file, loading into memory, 72

DLL (Dynamic Link Library), 16
DLL file name extension, 150
DOC file name extension, 150
DOS, 10-11
   BIOS (*B*asic *I*nput/*O*utput
      *S*ystem), 11
   command line, 302
      switches, 302
   commands, 10
      ATTRIB, 13, 30, 145, 217
      BACKUP, 27
      CHKDSK, 22, 43, 57, 96-97,
         107, 119, 141-143, 148, 176,
         197, 244-245, 281-282,
         295-296
      DEFRAG, 58, 119, 144-146
      DELTREE, 143, 295-296
      DEVICE, 72, 218
      DEVICEHIGH, 72-74, 218
      DIR, 23, 43, 95-96, 242-244
      FASTOPEN, 176
      FDISK, 68-69
      FORMAT, 68-69
      INTERLNK, 61, 63
      LABEL, 54, 175
      MEM, 75-76, 220-221
      MEMMAKER, 136, 288
      REPORT, 246-247
      STACKS=, 136, 288-289
      SUBST, 61, 63
      UNDELETE, 30, 145-147,
         296-297
   compressed disks, from prompt
      changing size, 126
      checking, 282-284
      compressing, 116-117
      creating, 121-122
      defragmenting, 129-130
      formatting, 133
      information, 97-99, 246-247
      mounting/unmounting, 102-104
      removing, 127-128
   device drivers, 11
   DoubleSpace CHKDSK utility,
      running from prompt, 131-132
   editing STACKER.INI file, 216-217

file management of compressed
   disks, 241-245
file system, 11-12
   disk clusters, 12
   disk partitions, 13-14
   drive letters, 13
   FAT (File Allocation Table), 12
   file attributes, 13
   physical/logical disk drives, 13
MS Anti-Virus, 45
MS Backup, 45
removable media disk drives,
   compressing from prompt,
   106-108, 257-258
SPACEMANager, 159-160
Stacker
   Tuner, 227
   utilities compatible, 263
Uninstall program, 32
DOS EDIT text editor, 217
double-clicking with mouse, 303
DoubleSpace, 9, 14-32
   CHKDSK utility
      running from DOS prompt,
         131-132
      running with menus, 132
   commands
      About (Help menu), 112
      /ALL switch, 79-80
      Change Size (Drive menu), 127
      Chkdsk (Tools menu), 132
      /COMPRESS switch, 88
      Contents (Help menu), 112
      Create New Drive (Compress
         menu), 122
      DBLFLOP, switches, 164-165
      DBLSPACE /COMPRESS, 108
      DBLSPACE /LIST, 78, 85,
         89-91, 140
      Defragment (Tools menu), 130
      Delete (Drive menu), 128
      Existing Drive (Compress
         menu), 108, 117
      Exit (Drive menu), 81
      Format (Drive menu), 134
      Index (Help menu), 112

Index   **327**

Info (Drive menu), 99
Mount (Drive menu), 104
Options (Tools menu), 87
Ratio (Drive menu), 80
/RATIO switch, 79-80
Unmount (Drive menu), 105
comparison of features with Stacker, 33-36
compatibility, disk repair programs, 44
compressed disks
  backing up, 110
  changing size from menus, 126-127
  changing sizes, 125-127
  creating additional, 115-125
  creating from free space, 120-125
  creating with menus, 122-125
  defragmenting with menus, 130
  formatting with menus, 133-134
  information at DOS prompt, 97-99
  information from menus, 99-100
  information from Windows File Manager, 100-101
  mounting/unmounting with menus, 104-105
  removing, 128-129
  size, 38
converting
  from DoubleSpace, 307-317
  from other disk compression programs, 66-70
  from Stacker, 66
  to Stacker, 195-202
CVFs (compressed volume files), 52-53
  labels, 54
device drivers
  relocating, 72-74
  verifying upper memory usage, 74-76
disk compression levels, 41-42

disk compression ratio, 79
  changing at command line, 79-80
  changing with DoubleSpace menus, 80-81
disk drives
  compressing existing, 60-63
  letter assignments, 81-87
  letters, 53-54
  new compressed, 63-66
  removable media, 87-88
disk utility compatibility, 110-111
file management, 93-97
files added to boot disk directory, 51-52
Help, 111
  context-sensitive, 111-112
  menu, 112
  navigating system, 112-113
improving with SMARTDRV program, 76-79
installing, 37
  changes to CONFIG.SYS and AUTOEXEC.BAT, 52
  Custom Setup, 59-66
  Express Setup, 56-59
  pre-installation steps, 54-56
memory, 40-41
  relocating device drivers, 71-76
program files, deleting before Stacker installation, 176-177
RAM disks, 88-89
  compressing by copying compressed volume, 90-91
  compressing with AUTOEXEC.BAT, 89
removable media disks
  changing disks 39-40, 108-109
  compressing, 106
  compressing with menus, 108
  in other computers, 109-110
  write-protected, 109
SPACEMANager add-in, 149-153
  compressing floppy disks from Windows, 165
  FortuneTeller free space estimator, 152

installing, 153-159
SelectCompress, 150-151, 162-163
starting from DOS, 159-160
starting from Windows, 160-161
SuperExchange, 151-152, 163-168
SuperMount, 151, 166-168
Windows integration, 152
System requirements, 46
tools, reporting, diagnostic, and maintenance, 42-44
troubleshooting
    compressed volume files (CVFs), 147-148
    compressed volume sizes, 144-146
    compressed volumes, recovering, 146-147
    cross-linked files, 142-144
    drive letter problems, 139
    lost clusters, 141-142
    problem prevention, 135-138
    Window swap files, 139-141
uncompressed disk drives, compressing with menus, 117-120
Windows, 44-45
DPMI (DOS Protected-Mode Interface) program, 151
drivers, device, 11, 303
    DBLSPACE.BIN, 52, 195, 203
    lost, 29-30
    memory-management program conflicts, 135-136
    preloading, 36
    RAMDRIVE.SYS, 235-236
    relocating DoubleSpace in memory, 71-92
    STACHIGH.SYS, 173
drives
    Bernoulli, 10, 301
    CD-ROM, 10, 301
    Floptical, 10, 304
    host, 304
    see also disk drives
Dynamic Link Library, *see* DLL

E

ED.EXE text editor, 215-216
EMM386 memory-management program, 30, 40-41, 73, 219-220, 288
EMS (Expanded Memory), 40-41, 304
    Stacker, 222
encrypted files, compression ratio, 16
EPS (Encapsulated PostScript) files, 15
error messages
    disk read, 298
        Drive G: is not a Stacker drive letter, 256
        Error reading drive..., 148
        No replaceable drives available, 255
        Not a Stacker drive, 249
        write-protected drive, 297
Error reading drive... messages, 148
ESDI hard disk drives, compatibility with DoubleSpace and Stacker, 38-39
Excel (Microsoft), 15
EXE file name extension, 150
Expanded Memory (EMS), 40-41, 304
Express Setup
    DoubleSpace, 37, 56-59
    Stacker, 177-182
        installation-final steps, 182-184
Extended Memory (XMS), 41, 304
    HIMEM.SYS, 219-220

F

Fastback (5th Generation), 175
FASTOPEN program, 176
FATs (File Allocation Tables), 12
FDISK (DOS), 68-69
file management of compressed disks
    DoubleSpace, 93-97
    Stacker, 241-245
File Manager, Windows
    compressed disk information, 100-101
    Stacker menu, 249-251

file-by-file compression programs, 17
FileMaker for Windows (Paradox), 15
files
    attributes, 13, 23
    AUTOEXEC.BAT, 36, 301
        compressing RAM disks, 89, 236-237
        DoubleSpace installation changes, 52
        Stacker installation changes, 172-173
    binary, 150
    chains, 12
    compression ratio, 14-18
    font, 16
    CONFIG.SYS, 36, 72, 302
        compressing RAM disks, 235
        DoubleSpace installation changes, 52
        local drive letters, 139
        Stacker installation changes, 172-173
        STACKS= command, 136
        STACKS= statement, 288-289
    cross-linked, 142, 282, 294
        causes, 294-295
        repairing, 143-144, 295-296
    CVFs (compressed volume files), 302
        DoubleSpace, 52-53
        recovering, 296-297
        troubleshooting, 147-148
    DBLSPACE.BIN, 51-52, 303
        adding to boot disk root directory, 172
        loading into memory, 72
        loading into upper memory, 218-221
    DBLSPACE.INI, 51-52, 82-85, 303
        editing, 85-86
    DBLSPACE.SYS, 72-76
    DBLSPACE.xxx, 303
    defragmenting, 303
        compatibility with DoubleSpace, 110-111
        programs compatible with Stacker, 263
    DoubleSpace, added to boot disk directory, 51-52
    listing with DIR or SDIR commands, 242-245
    SPACEMANager, 154-155
    STACHIGH.SYS, moving DBLSPACE.BIN file, 218-220
    STACKER.EXE, 257, 260
    STACKER.INI, 203-206, 246, 305
        adding to boot disk root directory, 172
        commands, 206-213
        disk compression levels, 228
        disk mounting parameters, 212-213
        editing, 214-217
        removable media disk drives, 233-234
    STACKER.LOG, 278
        adding to root directories, 172
    STACVOL.xxx, 305
    swap
        problems with DoubleSpace, 139-141
        troubleshooting problems, 291-293
    System, synchronization, 36
    text, 150
    Windows, SPACEMANager installation changes, 153-155
fixed disk drives, 10, 304
floppy disks, 13
    compatibility with DoubleSpace and Stacker, 38-39
    compressed, mounting with SuperMount, 152
    compressing from Windows, 165
    see also compressed disks; disks; hard disks; removable media disk drives
Floptical disk drives, 10, 304
    compatibility with DoubleSpace and Stacker, 38-39
    mounting, 28
FORMAT, *see* DOS commands, FORMAT
formatting compressed disks, 133-134

FortuneTeller free-space estimator, 152
fragmented disks, 304
    programs compatible with Stacker, 263
    Stackometer, 252
free space
    compressing, 192-194
    creating compressed drives, 120-125, 174
full backups, 319

G-H

GEM, Stacker utilities, 253
Generic CADD, 16
GEOworks, Stacker utilities, 253
GIF (Graphics Interchange Format) files, 16
graphics files, compression ratio, 15
hard disk drives, *see* compressed disks; disks
hardware
    disk compression, 21-22
    requirements, SPACEMANager installation, 155
Help
    DoubleSpace, 111-113
    Stacker, 264
Hidden file attribute 13, 23
HIGHSCAN switch, 298
HIMEM.SYS memory management program, 41, 73-74, 219
host drives, 304
hot links, Help, 112

I-K

IDE hard disk drives, compatibility with DoubleSpace and Stacker, 38-39
incremental backups, 319
installing
    DoubleSpace, 37
        Custom Setup, 59-66
        Express Setup, 56-59
        pre-installation steps, 54-56
    SPACEMANager, 153-159
    Stacker, 37
        pre-installation guidelines, 175-177
        with Express Setup, 177-184
INTERLNK, *see* DOS commands, INTERLINK
internal integrity, *see* logical integrity

L

Lantastic peer-to-peer networks, 14
Lempel-Ziv (LZ) compression algorithm, 18-20
local disk drives, names, 139
    problems, 291
logical disk drives, 13, 24, 304
logical integrity, compressed disks, 131-132, 281-282
    checking from Toolbox (Stacker), 284-285
    checking with CHECK (Stacker), 282-284
lost clusters, 282
    causes, 293-294
    problems with DoubleSpace, 141-142
    repairing, 294
Lotus 1-2-3, 15
LZ (Lempel-Ziv) compression algorithm, 18-20, 304
LZS alogrithm, 304

M

media disk drives, *see* removable media disk drives
MEMMAKER, *see* DOS commands, MEMMAKER
memory
    allocating for stacks, 288-289
    amount used
        DoubleSpace/Stacker, 40-41
        verifying with MEM command, 220-221

conventional, 30-31, 302
    freeing with Stacker, 218-222
DoubleSpace, relocating device
    drivers, 71-76
EMS (expanded), 40-41, 304
    Stacker, 222
extended, 304
    HIMEM.SYS, 219-220
UMBs (Upper Memory Blocks), 31, 305
    conflicts with device drivers, 135-136
    device driver conflicts, 287-288
    loading DBLSPACE.BIN file, 218-221
    loading device drivers, 72-76
memory-management programs, 30, 40-41, 71-73, 219-220
    conflict with device drivers, 135-136
    EMM386, 288
    QEMM, Optimize, 288
    troubleshooting, 287-288
MFM hard disk drives, compatibility with DoubleSpace and Stacker, 38-39
mounting
    compressed disk drives, 101-102, 253-255, 304
        at DOS prompt, 102-104
        parameters, STACKER.INI file, 212-213
        with DoubleSpace menus, 104-105
        with SuperExchange, 165-166
    removable media disk drives, 28
        disabling, 222
        with Stacker, 256-257
    see also unmounting
mouse
    clicking, 302
    double-clicking, 303
MS Anti-Virus, 45
MS Backup, 45
MS PaintBrush, 15
MSBACKUP, 27

N

NCache (Norton), 28
networks
    client/server, 14
    disk compression, 14
    drive name problems
        DoubleSpace, 139
        Stacker, 291
    peer-to-peer, 14
nonremovable media disk drive, *see* fixed disk drive
Norton Backup, 9
Norton Disk Doctor, 22, 138, 290
Norton Speed Disk, 191-193
Norton Utilities (Symantec), 30, 44
Novell, client/server networks, 14

O

on-the-fly, compressing/
    decompressing files, 15
Optimize, QEMM memory-
    management program, 136, 288
optimizing disks, 303
    compatibility with DoubleSpace, 110-111
OVL file name extension, 150

P

Paradox (Borland), 15
partitioning disks, 13-14, 303
password-protected compressed
    volumes, 260
passwords, Stacker, 260-262
PC Backup (Central Point), 9, 175
PC Tools (Central Point), 22, 30, 44, 138, 290
PCX files, 15
peer-to-peer networks
    Lantastic, 14
    Windows for Workgroups, 14

permanent swap files
　compression ratio, 17
　problems with DoubleSpace, 140-141
　troubleshooting problems, 291
physical disk drives, 13, 24, 305
PKZIP, 17
program files, 23-26
　compression ratio, 16
　DoubleSpace, 176-177
Program Manager, Windows
　starting Express Setup (Stacker), 179
PROGRAM.INI file, SPACEMANager installation changes, 153-155
programs
　Access, 15
　ADDX, switches, 163-164
　AutoCAD, 16
　AutoSKETCH, 16
　cache, write-delay, 289-290
　CHKDSK, 43, 141-143, 148
　CorelDRAW, 15
　CREATE (Stacker), 273-274
　defragmentation, compatibility with DoubleSpace, 110-111
　DESQview, 253
　disk cache, 28-29, 176
　disk compression, selection criteria, 47
　disk optimizers, compatibility with DoubleSpace, 110-111
　disk utilities, 44
　　compatible with Stacker, 263
　DOS
　　BACKUP, 27
　　CHKDSK, 96-97, 107, 119, 244, 281-282, 295-296
　　DEFRAG, 58, 119, 144-146
　　FASTOPEN, 176
　　FDISK, 68-69
　　FORMAT, 68-69
　　INTERLINK, 61-63
　　MEMMAKER, 288
　　SETVER, 138, 290
　　UNDELETE, 145-147, 296-297

DoubleSpace, 9, 14-32
　CHKDSK, 131-132
　comparison of features with Stacker, 33-47
　converting from others, 66-70
　converting from Stacker, 66
　files added to boot disk root directory, 51-52
　installing, 54-66
　write-delay disk cache problems, 137-138
DPMI (DOS Protected-Mode Interface), 151
Excel, 15
Fastback, 175
FileMaker for Windows, 15
Fortune Teller, 152
GEM, 253
Generic CADD, 16
GEOworks, 253
Lotus 1-2-3, 15
MEMMAKER, 136
memory-management, 40-41, 71-73
　conflict with device drivers, 135-136
　EMM386, 288
　troubleshooting, 287-288
MS Anti-Virus, 45
MS Backup, 27, 45
MS PaintBrush, 15
NCache, 28
Norton Backup, 9
Norton Disk Doctor, 22, 138, 290
Norton Speed Disk, 191-193
Norton Utilities, 30, 44
Optimize, 136
Paradox, 15
PC Backup, 9, 175
PC Tools, 22, 30, 44, 138, 290
PKZIP, 17
Quattro, 15
SMARTDRV, 28-29, 137-138
　improving DoubleSpace, 76-79
　improving Stacker, 223-226

Sound Recorder, Windows 3.1, 16
SpinRite, 44
SpinRite II, 22
Stacker, 9, 14-32
   Anywhere, 40, 257, 260
   CHECK, 281-285, 295
   converting from DoubleSpace, 195-199
   converting from other disk compression, 199-202
   DOS 6 start-up disks, 194-195
   installing, 177-184
   REPORT, 246-247
   SCREATE.SYS, 235-236
   SDEFRAG, 277-279
   SDIR, 43
   Setup, 171-173
   SGROUP (Stacker), 238-239
   STACKER.INI file, 203-217
   Stackometer, 45, 251-257, 281
   Toolbox, 258-274, 280
   Tuner, 45, 227-228
SuperExchange, 40, 151-152, 163-166
SuperMount, 40, 45
TSR (Terminate-Stay-Resident), 30, 305
Uninstall, 32
VCache, 28
XtraDrive, 67

Q-R

QEMM/QEMM-386 memory-management program, 30, 40-41, 72-73, 219-220
   Optimize, 136, 288
Quattro (Borland), 15

radio buttons, 305
RAM disks, 305
   DoubleSpace, 88-91
   drive names, 139
   Stacker, 234, 239
      compressing by copying compressed volumes, 237-238
      compressing with AUTOEXEC.BAT, 236-237
      compressing with CONFIG.SYS, 235-236
RAMDRIVE.SYS device driver, 235-236
Read-Only file attribute, 13, 23
read-only passwords, 260-262
read/write head, disk drives, 10
read/write passwords, 260-262
registration of software, Stacker, 180-181
removable media disk drives, 10, 233-234, 305
   changing disks, 108-109
   compatibility with Stacker and DoubleSpace, 38-39
   converting from Stacker to DoubleSpace
      at DOS prompt, 314-315
      insufficient uncompressed free space, 315-317
      with DoubleSpace menus, 315
   DoubleSpace, 39-40, 87-88, 106-108
   mounting
      with Stacker, 256-257
      with SuperMount, 151
   Stacker, 39-40
      internal integrity, 244-245
   SuperExchange (SPACEMANager), 151-152, 163-166
   write-protected, 109
removing compressed disks, 30, 127, 276-279
   from DOS prompt, 127-128
   with DoubleSpace menus, 128-129
reporting tools, DoubleSpace/Stacker, 42-44
root directories, boot disk, adding Stacker files, 172

S

SCREATE.SYS (Stacker), 235-236
SCSI hard disk drives, compatibility with DoubleSpace and Stacker, 38-39
SelectCompress, 150-151, 162-163
SETVER, *see* DOS commands, SETVER
SMARTDRV disk cache program, 28-29, 137-138
    improving DoubleSpace, 76-79
    improving Stacker, 223-226
software
    disk compression, 20-21
    registration, Stacker, 180-181
    requirements, SPACEMANager installation, 155
sound files, compression ratio, 16
Sound Recorder, Windows 3.1, 16
SPACEMANager, 33, 149-153
    commands
        Automatic Floppy Mount (Options menu), 167
        Compress a Floppy (File menu), 165
        Compression Levels (Options menu), 162
        Load SelectCompress TSR on System Startup, 162
        Make Floppy Exchangeable (File menu), 164
    comparison of features with DoubleSpace and Stacker, 33-36
    compressing floppy disks from Windows, 165
    compression levels, 41-42
    FortuneTeller free space estimator, 152
    installing, 153-159
    SelectCompress, 150-151, 162-163
    starting
        from DOS, 159-160
        from Windows, 160-161
    SuperExchange, 40, 151-152, 163-168
    SuperMount, 40, 45, 151, 166-168
    System requirements, 46-47
    Windows, 44
        integration, 152
SpinRite (Gibson Research), 44
SpinRite II (Gibson Research), 22
spreadsheet files, compression ratio, 15
STACHIGH.SYS device driver, 173
STACHIGH.SYS file, moving DBLSPACE.BIN file, 218-220
STACINI.BAT DOS batch file editing tool, 215-216
Stacker (Stac Electronics), 9, 14-32
    Anywhere, 40, 257, 260
    AutoMount, 39, 45
    commands
        CHECK, 244-245, 281-285, 295
        CREATE, 257-258, 273-274
        REMOVDRV, 278-279, 296
        REDIRECT, 222-223
        REPORT, 246-247
        SDEFRAG, 277-279
        SDIR, 43, 242-244
        SGROUP, 238-239
        STACKER, 246-247, 253-256, 264, 292-293
    comparison of features with DoubleSpace, 33-36
    compatibility, disk repair utilities, 44, 263
    compressed disks
        backing up, 262-263
        file management, 241-245
        information from Windows, 248-252
        labels, 175
        levels of compression, 41-42, 226-228
        passwords, 260-262
        removable media, 259-260
        size, 38
    Compression Report (Toolbox), 247-248
    converting
        from DoubleSpace, 195-199, 201-202

Index

from other disk compression
  programs, 199-202
to DoubleSpace, 66-70, 307-317
Custom Setup program, 184
  installation, final steps, 189-194
  starting from DOS prompt,
    185-186
  starting from Windows, 187-189
device drivers loading into upper
  memory, 218-221
disk drives
  letter assignments, 174-175,
    231-233
  removable media, 233-234
DOS 6 start-up disks, 194-195
DOS disk commands, redirecting,
  222-223
Express Setup program, 177
  installation-final steps, 182-184
  starting from DOS prompt,
    178-179
  starting from Windows, 179-182
Help system, 264
improving performance with
  SMARTDRV.EXE, 223-226
installing, 37
  pre-installation guidelines,
    175-177
memory
  EMS (expanded), 222
  usage, 40-41
RAM disks, 234
  compressing by copying
    compressed volumes, 237-238
  compressing with
    AUTOEXEC.BAT, 236-237
  compressing with CONFIG.SYS,
    235-236
removable media disk drives, 39-40
  compressing, 257-259
  mounting automatically,
    256-257
reporting, diagnostic, and
  maintenance tools, 42-44

Setup
  adding files to boot disk root
    directory, 172
  changes to CONFIG.SYS and
    AUTOEXEC.BAT, 172-173
  volumes, 173
STACKER.INI file, 203-206
  commands, 206-213
Stackometer, 45
  changing compression ratio,
    230-231
  compressed disk information,
    251-252
  defragmenting compressed
    disks, 281
System requirements, 46
Toolbox
  changing compression ratio,
    229-230
  changing size of compressed
    disks, 275-276
  checking integrity of
    compressed disks, 284-285
  compressing disks drives,
    267-273
  compressing removable media
    disks, 258-259
  defragmenting compressed
    disks, 280
  passwords/compressed
    volumes, 261-262
troubleshooting problems
  cross-linked files, 294-296
  CVFs (compressed volume
    files), 296-297
  disk read errors, 298
  drive letter problems, 290-291
  lost clusters, 293-294
  memory, 287-288
  memory allocation for stacks,
    288-289
  software compatibility with
    Stacker, 290
  Windows swap files, 291-293
  write-delay cache programs,
    289-290

write-protected drive error
messaages, 297
Tuner, 45
Windows, 44-45
program group/icons for
utilities, 238-239
STACKER.EXE program file, 257, 260
STACKER.INI file, 203-206, 246, 305
adding to boot disk root directory,
172
commands, switches, 206-212
disk compression levels, 228
disk drives
mounting parameters, 212-213
removable media, 233-234
editing, 214-215
with DOS, 216-217
with ED.EXE and
STACINI.BAT, 215-216
STACKER.LOG file, 278
adding to root directories, 172
Stackometer (Stacker), 45
changing compression ratio,
230-231
compressed disk information,
251-252
defragmenting compressed disks,
281
STACKS= statement, CONFIG.SYS
file, 288-289
STACVOL.DSK compressed disk
drives, 173
mounting, 253-255
unmounting, 255-256
STACVOL_DSK volume label, 175
STACVOL.xxx files, 305
start-up disks, DOS 6, Stacker,
194-195
starting
from DOS prompt
Custom Setup (Stacker),
185-186
Express Setup (Stacker), 178
SPACEMANager, 159-160

from Windows
Custom Setup (Stacker),
187-189
Express Setup (Stacker),
179-182
SPACEMANager, 160-161
strings, 19
suggest drives, 305
SuperExchange (SPACEMANager),
40, 151-152, 163-166
SuperMount, 40, 45, 166
enabling/disabling, 166-168
mounting, 151-152
swap files
compression ratio, 17-18
problems with DoubleSpace,
139-141
Windows, troubleshooting
problems, 291-293
switches
commands
CHECK (Stacker), 282-284
CHKDSK, 131-132
DBLFLOP, 164-165
DIR or SDIR, 242-244
STACKER.INI, 204-212
compressed disks, 95-96, 102,
121-122, 126
DoubleSpace, 97-99
synchronization, System files, 36
Syquest drives
compatibility with DoubleSpace
and Stacker, 38-39
mounting, 28
SYS file name extension, 150
System
attributes, 13, 23
files, synchronization, 36
requirements
DoubleSpace, 46
SPACEMANager, 46-47
Stacker, 46
SYSTEM.INI file, SPACEMANager
installation changes, 153-155

T

Tagged Image Format File, *see* TIFF
temporary swap files
   compression ratio, 18
   problems with DoubleSpace,
     140-141
   troubleshooting problems, 291
text boxes, 305
text editors
   DOS EDIT, 217
   ED.EXE, 215-216
text files, 150
   compression ratio, 15
TIFF (Tagged Image Format File)
  files, 15
title bar
   Stackometer, 251
tokens, 18-20
Toolbox (Stacker)
   changing compression ratio,
     229-230
   changing size of compressed disks,
     275-276
   checking logical integrity of
     compressed disks, 284-285
   compressing disks drives,
     267-273
     removable media disk drives,
       258-259
   defragmenting compressed disks,
     280
   Help, 264
   passwords/compressed volumes,
     261-262
   report utility, 247-248
tracks, 10
troubleshooting
   CHKDSK program, 244-245
   compressed disks
     with CHECK (Stacker),
       282-285
   cross-linked files, 294-296
   CVFs (compressed volume files),
     296-297
   disk read errors, 298

   DoubleSpace
     compressed volume files
       (CVFs), 147-148
     compressed volumes,
       recovering, 146-147
     compressed volumes sizes,
       144-146
     cross-linked files, 142-144
     drive letter problems, 139
     lost clusters, 141-142
     problem prevention, 135-138
     Window swap files, 139-141
   drive letter problems, 290-291
   lost cluster problems, 293-294
   memory managers, 287-288
   software compatibility with
     Stacker, 290
   stack memory allocation, 288-289
   upper memory, 287-288
   Windows swap file problems,
     291-293
   write-delay cache programs,
     289-290
   write-protected drive error
     messages, 297
TrueType fonts for Windows 3.1, 16
TSR (Terminate-Stay-Resident)
  programs, 30, 305
TSRs
   SuperExchange, 151-152, 163-165
   SuperMount, 166
Tuner (Stacker)
   DOS, 227
   Windows, 227-228
TXT file name extension, 150

U

UMBs (Upper Memory Blocks), 31,
  305
   device drivers, conflicts, 135-136,
     287-288
   loading DBLSPACE.BIN file, 72-76,
     218-221
uncompressed disk drives, *see*
  compressed disks

UNDELETE, *see* DOS programs, UNDELETE
unmounting
    compressed disk drives, 101-102, 255-256, 305
        at DOS prompt, 102-104
        with DoubleSpace menus, 104-105
utilities, *see* programs

V-W

VCache (Golden Bow), 28
video files, compression ratio, 17
volumes, *see* CVFs, 306

WAV files, 16
Windows
    compressed disks, 165
        information, 248-252
    DLL (Dynamic Link Library) files, compression ratio, 16
    DoubleSpace/Stacker, 44-45
    File Manager
        compressed disk information, 100-101
        Stacker menu, 249-251
    mounting disks with SuperMount, 152
    SPACEMANager installation changes, 153-155

Stacker
    changing compression ratio with Stackometer, 230-231
    program group/icons, 238-239
    Tuner, 227-228
    utilities, 253
starting
    Custom Setup (Stacker), 187-189
    Express Setup (Stacker), 179-182
    SPACEMANager, 160-161
swap files, troubleshooting problems, 139-141, 291-293
Workgroup for Windows, peer-to-peer networks, 14
working drives, 242
write-delay cache programs, problems
    DoubleSpace, 137-138
    Stacker, 289-290
write-protected removable media disk drives, 109, 259

X-Z

XMS (Extended Memory), 41
XtraDrive (ITT), 67

ZIP file name extension, 151